Northsiders

Northsiders

*Essays on the
History and Culture
of the Chicago Cubs*

Edited by
GERALD C. WOOD *and*
ANDREW HAZUCHA

McFarland & Company, Inc., Publishers
Jefferson, North Carolina, and London

LIBRARY OF CONGRESS CATALOGUING-IN-PUBLICATION DATA

Northsiders : essays on the history and culture of the Chicago Cubs /
edited by Gerald C. Wood and Andrew Hazucha.
p.   cm.
Includes bibliographical references and index.

ISBN 978-0-7864-3623-1
softcover : 50# alkaline paper ∞

1. Chicago Cubs (Baseball team)—History.   2. Chicago (Ill.)—Civilization.
3. Baseball players—United States.   I. Wood, Gerald C.   II. Hazucha, Andrew, 1960–
GV875.C6N67 2008   796.357′640977311—dc22   2008027643

British Library cataloguing data are available

Cover art: "Let's Play Two at Wrigley Field" ©2008 DannyOart.com

Manufactured in the United States of America

McFarland & Company, Inc., Publishers
Box 611, Jefferson, North Carolina 28640
www.mcfarlandpub.com

For Jeannette Palmer,
a Cubs fan from Grenada, Mississippi, since 1931,
who managed the pain by choosing
the Yankees as her American League team.

For Carl Roeske,
late of Boone Grove, Indiana,
who always was on the side of the Cubs
against the White Sox at the family softball games.

And for Rudolph and Winifred Hazucha,
Northsiders by birthright,
who taught their son that to love the Cubs
is to learn to accommodate loss.

Acknowledgments

A project involving many different approaches and disciplines, as this one does, relies on the advice of many talented people who, finally, for many reasons, don't have essays in the book. Nevertheless, they served as catalysts for the final edition. Tom Porter and Steven Riess should be mentioned. We wish also to thank Allen Nye for his suggestion that we contact Joe Price about issues of religion and baseball, and Ralph Savarese for putting us in contact with Steve Andrews about the intersecting histories of Cap Anson and Moses Fleetwood Walker. John Raeburn and Ed Folsom, both of the University of Iowa, were enthusiastic in their support and had many useful suggestions. Similarly, Dudley Andrew at Yale University, a talented baseball player and film scholar of international reputation, was helpful with our questions about minority issues. Tim Wiles of the National Baseball Hall of Fame was a repeated source for many topics, from baseball and politics to broadcasters to pictures. Andrew Newman, the Assistant Photo Archivist at the Hall of Fame, was instrumental in helping us procure many of the photos for this book.

In the preparation of the text, we want to thank Matt Cheney, a student assistant at Carson-Newman College, and Edra Garrett, Director of the Family Enrichment Institute at the same institution, for help with research, formatting, and proofing.

Finally, for her constant support, editorial suggestions, and tolerance of our late-night phone conversations over which most of the important decisions involving this book were made, we thank Emily Hester.

Table of Contents

Introduction

We are aware that the title of this book is slightly misleading. The Chicago team we are discussing was originally called the White Stockings, not the Cubs. Later they were known as the Orphans, when they lost their leader Cap Anson, and then the Colts when the subsequent team fielded many young players. Like many teams in their league after the rise of the American circuit, they sometimes were also called the Chicago Nationals. Equally significant is the qualifier that they were not always Northsiders; for though they did first play baseball on the north side of Chicago, they also played elsewhere in the city, including across the street from what has been the Mecca of *Southside* baseball, Comiskey Park/U.S. Cellular Field.

We use the term *Northsiders*, even with these qualifiers, because this collection focuses on the relationship between a team we seemingly forever will call the Cubs and its city, Chicago, which is very conscious, even self-conscious, about its neighborhoods. One of the most recognizable, and now desirable, areas of the city is Wrigleyville, a part of Lake View, which itself lives in the history and folklore — and economic plans and opportunities — of the city. In addition, the team's history has been informed by sociological forces which, while not unique to Chicago, are nuanced in ways specific to that major city and its people. Ethnic trends, patriarchal rule, racial discrimination, corporate policies, and the media, for example, have all brought distinct pressures to bear upon the franchise and fans who have supported it across the decades.

The Cubs can trace their history to the first days of the National League. The team was formed in 1876 by William A. Hulbert, who culled the best players from the National Association, including Albert G. Spalding and Cap Anson. Blackballed by the owners of the Association, Hulbert joined seven other owners to create the National League, with franchises in St. Louis, Boston, New York, Philadelphia, Cincinnati, Hartford, and Louisville. Hulbert's team was not the Cubs, of course. They were the White Stockings, and they dominated the NL in the early years. With Spalding serving as both manager and pitcher (he pitched in 61 of the team's 66 games, winning 47) and Ross Barnes leading the league with a .429 batting average, the White Stockings won the first NL championship by six games over St. Louis. In fact, they won six championships in the first eleven years of the National League, including consecutive wins in 1880–82 and 1885–86.

Before the losing habits that define the Chicago Cubs these days became so well entrenched, winning was common for the Chicago National League team. As one would expect, given their early dominance, the Cubs were responsible for the first shutout (Spalding) and first home run (Barnes). But they also hold other long-standing records: most runs scored in a game (36 against Louisville in 1897), and most runs in an inning (18 against Detroit in 1883) (*Few and Chosen* xxi-ii). They also own the major league record for consecutive victories, 21, which they did twice, as the White Stockings in 1880 and Cubs in 1935, as well as most victories in a year, 116, in 1906 (they actually share that record with the Seattle Mariners, but the Mariners played eight more games) (xxiii). Cubs fans are quick to remember that their team played in three consecutive World Series (1906–8), winning the last two. Even after those golden years, the team returned as NL champions in 1910, 1918, 1929, 1932, 1935, 1938, and finally 1945.

Crucial to this history is Wrigley Field and the neighborhood where it is located, Lake View. Wrigley Field was originally called Weeghman Park, built by Charles Weeghman for the Chicago entry in the Federal League, the Whales, in 1915. It cost $250,000 and had seating for 14,000. It was still Weeghman Park when the Federal League disbanded and the Cubs moved there in 1916. Four years later, in 1920, the team renamed its facility Cubs Park. It wasn't named Wrigley Field after its then-owner William Wrigley, Jr. until 1926 (*Few and Chosen* xxii–iii). Typical of the arrested development of Cubs teams, fans, and ownership, that venue has the distinction of being the final holdout against night baseball, the first game under the lights at Wrigley occurring on August 9, 1988.

While the essays contained in this collection reveal a variety of social and political views of the writers, less obvious, but no less significant, is the diversity in their voices and styles. Some, like Bob Boone and Jerry Grunska, focus on the intimate details, the personal and specific connections between the players and the local people. Others, like William F. McNeil, place the careers of iconic players in the context of national and even world events, like Prohibition, the Depression, and the rise of Hitlerism. Contributors Margaret Gripshover and Steve Andrews offer impressively researched scholarly interpretations of American history and culture. Curt Smith, on the other hand, offers a breezy, epigrammatic exploration of media personalities that reflects his passionate love for old-fashioned baseball, especially on the radio.

While the approaches and voices are distinct, there are points of view repeatedly visited in these essays that give the book a kind of narrative thread. Most of the contributors, for instance, recognize the retro nature of the Cubs team and its park which, depending on one's view, can be variously refreshing or rigidly nostalgic in this electronic, postmodern age. Consequently their analyses return time and again to the pressure of the media to sanitize, repackage, and even spin the action on and off the field. And even though the essayists had little or no knowledge of the other contributions, collectively they developed a sense of the franchise as chronically behind the curve of social change. As early as 1887 Spalding sold his best players, including Mike Kelly (for $10,000) and John Clarkson, to Boston for moral and economic ends, thus eliminating the chances that his club would resume its winning ways (*Wrigleyville* 62–69). Later the Cubs trailed the Cardinals, Dodgers, and Yankees in developing talented players through the emerging farm systems of the 1940s. Similarly, they didn't integrate as quickly as the Dodgers, Indians, and, most significantly for Chicago, the White Sox. Now a giant conglomerate Tribune uses the profitable Cubs sector to feed other less lucrative, even money-losing enterprises. Meanwhile the fans call for a savior from among the super-rich sports fanatics, the new wave of post-conglomerate owners like Jerry Colangelo, Mark Cuban, or even Donald Trump.

The first section brings together essays having historical and political foci. Margaret Gripshover's essay explains the history of Lake View, both before and after the arrival of the Chicago Cubs. She notes the changing ethnicity of that place, the various experiences of baseball there, and how the Cubs have been received, with both enthusiasm and harsh criticism, by that community. Within that context, David Bohmer explains how the Cubs first got behind the curve on the rights of the players, noting (as do other writers) that the reactionary tone of ownership has perhaps been the real curse of the Cubs. But there is a complementary argument, one offered by Joseph L. Price, that Wrigley Field offers more than business and politics. In an increasingly secular world, Price notes, the field and experience itself takes on a sense of the sacred that is rare in the increasingly materialistic and imagistic twenty-first century. In either case, as George Castle convincingly argues, the crucial figure is Philip K. Wrigley, who failed for personal and financial reasons to continue the winning tradition of his father. Especially since most successful franchises today are under the control of a sports-obsessed aristocrat in the manner of William Wrigley, the negative legacy left by his son is now clearer than ever. One of the silliest examples of such failed leadership under Phil Wrigley is the College of Coaches, the last experiment on a rudderless ship, as explained by Andrew Hazucha.

No better example exists of the connections between the social backwardness of the Wrigley patriarchy and its failure to take a giant step towards winning than the Wrigley dynasty's attitudes regarding race and ethnicity. Steve Andrews establishes the deep histori-cal and cultural sources of racism in baseball, particularly through the influence of the early Cubs hero and manager, Cap Anson. Through the narrative of the sad history of Anson's treat-ment of Moses Fleetwood Walker, Andrews demonstrates the heavy burden of racism passed to future Cubs fans, players, and management. How this burden was realized in Chicago is the subject of Brian Carroll's study of the different approaches to integration taken by the White Sox and Cubs, especially as described and judged by the black newspaper *The Chicago Defender*. In his essay Carroll examines the events that led to the relatively late integration of the Cubs in 1953, six years after Jackie Robinson had broken major league baseball's color line. Focusing on the ways the black press represented this historic event in Chicago, Carroll points out that because the crosstown rival White Sox had preceded the Cubs by two years in integrating their club, the Cubs' move was seen as anti-climactic, even irrelevant to many in Chicago's African-American community. An even more specific instance of race and racism at work is the career of Ernie Banks, in comparison with those of Gene Baker and Jackie Robin-son, as explained by Gerald C. Wood. Jewish players such as Ken Holtzman were also impli-cated in patterns of bigotry and discrimination. As Terry Barr explains in his personal and engaging style, Holtzman was brave and adamant in his expression of his faith, especially in the context of social forces that tended to make Jews invisible in Chicago, beginning with Johnny Kling.

The third section contains essays that attempt to explain how and why the Cubs have become legendary in the arts and social history of the area. Essayist Jim Davis, using the long-running play *Bleacher Bums* as his primary source, explores the desire of Cubs fans for a sense of authenticity and community in the face of commercialism and exploitation. It is a play, he discovers, with a powerful expression of melting pot ideology, yet it is a dated piece that at the dawn of the twenty-first century is finally becoming nostalgic as it drowns beneath the ineluctable tide of corporate and media politics. The bleachers as renovated by the Tribune Company are now the Budweiser Bleachers, and the new bums are wealthy yuppies who (along with telecubbies) are a far cry from the blue-collar fans who inspired the original Bums and play. Tim Morris finds surprisingly few appearances of the Cubs in modern fiction. While the team appears in these works, it tends to be peripheral to the main action and statement. One wonders why, given the Cubs' long, storied history and the massive media attention given to the club in recent times. Curt Smith describes the history of Cubs' broadcasting, empha-sizing the radio voices, from the glory days when the team seemed to win the NL pennant every other year until Harry Caray and beyond, including the radio re-creation employing Ronald Reagan and others. In his essay on the Tribune ownership era, Ron Kates argues that the Tribune Company, which bought the Cubs in 1981, has increasingly highlighted periph-eral activities at Wrigley Field rather than the on-field action. A baseball viewing experience that for decades emphasized the players and their performance is now, as Kates notes, a kind of postmodern theater. And in her essay on the bleacher regulars, Holly Swyers describes the social function of the scorecards that the regulars use to follow the game on the field. Following the anthropologist Arjun Appadurai, Swyers traces the social history of scorecards in the bleachers and offers a fascinating reading of their form and meaning.

The following section studies individual players as expression of Chicago culture. Shawn O'Hare recovers the career of John Clarkson, a relatively obscure player in Cubs history but a man whose personal problems and eccentricities made him one of the most colorful and (in his peak years) greatest pitchers of all time, that is, before the pitching mound was relocated. In the late 20s and early 30s Hack Wilson was as famous as Mordecai Brown was in the first decade, albeit more for his volatility than charm. As Bob Boone and Gerald Grunska describe, in "Hack Wilson in Chicago," Hack confronted pitchers, umpires, and even White Sox players while playing on the edge between excellence and self-destruction. And in his essay on Gabby Hartnett, William F. McNeil offers a convincing argument that Hartnett was the best catcher ever to play in the major leagues. But equally interesting to McNeil are the connections between Hartnett's achievements and the cultural history of Chicago and the nation during the 1920s, 30s, and 40s. Ron Santo and Ryne Sandberg, on the other hand, represent the traditional, dominant culture of late-twentieth-century Cubs fans. But there are significant differences even there, Gerald C. Wood argues. While Santo personifies a blue-collar ethnicity and its "character" ideology, Sandberg is the creation of the Tribune media culture, a posterboard cutout who lacks the grit, struggle, and political agendas of Santo's story.

Rick Moser provides the final word in this volume, arguing quite convincingly and in painstaking fashion why the Cubs' near-century of futility is unparalleled in the history of sport. Rather than lament this long durée of utter winlessness, Moser finds beauty and hope and karmic grace in the Cubs' holding out for an even century of no Worlds Series rings. For Moser, and for the editors of this volume, we trust that the 2008 Cubs will inaugurate a new century of exciting and record-setting baseball in the Friendly Confines, a century that promises each new season, as the bard would say, to be "such stuff as dreams are made on."

Cubs Timeline

12 Oct. 1869	Creation of the Chicago Base Ball Club, the forerunner of the White Stockings/Cubs.
1871	Play as one of original teams of the National Association, the White Stockings, until Union Grounds consumed in the Chicago Fire, October 9, 1871. Team out of league until 1874–75.
1876	Still called the White Stockings, the team became charter member of the National League, formed by club president William Hulbert. Played first game on May 10 at 23rd Street Grounds, at 23rd and State, beating Cincinnati 6–0, and eventually winning National League pennant.
1877	Move to Lakefront Park, Randolph and Michigan, site of Lake Park, where earlier teams had played until 1871 Chicago Fire. With expansion, park seated 10,000 in 1883. That year's team set Cubs' team record for home runs in a season, 131, which stood until 1970.
1880–82	White Stockings win three consecutive pennants under leadership of Cap Anson, who had become manager in 1879.
1885	Moved to West Side Park, Congress and Throop, patterned after Lakefront Park, where they also win pennants in 1885 and 86.
1891–93	Play at both West Side Park and South Side Park, 35th and Wentworth, former home of Chicago Pirates of the Players League. On West Side for Monday, Wednesday, and Friday games; on South Side, near eventual site of Comiskey Park, on Tuesday, Thursday, and Saturday games. Called Colts in 1892 because of their youthful players, the team that year began playing Sunday games at new field, West Side Grounds, Polk and Lincoln (now Wolcott).
1894	Stadium partially burned, suspected arson by Sunday Observance League.
1898	Cap Anson fired as manager.
1906–8	After brief designation as Orphans in early 1900s, the team called the Chicago Cubs, managed by Frank Chance, wins three consecutive National League Championships, including 116 wins in 1906 and the World Series in both 1907 and 1908. Stars include double play combination of Tinker (ss), Evers (2b), and Chance (1b) as well as pitcher Mordecai "Three-Finger" Brown.

1910	Cubs win pennant again but this time lose to the Philadelphia Athletics 4 games to 1 in World Series.
1916	Move to Weeghman Park (also called North Side Ballpark and Whales Park), former home of Federal League Whales, who had been managed by former Cub Joe Tinker and starred Mordecai Brown. Team purchased by Charles Weeghman, who had owned Whales during their two years of existence.
1918	Cubs win NL pennant but lose to Boston Red Sox (led by pitching of Carl Mays and Babe Ruth), 4 games to 2, in World Series.
1921	William Wrigley, Jr., of the chewing-gum dynasty, gains controlling interest in the Cubs.
1926	Field name changed to Wrigley Field.
1929	Cubs win pennant under Joe McCarthy with team led by Rogers Hornsby, Hack Wilson, and Kiki Cuyler. Lose World Series to Philadelphia Athletics, 4 games to 1.
1932	Philip Wrigley, son, becomes owner in 1932 and Cubs win pennant, with Gabby Hartnett and Billy Herman as key players, but lose to Babe Ruth and Yankees in World Series sweep, 4 games to 0.
1935	With Hartnett as manager (appointed during season) the Cubs win pennant again, with Hartnett as NL MVP and Phil Cavarretta as star rookie, 18 years old. They lose to Detroit Tigers in World Series, 4 games to 2.
1937	Ivy planted at Wrigley Field by Bill Veeck, first general manager of the team, and scoreboard added to center field. Addition of center-field bleachers also shortened center-field wall from 447 feet to 400.
1938	Following Hartnett's "Homer in the Gloamin'," Cubs yet again win pennant, but are swept by Yankees in World Series.
26 Apr. 1941	Organ installed at Wrigley Field.
8 Dec. 1941	Date for beginning of construction on lights at Wrigley, but Japanese attack on Pearl Harbor previous day leads Philip Wrigley to donate materials to war effort.
1945	Cubs go to World Series for last time, but lose to underdog Detroit Tigers 4 games to 3.
17 Sept. 1953	Ernie Banks, 22 years old, starts at shortstop and color barrier is broken on the Cubs.
1958 and 59	Banks wins back-to-back NL MVP Awards amidst 22-year period (1947–66) in which team has only one winning season (1963).
1961–62	Experiment with rotating system of managers, called College of Coaches, fails to inspire players or win games.
1966	Leo Durocher hired as manager.
1969	Cubs, led by aging Banks, Billy Williams, Ron Santo, and Fergie Jenkins, lead NL for most of season before losing to Miracle Mets in final weeks.
1977	Death of Philip Wrigley.

1981	Chicago Tribune Company buys the Chicago Cubs.
1983	Completes another ten-year period of losing records, including four last-place finishes.
1984	Following crucial trades by GM Dallas Green, team led by Ryne Sandberg, Leon Durham, and Rick Sutcliffe wins division title, but then loses League Championship Series to San Diego Padres after leading five-game playoff 2–0.
8 Aug. 1988	First night game with new lights at Wrigley Field. Game called that night in 4th inning with Cubs ahead 3–1. Next night they beat the Mets 6–4.
1989	Cubs win division again, managed by Don Zimmer and led by Mark Grace, Greg Maddux, and Ryne Sandberg, but again lose in playoffs.
1994	Harry Caray dies on February 18 at age 84.
15 Nov. 1999	Don Baylor hired as first black Cubs manager.
1998-2001	Sammy Sosa hits 243 home runs, including 66 (1998), 63 (1999), and 64 (2001).
2003	Cubs hire Dusty Baker as manager and go to finals of National League Championship, losing 4–3 games, after leading 3–1. Bartman ball rekindles talk of a curse.
2006	Nearly 1800 seats added to Wrigley Field's outfield bleachers, which are renamed the Budweiser Bleachers. GM Jim Hendry given two-year extension on his contract. With key players on DL, Cubs again flounder and Baker is fired at end of season.
Oct. 2006	Lou Piniella given three-year contract as manager.
2007	Team spends over $300 million on players, including 8-year, $136 million contract to free-agent Alfonso Soriano, in order to rebuild. Cubs still lose in first round of playoffs.
2008	With signing of Japanese star Kosuke Fukudome, Cubs expected to contend for post-season play. Team offered for sale by the Tribune Company, with naming rights to Wrigley Field reserved for separate auction.

PART I

THE CUBS, WRIGLEY FIELD, AND P.K. WRIGLEY

Lake View, Baseball, and Wrigleyville: The History of a Chicago Neighborhood

Margaret Gripshover

Wrigley Field is located on the North Side of Chicago in a small neighborhood, commonly called Wrigleyville, a part of the more historically significant Lake View area. Since the blocks around Wrigley Field contain a lively mix of residences, retailing, services, and restaurants, as well as a hyperactive bar scene, many people assume that it is Wrigley Field that has made Lake View the prosperous community that it is today. In fact, Lake View existed as a township, was incorporated, and thrived long before Wrigley Field was built. Even today it is more likely that Lake View's proximity to Lincoln Park and the Loop, as well as its eclectic mix of architecture and amenities, make it one of the most desirable neighborhoods in Chicago, rather than Cubs baseball, save for those seeking to relive their lost youth in the fraternity party fantasy world described in Kevin Kaduk's *Wrigleyworld*. With or without the Cubs, Lake View is an ideal example of the neighborhood that New Urbanists strive to achieve through land use and architectural alchemy. Because it offers almost every commodity or service—trendy or mundane, rowdy or urbane—within a few blocks of most residences, Lake View has become one of the most desirable residential neighborhoods in Chicago.

The historical truth of the matter is that the Lake View neighborhood existed as a separate entity with its own identity well over one hundred years before the term "Wrigleyville" came into use. The mythology of Wrigley Field and its surrounding neighborhood wouldn't have existed without Lake View's evolution as a destination for Chicago's pleasure seekers and sports fans long before 1914, the year Charles Weeghman built for his Federal League Whales a ballpark that would later become Wrigley Field, home of the Cubs. Wrigleyville is a relatively new neighborhood name, having been created mainly as a marketing ploy by real estate agents during the 1980s. Today "Wrigleyville" is used to evoke the culture of Wrigley Field as a lifestyle for young, affluent (and mostly childless) professionals in the highly desirable, expensive apartments and condominiums near the ballpark. For those who couldn't imagine living anywhere else, Wrigleyville is the Land of Oz, where there is no place like a home near home plate. Peter Golenbock says it best when he describes Wrigleyville as more than just a place; it is an eminently marketable "state of mind" (xv).

By the mid-nineteenth century, the community that would serve as the future home of Wrigley Field was sparsely settled countryside. One of the few commercial ventures in the area was Lake View House, a hotel and namesake of the Lake View neighborhood, opened in 1854 just north of where Wrigley Field stands today. It would take two years for a stage-coach line to connect the Lake View House to the City of Chicago and three years for the first horse-drawn omnibuses to serve the area. Prior to incorporation as a township in 1857, Lake View's only other major claim to fame was being part of the "celery growing capital of the world" (Pacyga 87). Celery growing doesn't sound quite as exciting as a Cubs game, but for the Luxembourger and German immigrant farmers who specialized in its production as early as the 1830s, it was quite an enterprise. By the 1840s, Chicago had the largest concentration of Luxembourger immigrants of any city in the United States (Conzen 496–97).

The original boundaries of Lake View Township were Fullerton, Western, Devon, and the shoreline of Lake Michigan (see map). As the area grew, new schools opened, the Lake View Town Hall was built, and immigrants — mainly northern Europeans — streamed into the area, establishing ethnic enclaves, churches, and businesses. In addition to newly arrived immigrants, Germans and Swedes began to relocate into Lake View from neighborhoods to the south. Some of these immigrant groups were looked upon as threats to the cultural and economic underpinnings of the area. Ethnic prejudice was directed especially at groups of Irish and German immigrants, both of which had settled in large numbers in Chicago. Scorn was heaped especially upon the Germans who gathered on Sundays in beer gardens. While Germans viewed Sunday drinking as wholesome family leisure time, it was viewed as a moral outrage by some in the community, especially those involved in temperance movements. Where and when alcoholic beverages could be sold in Lake View would become a recurrent point of contention throughout the neighborhood's history, the source of division between different areas of the neighborhood. The effects of alcohol consumption on public behavior proved to be a perennial issue in Lake View, right up to the present day, with neighborhood concerns about alcohol-related fan rowdiness in Wrigleyville.

By the 1860s, the early celery farms of Lake View gave way to a first wave of residential development. Graceland Cemetery was established in 1860, quickly serving not only as a resting place for the dead but a popular picnic grounds. Even though it was remote enough to be perceived by the city as a favorite dumping ground for the city's waste ("Scavenger Nuisance" 3),[1] public spaces such as Graceland and various groves led Lake View to be "justly celebrated," according to the *Chicago Tribune*, "for its beauty of location, Sab-bath quiet, and its pride in a being a suburb of Chicago." The area offered "attractive fea-tures to real estate dealers," and consequently, "the price of land" was "on the increase throughout the town." While such a place "afford[ed] quiet homes for the wealthy, the *Tri-bune* continued, "the less favored citizens" also "find here [...] a lounging place." By 1869, baseball was becoming a part of the Lake View landscape as the locals enjoyed "the myster-ies of the "bat and ball," "a friendly game of the 'base'" and "a practicing game at Wright's Grove" ("Recreation" 4).[2]

But baseball was not the only form of lounging. Lake View was also home to a sharp-shooting club, a popular nineteenth-century leisure activity enjoyed by German immigrants. National sharpshooting meets were held in Lake View for many decades, some on the site of the Lake View Hotel.[3] In 1866, *The Chicago Tribune* reported that cockfights were being held in Lake View and illegal Keno gambling was taking place at the Lake View House. Two years later the *Tribune* ran a sensational headline that read, "The Groves of Lake View Scene of Debauchery" ("Pandemonium" 4). The "debauchery" in question referred to the public con-sumption of alcohol at Lake View picnic groves by Germans on Sundays.[4] Enjoying sports and beer in an outdoor setting in Lake View predates major league baseball's arrival by over half a century. Beer gardens were not known for an exclusively genteel clientele; they attracted "ruffians" from other parts of the city who came to enjoy the party atmosphere before returning to their homes.

By the 1870s, the rural character of Lake View was beginning to fade. A significant impetus for change was the Great Chicago Fire of 1871. Untouched by the fire, and not annexed by Chicago until the late 1880s, Lake View was not subject to the city's strict new fire ordinances, making inexpensive balloon-frame construction perfectly legal in the township. Keenly aware of their fortuitous location with respect to downtown Chicago, Lake View residents fought to keep certain types of land uses out of the township. In 1871, local developer S.H. Kerfoot and others opposed a plan to expand Graceland and Rosehill Cemeteries, believing that such a move would lower property values. Reflecting the new urban focus, the Lake View Board of Trustees in 1874 passed an ordinance to prohibit cattle from running free in the various sections of the township.[5]

Pointing to such ordinances, Lake View promoted itself as a "respectable and desirable residence suburb, where the tired business man [sic] can spend his Sundays in the quiet retirement of home, and not the tramping-ground for the roughs and loafers of the city" ("Local Miscellany" 22 May 1874: 3).

Law enforcement was seen as a mechanism by which local behavior could be moderated. The Lake View Police were issued their first official uniforms in 1874 in the hope that the more professionally appearing officers would "have a healthy moral effect on the minds of the city-roughs who go to Lake View for their Sunday's fun and have not hitherto been much impressed by the sight of a country official in citizen's clothes" ("Local Miscellany" 16 June 1874: 3). Locals looked to the police to enforce proper behavior and warned that property values would fall if immoral activities were left unchecked. Racing horses along Lake View roads was, for example, a popular weekend activity, much to the chagrin of the local police. And summertime seemed to bring out some of the most colorful visitor behavior. For example, in the summer of 1878, the *Tribune* noted that "There have been quite a number of arrests, since the commencement of the heated term, of parties swimming along the shore in a nude state, all being parties from the city, who think there are no ordinances restricting them after they once leave the city limits" ("Suburban" 6 June 1878: 8). Even the Lake View Glee Club came under suspicion when members were discovered "taking advantage of the moonlight evenings to do some serenading." According to a *Tribune* report, "Real Estate dealers will not be surprised by the low valuation of property near the corner of Halsted Street and Diversey Avenue when they learn that the [Lake View Glee] Club is in the habit of rehearsing in that vicinity" ("Local Miscellany" 30 June 1874: 3).

Baseball truly becomes a part of Lake View's sports life in the 1870s. Prior to the 1870s, there was only an occasional mention of "base ball" being played in Lake View, even as the city of Chicago was experiencing its golden age of amateur baseball (Freedman 42). But by the mid–70s Lake View earned its reputation as a leisure destination because it possessed the "Purest of lake water, accessible from all the principal streets, and nineteen saloons similarly accessible for the thirsty, shady groves with meandering walks for the sentimental, base-ball for the muscular Christians" ("Lake View" 12). During those summer months, there were almost daily reports of rosters and scores. At first, the players were local (sometimes college teams were the opponents), the games informal, the scoring high, and the players, more often than not, engaged in business professions. But during this decade the results of the "Lake Views" baseball team began to appear in Chicago newspaper reports, especially when they played against the Ravenswood Base-Ball Club.[6] During the 1875 season, the Lake Views were considered as one of the top "amateur nines" in Chicagoland, having "suffered only one defeat this summer, although playing two or three matches every week" ("Suburban" 28 July 1875: 8). At the end of the 1875 season, the "Lake View Brown Stockings" were organized to play the following year and would soon be viewed by many as the finest Chicago area amateur team of its era. Of course, by then, across town, the Chicago White Stockings, the baseball club that would eventually become the Chicago Cubs, had been playing since 1870.

Lake View experienced dramatic changes during the 1880s, culminating in its annexation by the city of Chicago in 1889. Throughout the nineteenth century the southern half of the township, being located closer to the Chicago city limits, tended to take on a much more urban character while the northern portion of Lake View, even as late as the 1870s, still had a more rural character, and farmers there continued to raise potatoes, pumpkins, and celery for Chicago markets.[7] By the 1880s, a second division was identifiable between the east and west, along Halsted, when saloons were banned to the east. The result was a "beer line" that concentrated saloons along an emerging commercial corridor following Halsted, Green Bay Road (now Clark Street), Belmont Avenue, Lincoln Avenue, Sheffield Avenue, and Diversey. As the *Tribune* noted in 1882, "While the western side of town is quickly filling up with manufacturing establishments, the eastern or residence part is also being improved to a greater extent than ever before" ("Manufactures at Lake View" 18). Today this divide is still visible on the landscape, with the east side of Lake View having fewer commercial establishments and more exclusive real estate, including tony Lake Shore Drive addresses, than neighborhoods to the west. Wrigley Field and Wrigleyville are located in the north end of Lake View, near this east/west divide.

In the 1880s, Lake View was promoted as an affordable neighborhood to prospective homebuyers, and local building and loan associations flourished. Lake View's population by 1884 stood at 12,824, one-third of whom were children. Two public schools and a high school were built in response to the influx of families with school-aged children. During this same decade, Lake View benefited from infrastructural improvements, including the first commuter rail lines connecting Lake View with downtown Chicago. New social organizations and churches as well as retail and services grew with the burgeoning population. The first graystones, elegant and substantial single-family homes and apartments with generous setbacks, were being built. Beer gardens and saloons continued to attract locals as well as outsiders. Although Lake View's public transportation system had improved, the suburb was still relatively remote from downtown Chicago, making it a favored escapist destination for those leaving the city for leisure as well as for medical treatment.[8]

Lake View was growing, and while many were profiting from real estate speculation and subdivision development, the costs of increased population and woefully inadequate infrastructure were beginning to wear on its residents. Lake View had resisted the notion of annexation for nearly twenty years. But finally, in 1889, after a bitter campaign waged by both sides of the debate, the residents of Lake View voted for annexation with the city of Chicago — largely as a result of public health concerns related to safe water and proper waste disposal. Subsequently, with the implementation of new fire codes, the graystones became even more attractive in the Lake View community.

Meanwhile, baseball continued to evolve in Lake View. The game was becoming more popular and was emerging as a major spectator sport in Lake View as teams competed for the City Championship.[9] The City Championship in 1880, for example, went to the Dreadnoughts, who "received $50 and A.G. Spalding bats and balls" ("Base-Ball" 7). In 1882, the Lake Views were renamed "Spalding's Amateurs," who, despite their name, retained little of their gentlemanly reputation of years past. For example, the June 14, 1882, *Tribune* reported that

Last Sunday the Lake View base-ball club which was reorganized this spring and its name changed, played a rival club at the North Side Driving Club, near Sheffield Avenue. After the game the boys started out to have some fun, visiting a number of saloons by the wayside and getting pretty well soaked with beer. On their way towards the city they entered a saloon on Lincoln Avenue, near Wrightwood, got into a row, pounded the saloonkeeper and his assistant, smashed the windows, beer tumblers, and some furniture, then left in pursuit of more "fun" ["Suburban" 8].

Reports of amateur baseball in Lake View begin to wane by the late 1880s and were replaced by news of games played by school-aged teams and professionals.

A most significant event for the future of the Cubs' organization occurred in 1886, from a surprising source. At the Lutheran General Council meeting, Reverend Dr. W. A. Passavant reminded the Council that fifteen years earlier he had donated four acres of land in Lake View, valued at $16,000, for the purpose of building a seminary. Plans were made to officially transfer the property to the Council. On the four-acre parcel bounded by Addison, Clark, Sheffield, and Waveland Avenue the purchasers planned to build the first English-language Lutheran seminary west of the Appalachians (Campbell 8). On this quiet, nearly rural land, the Lutherans completed the first seminary building, the president's residence, at the corner of Sheffield and Waveland Avenues. The opening ceremonies were held in October 1891, and the *Tribune* noted that "altogether the school has a good outlook" ("Lutheran Theological Seminary" 3). In less than twenty-five years this site would become home to Weeghman Park, and ultimately, Wrigley Field. It is no wonder, given the provenance of the property, that many people view attending a Cubs games as something akin to a religious pilgrimage.

About the time that the Lutherans were setting cornerstones for a seminary on the North Side, the neighborhood was gaining a reputation never imagined by that religious group. In 1890, an article in the *Chicago Tribune* describes the North Clark Street and Sheffield Avenue area as "Funeral Avenue," noting that the routes through Lake View to Graceland, Rose Hill, Calvary, Jewish, St. Boniface, and the German Catholic cemeteries were lined with saloons that catered to the mourners returning from burying their dearly departed. There were an estimated fifty such "cemetery saloons" along Funeral Avenue, many of which had a "Ladies' Entrance" and long sheds that could accommodate buggies and horse-drawn hearses, some large enough for a funeral cortege of one hundred vehicles ("Funeral Avenue Bars" 3). In addition to the saloons that lined the Avenue, beer gardens were another popular destination to relax and enjoy drinking, dancing, and even outdoor sporting events. In 1893, De Berg's Garden at Grace and Halsted, a popular beer garden, hosted "Volksfest" for the Bavarian Society of Chicago and offered outdoor bowling alleys. De Berg's would later be renamed Bismarck Garden and then renamed yet again during the anti–German agitation of World War I as Marigold Garden, which became famous for its boxing matches.

By the end of the nineteenth century Lake View had built the foundation for the introduction of major league baseball to the neighborhood at the beginning of the twentieth century. Throughout the 1800s, the township attracted non-residents from a variety of ethnic and economic backgrounds who sought everything from a few hours' to a few days' escape from the noise, pollution, violence, and chaos that plagued nineteenth-century Chicago. Lake View was especially noted for its sporting events, from "base ball," horse racing, and rifle shooting to all manner of illegal diversions. By the 1890s, amateur baseball was replaced by amateur adult and boys' teams that began placing the equivalent of contemporary "singles ads" in the *Chicago Tribune* requesting "dates" with other teams.[10] Another twist in the sport by the 1890s was the improbable popularity of indoor baseball. And when just about every marketing angle to attract new fans to baseball had been tried, in 1890 the Chicago City League

In the early 1900s, the Lutheran Seminary was on the site of today's Wrigley Field (courtesy Evangelical Lutheran Church in America).

advertised their games as "ladies days" with free admission for the distaff side ("The City League" 6).

Not everyone merrily embraced the changes that were occurring in Lake View by the 1890s. In 1894, residents along Evanston (Broadway) were successful in killing plans for a new trolley line. Another issue that polarized Lake View in the 1890s was the plan to relocate the famous World's Fair Ferris wheel in the neighborhood as part of a new amusement park. The *Tribune* reported that there was "considerable probability [...] that Lake View is to become the great amusement center of the city" ("New Street in Cairo" 8). "Ferris Wheel Park" at Clark and Wrightwood opened in 1896, and from the outset was fraught with problems ranging from the granting of liquor licenses to neighborhood disdain. In 1896, Lake View residents formed The Improvement and Protective Organization (IPO) to "prevent further invasion of such nuisances which invariably follows anything of the kind" ("Fight on Ferris Wheel Sideshows" 5). The IPO got its wish when Ferris Wheel Park went bankrupt in 1900, and the wheel was sold to St. Louis, where it was featured at the Louisiana Purchase Exposition (St. Louis World's Fair) of 1904, and ultimately was demolished for scrap in 1906. The IPO battles against Ferris Wheel Park were precursors to the battles fought by the Lake View Citizens' Council (LVCC) for neighborhood preservation and a group that called itself Citizens United for Baseball in the Sunshine (CUBS) that fought to restrict night baseball in Wrigley Field.[11]

The twentieth century debuted in Lake View with the first elevated (El) train lines to serve the western part of the neighborhood, physically reinforcing the cultural divide between the east and west sides of Lake View. A second El connection to the Ravenswood line in 1908 proved a boon to commuters, retailers, and developers. The western section of the neighborhood continued to be more commercial (with mostly lower-quality frame housing) than East Lake View, which was graced with elegant graystones and estate homes along Lake Shore Drive. But the arrival of the El in Lake View would do more than just divide the neighborhood. Proximity to the El proved to be one of the reasons why the Chicago Lutheran Seminary decided to vacate its property, and one of the major reasons why that same location was so attractive to Charles Weeghman.

The Chicago Lutheran Seminary's decision to vacate its property in 1910 was prompted by the boisterous commercial district that had emerged around it. The land upon which the seminary built was, by 1910, much more desirable for commercial development than when the Lutherans acquired it nine years earlier. When the seminary was built, there was no elevated train service to Lake View. By 1910, the El line clattered along within earshot of seminarians, bringing with it crowds of transients, recreation seekers, and commuters. Improved transportation, increasing population, manufacturing and retail expansion, plus the growing popularity of nearby beer gardens and their singing groups and boxing matches, increasingly encroached upon the peaceful confines of the Chicago Lutheran Seminary. The Synod decided that the area was becoming unsuitable for meditative study and relocated the entire seminary to Maywood, Illinois (Shea 6).

Who would be interested in buying the property given all its "faults"? The initial purchaser of the seminary property was Charles Havenor, owner of the Milwaukee baseball club of the American Association. The *Tribune* reported the sale in 1909. But in his 1941 reminiscences about the transfer, Rev. Dr. Frank E. Jensen more accurately dated the sale as 1907, saying he kept the sale secret (even from the seminary leadership) at Havenor's request. Havenor was worried about possible objections to his franchise in Chicago. Rumors were rampant that Havenor wanted to establish a new club on the North Side or, alternatively, that a railroad was interested in developing the site. Neither of those plans came to fruition, as Havenor died before he could build a ballpark in Lake View, and his business partners eventually sold the land to "Lucky Charlie" Weeghman.

In 1913, Charles H. Weeghman, owner of a string of successful lunch counters and the Federal League Whales, stepped in and signed a deal to acquire the land to build a ballpark at the corner of Clark and Addison. While there was initial resistance to the construction of the baseball "plant" by its immediate residential neighbors, Weeghman's vision was endorsed by the local business community (Green and Jacob 95). Weeghman enlisted Zachary Taylor Davis, designer of Comiskey Park, as the architect, and Weeghman Park opened on April 23, 1914. Weeghman saw the neighborhood as an asset to conducting business, not a liability as had the seminarians. What better way to complement a sporting venue than with nearby saloons and beer gardens? Unlike the South and West sides of the city, the North Side could not claim a professional baseball team. Add to that an El stop just steps away from the park and you have a perfect location for a baseball stadium in the early twentieth century, given that most fans either walked or took public transportation to reach their destination.

Weeghman's short tenure as a baseball magnate nearly ended in 1915, however, when the Federal League collapsed and his Chicago Whales became defunct. Not missing a beat, Weeghman capitalized on an opportunity to purchase the Cubs and moved them from the West Side to Weeghman Park for the 1916 season. After buying the team, however, "Lucky Charlie" seems to have lost his Midas touch. His luck ran out and his personal life and fortune went into a tailspin. By 1920, he had lost control of the Cubs to William Wrigley, Jr., and his restaurants were in receivership. Weeghman went from owning a mansion on Sheridan Road in Chicago in 1917, to renting a studio apartment in 1930 in New York City, where he failed in his efforts to restart his restaurant empire. Weeghman died in 1938 in Chicago from the effects of a stroke. The headlines for his obituary summed up his story: "C.H. Weeghman, 64, Dead in Chicago — Former Owner of the Cubs Was Among First of 'One-Arm'-Lunch Operators — Built Restaurant Chain — Met Reverses After Entering Baseball" ("C. H. Weeghman" 23). If there has ever been a curse on the Cubs, don't look to a goat; look to "Lucky Charlie."[12]

Lake View in the 1910s and 1920s continued to prosper, and the older western side of the neighborhood — now bisected by busy El lines — was the focal point for commercial development. On Lincoln Avenue, Wieboldt's opened an eight-story department store that anchored a shopping district known as the "Triple Transfer Corner." The Lincoln-Belmont area developed as the largest retail furniture district outside the Loop. And the beginnings of a gay and lesbian district of North Halsted also surfaced in the 1920s as gays and lesbians found it relatively easy to blend in with single transient workers living in boarding houses and apartments in the commercial and industrial sections of Chicago such as Lake View (Meyerowitz 112).

Bismarck Garden, not the nearby Weeghman Park, was the main source of disdain for neighbors in the northern end of Lake View during the 1910s. The Bismarck burned in 1913, and residents of the neighborhood protested the rebuilding of the bandstand and cabaret stage ("Bismarck Garden Damaged by Fire" 9).[13] In that same year, another problem surfaced at the Garden — the beginning of the parking issues that continue to vex Wrigleyville, and the Lake View neighborhood in general, to this day. Bismarck Garden was built before the "Auto Age," so parking wasn't a consideration. But eventually the increased demand for automobile parking spawned illegal activity such as "tip trusts" that involved charging someone to park on public streets. Lack of on-street parking was becoming a major annoyance to local residents who found the free curb space in front of their house occupied by a Bismarck Garden patron, thus leaving the owner without a spot for the family Model-T.[14] The same year that parking bribes were causing an uproar in Lake View, Bismarck Garden changed its name to Marigold Garden, following the trend of such businesses to distance themselves from their Germanic roots at the onset of World War I. What finally put an end to Marigold Garden was not neighborhood pressure or backlash against German-style beer gardens; it was Prohibition in 1923.

Beer gardens weren't the only landmarks that changed their names during this period. In 1920, William Wrigley purchased the Cubs from Charles Weeghman, and the ballpark was officially renamed Wrigley Field in 1926. The following year, an upper deck was added, bringing the seating capacity up to 40,000. The addition of seats brought more congestion to the Wrigley Field area as it was becoming more common to arrive at Cubs games via personal transportation. When the park was built, no one could have envisioned the shift away from the El to private automobiles, except for, say, Henry Ford. So, with each ensuing decade, the friction between Wrigley Field patrons and Lake View residents over parking issues continued to escalate. "Tip trusts" that began around 1917 continued unabated.[15] And this group was soon followed by the parking hustlers known as the "Watch yer car?" barkers.[16]

By 1930, Lake View's population had grown to 114,872, nearly ten times the population just prior to annexation. The neighborhood remained overwhelmingly white, and 29 percent of its residents were foreign-born. New immigrants and poorer migrants continued to live mainly in the older western part of Lake View, where housing was still predominately frame construction and less expensive than East Lake View, which was dominated by pricier brick and stone construction. The repeal of Prohibition in 1933 was certainly welcome news to many thirsty souls. Bars and clubs reopened (or at least now operated legally), and the uninhibited character of the neighborhood surrounding Wrigley Field was revived. The 1930s also signaled major changes for the Cubs. William Wrigley, Jr., died in 1932. Wrigley's son, Philip K. (P.K.) Wrigley, set about revamping Wrigley Field to "fit his vision of a backyard family playground" ("Cubs Timeline: 1930s," par. 2). New bleachers and a scoreboard were installed. In 1937, P.K. hired Bill Veeck as manager. And while Veeck failed to bring a championship home to the North Side, he did plant the now-famous ivy that covers the outfield brick walls.

The War years of the 1940s were quiet ones for Lake View. The Cubs made their last World Series appearance in 1945, losing once again — to the Detroit Tigers. In 1941, the first attempt was made to install lights at Wrigley Field, but those plans were scuttled after the attack on Pearl Harbor. Philip K. Wrigley donated what were to become the lights for Wrigley Field to the U.S. government to support the war effort, and the tradition of "day games only" continued. By 1948, the Chicago Cubs were the only team in major league baseball without night games on their home schedule. The Cubs' potential fan base expanded in 1948 with WGN-TV's premier broadcast of a Cubs game. The Cubs lost the game, but WGN ultimately ended up as the winner. By the 1980s, WGN emerged as a "super-station," gaining access to markets beyond Chicago and creating a new demographic of Cubs fans via cable television outlets.

The population of Lake View in 1950 had reached 125,000, the highest ever for the neighborhood, and there were 2,000 more cars in the neighborhood than spaces to accommodate them. The type of housing was also changing. High-rise apartments were being constructed along Lake Shore Drive in East Lake View while historic single-family graystones became "tear down" targets to be replaced by the much-maligned "four-plus-one" apartments, four-story apartments with the "one" being a parking area underneath. Four-plus-ones were inexpensive housing for urban singles and often lacked any architectural sympathy for their neighborhood contexts. In the opinion of many Lake View residents, the four-plus-ones were not only ugly but also represented a threat to the visual character of Lake View and would increase population density.[17]

In 1952, a group of Lake View residents, believing the integrity of their neighborhood was at stake, organized to confront the developers of both four-plus-ones and high rises. The Lake View Citizens' Council was an early entrant into the historic preservation movement and successfully lobbied to limit the intrusion of four-plus-ones and the destruction of older residences. While concerns about Wrigley Field and its associated activities were not a part of the LVCC's original agenda, the organization campaigned successfully for historic neighborhood preservation into the 1960s (Spirou and Bennett 16).

But the character of the neighborhood was starting to shift beneath their feet. The 1960 Census revealed a slight decline in population from the peak year a decade earlier. In 1961, it was estimated that at least 64,000 people lived within a half-mile radius of Wrigley Field, perhaps the first reference to a distinct neighborhood associated with the ballpark. The common use of the term "Wrigleyville" was still a decade or more away, but there was a certain awareness of an emerging Wrigleyville even before it became a part of real estate agents' vernacular. The site of the infamous Marigold Garden, for decades a popular destination for beer drinkers and sports enthusiasts, received the ultimate conversion in 1963 when the building was converted to the Faith Tabernacle Church. Old German-style beer gardens had fallen out of favor, and consumer preferences shifted toward indoor clubs and bars that offered more privacy and the comforts of air conditioning. Parking continued to prove nettlesome for fans and residents alike in the 1960s.[18] And the 1960s ended for the Cubs much like the 1950s — no World Series rings.

By 1970, Lake View's population had fallen a bit further, to 115,000, close to the level in 1930. The neighborhood was, however, in the middle of transition period from a blue-collar, older working-class and ethnic community to a white-collar, youthful, affluent, and diverse area. And that trend would persist. Over one-third of the residents were now employed in white-collar professions. Few churches remained that could claim a single ethnic heritage. Trinity Lutheran, which had offered services in Swedish as late as the 1960s, by the 1970s had become the *Iglesia del Valle* parish. What was once a Swedish neighborhood around Belmont and Sheffield was now becoming a Latino enclave, and the name "Boys Town" emerged to refer to the gay and lesbian residential and commercial district between 3100 and 3800 North Halsted.

In the midst of all the social changes in the neighborhood, gentrification came to Lake View in the 1970s and 1980s. The redevelopment successes of Lincoln Park spilled over into then more-affordable Lake View. By the end of the 1970s, older stores, many operated by immigrants or their descendants, closed and were replaced with upscale boutiques and shops catering to the new class of young urban professionals, the "Yuppies" who found Lake View an affordable alternative to Lincoln Park and a much more fashionable alternative to Uptown, located to the north. The term "Wrigleyville" began to appear in real estate advertisements aimed at a largely single, young, and relatively affluent groups of would-be residents to embody the hip, fun, and accessible possibilities of the neighborhood. Speculation, combined with strong demand, drove up the price of housing in Lake View and forced some renters out as more and more properties were "going condo." The average value of owner-occupied housing in Lake View jumped from $16,000 in 1960s to over $52,000 in the 1970s. In the 1970s and 1980s, young urban hipsters were attracted to the historic graystones of Lake View at the same time that their demographic counterparts in New York and Washington, D.C., were busily converting downtrodden brownstones into highly desirable and trendy neighborhoods.

What was happening to the Cubs as all this renewed interest in their backyard was swirling about them? P.K. Wrigley, son of William Wrigley, died in 1977. While P.K. was generally reviled by Cubs fans for his detached ownership style and the club's decline, he did attempt to be a good Lake View neighbor. He promised that as long as he was alive, Wrigley Field would be a day-game only park. P.K. did not, however, solve the perennial parking problems associated with Wrigley Field.[19] The death of P.K. set into motion a series of events that would ultimately change the way the Cubs organization operated and the nature of its relationship with the Lake View neighborhood.

The 1980s brought as much change to the character of the Lake View neighborhood as did the period of the 1880s. During the 1980s, for the first time in Lake View history, the majority of its residents were employed in white-collar occupations. The percentage of white residents dropped to a historic low of less than 75 percent (6.9 percent were now African-American and 18.8 percent Latino). Yet Latinos and other minorities, who had moved into

Lake View after 1950 but before the real estate boom of the 1970s, were now finding themselves increasingly priced out of the housing market. With more singles living in the neighborhood, school enrollments began to drop. And cultural shifts continued to affect the neighborhood during the 1980s. The former Norwegian Lutheran Church on W. Roscoe became the North Side Islamic Mosque. The Elim Swedish Methodist Episcopal Church on W. Barry went condo. In 1982, the first "Northalsted Market Days" were held celebrating gay and lesbian culture. The Music Box Theatre and the Victorian Theatre each experienced restoration and revival as a renewed interest in the arts paralleled the growing diversity and affluence in Lake View.

Meanwhile, a few blocks away from North Halsted's Boys Town, things were also changing at Wrigley Field. Upon learning he owed over $40 million in estate taxes, P.K. Wrigley's son, William Wrigley III lightened his debt in 1981 by selling his grandfather's beloved Cubs to the Tribune Company for $20.5 million. It seemed that overnight the Cubs had gone from a business owned by a neighbor to yet another corporate acquisition of a large media conglomerate. The Tribune was not just a newspaper company; it also owned WGN. Under the Tribune Company's ownership, in 1984, the Cubs, for the first time since 1945, found themselves in the National League playoffs. While that may have seemed like a very good thing at the time, the lack of lights at Wrigley Field and the inability to broadcast playoff games for primetime viewing on television ignited a controversy that still simmers and occasionally boils over. The bottom line was that the time had come for night games at Wrigley Field.

Lake View residents were keenly aware of the implications of the sale of the Cubs to the Tribune Company, including the fact that night baseball was becoming a real possibility. There were calls for a provision in the new deed to Wrigley Field that no night games would ever be played at Wrigley Field. Some residents tried to use level-headed arguments for maintaining the Cubs' tradition of day games at Wrigley with statements such as "This is a viable neighborhood, the only one in the major leagues, and one of the reasons is that Cubs only play day games."[20] Others were more confrontational and political. The Tribune Company's effort to bring night baseball to Wrigley Field in 1985 was met with fierce resistance from the LVCC and a new group, "Citizens United for Baseball in the Sunshine" (CUBS). Neighborhood representatives claimed that night baseball would create undue hardships to the citizens of Lake View including noise, trash, public drunkenness issues, parking problems, and last but not least, lower property values.[21]

Wrigley Field, unlike nearly every other major league baseball stadium, is not a baseball "oasis" surrounded by acres of parking lot "desert." Until 2005, no plans were approved for a Wrigley parking garage. Daytime games were always problematic when it came to parking. But those events were held while many Lake View residents were at work. The prospect of returning home in the evening and having your coveted on-street parking space occupied by a non-neighborhood resident who dumps beer cans and vomit in your yard was a little tough to swallow, not to mention worries over possible declining property values. Parking in the neighborhood, even without a Cubs game being played, was a challenge. Jim Finks, Cubs President in 1984, assured Lake View residents that, "There will be no lights at Wrigley Field as long as I am with the Cubs" (Jauss C2). Finks was true to his word. He resigned in December 1984.

The Tribune Company's plans were attacked by the LVCC and CUBS as well as the courts. Judge Richard Curry, in his 1985 ruling against the Tribune Company's request for lights at Wrigley Field said, "Tinkering with the quality-of-life aspirations of countless households so that television royalties might more easily flow into the coffers of 25 distant sports moguls is [...] repugnant to common decency" (Spirou and Bennett 682). But lights were ultimately installed at Wrigley Field, and the first night baseball game on the North Side was played on August 9, 1989. Ironically, or perhaps appropriately, the game was called in the early innings because of a lightning storm. The LVCC and CUBS did win some concessions from the Tribune Company, though. The Cubs were limited to twenty-two night games, and an elaborate parking permitting plan for the neighborhood was put into place with severe penalties imposed on violators.

In the post-lighting controversy years, Lake View and the Cubs have co-existed in a tense standoff. The move to install lights and hold night games at Wrigley Field has paid major dividends for the Tribune Company and WGN. The Cubs themselves have resurged and won the National League Central title in 2003 and had back-to-back winning seasons in 2003 and 2004 ("Cubs Timeline: 2000s," pars. 14, 18). In 2005, the Chicago City Council gave the Cubs permission to expand the bleacher section by 1,790 seats and add a 400-space parking garage and shopping complex across the street from Wrigley Field. In return, the Lake View neighborhood will get a new park, improved pedestrian pathways, and traffic lights at Clark and Waveland.

During the 1990s, Lake View's population continued a general decline, down to 91,031. But the percentage of whites in the neighborhood increased to 82 percent while foreign-born residents dwindled to 15 percent, a group least likely to find affordable housing. By 1990, nearly one-quarter of the neighborhood's population consisted of people ages 25–44 and living in "non-family households." Ironically, the much reviled four-plus-ones of the 1950s and 1960s became prime teardown targets to be replaced by taller four- to five-unit condominiums that were even more out of scale and became the new objects of scorn for older residents.

The 2000 Census confirms the trend for less racial diversity in Lake View: it notes declines in the percentages of African-Americans and Latinos in the neighborhood and just a slight increase in the percentage of Asian-Americans. Lake View was 84 percent white in 2000, up two percent from the previous decade. The fears of the LVCC and others concerning the potential negative impacts of night baseball on the neighborhood property values have proved unfounded. In fact, Lake View ranks second only to Lincoln Park in the value of residential loans among all Chicago neighborhoods. But the problems that have resulted from night baseball at Wrigley Field are indeed some of the ones that the members of the LVCC and CUBS feared—increased public intoxication, trash, crime, and parking problems. Some of the bigger losers in the continuing neighborhood transition, however, are retailers and restaurants that do not cater to the baseball crowds. They have seen declines in revenue on nights when the Cubs are playing at home. They claim that their customers fear the traffic and parking problems on game nights and thus are less likely to venture into the Lake View area.

Since the mid-nineteenth century, Lake View has seemed driven by history to become the complicated place that it is today — a livable, progressive, gentrifying, and upwardly mobile neighborhood that also functions as a place of pilgrimage for thousands of devoted Cubs fans. Many come to Wrigley Field to be wrapped in the aura of Cubs history, to cheer with the ghosts of Hornsby, Grimm, and Wilson, to imagine that they themselves can still see the "Homer in the Gloamin'," or hear Ernie Banks say, "Let's Play Two." But just as many come as peeping toms, peering into Wrigley Field from rooftops across the streets, baptized in beer and the party atmosphere that spills out of the ballpark and into the Wrigleyville neighborhood, where it often escalates into public drunkenness, fights, and destruction of property.

If you ask Lake View residents what they think of Wrigleyville, the usual responses include comments like, "I wish they wouldn't even call it Wrigleyville" or "I wish the Cubs would leave the neighborhood." Their thought is that if Wrigley Field were not located in

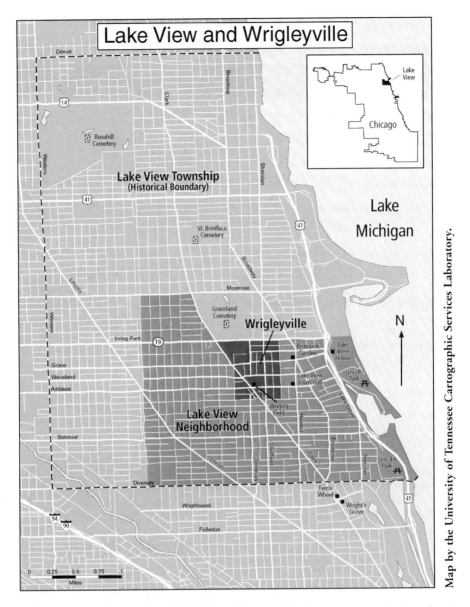

Map by the University of Tennessee Cartographic Services Laboratory.

their backyard, the neighborhood would be the peaceful, family-oriented place that it used to be. The trouble is that their nostalgic, romantic, and rear-view mirror image of Lake View is quite flawed. Before there ever was a Wrigley Field, that same part of Lake View was dotted with open-air beer gardens, outdoor boxing matches, plenty of noise, and drunken patrons staggering onto the streets. It should be remembered that those nineteenth- and early twentieth-century rowdies and ruffians were the ones who chased the Lutheran Theological Seminary out in the first place, making way for Wrigley Field.

NOTES

1. "Scavengers" was the name given to those who collected garbage, human "night soil," and animal carcasses, frequently depositing their loads at night just over the city limits in Lake View.

2. Wright's Grove was located north of Lincoln Park and south of Graceland and was a popular

Sunday resort and picnic spot that attracted thousands of weary Chicagoans each weekend, characterized in the *Tribune* as being "Germans and Americans from the industrial classes" ("Sunday Resorts" 3).

3. The Lake View Sharpshooters Club eventually became the site of Riverside Park.

4. "Nearly all of the German population seek occasional amusement and recreation at some of the concert saloons which are met with every few steps in passing up North Clark street" ("Sunday Amusements" 4). One *Tribune* writer went so far as to say that Germans can "out-Herod Herod" given their predisposition to consuming beer on Sundays ("Pandemonium" 4).

5. Despite attempts to keep cows in their places, dairy cattle rustling in Lake View persisted into the 1880s ("Suburban" 25 June 1880: 8).

6. For example, this rather humorous accounting of a game played in August, 1875 appeared in the *Tribune*. "The Ravenswood Base-Ball Club invited the Lake Views to come up last Saturday to get beaten, a large number of the Ravenswooders turning out to see it done. Contrary to their expectations, however, the Lake View Boys walked away with their pets by a score of 16–4. If the villagers of Sec. 17 wish to play ball, they should come southward and learn how" ("Other Suburbs: Lake View" 8).

7. Celery was, in fact, described as being a popular "nerve-restoring esculent" ("Lake View: General Gossip" 9).

8. In 1882, "The Martha Washington Department of the Washington Home — an institution wherein are to be treated inebriated and opium-eating women — was formally opened yesterday [July 1st] afternoon. It is located near the corner of Graceland and Western Avenues in the Town of Lake View and admirably adapted to the purpose" ("Martha Washington" 3).

9. The *Tribune* noted that "[T]he Lake Views and the Franklins will play their first game of the series for the amateur championship at White-Stockings Park tomorrow afternoon for the benefit of the Half-Orphan Asylum. Admission 25 cents and 15 cents. Aside from the charitable object of the game base-ball lovers will doubtless witness a good contest, as neither club has thus far lost a game this season" ("Ball Gossip" 8.). The Lake Views won the game, 9–8, but a few weeks later went down to their first defeat of the year at the hands of the Franklins.

10. Examples of such ads include the following three: (1) "Two or three good ball-players 18 or 19 years of age, living in Lake View or on the North Side, and wanting to play with a good uniformed club, can address Sam Wolf, No. 1347 Lincoln Avenue, or call Sunday 2 P.M. at the above address" ("Northwestern Suburban Games: Amateur Notes" 4); (2) "The Union Boys of Lake View would like to hear from some 14-year old clubs on the North Side" ("Amateur Notes" 5 June 1890); and (3) "The Warriors want games from the American Maroons, Young Diamonds, Fort Dearborns, Valley Boys, and Union Boys of Lake View" ("Amateur Notes" 23 June 1890).

11. And speaking of "baseball," 1892 was the first year the *Tribune* printed the sport's name as one word, "baseball," instead of the previous iterations that included "base ball," and "base-ball."

12. Weeghman's story is compelling. He arrived in Chicago from Richmond, Indiana, with a few dollars in his pocket and within 15 years went on to become a millionaire and owner of two baseball teams, the Federal League Chicago Whales and the Chicago Cubs. His Horatio Algeresque life did not have a perfect ending, and Weeghman died in near obscurity.

13. A year later, Anheuser-Busch purchased Bismarck Garden and announced plans for "winter garden" festivities and a large theatre was planned for a site across the street ("Begin Work on $300,000 Block on Broadway" 18). In 1916, Bismarck Garden was warned for "sneaking drinks" to patrons on Sundays, which were to be alcohol-free days. In 1917, striking union waiters were implicated in a plot to blow up Bismarck Garden.

14. "Neighbors of the Bismarck garden did not hesitate to proclaim the automobile convention in the vicinity a nuisance to those seeking repose. The honking of horns, the shrieking of women, and the constant clatter of exhausts is enough to drive us crazy, said C.W. Mains of 848 Grace Street. "I have complained time and again, but it's no use. The racket is terrible" ("Police Put Soft Pedal Upon Tip Trust Bandits" 8). One wonders if Mr. Mains could have even contemplated the complex on-street parking situation around Wrigley Field today.

15. One might even argue that tip trusts served as entrée into the world of crime for some juveniles in the neighborhood as evidenced in this amusing news item: "It was only yesterday that Miss Mary Capelli, 15 years old, a Lake View High School student, found prospects for thriving business in the rear of her home at 3554 Wilton Avenue. Today she is in the juvenile home, her business gone to smash. Robert, 7744 Stony Island Avenue, parked his car back of Mary's house yesterday while he spent the afternoon at Cub's park. After the game he returned to the machine to find Mary waiting. 'It'll cost you 25 cents for

parking here,' she informed McMillan. He refused to pay. 'All right,' shrilled Mary, and with an ice pick she put four holes in one of his tires. McMillan called the Town Hall police who took the girl to the juvenile home" ("Girl Punches Holes in Tires" 1).

16. Although parking restrictions were announced for the 1938 World Series, and car barkers were finally threatened with arrest, those actions did little to solve the long-term parking issues in the neighborhood ("Traffic Control is Mapped for Series Games" 5). And a letter to the *Tribune* editor in 1949 provides evidence that in the ensuing years nothing had been done to alleviate the parking problems around Wrigley Field. In fact, there was a spike in the number of newspaper articles concerning Wrigley Field and parking issues beginning in 1949 and continuing to the present. The growing demand for parking spaces reflected the increases in automobile ownership in the post–World War II period. "I went to a Cubs ball game and had to leave my car four blocks away to find a legal place to park. At Sheffield and Waveland there was a Cadillac parked on the sidewalk. There are a lot of parking violations around Wrigley Field" ("Wrigley Field Parking" A6). Parking problems extended to Bears games as well. Mrs. H.J. Conroy wrote, "Every time there is a football game at Wrigley Field our alleys are full of cars, despite warning signs all over the alleys, put there by the city council" (Conroy 20). Another irate resident wrote, "Can someone tell me who receives the payoff from parking operators near Wrigley Field who operate in the area beneath the elevated tracks? They charge 75 cents ($1 on double-header days) for parking under signs reading "No parking at any time" (Newman B24).

17. While no one seemed to come right out and say it, it was implied that four-plus-ones would attract the less affluent, more singles, and non-white residents.

18. A letter to the *Tribune* editor by Edward G. Carter stated that "Professional ball parks should furnish their own parking lots. Cars now swarm all over the surrounding area, taking the parking spaces normally used by the residents. Besides, there is price gouging at the limited off street lots" (Carter C4).

19. Illegal parking around Wrigley was even the focus of a grand jury investigation in 1974 when unlicensed lot operators testified about payoffs to Chicago police (Mount A1).

20. But one East Lake View resident advocated a more strident approach when he said, "Stanton Cook (Tribune CEO) is going to have to listen to us. And, if we have to, we have our own little guerilla warfare plan [...] But given a choice, I'd rather have them move the Cubs somewhere else than ruin the neighborhood by playing night baseball" (Milbert C3). Yet other residents tried to extend an olive branch to the new Cubs owners with that caveat that "We hope that the new owners will continue the spirit of cooperation we always have enjoyed with the previous ownership" (Geske et al A6).

21. But not everyone was against night baseball at Wrigley. A letter to Mike Royko's column in 1984 essentially tells the people of Lake View to get a life and realize that Wrigley Field was there before most of them moved there so what gives them the right to complain about it now? The letter writer goes on to say that he was a former resident of Lake View and moved out because he believed the neighborhood had gotten so rough that he would have rather run into "a drunken Cub fan on a dark street than a cut-throat hooker and her pimp" (Royko 3).

WORKS CITED

"Amateur Notes." *Chicago Tribune* 5 June 1890: 3.

"Amateur Notes." *Chicago Tribune* 23 June 1890: 3.

"Ball Gossip." *Chicago Tribune* 1 Aug. 1880: 8.

"Base-Ball: Winter Notes About the Game." *Chicago Tribune* 5 Dec. 1880: 7.

"Begin Work on $300,000 Block on Broadway: Big Structure Opposite Bismarck Garden to Contain Theater." *Chicago Tribune* 8 June 1915: 18.

"Bismarck Garden Damaged by Fire." *Chicago Tribune* 30 June 1913: 9.

Carter, Edward G. "Wrigley Parking." *Chicago Tribune* 9 Nov. 1862: C4.

"C. H. Weehgman, 64, Dead in Chicago: Former Owner of the Cubs Was Among First of 'One-Arm' Lunch Operators: Built Restaurant Chain: Met Reverses After Entering Baseball: Associated with Enterprises Here." *New York Times* 3 Nov. 1938: 23.

"The City League: The Clubs Rapidly Getting Into Shape for the Season's Work." *Chicago Tribune* 24 Mar. 1890: 6.

Conroy, Mrs. H. J. "'No Parking' Meaningless." *Chicago Tribune* 15 Nov. 1949: 20.

Conzen, Kathleen Neils. "Luxembourgers." *Encyclopedia of Chicago*. Ed. James R. Grossman, et al. Chicago: U of Chicago P, 2004.

"Cubs Timeline: 1930s." Cubs History. Official Site of the Chicago Cubs. <http://chicago.cubs.mlb.com/chc/history/timeline05.jsp>. 27 May 2006.

"Cubs Timeline: 2000s." Cubs History. Official Site of the Chicago Cubs. <http://chicago.cubs.mlb.com/chc/history/timeline05.jsp>. 27 May 2006.

"Fight on Ferris Wheel Sideshows: Property Owners of the Seventeenth Precinct of the Twenty-Fifth Ward to Form Protective Association." *Chicago Tribune* 6 June 1896: 5.

Freedman, Stephen. "The Baseball Fad in Chicago, 1865–1870: An Exploration of the Role of Sport in the Nineteenth-Century City." *Journal of Sport History* 5.2 (Summer 1978): 42–64.

"Funeral Avenue Bars: Saloons in Close Proximity to Cemeteries." *Chicago Tribune* 6 Nov. 1890: 3.

Geske, Herbert E., Paul J. Kendall, and Marilyn D. Krausas. "The Cubs' Neighbors." *Chicago Tribune* 5 July 1981: A6.

"Girl Punches Holes in Tires: Taken By Police." *Chicago Tribune* 13 Sept. 1927: 1.

Golenbock, Peter. *Wrigleyville: A Magical History Tour of the Chicago Cubs.* New York: St. Martin's Griffin, 1999.

Green, Stephen, and Mark Jacob. *Wrigley Field: A Celebration of the Friendly Confines.* Chicago: Contemporary Books, 2003.

Jauss, Bill. "Baseball: Finks De-Lights C.U.B.S." *Chicago Tribune* 24 Feb. 1984: C2.

Kaduk, Kevin. *Wrigleyworld: A Season in Baseball's Best Neighborhood.* New York: New American Library, 2006.

"Lake View." *Chicago Tribune* 23 July 1876: 12.

"Lake View: General Gossip." *Chicago Tribune* 1 Oct. 1876: 9.

"Local Miscellany." *Chicago Tribune* 22 May 1874: 3.

"Local Miscellany." *Chicago Tribune* 16 June 1874: 3.

"Local Miscellany." *Chicago Tribune* 30 June 1874: 3.

"Lutheran Theological Seminary." *Chicago Tribune* 2 Oct. 1891: 3.

"Manufactures at Lake View." *Chicago Tribune* 23 Apr. 1882: 18.

"Martha Washington: Formal Opening of the Home for Female Inebriates and Opium-Eaters." *Chicago Tribune* 2 July 1882: 3.

Meyerowitz, Joanne J. *Women Adrift: Independent Wage Earners in Chicago, 1880–1930.* Chicago: U of Chicago P, 1988.

Milbert, Neil. "Cubs' Neighbors Oppose Lights." *Chicago Tribune* 24 June 1981: C3.

Mount, Charles. "Parking Operators Tell Jury of Payoffs." *Chicago Tribune* 7 June 1974: A1.

Newman, Al. "Voice of Traffic: Wrigley Field Parking." *Chicago Tribune* 6 Aug. 1950: 24.

"New Street in Cairo: Reproduction to be Erected Close to the Ferris Wheel: Lake View Property Owners Grieve." *Chicago Tribune* 6 Apr. 1895: 8.

"Northwestern Suburban Games: Amateur Notes." *Chicago Tribune* 25 May 1890: 4.

"Other Suburbs: Lake View." *Chicago Tribune* 11 Aug. 1875: 8.

Pacyga, Dominic A., and Ellen Skerrett. *Chicago: City of Neighborhoods.* Chicago: Loyola UP, 1986.

"Pandemonium: The Groves of Lake View: How the Sabbath Was Observed by the Democracy: The Groves of Lake View a Scene of Debauchery." *Chicago Tribune* 27 July 1868: 4.

"Police Put Soft Pedal Upon Tip Trust Bandits: Bismarck Garden Visitors Allowed to Park in Grace Street." *Chicago Tribune* 12 Aug. 1917: 8.

"Recreation." *Chicago Tribune* 20 June 1869: 4.

Royko, Mike. "Lighten Up, You Cub Neighbors." *Chicago Tribune* 10 Sept. 1984: 3.

"The Scavenger Nuisance in Lake View." *Chicago Tribune.* 27 Apr. 1866: 3.

Shea, Stuart. *Wrigley Field: The Unauthorized Biography.* Washington, D.C.: Brassey's Inc., 2004.

Spirou, Costas, and Larry Bennett. "Revamped Stadium ... New Neighborhood?" *Urban Affairs Review* 37.5 (May 2002): 675–702.

"Suburban." *Chicago Tribune* 28 July 1875: 8.

"Suburban." *Chicago Tribune* 17 June 1878: 8.

"Suburban." *Chicago Tribune* 25 July 1880: 8.

"Suburban." *Chicago Tribune* 14 June 1882: 8.

"Sunday Amusements: How the Sabbath was Spent by Our German Fellow Citizens." *Chicago Tribune* 8 June 1868: 4.

"Sunday Resorts: Where and How the People Spend the Sabbath." *Chicago Tribune* 18 July 1869: 3.

"Traffic Control is Mapped for Series Games." *Chicago Tribune* 5 Oct. 1938: 21.

"Wrigley Field Parking." *Chicago Tribune.* 21 Aug. 1949: A6.

Wrigley Field: An Historical Basis for the Cubs' Curse?

David Bohmer

On the morning of March 14, 1914, a crew of 500 workers assembled on the city block of the Chicago north side bounded by Waveland, Sheffield, Addison and Clark. Their mission was to construct a 14,000-seat ballpark to be ready for play by April 23, the opening home game for the Chicago entry in the newly formed Federal League of Baseball. The financing of the new ballpark was provided by Charles Weeghman, the owner of the new Chicago team, soon to be known as the Chi Feds and later the Whales. Weeghman, originally from Indiana, had moved to Chicago in the 1890s, working initially as a waiter. By the time he invested in the Federal League, he owned a chain of luncheon restaurants in Chicago, the largest of which served up to 35,000 customers a day. The ballpark was constructed on land leased from the Lutheran Church, which had built a theological seminary on the site in 1891. In 1910, the town of Maywood, Illinois put up funds to convince the seminary to move, so the site was vacated well before construction started. Weeghman contracted with the architectural firm of Davis and Davis based in Aurora, Illinois. The firm's premier architect, Zachary Taylor Davis, was already well regarded for his design of the new ballpark on the south side of Chicago that housed the American League White Sox. In spite of Chicago's fickle spring weather and a two-day strike, the new ballpark was finished three days ahead of the opener (Jacob 1–7).

In the opener, the Chi Feds met the Kansas City Packers before an overflow crowd of 20,000 that squeezed into the new park, perhaps filling the open areas around the perimeter of the outfield (Jacob 5). They were managed by the great Cubs shortstop, Joe Tinker. In 1907 and 1908, Tinker had helped the Cubs win back-to-back World Series. Now he had gotten his chance to manage, as had the other members of the great double play combination, Evers and Chance, who both had managed the Cubs previously. The large crowd foreshadowed a good first season at the gate. Before the next season, capacity was expanded to 18,000 at Weeghman's "edifice of beauty" (3).

The Chicago team won the opening game 9–1, starting a pattern of success on the field for the new franchise during its first two seasons (Jacob 4). In the first year, the team finished with an 87–67 record, a game and a half behind the winning Indianapolis franchise. During the second season, the re-named Whales finished in first place by half a game when the struggling league decided not to make up rainouts. Playing two fewer games than the 87–67 St. Louis team, the Whales finished 86–66 and were declared the champions. They were helped in that successful season by the addition of another ex-Cub, pitcher Mordecai "Three

Finger" Brown, whom St. Louis had fired as their manager the previous year. It would be the first and last time that a baseball team playing in the ballpark now known as Wrigley Field would win a complete championship (*Baseball Encyclopedia* 197–99, 203–5).

When the Federal League folded after the 1915 season, the Major League owners bought out most of the financial backers or enabled them to buy existing franchises. The St. Louis owners were able to purchase the local American League Browns, resulting in that team's manager, Branch Rickey, jumping over to the Cardinals, beginning perhaps the greatest career ever for a baseball executive. Weeghman, with the help of minority partners, including William Wrigley, Jr., was able to purchase the Cubs from the Taft family of Cincinnati. He immediately vacated West Side Park where the Cubs had played since 1893 to have his newly acquired team perform in the recently constructed ballpark that was now called "Weeghman Park" (Jacob 6). The Cubs opened the 1916 season there, starting what is now a ninety-year run. The new owner brought with him his Federal League manager, Joe Tinker, who proved to be less successful than during his Federal League tenure, as the club finished in fifth place in their new park, twenty-seven games behind the pennant-winning Dodgers. It was to be the final season in major league baseball for both Tinker and "Three Finger" Brown, the last remnants of the 1908 world champions (*Baseball Encyclopedia* 207).

In the ensuing years, the Cubs would go on to win six National League pennants but never a World Series. Even the pennants ended after the 1945 season when William Sianis, a Chicago tavern owner, placed a curse on the Cubs for preventing him from bringing his pet goat into Wrigley Field for a World Series game. In spite of two efforts by Sianis's son to break that curse with another goat in the 1980s and 1990s, Cubs seasons have continued to end fruitlessly (Jacob 30). Today, the legend of the curse has taken on a life of its own, punctuated by a major collapse in 1969; a frustrating, losing playoff series with San Diego in 1984; and the infamous foul ball interference by Steve Bartman in 2003. The last two saw the Cubs within a few outs of making it to the World Series. They have certainly not been alone in being "cursed." The Boston Red Sox had not won a World Series since 1918, though they had played in four between 1946 and 1986. They supposedly bore the "curse of the Bambino" for having sold Babe Ruth to New York a year after that championship. Likewise, the Chicago White Sox supposedly bore a curse for having thrown the 1919 World Series, often blamed on their owner, Charles Comiskey. They had only won one pennant, forty years later in 1959, and no World Series. Of course, both of these "curses" have been broken, first by the 2004 Red Sox and then by the 2005 White Sox. Only the Cubs remain with an amazingly long drought, now a century since winning a World Series and over sixty years since a pennant.

Cubs fans differ as to what the curse actually is. The goat is often mentioned, especially by the national media, probably in part caused by the *Saturday Night Live* skit about the Billy Goat Tavern in Chicago. Many fans suggest that Wrigley Field itself is the curse. The beautiful park, surrounded by an old-time Chicago neighborhood, with the traditions of the bleachers, scoreboard, and ivy, draws large crowds regardless of how the team performs. Essentially the Tribune Company, which purchased the Cubs in 1981, doesn't need to invest seriously in a winning team to draw fans. Both curse theories will remain as long as the Cubs fall short. However, if there is any basis to a curse, it probably lies in the early history of Wrigley Field far more than in the goat or the current owner of the team. That story starts with the Federal League, the reason why the ballpark was built in the first place.

When James A. Gilmore and the owners of the eight Federal franchises organized the league during 1913, there was every reason to expect success. The two major leagues were doing very well, and the popularity of the game was on the rise. History also seemed to be on their side. The American Association was formed in 1882, six years after the National League had been founded. The two coexisted for almost a decade, and when the American Association floundered, four of its eight franchises were absorbed into the other league. In 1901, the American League emerged to compete with a more streamlined National League. The new league proved an instant success, and two years later the highly popular World Series was created. There was little in the past to suggest a serious risk of failure.

The Federal League began in a fashion similar to the way previous leagues had started. Players in the existing leagues were offered much higher salaries, often more than double what they were currently making, to jump to the new league. The reserve clause, which gave a team the right to reserve the services of a player for the following season, even if a contract could not be negotiated, became moot with the new competition. Since the reserve clause was a major source of discontent with players, the new league implemented a form of free agency to make it even more attractive. Close to one hundred players jumped to the new league. More significantly, many of the star players, such as Ty Cobb, Eddie Collins, and Tris Speaker, saw their salaries more than double to keep them from jumping. Owners of the existing two leagues threatened players who jumped with being blacklisted, banned from returning if the Federal League were to fold. When players did jump, Federal League owners were frequently faced with costly lawsuits filed by the previous owners of the players. While the courts ultimately decided in favor of the Federal owners, the suits were costly nuisances. In the most extreme case, Charles Comiskey, owner of the Chicago White Sox, gave Clark Griffith, owner of the Washington Senators, $10,000 so he could afford to keep his star pitcher, Walter Johnson. Far from being generous, Comiskey didn't want Weeghman to sign Johnson for the Whales, fearing it would draw Sox fans to the new north side team to watch the great pitcher at his team's expense. Through it all, players were the clear winners, making far more money and having much greater freedom to sign with whom they wanted (Burk 195–206).

While the Federal League was competitive, well financed, and well organized, it failed. Part of that failure came from the collusive efforts of National and American League owners to keep players from jumping. Part of it was due to the costly court cases Federal owners had to endure to protect their newly signed players. Beyond these problems, none of the new owners could have anticipated the outbreak of World War I in 1914 or the ripple effects the European war would have in America. The impact on the economy, on discretionary income, and on the popularity of baseball all helped to retard the growth of the new league. Still, the Federal League had drawn fans at levels similar to the other leagues, and the owners felt they could stabilize their situation if they could stop the collusion efforts. They filed an anti-trust suit in Chicago Federal Court before Judge Kenesaw Mountain Landis, a notorious trust-buster. Little did they know that Landis was also a huge fan of baseball. Fearing that an unfavorable ruling would hurt the game, he delayed a decision on the case, hoping the owners could work out a resolution (Burk 207–8). The resulting uncertainty, coupled with war fears and higher than anticipated costs, helped cause the Federal League to fold. The collapse was facilitated even further by the willingness of the senior leagues' owners to buy out the Federal investors in seven of the eight teams (Ward and Burns 123).

The outcome for the players was predictable. Unless they had long-term contracts, player salaries returned to what they had been before the Federal League had formed. Overall, salaries were less than half what they had been with the competition. The dreaded reserve clause once again took effect, binding an unsigned player to the team for which he had played the previous season. The fledgling players union, growing stronger before the appearance of the new league, was now in shambles. By every measurable standard, the condition of the players was as bad as or worse than it had been in 1913. The discontent that this caused with ballplayers was a major factor in the increasing involvement of gamblers in baseball that culminated in the Black Sox scandal, the fixing of the 1919 World Series by eight players on the Chicago White Sox (Burk 210–14).

What was terrible news for the ballplayers was not initially good news for the owners of the remaining sixteen major league teams either. The threat and subsequently the outbreak of World War I continued to reduce gate revenues and ultimately took away some of the star players, who were called to military service. Only when the war ended did the game's financial health begin to improve in any appreciable fashion, which came as a major surprise to the owners during the 1919 season. At that point, professional baseball was at the beginning of a decade of unprecedented success (James 105–6).

The only major cloud on the horizon in 1919, other than the Series scandal, was a lawsuit that carried over from the demise of the Federal League. The owners of the Baltimore Terrapins franchise either had been left out of the deal that bought out the other owners or weren't happy with whatever offer they had received. In either case, the owners of the Terrapins decided to sue the major league owners, alleging that the buyout was a violation of the Sherman Antitrust Act. The case formally became known as *The Federal Baseball Club of Baltimore, Inc. v. National League of Professional Baseball Clubs, Inc.* It took until September of 1919 before a decision was reached in the District Court of Columbia. That court found that the practices of organized baseball indeed constituted an attempt to monopolize the business of the game. Damages were fixed at $80,000, a sum immediately tripled under the Sherman Act. When attorneys' fees were added, organized baseball owed over $264,000 to the Baltimore club owners (Seymour 244).

The precedent was as disturbing as the dollar amount of the award, and the owners quickly appealed the decision to the Court of Appeals of the District of Columbia. That court overruled the decision. Foreshadowing the eventual Supreme Court decision, the court ruled that baseball more resembled the entertainment industry than business, stating that the game "is as far removed as possible from the commonly accepted meaning of trade and commerce." The most compelling point about this decision was the differentiation of sport from commerce. It was now the Terrapin owners' turn to appeal, this time taking the case to the Supreme Court (*National League v. Baltimore* par. 17).

It took until May of 1922 for the Supreme Court to render an 8–0 decision, written by Justice Oliver Wendell Holmes. By that time, news of the Black Sox scandal had broken in late September of 1920, Kenesaw Mountain Landis had been hired as the first commissioner of Major League Baseball, the eight players who had fixed the 1919 series had been found innocent in court in 1921, and Landis had immediately banned all eight from the game for life. It is not possible to gauge how much these events may have weighed on the minds of the eight justices who rendered the unanimous decision, but it is difficult to imagine that they didn't factor into the vote. Borrowing from the lower court's ruling, Holmes wrote that the peculiar nature of baseball separated it from commerce as it was commonly defined. While players and fans may have crossed state boundaries to play and watch games, that did not sufficiently constitute interstate commerce. And if baseball did not engage in interstate commerce, the Sherman Act did not apply. In essence, not only did the Terrapin owners lose, but also major league baseball was granted an exemption from anti-trust laws that it still possesses today (*Baltimore v. National League* 208–9).

While this court case was winding its way through the system, the ownership situation with the Cubs was certainly not stagnant. For a variety of reasons, probably including World War I, Weeghman's restaurant business was not faring well. Even though the Cubs won the pennant in 1918, falling to the Red Sox in the World Series, Weeghman was losing control of the team. By 1919, an aggressive William Wrigley, Jr., had managed to increase his ownership stake and gained the support of other investors, finally reaching the point where he was able to assume majority control of the team. In 1920, he changed the name of the field to Cubs Park, and in 1926, after major renovations, including the construction of the upper deck, he changed the name again, this time to Wrigley Field (Jacob 6–7). The park now looked much as it appears today, and the name has endured for eighty years. The ownership has changed, lights and skyboxes have been added, ivy grows on the walls, and minor seating renovations have been made. Little else has changed.

That was certainly not the case with the aftermath of the 1922 decision granting baseball its anti-trust exemption. In one powerful ruling, the Supreme Court had profoundly changed the dynamics of the game from the first five decades of professional baseball. The reserve clause had existed almost as long as the National League. Initially popular with the better players, it soon became a major issue of contention when owners assumed it carried over year after year as long as they desired. When players contested the reserve clause in court, they won as often as they lost (Winand 4–29). More importantly, when new leagues provided competition, as they did in 1882, 1890, 1901, and 1914, they rendered the reserve clause moot. There was no way to keep players from jumping to teams in the new league. Between the courts and competition, then, players could expect to see both salary improvements and more freedom if they played long enough. Thanks to the Supreme Court Decision in 1922, this was no longer the case.

After that ruling, the possibility of competition for the major leagues was greatly reduced. The decision known as *Federal Baseball v. National League* made it extremely difficult for any new league to organize. With anti-trust exemption, owners were free to take any number of steps to block competition. Without either an act of Congress or a subsequent Supreme Court overruling itself, this situation was unlikely to change. Even the National Labor Relations Act of 1935 did not apply to baseball players as a result of the ruling that the game did not engage in interstate commerce (Winand 44). Without the threat of competition and free from federal labor laws, the owners could interpret the reserve clause to maximize their interests. Not surprisingly, club owners and management concluded that players were bound for life to the team that held their last contract.

History, too, conspired against the players after the 1922 ruling. The prosperity of the 1920s, coupled with the cult following of Babe Ruth and the interest he generated in the game, all created a somewhat better environment in the second decade of the twentieth century for salaries if not player freedom. Perhaps if that prosperity had continued, there would have been another attempt at a competitive league even with the obstacles of the Federal League decision. However, with the end of the 1929 season came the onslaught of the Great Depression. Baseball suffered like other businesses. Dwindling crowds brought some teams to the edge of bankruptcy. No one dreamed of any effort at competition, and few players complained about salaries. They were happy to have jobs that still paid much better than the normal worker. And, of course, World War II came on top of the Depression, again postponing attempts to either contest the reserve clause or start a competitive league.

The end of World War II and a return to more prosperous times opened the door to the first challenges of the reserve clause and the hold it had on ballplayers. In 1946, Danny Gardella, a back-up outfielder with the New York Giants, jumped to the Mexican League. When he attempted to return to the Majors the following year, no team would sign him. In effect, he was blacklisted, a policy obviously still very much in force in organized baseball. Gardella sued. In the case *Gardella v. Chandler*, he initially lost in U.S. District Court. Gardella appealed and won a 2–1 decision that concluded that baseball engaged in monopolistic practices. Rather than take the case to a higher court, Major League baseball settled the case with Gardella, ending any immediate threat of change to the Federal Baseball Decision (Quirk 187).

Only two years later, another case was filed, this time by George Toolson, a good New York Yankee minor leaguer who felt blocked from the majors by his organization's deep talent of ballplayers. This time, the case made it all the way to the Supreme Court in *Toolson v. New York Yankees*, decided in 1953. The Court ruled by a 7–2 margin against Toolson. While acknowledging that Federal Baseball was a highly questionable decision, the Court felt that Congress, not the courts, should take on the role of addressing baseball's anti-trust status and thereby include the game under its laws. The Court was not going to act on its predecessor's thirty-year precedent (*Toolson v. New York Yankees* 357). The reserve, thanks to Federal Baseball, remained as powerful as ever.

Congress did hold hearings around the same time that the Toolson case was ruled upon, but took no action (*Report of Subcommittee* 98). The issue returned before the nation's capital in 1959, when potential owners in a number of growing markets without major league franchises attempted to form the Continental League to offer professional baseball on an equal level with the sixteen existing teams. The aspiring owners hired Branch Rickey to be their commissioner. The new league immediately ran into difficulty since the reserve clause was applied by major league owners to all of the hundreds of ballplayers in each team's organization. Thus, there was almost no professional talent free to sign with the new league unless the 1922 decision were overturned or Congress could make some change. An attempt was made in the House of Representatives to reduce dramatically the number of players a team could reserve, but it died in committee (Nevard par. 5–8). Once again, the influence of the major leagues and the protection provided by Federal Baseball prevailed.

The most famous attempt to challenge the anti-trust status, of course, was by Curt Flood. After twelve years with the Cardinals and fourteen in the National League, Flood was traded to the Philadelphia Phillies. He refused to report, instead deciding to challenge the reserve clause in the courts. In *Flood v. Kuhn*, the Supreme Court once again had the opportunity to reconsider baseball's anti-trust status. In 1972, the Court ruled against Flood in a 5–3 decision. Harry Blackmun penned the majority decision, which included a preface filled with nostalgic references to the game of baseball. It acknowledged that baseball's exemption from anti-trust was an anomaly, but suggested it was inappropriate to overrule a decision that the game had depended upon to develop over the last fifty years. Essentially the Court recognized that the Federal League ruling had been incorrect, but it did not want to upset the structure of the game by overturning the previous judgment (*Flood v. Kuhn* 282). Once again, baseball had dodged a bullet, but this time not for much longer.

Three years later, in December 1975, Marvin Miller, director of the Major League Players Union, won a favorable ruling under binding arbitration. The decision declared the reserve clause to be nothing more than what it stated on paper — the right to reserve an unsigned player's service for one more year. After that, a player was free to take his services wherever he chose. Over fifty years after an anti-trust exemption had allowed Major League Baseball to claim the reserve clause bound a player to a team as long as the team desired, Miller established that it was really a paper tiger. Ballplayers were finally free to prove their real value in the marketplace. What the U.S. Congress and Supreme Court couldn't or wouldn't do, was in fact accomplished by the leadership and savvy of one union leader. The reserve clause was dead (Miller 238–53; Ward and Burns 434–35, 443).

That same year, 1975, the Chicago Cubs finished fifth in the National League East's six-team division, marking thirty empty years since their last World Series appearance (*Baseball Encyclopedia* 451–52). Another thirty have passed since players received their freedom from the reserve, still without a Cubs appearance in the Series. Something continues to maintain a hold on the longest drought in baseball.

Perhaps that something is the Federal League of Baseball, from which Wrigley Field is the last surviving ballpark. For two years the Federal League was a strong competitor to the two older leagues. It enabled salaries of ballplayers to more than double while it existed. It rendered the reserve clause meaningless. It also offered its players an opportunity eventually to become free agents, unheard of before it existed and again for six decades after it folded. But these short-term benefits proved to be just that — short term. Without the competition, salaries dropped back to 1913 levels and the reserve clause again became formidable. Player discontent from the return of this situation led in part to the Black Sox scandal in 1919, which shaped the game profoundly in subsequent decades (Asinof 12–15). And the appeal of the one group of unsatisfied Federal League owners resulted in a Supreme Court decision that gave baseball its unique anti-trust status. That status exempted professional baseball from any federal laws dealing with business or labor that could have been used to improve the bargaining position of ballplayers. In essence, it kept generations of players under the so-called "plantation system" for over fifty years. Even in the best of times, players, including the great ones like Ruth, Gehrig, DiMaggio and Williams, were never compensated close to what they were worth and never had a say about where they played. The Federal League, a short-term boon for players, became a half-century disaster in the fallout it created.

Today, there are three major league teams that play in ballparks not built for them. Until March 30, 2008, the Washington Nationals played in RFK Stadium. The Marlins, never satisfied with Joe Robbie Stadium, will either get a new park in Miami or move to a city that builds them one. The third team is the Cubs, pulled from their old stomping groups on the near west side of Chicago after the Federal League folded to arrive at their current home. Today, Wrigley Field stands as the only remaining monument to that almost forgotten league. As such, it is also a monument to the grossly unfair treatment of thousands of ballplayers from 1916–1975 who suffered from what the Federal League wrought. While this is not to suggest that Wrigley itself is cursed, it does provide some historic context for what the park symbolizes from its rich past. It also explains why that past is more complicated than the perceptions we hold of the wonderful old-fashioned ballpark, that "edifice of beauty," in which we enjoy baseball today.

Works Cited

Asinof, Eliot. *Eight Men Out: The Black Sox and the 1919 World Series*. New York: Henry Holt & Company, 1963.

The Baseball Encyclopedia. Eighth Edition. New York: Macmillan, 1990.

Burk, Robert F. *Never Just a Game*. Chapel Hill, NC: U of North Carolina P, 1994.

Federal Baseball Club of Baltimore, Inc., v. National League of Professional Baseball Clubs, et al., No. 204, Supreme Ct. of the U.S. 29 May 1922. United States Reports Vol. 259, Washington: G.P.O., 1923.

Flood v. Kuhn, No. 71–32. Supreme Ct. of the U.S. 19 June 1972. United States Reports Vol. 407, Washington: G.P.O., 1973.

Jacob, Mark. *A Celebration of the Friendly Confines*. New York: McGraw Hill, 2003.

James, Bill. *The New Historical Baseball Abstract*. New York: The Free Press, 2001.

Quirk, James P. *Pay Dirt: The Business of Professional Team Sports*. Princeton, NJ: Princeton UP, 1997.

Miller, Marvin. *A Whole Different Ball Game: The Sport and Business of Baseball*. New York: Carol Publishing, 1991.

National League of Professional Baseball Clubs, et al. v. Federal Baseball Club of Baltimore, No. 3368. Court of Appeals of District of Columbia. 6 Dec. 1920. Online. Lexis Nexis Academic. 28 Aug. 2006.

Nevard, David, "The Continental League." <http://webpages.charter.net/voekuras/continental.htm>.

Report of the Subcommittee on Study of Monopoly Power, House Committee on the Judiciary, 1952.

Seymour, Harold. *Baseball: The Early Years.* New York: Oxford UP, 1967.

Toolson v. New York Yankees, No. 18. Supreme Ct. of the U.S. 9 Nov. 1953. United States Reports Vol. 346, Washington: G.P.O., 1954.

Ward, Geoffrey, and Ken Burns. *Baseball: An Illustrated History.* New York: Alfred J. Knopf, 1994.

Winand, Christopher J. *Baseball and the Reserve: The Legality and Legacy of the Reserve Clause.* Honors Thesis, DePauw University, 2003.

Hallowed Ivy and Sacred Sun:
The Iconic Character of Wrigley Field

Joseph L. Price

Wrigley Field: To baseball fans the invocation of its name immediately evokes ethereal images of ivy climbing brick walls, of sunlight bathing the bleachers, of the unreachable score-board with a post-game white flag featuring a large blue "W" flying above the intersection of Waveland Avenue and Sheffield, of Cubs banners with the names and numbers of Banks, Santo, and Williams flying from the foul poles, and of the statue of the largely bespectacled Harry Caray waving his microphone and cueing the crowd with, "Let's hear it now. Ah one, ah two, ah three. Take me out to the ballgame...." These images of Wrigley Field are as alluring as a dream, but not just any dream. To baseball fans, the dreams are like those of children imagining Disneyland, the place where dreams come true.

Among such devout baseball lovers is Lonnie Wheeler, who spent a summer attending every game at Wrigley Field in the summer of 1987. He confesses this attitude in the opening lines of his book *Bleachers: A Summer in Wrigley Field*, which began as a diary of a season of his devotion: "I'd always thought of Wrigley Field's bleachers," he writes, "as the place where real baseball fans go when they close their eyes and click their heels three times" (3). But on opening day in 1987, Wheeler discovered that bleacher bums were like the ever penitent clotting the mourning bench at a tent revival; for the thousands of faithful believers who packed the backless pews and stood in the aisles, "the bleachers were much more than benches beyond the outfield. They were a neighborhood, a bar, a depot, a beach, an office, a church, a home[....] People hugged each other, [as] friends lost over the grim Chicago winter and found again with the first pitch" (4).

Unlike the uniform, circular, multi-purpose stadiums made popular in Major League cities in the third quarter of the twentieth century, and even in contrast to the retro-style ballparks constructed to replace them at the century's next turn, Wrigley Field does not enjoy acres of adjacent parking, wide ramps, and easy freeway access. Instead, it is "a place settled and developed by a city and a sport, indigenous turf, a tract of Americana whose essential nature could not be contained by the brick walls of Wrigley Field, or the streets named Clark, Addison, Waveland, and Sheffield" (Wheeler 4). Although Camden Yards and San Francisco's new ballpark, presently called AT&T Park, feature superb sight lines and improved proximity of the seats to the field of play, Wrigley Field has the patina of authenticity and the history of major on-field accomplishments rather than mere franchise memorials.

Whether emboldened by the wind blowing out or dismayed by the near-miss home runs with the wind blowing in, whether in victory or in defeat followed by the flying of a blue flag with a white "L" atop the centerfield flag pole, Wrigley Field serves as an icon of baseball, its history and myths, its communal values, and its enduring possibilities. It exemplifies the purity of baseball since its erection predates baseball's first major trauma — the Black Sox scandal. It represents the simplicity of the game, even with today's electronic fascination, since its scoreboard has no video screen and since its games are played most often under afternoon sunlight rather than network television spotlights. It celebrates the intimacy afforded between fans and players since the ballpark features every seat within shouting distance of a player's position and a kind of intimacy between the community and the game itself since the ballpark is nestled into a square block of the Lake View neighborhood. Wrigley Field emblematizes the recurrent human experience of suffering and defeat (as the home of the team longest absent from the reward of the World Series) while persisting in hope. The tenacious character of hope is such that one devout Cubs fan noted that "being a Cub fan is like getting married for the second time — hope wins out over experience" (qtd. in Wheeler 171).

That Wrigley Field is a cultural icon at the turn of the twenty-first century is seemingly beyond question: it surely exudes the sacred character that fans and pundits so keenly experience and ascribe to it. But how and why it acquired this iconic character — and what this sacral character suggests — are issues and questions that arise in response to its popularity. Has it always been experienced as a place where the Other can be engaged, where transcendence seems palpable, where the prospects of inevitable defeat of the Cubs intimates the fate of death that all must experience, nonetheless with hope for victory beyond defeat, for life after the torment of death? Like genuine symbols that are not intentionally created but emerge in response to social needs and assume their referential power to address cultural issues,[1] Wrigley Field has attained its symbolic significance, or its iconic character, because of its constitution (its setting and its architecture), its historic and mythic character, its ritual significance, and its communal ethos — its flair for facilitating friendship.

Its Constitution — A Cathedral on Holy Ground

Above the entry to the third floor exhibition at Baseball's Hall of Fame in Cooperstown, New York, is the simple phrase "Sacred Ground." The gallery features historic ballparks, among which, of course, is Wrigley Field. Its history and charm are featured because fans often identify a special character of their experience there, as though their being there placed them, as the entry to the Hall of Fame's gallery puts it, on "sacred ground." Throughout history and across diverse cultures, people have identified a sacred character with a place, even as its specific use might be transformed from one purpose to another. And to protect the special sense of power that devotees experience in a place, rites of deconsecration are performed in various traditions when a facility or site is "returned" to the secular order. And on other occasions, the sense of the sacred is retained when a site transitions from a worship center for one tradition to another; for instance, in Jerusalem, as is well known, the mosque of the Dome of the Rock lies at the site of the earlier ancient temple of Solomon, and in Damascus, the former Cathedral of St. John, which was erected on the site of an ancient Roman temple, was itself adapted to new usage as the Great Mosque of Damascus when Amr conquered the city in the late seventh century of the Common Era. Although lacking the historic gravity of the modifications of these two sample sites, the placement of the ballpark at the intersection of Addison and Clark is similar in the sense that in the late nineteenth century, the site was selected because of its pastoral setting. Then, the facilities of a Lutheran seminary were constructed there to provide a place for retreat and contemplation for the students preparing for ministry.

A ballpark's location also often suggests a reverential response in ways similar to the placement of medieval cathedrals in their respective communities. Like European cathedrals, ballparks are often situated in ways that orient the city to them. In earlier epochs, cathedrals and churches often rose above the landscape because their spiritual magnitude dominated a community and, thus intentionally, the height of their spires provided a singular point of reference for a city. A steeple could be seen from afar, providing a point of reference for knowing how to get to the spiritual center of a city. Like medieval cathedrals whose grandeur was architecturally unmatched in a community, ballparks are prominently featured in the landscape — with the Cincinnati and Pittsburgh ballparks dominating riverfronts, with new stadiums in San Francisco and Baltimore perching above waterfronts, with stadiums in Milwaukee and Anaheim adjacent to the confluence of freeways. And Dodger Stadium, now the second oldest National League ballpark, is situated atop Chavez Ravine, overlooking downtown Los Angeles against a backdrop of the San Gabriel Mountains. In each of these instances, the placement of the ballpark is a significant feature of its architecture: it seeks to dominate, to rise above the landscape in a way that renders it magnificent, approaching transcendence. Yet Wrigley Field does not dominate the Chicago skyline. Instead, it blends in with the height of the commercial storefronts on Clark Street, and it does not rise far above the rooftops of the apartments on Waveland and Sheffield. Within Chicago, Wrigley Field serves as a democratic or popular symbol for the way that a ballpark can fit into a community while providing its heart.

Throughout recent years baseball fans and writers have described ballparks — especially the ones embedded in communities and imbued with historical significance — in religious terms, often referring to them as "green cathedrals." Recognizing the ethereal experience often evoked by a ballpark, Edward J. Reilly has identified some design elements that align ballparks with cathedrals. Specifically, he notes that a "domed roof or open air [stadium] parallels the vaulted roof of a medieval cathedral built to approximate the eternal vault of the heavens" (253). Sensing a similar spiritual ethos at ballparks, Philip Lowry began to recognize the resemblance of ballparks to houses and places of worship as he undertook his study of hundreds of historic and contemporary baseball stadiums (1–2). Although he perceived architectural similarities between ballparks and cathedrals, he did not specify what the particular design elements were that prompted spiritual responses by fans.

The reverential response evoked by a ballpark has also been perceived by W. P. Kinsella, who attributes the spiritual sensation to his fictive hero Ray Kinsella. The author Kinsella has the protagonist Kinsella, who is among other distinctions a generation younger than the author, muse about the sacred sensation that a ballpark elicits. W. P. Kinsella, of course, is himself a lover of the Cubs, having fixated on them in two other works. In the short story "The Last Pennant before Armageddon," Kinsella imagines a Faustian dilemma for the Cubs manager, who is faced with the possibility of winning the pennant, perceiving that it would precipitate the cosmic conflagration at the end of the world. Also featuring the Cubs, Kinsella's novel *The Iowa Baseball Confederacy,* which plots the 2000-inning epic contest in Big Inning, Iowa (punning with the idea that the idea of the game was a kind of cosmogonic event, a *beginning*) between the mythic all-star team from the Iowa Baseball Confederacy against the Chicago Cubs. In his novella *Shoeless Joe* Kinsella narrates a moonlit visit of Ray Kinsella, J.D. "Jerry" Salinger (modified in the film version to become the author-turned-computer-programmer Thomas Mann), and Archie Graham to old Metropolitan Stadium in Bloomington, Minnesota. In the scene, which was omitted in the filmic version popularly received as *Field of Dreams,* Kinsella asks his traveling companions if either of them has spent time in an empty ballpark. "There's something both eerie and holy about it," he asserts. "A ballpark at night is more like a church than a church" (Kinsella, *Shoeless Joe* 135).

History and Myth— The Construction of the Park and the Feats of Heroes

According to Mircea Eliade, the perception and identification of a particular place as sacred is tied to its association with power, with an experience of alterity or Otherness that serves to organize and orient the lives of the people who recognize its centrality. By virtue of its "otherness," a sacred space is able to transform chaos into cosmos, to render disorder into order, to change the clutter and clatter of daily living in an urban center like Chicago into a source of energy and innovation for those who perceive its distinction. In effect, sacred spaces symbolize and replicate the center of the world, the point where creation (in mythic terms) began as an expression of divine power and where hope continues to be engendered. As a symbolic center of the world, a sacred space also becomes a focus for pilgrimage (29–65).

The lure and power of sacred spaces are associated with unique events—especially their discovery or their founding—and heroic acts that occur there and in their telling the attributes of the space itself and the accomplishments centered there grow in time to mythic status. As the myths begin to form about the heroes who have exercised particular power at a place, the history of the origin of the space itself developed. Its own creation or construction assumes mythic status. Such is the case, too, with Wrigley Field. Prior to its development as a ballpark, the site had been used for a pastoral retreat from urban life. In the early 1890s Chicago physician William Passavant donated the plot of prairie in the region then becoming known as Lake View for the construction of a Lutheran Seminary, which then occupied the site for almost two decades. By the end of the first decades of the twentieth century, however, the area was deemed too noisy and dirty for the seminary students to be able to focus on their devotional studies and their practices of piety. In large part the distractions resulted from the extension of the El to the area and from the acrid air generated by a coal yard nearby.

Following Charles Weeghman's purchase of the site to build the ballpark for his Chicago entry into the Federal League, the construction crew tore down the four seminary buildings in late February 1914. Seven weeks later the ballpark now known as Wrigley Field was completed at a cost of $250,000, and it provided a new destination for baseball fans in Chicago, offering capacity seating of 18,000. Over the years Wrigley Field has been expanded time and again, reaching its maximum seating capacity during the twentieth century of 40,000 in 1928. A decade later, for the World Series, owner P. K. Wrigley placed a number of temporary seats that brought the capacity above 40,000. For most of the following half century, the seating capacity fluctuated within two thousand seats of that number. But prior to the 2006 season, expansions above sidewalks and beyond the catwalks in left field and right field enlarged the capacity to more than 41,000 seats.

Like the gradual emergence into lore of the feats that heroes have accomplished at the Friendly Confines, a number of architectural features and landscaping distinctions of Wrigley Field have evolved over the years—like the reconfiguring of the outfield walls to include the "wells," where the bleachers end and curve back into their respective outfield corners, and the planting of the ivy along the brick faces of the outfield walls.

To open the ballpark for the ChiFeds in April 1914, Weeghman designed a series of festivities that included performances by ten brass bands and culminated with a parade of VIPs from Grant Park to Clark and Addison. At the ballpark itself, twenty members of a women's patriotic league carried a thirty-foot American flag around the ballpark while one of the brass bands played "The Star Spangled Banner," which would become the National Anthem fifteen years later (Shea and Castle 49).[2] Following the dissolution of the Federal League after the 1915 season, Weeghman purchased the National League franchise at a record price of $500,000 and moved the Cubs into the Northside ballpark for the start of the 1916 season. At that time Weeghman again staged a huge parade to mark the occasion. By so doing he not only garnered attention for his enterprise; he also effectively brought a kind of civic sanction to the ballpark, especially since the motorcade was escorted by ten police vehicles (Shea 72–73).

Before the 1923 season, the first major expansion of the ballpark was undertaken. To accomplish the expansion of the grandstand and the extension of the outfield, the grandstands were cut into three sections near the first and third base dugouts, and then they were rolled toward Addison and Clarke Streets about a hundred feet. The project enlarged the seating capacity to the point that Cubs Park, as it was still known at that time, became the largest single-decked ballpark in the country. Although Bill Veeck indicated at that time that an upper deck would not be added, the foundations and support were put into place to accommodate that expansion, which occurred four years later. The erection of the second tier of seating enabled the Cubs in 1927 to become the first National League team to exceed the million mark in a season's attendance. When the grandstands had been expanded in 1923, home plate was also moved from a position near the present pitcher's mound to its current location, in effect pushing back the outfield fences (Shea 109).

In 1937 several of the distinctive features of Wrigley Field were added. Inspired by the model of the ivy-covered walls at Perry Stadium in Indianapolis and the popular fascination with National Parks, owner P.K. Wrigley authorized the modification of the ballpark. Most significantly, the bleachers were constructed beyond the brick walls edging the outfield, ivy was planted to cover the fence, and the scoreboard was raised beyond the upper portion of the centerfield bleachers. Four years later, the distinctive clock was added atop the scoreboard, which is still hand operated. Although Sam Snead once hit a golf ball off the scoreboard from a tee placed at home plate, no baseball has ever struck the scoreboard. The nearest misses were a shot off the bat of Roberto Clemente that sailed to the left and onto Waveland Avenue, and a blast by Sammy Sosa that landed atop the television camera canopy near the base of the scoreboard (Peterson 62).

Back in 1937, when Bill Veeck discovered that ivy could not be planted effectively in a day, he and groundskeeper Bob Dorr interlaced bittersweet through wires that crossed the bricks and held the vines in place. In years since the vines have grown thick, balls have gotten lost in the ivy — among them a drive by the Tigers' Roy Cullenbine in the 1945 World Series that was retrieved by Andy Pafko, and decades later one hit by Bill Buckner that turned into a home run. Since then, a lost vine ball has been ruled a double — with outfielders often throwing hands aloft and acting as though they could not see ivy balls, thereby turning potential triples into ground-rule doubles (Wheeler 48). Perhaps the most unusual ivy play occurred at mid-century when Ralph Kiner, who was approaching the end of his career, tried to make a leaping catch against the wall, but got stuck in the vines. A final addition to the outfield walls appeared in 1970, when "the basket," a wire fence extending at an angle from the top of the wall, prevented fan interference with an outfielder. It became possible then to hit a home run into the basket, with the ball landing a few feet in front of the bleachers but encased above the outfielder's reach (Shea 270).

One of the renovations that had been planned for Wrigley Field in the 1940s was the

installation of lights, meaning that Wrigley Field would have been able to enjoy night baseball before the fans in Detroit. In preparation for the 1942 season, P.K. Wrigley had purchased
light standards, whose erection was scheduled to begin in December 1941. But following the
attack on Pearl Harbor, Wrigley donated the equipment to the War Department, and Wrigley
Field remained the only Major League stadium without lights for four decades, thus creating
its distinctive niche not only for the time of games but also for the telecast of games that
began in the 1940s (Shea 182–83). Not until 1988 were lights installed at Wrigley — and then
to meet Major League stipulations related to television contracts for prospective post-season
play. If it were not possible to play post-season night games for live, Prime Time telecast from
Wrigley Field, the Cubs would have been required to play their "home" games in the postseason not from Comiskey Park on Chicago's South side (as the National League had required
for the Cubs' World Series play in 1918) but in St. Louis.

As a place of innovation and power, Wrigley Field has made a number of creative contributions to baseball, and it has witnessed heroic feats throughout its history. While it served
as the home of the ChiFeds and Whales during the last few years of their existence, the ballpark introduced several rituals that subsequently became standard for the Cubs for many
years. Among other innovations, in 1914 Weeghman instituted the idea of Ladies Day on Fri-
days for his Federal League team in an effort to increase attendance and to "gentrify" baseball itself. In part, Weeghman also hoped to lure fans away from the Cubs, who at that time
were prohibited by National League restrictions from engaging in such a promotion. The free
admission offered to women on Ladies Days became a successful marketing strategy that continued for about fifty years. In fact, the largest crowd ever to see a ballgame at Wrigley Field
was 51,556 when the Cubs played the Brooklyn Dodgers on Friday, June 27, 1930 — a "Ladies
Day" when more than thirty thousand of the attendees were women who had been admitted
free (Peterson 15).

Building upon the success of the Ladies Day promotion, Weeghman's successor William
Wrigley, Jr., established the policy of providing free admission on weekdays other than Fri-
days to the first four thousand children up to the age of sixteen — even on schooldays in late
spring and during September. Apparently, the practice was endorsed by the school board and
"the athletic committee" of the Chicago City Council (Shea 133). As a result, even as women
began to follow the Cubs in greater numbers than other teams enjoyed, so too did thousands
of young Chicagoans become avid fans of the Cubs since they offered an afternoon at the
ballpark rather than the classroom.

In addition to these attendance initiatives at Wrigley Field, Weeghman had also sought
to improve fans' experience at the ballpark by drawing upon his success in having developed
a franchise of lunch counters throughout Chicago. He was the first owner to coordinate and
incorporate concession kiosks adjacent to the ballpark where food and refreshments could be
purchased. Continuing his efforts to enhance fans' experience at the ballpark, in the summer
of 1916 Weeghman established the practice of allowing fans to keep balls hit into the stands
(Shea 58).

Within a few years attempts to elevate the culture of the ballpark were continued by
William Wrigley, Jr., who, after assuming ownership of the Cubs, made sure that all ballpark
employees wore attractive uniforms, and he sought to make the ballpark like a park itself by
planting the ivy to climb the outfield walls and by planting elm trees in the upper walkways
in the centerfield bleachers. In the early 1940s Wrigley Field also introduced organ music to
baseball games. Previously, the musical instruments had been identified exclusively with
churches, theaters, and concert halls. By introducing organ music into the ballpark, Wrigley
Field added an entertaining element to the atmosphere, while it also intimated to many fans

the quasi-sacred character of the facility — since the other place where they most frequently had heard organ music was in a church sanctuary.

Among the other innovations that Wrigley introduced was that of a corporate name for the ballpark. At the time of its construction, the ballpark had been called Weeghman Park in recognition of its owner, Charles Weeghman. When his financial woes forced him to sell the majority ownership to William Wrigley, the ballpark's name then shifted, like a number of other ballparks at the time, to that of the team: Cubs Park. But Weeghman persuaded Wrigley that by naming the ballpark after himself, Wrigley would enjoy free advertising for his chewing gum empire. With that in mind, then, Wrigley authorized the change of the name of the ballpark to Wrigley Field in 1926. A few years earlier, Wrigley had introduced implied advertising for his gum to the ballpark. For Opening Day in 1923, two pixie baseball figures representing "The Doublemint Twins" were positioned at both ends of the scoreboard in centerfield. On the left one posed with a bat awaiting a pitch from the one at the opposite end. About this time, the vendors also started to wear Wrigley Gum hats in addition to their white-coat uniforms (Shea 110).

Like other ballparks, however, Wrigley Field magnified its special character or sacred aura because of the historic feats by heroes. Several of the historic performances at Wrigley Field rise above all others in terms of their uniqueness or their mythic quality — such as the double no-hitter, Babe Ruth's called shot, and Gabby Hartnett's "Homer in the Gloamin'." Other remarkable milestones were reached and accomplishments realized at Wrigley Field, but these are distinguished because of their elevation to mythic status.

Shortly after the ballpark became the home of the Cubs, Wrigley Field witnessed the only double no-hitter in history. In 1917 the Cubs' Jim "Hippo" Vaughn tossed a no-hitter for nine innings, which was matched frame for frame by the Reds' Fred Toney. In the tenth, however, the Reds' shortstop singled and later scored, following sloppy fielding by the Cubs, on a dubious hit by Jim Thorpe. Other incredible feats that have acquired mythic status at Wrigley Field are two dramatic home runs: the famous "called" shot by Babe Ruth off Charlie Root in the fifth inning of the third game in the 1932 World Series and Gabby Hartnett's "Homer in the Gloamin'" in late September a few years later. After having hit a home run in his first at bat, Ruth came to the plate in the fifth inning amidst a good bit of razzing from the Cubs' bench. After taking two strikes, Ruth, as shown in film clips, stepped out of the batter's box and gestured generally toward centerfield. According to most historic accounts, Ruth did not actually point to a spot where he then hit the next pitch for a gargantuan home run, to the right of the unreachable scoreboard. But the batter was Ruth, the blast was Herculean, and the timing was with the world watching. Years later, Ruth refused to deny that he had called the shot, but he did remark that he was pleased that the "good Lord" let him hit it. All the stuff of myth.

Like Ruth's home run, the mythic character of Gabby Hartnett's homer resulted from its improbable timing. With the score tied 5–5 with two outs and two strikes in the bottom of the ninth inning while darkness descended on Wrigley Field the evening of September 28, 1938, Hartnett's home run catapulted the Cubs past the Pirates, who had begun the game a half game ahead of the Cubs in the National League pennant race. Hartnett's home run capped a remarkable comeback by the Cubs, not only in terms of overtaking the Pirates with their victory, since they had been three and a half games behind only ten days earlier, but also fighting back twice against the Pirates, who had taken a two-run lead in the eighth inning. Add to this dramatic recovery the kind of preparation that had permitted Hartnett to come to bat, and his home run seems to manifest a cosmic anticipation. After the Cubs had beaten the Pirates in the first game of their series on the previous afternoon, officials had moved up the start time for the game on the 28th, shifting it from 3:00 P.M. to 2:30 P.M. to minimize the threat that the game would be called because of darkness.

Other milestone accomplishments were also realized at Wrigley Field and thus enhanced the ballpark's mythic status. Among other records that were set there, some of the more distinct ones include the highest scoring game in major league history in 1922, when the Cubs beat the Phillies 26–23. A little more than fifty years later, the Cubs and Phillies would lock together in two other incredible offensive displays, with the Cubs blowing an 11-run lead against Philadelphia, losing 18–16 on the strength of Hall of Famer Mike Schmidt's four home runs, a feat that he almost replicated in a 23–22 Phillies' win three years later. And in one of the games that I had the privilege of seeing at Wrigley Field, I watched John Candelaria and the Pirates on September 16, 1975, post the most lopsided shutout in major league history. In the Pirates' 22–0 clobbering of the Cubs that day, Rennie Stennett went 7 for 7 in a nine-inning game.

Single-game milestone and records were also turned in by the Cubs: Ernie Banks hit his 500th home run at Wrigley Field, Kerry Wood struck out 20 Astros in only his fifth major league start, and Sammy Sosa hit home runs 61 and 62 in the same afternoon to surpass Roger Maris only a week after Mark McGwire had eclipsed the record. And, of course, the Cubs suffer the ignominy of having refused Billy Sianis's goat admission to the World Series in 1945 and having blown the lead after Steve Bartman reached for the foul ball and prevented Moises Alou from recording an out in the Cubs' playoff pursuit of the 2003 pennant. Each of these milestones, records, and achievements marks Wrigley Field with yet another significant historical moment that, in its telling and retelling, becomes a part of the myth.

Ritual — The Community of Ever Faithful "Bleacher Bums"

While public endorsements and ceremonial presentations inaugurate each season, some of the ritual components that Lonnie Wheeler identified on Opening Day in 1987 were space and time. With the first pitch, he observed, people found each other as friends who had been separated throughout Chicago's winter; and they found themselves together as friends because they were not anywhere, but somewhere. Indeed, as he puts it succinctly, "the bleachers were *somewhere*" (4). They enabled reunion, gathering people together as a community in ritual space.

As the place where myths are born, where transformation becomes possible, and where communal bonding is established, sacred spaces also facilitate an experience of sacred time, a sense of timelessness that offers retreat from the hectic pace of daily living and connects one with previous generations through a kind of embodied memory, a way of making the past present in a real way. Typifying the experience of many devout Cubs fans, Chicago native Tom Dreesen has expressed this atemporal power of Wrigley Field. "In the hustle and bustle of human life," he remarks, "[Wrigley Field] is also the place where you can take your son and put him in a seat that you sat in as a child and his grandfather sat in and, in fact, his grandfather's grandfather sat in. He'll watch a game that all those before him watched. For a moment — for a precious wonderful moment — time stands still" (67). In a very real sense, Wrigley Field is a "hand-me-down ballpark," intimate and passed on from one generation to another.

One of the facets of ritual is that it functions within a community while shaping the community in which it is embedded. Rituals involve shared symbolic gestures — sets of meaning. In popular usage the word "ritual" is often used to describe a repeated idiosyncratic action, but a more precise description would be a recognized habit because a ritual conveys and participates in a shared symbols system. It is not an individual's distinct pattern of behavior. Ritual emerges out of and refers to the shared meaning of a community, and in so doing it generates a sense of community.

Certainly that is the character of Wrigley Field, especially as it was experienced in the bleachers by Lonnie Wheeler on Opening Day 1987. Focusing on the communal bonding that he observed in the bleachers, he understood that there was seemingly a sacred character about the space itself, about the climbing ivy on the brick walls beyond the warning track and the sunshine confirming an end to winter. His observations were recorded a year before the construction of the light standards atop the grandstands that somehow blasphemed the divine act of creating the natural light of the sun and profaned the simplicity and elegance of daytime baseball.

Although the bleachers had been an inviting place since the improvements to the park in the 1930s, the outfield pews did not always fill with the faithful during fallow seasons, which were more frequent than the fruitful ones. In fact, during the mid–1960s, when the Cubs were mired near the bottom of the National League, it was possible to find fewer than two dozen fans seated there. On such occasions the section looked like an ignored mourners' bench at an evangelistic service. On one particularly dismal afternoon when the Cubs were vying with the Mets for ninth place, there were only thirteen fans in the bleachers — so few, in fact, that Cubs' outfielder Billy Williams started playing catch with one of them.

Finally in 1967 the Cubs' popularity began to swell, especially as they climbed to first place in late July. Yet the group's identity as "Bleacher Bums" did not result from self-designation. Instead, the name was uttered by one of the regular bleachers fans when a reporter noted the camaraderie among the fans there and called out to them, "Who are you guys?" Brushing off the inquiry, they told the reporter to leave, replying facetiously that they were merely a bunch of bums because daily they lounged in the sun, drank beer, and bemoaned the losing ways of the Cubs. The following day, a newspaper headline read "Bleacher Bums," and within days national news crews from television networks as well as non-sports oriented newspapers, like the *Wall Street Journal*, pressed them for stories. Mike Murphy, the self-designated bleacher historian among them, recalls, "We didn't set out to make ourselves a group. The press made us a group. The press created us." And soon, the name "Bleacher Bums became synonymous with Cub fans in general" (Wheeler 14).

As the Cubs' on-field performance improved in the late 1960s, the actions of the Bleacher Bums became more provocative. Talking with the enduring devotees two decades later, Wheeler learned that back then, acting like Bums, they had thrown "frogs at Cleon Jones, white mice at Lou Brock, [and] hot dog buns at Willie Stargell." While they taunted Pete Rose with "fairy" language, they had "tossed a softball around, and they [had thrown] their beers up in the air when the Cubs hit a home run." Although their antics were disruptive, Wheeler concludes, "All of it was natural to them because they had grown up together laughing and cursing in the bleachers. They had grown up together as kids who cared about something, and not because it was on TV; as an open frontier back then, the cheap seats were not as photogenic as they would later become. The bleacher boys cared about baseball for one reason only: because they did" (Wheeler 131).

Among the practices of bleacher fans that have persisted into the twenty-first century is throwing opponents' home run balls back onto the field, rejecting them as though they were heretical acts. When the custom of throwing back opponents' home run balls began, "bleacher fans would take up a collection and pay somebody forty or fifty dollars to toss the ball down; but the philanthropy soon passed, and now the throw-back was considered a Cub fan's moral obligation." The true Cubs fans can be distinguished from other baseball fans by their willingness to throw the home run ball back without receiving compensation. Among the baseball fans who regularly sat in the bleachers during Wheeler's season in the sun was one fellow who brought an old ball with him each day so that, if he caught a home run, he could keep the genuine game ball and toss back the old ball, thus without suffering harassment from the true Cubs fans (Wheeler 93, 109).

To gain a different perspective on a game, the ballpark, and the bleachers themselves, Wheeler shifted one afternoon in June, moving from his normal bench to the grandstand. From there, he had two immediate impressions — one, how the outfield still looked Edenic, lush and green and bathed in sunlight, but now more remote, less intimate than the view from the bleachers; and the other, how the Bleacher Bums enjoyed a camaraderie that was lacking in the grandstand (Wheeler 120).

Not only have the Bleacher Bums created a distinct identity and community, but so too have the residents and fans in the "peanut gallery," the rows of apartment buildings overlooking Wrigley Field along Waveland and Sheffield. Throughout the history of the ballpark, folks in the apartment buildings along Waveland and Sheffield have watched the Cubs' games from their perches behind upper-room windows and on rooftops. Reporting about the Cubs' move to Weeghman Park in 1916, the *Chicago Tribune* reported that hundreds of fans had viewed the Opening Day game "from the roofs and windows of flat buildings across the street from the ballpark" (qtd. in Shea 78). By 1932, the practice of viewing the games from the nearby upper-floor apartments and rooftops had become so profitable that the Chicago Department of Revenue announced that it would collect a tax from the fans who watched games from the buildings. For the 1938 World Series, following Gabby Hartnett's remarkable dusk-defying two-out home run in the bottom of the ninth to give the Cubs the National League lead with less than a week to go in the season, spaces in the apartments sold for more than ballpark tickets during the season. On Sheffield Avenue, one apartment resident sold more than forty admission tickets for fans, many obstructed by others standing between themselves and the apartment windows, to view the game. And another woman on Waveland reported crowding fifty-seven faithful fans into her front two rooms (Shea 140, 177).

By the 1990s the practice of selling admission tickets for rooftop viewing expanded when the owners of some of the apartment buildings began to erect bleachers of their own atop their buildings. At that point the Cubs began to threaten legal action against the owners, and subsequently they started to place opaque screens above the outer walls of the ballpark in order to block the view of the rooftop fans. Community mediation worked, however, as the building owners agreed to share their proceeds, and in return, the building owners would not object to a plan that the Cubs submitted for extending their own outfield bleachers above the sidewalks along the streets — a project that was completed prior to the 2006 season.

A few years before the peanut gallery began to take on a life of its own, the bleachers started to fill to capacity on a daily basis. Prior to the 1985 season, bleacher tickets were sold only on the day of the game. As the popularity of the bleachers increased, in part from the expanded television coverage available through the superstation transmission of Cubs' home games, so did the length of the lines of fans awaiting their opportunity to purchase tickets. Consequently, in 1985 the Tribune Company, a media conglomerate that had recently acquired majority ownership of the Cubs, shifted the policy and began to sell tickets in advance. Not surprisingly, scalpers started to buy up large blocks of bleacher seats, prices increased dramatically with the increased demand, and the character of the bleachers changed from being the spontaneous "communitas"[3] that the Bleacher Bums had enjoyed together for decades to a more yuppie place to go and be seen. So certain was he that the character of the bleachers would be gentrified by the new procedure that, in response to the new policy, Bill Veeck boycotted the ballpark.

Holy Cow!—The Media Polishes the Icon

Part of the appeal of sitting on the sun-bleached planks beyond the outfield walls was that it still generated the sense of camaraderie that fans from afar had seen on their cable—and satellite—reception of the games. "By 1987," Wheeler writes, "sitting in the bleachers at Wrigley Field had become a ceremonial participation in a rite endorsed and glorified by television" (23). For most of their first half-century, in fact, the bleachers had merely been "benches without backs, hard wooden accommodations for the lonely lovers of baseball and the occasional crowd that overflowed the grandstand" (143).

By the late 1980s some of the bleachers ticket holders attended the game primarily to join charismatic Harry Caray, the late-century evangelist for the Cubs, in singing "Take Me Out to the Ballgame." That experience, not unlike singing the Doxology or the Gloria Patri in ecclesiastical services, unified the faithful in a celebrative ritual. So imprecise and charming was Harry's rhythm in leading the singing during the seventh inning stretch that the chorus often sounded like a liturgical canon, with antiphonal responses and repetition in rounds (Wheeler 68).

Grounded in its location, history, and rituals, the iconic perception of Wrigley Field has been intensified and polished by the media—initially radio broadcasts, then multiple local telecasts, and most recently cable and satellite transmission on Superstation WGN. In addition, it is not insignificant that a new generation of popular culture aficionados has come to revere Wrigley Field through two blockbuster films in the 1980s, each of which affirmed the idyllic character of the ballpark in distinct ways. One was *Blues Brothers* (1980), and the other was *Ferris Bueller's Day Off* (1986). In the former comedy, the brothers Jake and Elwood Blue set out to avoid the law while raising money to rescue their childhood home, which was run by nuns, from being sold. Among the scams and skirmishes that they encounter with legal proceedings and documents, Elwood claims 1060 W. Addison as his home address on his driver's license. Of course, that is the mailing address for Wrigley Field.[4]

The other popular film that features Wrigley Field as an icon involves high school student Ferris Bueller fulfilling various adolescent fantasies related to popularity and extravagance: ditching school, befuddling the Dean of Students, driving a red Ferrari for a day, leading a parade, dining in elegant style, and attending a sun-soaked game at Wrigley Field between the Cubs and the Montreal Expos. Like *The Blues Brothers*, this film used Wrigley Field as a visual punch line for some of the comedic twists in the popular script.

Three decades after implementing Weeghman's innovative marketing strategy of providing free admission to women for Friday games at Wrigley Field, Cubs' games began to be telecast on WBKB in 1946, which followed the season during which the Cubs appeared against the Tigers in the World Series. The next year, the station telecast most of the home games and introduced eventual Hall of Fame broadcaster Jack Brickhouse to the microphone. Since the Cubs did not sell exclusive rights to broadcast and telecast their games, in 1948 three Chicago stations offered telecasts of Cubs games. Rather than considering the market saturation a detriment to Cubs' attendance, owner P. K. Wrigley viewed the extensive schedule of telecasts as an opportunity to create more Cubs fans who, eventually, would want to attend games at Wrigley Field. With a last-place team in 1949, the Cubs demonstrated the wisdom of Wrigley's vision as they drew more than a million fans to their home games (Wheeler 122,

198–99). By contrast, throughout the 1950s the Pittsburgh Pirates telecast no home games because they feared that the television audience would supplant stadium attendance. Four decades later, the Pirates enjoyed the second highest local TV rating among major league teams; yet because they had not created a broader fan base beyond the local area, Pittsburgh was considered a "small market" city (Bellamy and Walker 31–45).

Although the Cubs drew more than a million fans annually to Wrigley Field in six of the seven years following their pennant in 1945, after that run they did not reach the million-fan attendance milestone again until 1968, a point at which the identity of the Bleacher Bums had been publicized and the year before they were overtaken by the Mets for the National League crown. In 1952, the final year of their attendance success for a decade, the Cubs awarded exclusive telecast rights to WGN, which had wooed Brickhouse to its station a few years earlier. It was during that year that Brickhouse, carried away with a moment of delight at seeing Hank Sauer hit a home run, spontaneously said, "Hey! Hey!," which subsequently became his signature call for Cubs' home runs.

So integral were telecasts to Wrigley Field and to the public perception of the Cubs that in July 1955 the Cubs designated a section of the left-field grandstand as the "TV Audio Section." In a mid–July issue of the Cubs newsletter, the story noted that from the TV Audio Section fans get "an excellent wide angle view of the field and game." The article goes on to indicate that that section of the grandstand "is equipped with modulated loud speakers which convey the voice of WGN-TV's telecast exactly as it is broadcast." In effect, the promotional piece concludes, "the people in this section will be members of a studio audience, seeing the actual performance as they listen to what goes on in the air" ("TV Audio" 1).

When the Cubs first began to telecast their games from Wrigley Field in the late 1940s, they enjoyed an immediate expansion of their audience, significantly among women who often tuned in while doing afternoon house chores or while waiting for their children to return home from school. In these years prior to Oprah, Mike Douglas, or Merv Griffin hosting talk and variety shows aimed at a female audience, many of the women established familiarity with Jack Brickhouse as a conversation partner. According to some observers, not only were women attracted to the Cubs because they could get a tan while watching the game from Wrigley Field's bleachers, but they also flocked to the regular afternoon telecasts because "a ballgame is ideal daytime television" since it is possible to turn one's back on the game and still keep up with the developing story whose ending is not specifically known even by the narrator (Wheeler 27).

Once the Cubs went on to cable as a superstation in 1982, they became an instant success, having lured Harry Caray from the cross-town rival White Sox to become the featured announcer. At Comiskey Park on Chicago's south side, Caray had enjoyed broadcasting from the ambiance of the ballpark that was older than Wrigley Field and, in its own way, with lights flashing and a fireworks-exploding scoreboard, equally eccentric as its north side sibling. But "without ivy and sunshine and apartment buildings on every side, people [had] just thought of Comiskey as an old ballpark rather than a sacred institution" (Wheeler 205).

In the years immediately following Caray's becoming the announcer for the Cubs' games, he enlarged the audience of viewers who previously had cared little about baseball or the Cubs. So popular did he and his partner Steve Stone become that they both opened restaurants in Phoenix, the home of the Cubs during spring training. Shortly thereafter, Harry opened his restaurant on Rush Street in Chicago and became the self-proclaimed King of Rush Street. Their popularity extended well beyond the upper Midwest and even the Southwest. Cable systems in Belize, for instance, began to transmit Cubs games during the mid–1980s, and almost immediately the Cubs became the national team there. According to the coach of the Belize women's softball team competing in the Pan American games in the late 1980s, "Eighty percent of the people in Belize love the Cubs. People take little televisions to their offices to watch the Cubs during the day. The work stops when the Cubs are on" (qtd. in Wheeler 161). During Caray's tenure as announcer, the magnetic lure of Wrigley Field became even more powerful in measurable ways. For one thing, after two years of Caray's broadcasting from the Cubs' ballpark, home attendance for the first time reached more than two million fans in a single year, and it exceeded that milestone in eighteen of the twenty subsequent years. Even after his death, the daily tributes to Harry from Wrigley Field kept alive his memory — and part of his personality — with guest non-musicians often called upon to lead the crowd with Harry's cadence and verve in singing "Take Me Out to the Ballgame" during the seventh-inning stretch. And in 2004 the Cubs became one of the few teams in major league history to draw more than three million fans, even though Wrigley Field's seating capacity is among the smallest in the major leagues.

Conclusion

Historically the site where mythic feats have been accomplished and storied milestones passed, architecturally akin to places of worship, and functionally the site where Bleacher Bums serve as prophets who endure suffering, persevere through adversity, call the faithful to gather, and engender hope, Wrigley Field has stood as a spiritual site for generations of Cubs devotees and more recently for the media-attracted fans drawn to the ballpark by the charisma and memory of Harry Caray. Not only does Wrigley Field serve these crowds as a kind of sacred place — a place where memory gathers and where hope is garnered — but it also serves as a place of eternal rest, quite literally for Steve Goodman, a die-hard (as he did) Cubs fan and musician and composer best known, perhaps, for having written Arlo Guthrie's hit song "The City of New Orleans." Goodman also wrote several songs about the Cubs: "Go Cubs Go" and "A Dying Cub Fan's Last Request." Following his death in 1984, Goodman's ashes were buried beneath home plate, thus fulfilling his final request.

Although he supervised the burial of Goodman's ashes beneath home plate, former groundkeeper Frank Capparelli, who served as the custodian of the temple for almost forty years, did not specifically refer to Wrigley Field as sacred space. Nonetheless, he describes it as a pilgrimage center, as the destination for "an outing, a place to spend the entire day, [... to] see the charisma of the park," he declares. "There's no place like it. That's why it's always packed" (qtd. in Smith 47). Or as photographic journalist Ira Rosen simply puts it: "Wrigley is unmatched for its physical beauty. An afternoon game [there] must be why baseball was invented" (Rosen 203–204). It's the place where hallowed ivy grows from vines planted by Bill Veeck and where the sacred sun still shines on most Cubs home games.

NOTES

1. Cf. Paul Tillich, *Dynamics of Faith* (New York: Harper and Row, 1952), pp. 41–54.

2. The first verified playing of "The Star-Spangled Banner" at a Major League game also is associated with the Cubs in Chicago. When the Cubs were hosting the Red Sox for the 1918 World Series, the home games were played in Comiskey Park. According to game summaries published in the *New York Times* the following day, during the middle of the seventh inning, a brass band struck up play of the future Anthem, prompting all to rise and players to heed the music.

3. See Victor Turner and Edith Turner, *Image and Pilgrimage in Christian Culture* (New York: Columbia University Press, 1978), pp. 250–55.

4. As odd as it might seem that someone might legally live at the ballpark, Bobby Dorr, the grounds-keeper for the Cubs in the 1920s and 1930s who had worked with Bill Veeck to plant the ivy along the outfield wall, actually had an apartment in Wrigley Field; but the doorway to his rooms was adjacent to the Waveland Avenue entry to the ballpark.

WORKS CITED

Bellamy, Robert V., Jr., and James R. Walker. "Baseball and Television Origins: The Case of the Cubs." *Nine: A Journal of Baseball History and Culture.* 10.1 (Fall 2001): 31–45.

Caparelli, Frank. *What Baseball Means to Me.* Ed. Curt Smith. New York: Warner Books, 2002. 47.

Dreeson, Tom. *What Baseball Means to Me.* Ed. Curt Smith. New York: Warner Books, 2002. 66–67.

Eliade, Mircea. *The Sacred and the Profane: The Nature of Religion.* Trans. Willard R. Trask. New York: Harcourt, Brace, and Company, 1959.

Kinsella, W. P. *The Iowa Baseball Confederacy.* Boston: Houghton Mifflin, 1986.

_____. "The Last Pennant before Armageddon." *The Thrill of the Grass.* New York: Penguin, 1985. 1–22.

_____. *Shoeless Joe.* New York: Ballantine, 1983.

Lowry, Philip. *Green Cathedrals: The Ultimate Celebration of All 273 Major League and Negro League Ballparks Past and Present.* Rev. ed. Reading, PA: Addison-Wesley, 1992.

Peterson, Paul Michael. *Chicago's Wrigley Field.* Chicago: Arcadia, 2002.

Reilly, Edward J. *Baseball: An Encyclopedia of Popular Culture.* Lincoln: U of Nebraska P, 2005.

Rosen, Ira. *Blue Skies Green Fields: A Celebration of 50 Major League Baseball Stadiums.* New York: Clarkson Potter, 2001.

Shea, Stuart, and George Castle. *Wrigley Field: The Unauthorized Biography.* Washington, D.C.: Brassey's, 2006.

Tillich, Paul. *Dynamics of Faith.* New York: Harper and Row, 1952.

Turner, Victor, and Edith Turner. *Image and Pilgrimage in Christian Culture.* New York: Columbia UP, 1978.

"TV Audio Section for Fans." *Chicago Cubs News* 20.3 (21 July 1955): 1.

Wheeler, Lonnie. *Bleachers: A Summer in Wrigley Field.* Chicago: Contemporary Books, 1988.

Philip K. Wrigley: Contrarian

George Castle

More than any other man, Philip K. Wrigley is the one responsible for the Cubs defying million-to-one odds against avoiding a World Series berth since 1945. He had absolute power to bring the endless seasons of losing to a close with a couple of capital expenditures here, a couple of key hires there, and the reconciliation of his tepid — if that much — interest in baseball with his desire to tinker and meddle rather than letting dynamic baseball men run his team.

But the transformation of the Cubs from stumblebums into proud athletes worthy of the stewardship of his father, William Wrigley, Jr., never took place because of the unique, eccentric, and singular personality of Philip K. Wrigley.

The Cubs could never get a head of steam up because of the contrarian nature of Wrigley's personality, expressed in so many different ways:

He was an intensely private, shy man with admittedly few close friends, without even a guest bedroom at his Phoenix mansion because he believed there was no need for anyone to stay overnight. He would have been repulsed had he entered his ballpark as Philip K. Wrigley, owner, with notebooks being filled, flashbulbs popping, cameras whirring, and microphones thrust his way. Yet he was astoundingly accessible for a man of his stature in business and baseball, with player Pete La Cock walking in off the street to see him, baseball writers easily reaching him at the office and home in Lake Geneva when he answered his own phone, and his responding with long written treatises to fan and media criticism.

He increased the profitability and reach of the William Wrigley, Jr., gum company that his father had first built into prominence. Wrigley held a chokehold on the gum market with lavish expenditures on marketing and advertising, the broadcast gum jingles among the most memorable of all time. But as well managed as the gum company was, the Cubs were run in Alice-in-Wonderland style. The team was starved for a decent operating budget while mossified executives, virtually assured of lifetime employment by Wrigley, ignored the blueprints for winning available right under their noses. The team tried the oddball and the unusual, but it never did the basic by acquiring and developing players better than its competitors. The contrast between the gum company's efficiency and profitability, and the Cubs' eternal ineptness is the most striking paradox of the Wrigley business empire.

He kept lights out of Wrigley Field even after planning to introduce night games for the

A version of this essay first appeared in George Castle, *The Million-to-One Team: Why the Chicago Cubs Haven't Won a Pennant Since 1945* (South Bend, IN: Diamond Communications, 2000). Reprinted with permission.

1942 season; he had donated the steel for the towers to the war effort. All other big league teams had lights by 1948. The lack of lights helped doom the Cubs to mediocre season attendance counts for much of the 1950s and 1960s, spurring a downward cycle of financial losses that fed on itself when Wrigley insisted the ballclub be self-supporting.

He believed that one strong man couldn't possibly run an effective business organization, that delegation and specialization was needed. Yet he was executive general manager of the Cubs, with no major player or financial move permitted unless he approved it. His employees were not empowered to act independently or with any ingenuity.

Wrigley's favorite all-time Cubs player was Ernie Banks, an African-American, and he loved Jose Cardenal, a colorful, Afro-adorned Cuban. Wrigley himself went on record opposing racial discrimination on his Catalina Island property. But his organization was particularly hard on African-American players who had indiscretions in their personal lives or spoke out about their salaries and playing conditions. They were dispatched in relatively quick order in trades or released. At the same time, few Latin players became Cubs on his watch, and scouting in the Caribbean was thin at best.

But perhaps the biggest contradiction was Wrigley's maintaining Cubs ownership throughout all the aggravation and financial losses and brickbats from players, fans, and media while continually spurning offers to purchase the franchise. It made little sense that self-described hermit Wrigley continued to own the Cubs, his every move subject to public scrutiny, his burden never lifting as the team continued to lose.

Although there is no conclusive evidence for it, perhaps Wrigley made a solemn vow to William Wrigley, Jr., at his father's deathbed to keep the Cubs in the family, like a treasured heirloom, maintaining it to fend off the ravages of time, but not fiddling with it or improving it. Phil Wrigley kept the Cubs out of an old-fashioned sense of duty, not out of a passionate urge to restore the near-dynastic status of the 1920s-1930s teams.

On January 26, 1932, the dynamic William Wrigley, Jr., died at age 70 in Phoenix. In his will, the elder Wrigley bequeathed the Cubs directly to his son.

"The club and the park stand as memorials to my father," Phil Wrigley was quoted in 1933 as proclaiming. "I will never dispose of my holdings in the club as long as the chewing-gum business remains profitable enough to retain it."

Decades later, he re-confirmed this position in a conversation with *Chicago Sun-Times* columnist Irv Kupcinet: "I inherited the Cubs from my father and I feel an obligation to carry on in respect to him. But I'll leave the team to my son Bill and he can do whatever he pleases."

Bill Veeck, who had worked as a jack-of-all-trades for Phil Wrigley throughout the 1930s, said in his 1962 book *Veeck: As in Wreck*: "Phil Wrigley assumed the burden out of his sense of loyalty and duty. If he has any particular feeling for baseball, any real liking for it, he has disguised it magnificently."

Wrigley never ended up building the Cubs, and maybe that wasn't possible given his inherent nature. Having not grown up around the game and with his shy personality, Wrigley was uncomfortable around the gregarious, often coarse, tobacco-chewing-and-spitting baseball people. He didn't know how to mix and blend in, despite his common-man interests. A man who once remarked that he'd like to live in a cave to get away from everyone wasn't going to survive in the backslapping — and backstabbing — world of baseball. Flushed into the spotlight due to his ultimate sense of family obligation, he dutifully kept the Cubs' door open for business, but certainly didn't dive into it with the passion required of an owner who wanted to win more than anything else. Passion and desire are like balls and strikes in the game. They're central to everything.

"You have to understand where Phil Wrigley was coming from," Cubs media relations director Chuck Shriver said. "He was not a baseball person. His approach to the Cubs was like being the main sponsor of a Chicago symphony orchestra. It was a Chicago resource to be maintained, but you don't waste a lot of money on it. It's entertainment, you keep it in business. That was his approach."

"The worst thing that tore down the Cubs were the Wrigleys," said former Cubs catcher Dick Bertell a few months before his death in 1999. "The Wrigleys weren't passionate baseball people." Bertell's batterymate from 1960 to 1964, Glen Hobbie, concurred. "It seemed like when Wrigley owned the Cubs, the feeling was it would be super if you won the pennant, but if not, no big deal, " said Hobbie.

Without a strong, willful baseball personality, Phil Wrigley was susceptible to all kinds of wacky ideas, like the College of Coaches, an athletic director, and an "evil eye" to put hexes on the Cubs' opponents. Meanwhile, the owner sweated the small stuff, including the appearances and personal behavior of players, rather than the big picture—building a consistent contender.

When some Cubs wore stylish blue socks obtained from the Dodgers, Wrigley ordered equipment chief Yosh Kawano to immediately replace the socks with the traditional stirrups. The players' desire to wear high insteps on their socks became a minor bone of contention on the Cubs in the early 1960s.

Around the same time, Dick Bertell had to pay close attention to his shin guards when he came to bat. "Usually, when you're in the on-deck circle with two out, you keep your shin guards on to save the trouble of taking them off and putting them back on if the batter makes the third out," Bertell said. "But the word came on down from upstairs to take the shinguards off. It looks bad, you showed no faith in your hitter if you kept them on."

With eccentric schemes and the cosmetic appearance of the players and ballpark taking center stage, basic player development and scouting became a neglected part of the Cubs' organization. Although his personal fortune was estimated to be $100 million with $50,000 weekly dividends from the gum company, Wrigley chose not to pour money into the team in an era when much lower costs prevailed. In the cottage industry that was Major League Baseball in the first two-thirds of the twentieth century, Wrigley could have outspent most, if not all, other owners by a wide margin. He did not choose to.

"If Wrigley had just spent a couple of hundred thousand more, we could have picked up a couple of star players who could have helped us," Bertell said. "I never saw us bringing in that kind of talent from the outside."

"The Cubs seemed to operate at a Mom and Pop store level," *Baseball Digest* editor Jack Kuenster said. "They operated at a level below everyone else."

For much of the first part of the million-to-one era, the fans cast their vote on Wrigley's management through the seas of empty seats. They'd come out a couple of times a year, but no more, to Wrigley Field when the team wallowed in the second division. And they often made the owner aware of their feelings. They may not have spun the turnstiles, but they were always close at hand. Most owners would have been moved off Square One by the combination of the fans' angry reaction and their informal boycott of the ballpark, but not Phil Wrigley, always ensured of his gum company's financial cushion.

A disgruntled fan named "Guido II"—no doubt a forerunner of the nickname-laden callers to sports talk radio four decades hence—aired a laundry list of complaints about Wrigley and the Cubs in a letter to the *Chicago Daily News* in July 1959. Guido II lambasted the owner's aversion to night baseball, his apparent tolerance of his baseball management's "stand pat" attitude, and the longtime feeling that Wrigley retained the Cubs as a tax deduction. The newspaper submitted the letter to Wrigley for his reaction. As was his custom,

Wrigley wrote a long response. On July 21, 1959, both the Guido II letter and Wrigley's reaction were published as the lead story on the *Daily News* lead sports page.

Wrigley, for one, suggested Guido II was expending too much energy worrying about the Cubs. In the process, he displayed he did not understand the mindset of his fans. Did he simply expect the fans to come on out, sheeplike, to have a picnic in the sunshine at Wrigley Field? The answer may be obvious. "The writer of this letter is fortunate that we still live in a comparatively free country where he has the right to limit his visits to Wrigley Field," Wrigley penned, "but what puzzles me is feeling the way he does, why doesn't he direct his time and attention to something else that would not get him so stirred up?"

Wrigley sloughed off fourteen years of failure by stating that other teams had lost for longer periods of time. "It is true that it has been 14 years since the Cubs won their last pennant, and none of us is very proud of that," wrote Wrigley. "But there are a lot of clubs that have been trying even longer and their owners are not in the gum business. No one connected with the Cubs has ever had a 'stand pat' attitude in spite of any articles that might have been written about it, and no one is satisfied with .500 ball [the Cubs' pace in mid-season 1959]."

The Cubs a tax writeoff? Wrigley's view: "I have heard this voiced before, and I would love to know how anyone can take a ballclub as a tax deduction as I have never found anyone who could figure this out, and I am sure that the Bureau of Internal Revenue would take a very dim view of anyone who thought he could."

A torrent of angry letters was received by the *Daily News* from fans reacting to Wrigley's response. They were published about a week later. Bob Springer of Chicago wrote that Wrigley didn't answer the tax and "stand pat" questions, sarcastically adding that the owner "didn't say a word about the man who drills for oil at third base." Mildred Walker of Bellwood, Illinois, said Wrigley "does not care if his club draws people and if he doesn't want a winning ballclub as much as any one of his fans, then I would say that he had better stick to making gum." Anita Petita Gonzalez of Cicero reasoned that "it doesn't take eons to build up at least a competent first division ballclub."

A few days later, a small-scale Cubs stockholder wrote in, getting lead *Daily News* sports page play. The stockholder said he had been stonewalled on some of the same questions during the annual shareholders meetings. "He excuses failure by stating other clubs have gone without winning a flag. Nuff said," wrote the stockholder.

To his credit, Wrigley did one important thing right as owner: he kept a regular schedule of ballpark upkeep that preserved Wrigley Field for decades to come. Longtime ballpark business and concessions manager Salty Saltwell supervised many of the off-season remodeling and reconstruction projects that included turning entire sections of grandstand seats down the foul lines to an angle facing home plate. In contrast to old Comiskey Park, which began falling down in the 1970s and 1980s due to maintenance neglect by cash-strapped ownerships, Wrigley Field was adequately rehabbed so that its lifespan, which began in 1914, could reach its 100th birthday in 2014 if the demands of baseball economics doesn't overwhelm it in the interim.

"When the club had a good year [financially], Mr. Wrigley put an awful lot into the physical structure of the ballpark," Saltwell said. Left out of all the construction projects, of course, were up-to-date and comfortable quarters for the players in the form of a larger clubhouse and dugout.

With attendance held down by bad teams and the no-lights policy, the Cubs' cash flow was hampered further by Wrigley's policy of encouraging television coverage of the team. Other owners had begun clamping down on the number of games televised, fearing a negative impact on gate receipts, after an initial burst of video coverage at the dawn of TV in the late 1940s. Braves owner Lou Perini, in fact, forbade any coverage, home or road, of games in the Milwaukee market. The only time Braves fans got to see their team on TV was during the 1957 and 1958 World Series, when the NBC-TV rights superseded the local deal, permitting broadcasts of home games.

But Wrigley opened the doors wide open to the camera's lenses — lots of them. In 1948, two stations, WGN-TV and WBKB-TV, each used their own equipment to televise the entire Cubs' home schedule. Jack Brickhouse was at the mike for WGN while "Whispering Joe" Wilson handled play-by-play for WBKB, which had been Chicago's first commercial TV station. In 1949, the brand-new ABC-owned station, WENR-TV (now WLS-TV) joined the orgy of televised baseball with the irascible Rogers Hornsby announcing the games. There were times when the Cubs game was the only telecast on the three channels on summer afternoons in 1949. Wrigley believed in exposing his product in the new video medium, and he did it more prolifically than any other owner.

Soon WENR and WBKB, the city's first CBS affiliate, dropped out due to mounting production costs and the encroachment of network daytime programming. WGN had exclusivity. The problem was that the Tribune Company-owned station did not have to pay through the nose in rights fees. Wrigley opted not to strike a hard bargain. Some called it a "sweetheart deal" for WGN. Saltwell admitted that "the radio-TV rights were undervalued, compared to what other clubs were getting. We probably should have gotten more."

Financial records could not be obtained, but longtime WGN-TV director-producer Arne Harris estimates that the station paid the Cubs around $5,000 a game (multiply that by 77 games in the old 154-game schedule) in the 1950s. "I heard we were paying the Blackhawks $10,000 a game in the early 1960s, and I don't think the Cubs were getting more than that," Harris theorized. Ward Quaal, then WGN's general manager, also cannot remember specifics of TV rights-fees numbers, but confirms he got a near-bargain. "It is true that it was modest, but Mr. Wrigley saw the value of TV exposure to build fans among kids and women," said Quaal, who now runs a Chicago consulting firm a stone's throw from the Tribune Tower.

Without rancorous rights-fees negotiations, the WGN-Cubs relationship became so close that many fans thought the two entities were under common ownership. They might as well have been, and it was made official when the Tribune Company bought the team in 1981.

WGN and the Cubs had further cemented their marriage in 1958 when the former's 50,000-watt clear-channel AM station landed the radio rights from longtime Cubs carrier WIND-Radio. With morning disc jockey Howard Miller helping make WIND the number one rated station in Chicago at the end of the 1950s, the station was a 5,000-watt outlet that had built up a huge Midwest network for baseball broadcasts to compensate for its lack of signal reach. WIND had paid the Cubs $75,000 a year for rights. Jack Brickhouse, who negotiated sports contracts on behalf of WGN at the time, had lobbied Quaal to fork up the modest amount of cash Wrigley wanted. The Cubs and the radio station settled for a five-year, $150,000 per year deal. "You might lose money the first year," Brickhouse later recalled telling Quaal, "but then you'll make money forevermore."

That was not a difficult prophecy. In a nearly one-way deal, Wrigley was providing a profit center and countless hours of reliable programming for WGN-TV and radio. The ratings enabled the stations' sales staffs to stock the commercial time slots during games with name sponsors.

New fans were created for the future, to be sure. But the Cubs' ledger books suffered during Wrigley's ownership due to the near-giveaway to WGN. The true market value of rights fees, the team's just-due portion of the healthy cash flow the broadcasting operation raked in, never came back to the team. And many still wonder if the same holds true under the Tribune Company umbrella.

Rejecting the available forms of cash flow and unwilling to subsidized the Cubs, Wrigley operated the team a lot more leanly than most major-market franchises. The financial squeeze often put on the Cubs by Wrigley and his son, Bill, privately exasperated some who worked under them. Fearing the price of dissent, they had to keep their feelings to themselves.

But the statute of limitations does run out. And so, twice in the late 1990s, Bob Kennedy, who had served father and son Wrigley as manager and general manager, rued the fact that the Cubs operated at the whims of multi-millionaires who would not use a fraction of the interest on their earnings to improve the team. And when Bill Wrigley was buffeted by $40 million in inheritance taxes after his father and mother, Helen Wrigley, died within two months of each other in 1977, the economic pressure was heightened just when the onset of free agency demanded more budget flexibility.

"I wish the Cubs had been owned by the gum company instead of the individual. Then there would have been more money available to it," Kennedy said as he watched spring training games and workouts near his retirement home in Mesa, Arizona. His wish would have never come true. Phil and Bill Wrigley kept the Cubs and the gum company separate, even to the point of not selling Wrigley's gum at the ballpark.

For all his egalitarian and pro-consumer stances, Wrigley did not believe in free speech for his staff or players. Dissidents were spun out of the organization.

In a quirky way, true to his contrarian personality, Wrigley virtually bought his players' silence in the 1960s by increasing the pay scales after keeping a lid on salaries under Wid Matthews in the early 1950s. The Cubs typically had very few holdouts in spring training. By 1968, players throughout the National League remarked how Wrigley treated his players better than those on any other team. But the happy, satisfied crew didn't last long into the 1970s with the coming of $100,000 salaries, agents, and free agency. Wrigley opposed salaries heading into the healthy six-figure range in multi-year deals. Players complained about their pay, and Wrigley dispatched them to the detriment of his ballclub.

All along, those who zipped their lips and dutifully carried on were rewarded. Loyalty to the owner and the organization seemingly was prized over creative thinking and initiative. Like a long-running TV show, the owner kept an ensemble of employees, some with ability, but always the same cast in an industry where change is often the byword. The end result was an inbred style of management that fell far behind the most progressive baseball organizations.

Former trainer Gary Nicholson, who worked for the Cubs from 1972 to 1976, summed up the Wrigley-era front-office attitude the best: "Don't rock the boat, do things as we've always done."

If an executive's, manager's, or coach's time was up in one job, Wrigley often would lateral him to another position in the organization, no matter whether the man merited continued employment. When Phil Cavarretta was fired as Cubs manager in spring training 1954, Wrigley offered him the manager's job at the Triple-A Los Angeles Angels. But with his pride wounded, Cavarretta rejected the position, going crosstown to play one more season for the White Sox. Despite Cavvy's twenty years of loyal service to the Cubs as player and manager, he never worked for the team again while other, lesser lights found employment with the Cubs.

"If you ever left the organization [on your own], quit on the organization and then wanted to come back, he wouldn't take you," Salty Saltwell said of Wrigley. "If you were fired by him, he would take you back."

The one man who logically could have moved Wrigley off square one was John Holland, in his role as general manager for nineteen years, from 1956 to 1975. But Holland was the absolutely wrong man to play off Wrigley. His low-wattage personality, innate conservatism, blundering trades, mishandling of homegrown players, and fear of offending Wrigley made him a close second to the owner in establishing the losing tradition that led the Cubs to million-to-one status.

"Wrigley easily could have spent $1 million to boost scouting and the minor-leagues, but he would have had to have someone to direct that money in the right direction," said Peter Golenbock.

Holland was not the right man for the job. He was decades behind the times. Yet he stayed on as Cubs GM until his retirement at 65, never once fielding a Cubs team that didn't have at least two major holes. Holland would have been fired by the majority of teams after his few years of failure, but he stayed subservient to Wrigley, and thus was rewarded with lifetime employment. If anything, he was even more conservative and cautious than Wrigley.

Holland did not act independently of Wrigley. When the owner took out an ad in Chicago newspapers defending embattled manager Leo Durocher on September 4, 1971, he said that he and his general manager were close. "John and I are like one," Wrigley said. "We don't do anything without talking it over."

Wrigley would make the final decision on whatever they were contemplating doing with the ballclub. Holland said that when he began with the Cubs, Wrigley gave him "carte blanche" in decisions involving player personnel. But in 1975, Salty Saltwell later revealed who had the last say: "Mr. Wrigley, of course, gives final approval on trades." Despite his lack of knowledge of the game's nuances and people, Wrigley also reportedly wanted Holland to call him after the end of every game, no matter what the time.

Wrigley kept Holland on the job so long he did not know where to turn for a replacement GM. He did not possess the social skills and connections in the game to snare a competent outsider. Wrigley always had promoted or recycled from within the organization with the major exception of Leo Durocher. And once Durocher established himself as a near-savior of the Cubs in the late 1960s, Wrigley adopted him as one of his own. He even toyed with the idea of bringing Leo the Lip back as general manager to succeed Holland in 1976, and turning over day-to-day operation of the Cubs to broadcaster Jack Brickhouse, a member of the Cubs' board of directors. Brickhouse wisely opted to retain the lifetime security of the broadcast booth.

A more likely scenario focused on Blake Cullen. He thought he was in line to replace Holland. After all, he had served as Holland's right-hand man for the previous few years, recommending trades and negotiating some contracts. He was led to believe he was Holland's successor by the GM's own words and in a conversation with Wrigley. Cullen had been approached by Lee Stern for a job with the latter's new pro soccer team, the Sting, in 1974. He told Holland of the offer.

"John said he was grooming me for the [GM] job," Cullen said. In another conversation with Wrigley, he was told there was no one else in the picture. Believing he was the next GM, Cullen turned down Stern.

But Cullen, his co-workers, and fans and media alike were soon in for a surprise. "As the 1975 season ended, John said he had bad news for me," Cullen said. "Salty Saltwell had the job."

"We all thought he'd get the job," Chuck Shriver said of the front-office employees' opinions of Cullen.

We thought it was a foregone conclusion. He was much younger and had a different way of thinking. He was not hidebound by old baseball traditions. He would have made changes, as best he could. We were all shocked when he didn't get the job. Maybe Blake was perceived as being from the hotel business [his employer prior to the Cubs], not the baseball business. I don't think John recommended him, and I don't think Wrigley would have made the decision on his own.

Cullen speculated of himself that he was too high-profile for Wrigley's tastes. His name had appeared in a gossip column when he attended a play, and he had been the subject of other articles. "Wrigley apparently didn't like people promoting themselves," Cullen said. "That wasn't the case with me, but to Wrigley maybe that's how it appeared."

Wrigley himself gave a contrary explanation for passing up Cullen and Whitey Lockman, then director of player development. "They were too close to the present management," he said. Interesting. Wrigley had kept that "present management" intact for nearly two decades.

Chicago sports media members were in near-shock with the news that Saltwell, who had worked on the business side of the Cubs for the previous two decades, was named GM. "It must be pointed out that he has watched the Cubs play ball every day for the last 10 years, both at home and on the road," the *Chicago Tribune*'s Robert Markus wrote of Cullen, contrasting that with Saltwell's desk-bound job at Wrigley Field that prevented him from watching entire games live. "He's seen every ballplayer in the National League and is well-acquainted with the Cubs' own personnel. So the fact he started life running a hotel doesn't mean he couldn't do a decent job wheeling and dealing players. After all, Charlie Finley, the most successful GM in the game, began as an insurance salesman."

Through the decades, the ranks of GMs have been rounded out by men who hadn't played professionally. Cubs president Andy MacPhail, for one, went directly into front-office work right out of college without any playing experience. Other GMs, such as former Dodgers chief Fred Claire, had begun as their teams' media relations directors. The Wrigley family themselves had hired two GMs — William Veeck, Sr., and Jim Gallagher — directly from the ranks of sportswriters.

"I can't guarantee you that Cullen would have been a successful general manager," Markus wrote. "But he at least has acquired the firsthand baseball knowledge that Saltwell obviously lacks."

Critics and fans called Saltwell a "peanut vendor" because he headed concessions. That had been his bailiwick since he joined the Cubs in 1958. Previously, though, Iowa native Saltwell had worked in baseball operations in the minor leagues. He had been executive vice president of the old Class A Western League before joining the Des Moines farm club in 1955 after John Holland had been promoted to Triple-A Los Angeles.

So why did Wrigley pick a GM who wasn't familiar, day to day, with big-league personnel? "Mr. Wrigley sensed what was happening in baseball with free agency coming around," Saltwell said. "His thinking was that somebody with a little business background was needed to work on the player end. He approached me. I had an interest in it. If he expressed enough confidence in your ability to do the job, you went along with it. I had no trepidations."

Wrigley also believed that Saltwell's no-nonsense style could stir an underperforming club — and duel the newly-empowered agents to a standstill. "I told him to get rough," the owner said. "And I think he will."

Wrigley cited the example of Leo Durocher's imperious tenure as manager. "The closest we came to winning was under Durocher in 1969," he said. "The players hated him. Maybe we're being too nice."

Saltwell's alleged toughness aside, he was an astute man, with a penchant for details of how the Cubs ran as a business. But at a crucial juncture in baseball history, the Cubs lost more by not promoting Cullen. He had worked his way up to the job.

"I still have notebooks that I compiled then on how to play the game in Wrigley Field," Cullen said.

> Also about the type of pitcher you need to win in that ballpark — big, tall, right-handed pitchers with sinkers. The left-handed pitcher seems to struggle there, and it has something to do with the angle of the ball coming out of the bleachers. High fastballs don't work in Wrigley Field. With free agency coming in, I had a real door set up with agents. Dealing with them never bothered me. I almost liked dealing with agents. You had to jump on the free-agent bandwagon, and it got away from the Cubs.

In picking Saltwell, Wrigley simply chose someone else from his longtime cast of characters, as per custom. But the Saltwell rein was brief, notable only for another disastrous trade (Andre Thornton to the Indians), the callup of Bruce Sutter, and Saltwell's being forced to get an unlisted number at his Park Ridge home when teenage girls called to plead with him not to trade Rick Monday.

Business-operations chief Bill Heymans left in the middle of the 1976 season for health reasons. "I got the whole bundle of wax, baseball and business end, because I was the only one in the front office with experience," Saltwell said. "After the end of the season, I told Mr. Wrigley that there was no way I could continue as general manager and business manager. I could do one or the other."

Wrigley gave him the choice. Saltwell selected business operations, but was asked to help choose his successor and work in negotiating baseball contracts. "He asked if I had anyone in mind," Saltwell said. "Bob Kennedy had been trying to get back into the organization. He had been doing a good job evaluating players for Seattle, which was then just starting as an expansion team. Mr. Wrigley asked me about what Kennedy was doing."

Kennedy, Cubs manager from 1963 to 1965, was hired as Phil Wrigley's last general manager. He hired Herman Franks as manager to replace Jim Marshall. Kennedy had worked for Franks as manager of the Triple-A Salt Lake City team Franks had owned back in 1962. Franks himself was a recycled Cub. He had served as a coach under Leo Durocher in 1970. Later, after quitting as Cubs manager with a week to go in the 1979 season, Franks returned again as a caretaker general manager to succeed Kennedy as Bill Wrigley sold the team to the Tribune Company.

Happy to get back to his native Chicago, Kennedy was not going to counter Phil Wrigley's dicta when stars Bill Madlock and Rick Monday wanted hefty raises for 1977. Wrigley ordered both traded. The Madlock deal was another long-run stinker. By this time, the 82-year-old Wrigley felt lost. The world had turned. "I have outlived my usefulness. Everything has changed," he said as salaries exploded and free-spending owners like George Steinbrenner reaped immediate benefits in the won-lost column.

The aggravation at the end of his life causes the question to be asked again: What pleasure, what ego-satisfying process did Phil Wrigley derive from continued ownership of the Cubs? The team lost for so long. Red ink flowed. Wrigley believed he tried everything to turn the franchise around. Nothing worked. Why not make the team someone else's burden, despite the commitment to his father's memory?

Wrigley did not lack for ways out of his predicament. He was always approached to sell the Cubs by some of the biggest names in sports, business, and entertainment.

McDonald's impresario Ray Kroc, a dyed-in-the-wool Cubs fan, made Wrigley offers he could refuse. When he had the chance to buy the San Diego Padres in 1973, Kroc enlisted

George Halas as an intermediary in another purchase attempt. Wrigley said "no," and Kroc went ahead with the Padres deal.

Halas, who rented Wrigley Field for his Bears from William Jr. and Phil Wrigley from 1921 to 1970, said he had approached Wrigley in the 1950s to buy the Cubs for himself. That would have been an emotional buy. Halas had played briefly in the majors for the New York Yankees and had long lived on Chicago's far North Side, not far from the ballpark. "At the time, he said he would give me not the first refusal but the last refusal," Halas said in 1977. "But nothing came of it."

Chicago radio talk show host Chet Coppock, whose family was close to Halas, said Papa Bear continued loving baseball through his decades of Bears stewardship. Halas had a drawing on one of his office walls at 233 W. Madison St. of Babe Ruth pointing before his "called shot" homer in the 1932 World Series at Wrigley Field.

Frank "Trader" Lane, the frantic baseball executive who once was general manager of the White Sox, reportedly made a $7 million bid to buy the Cubs. Saltwell said he heard rumors that Bob Hope, who at one time had an ownership interest in the Cleveland Indians, had made an offer to Wrigley. Jack Brickhouse expressed interest in buying the club on several conversations while driving in his car with Coppock and his father, Charles. "He probably had 25 serious offers and 1,500 inquiries about buying the team," Chet Coppock said.

Maybe Wrigley didn't understand the passion of Cubs fans. He should have if he was slipping into the ballpark incognito. The gap between the owner's desire to win and that of his fans was light years wide. The frustration of the fans was so great by 1964 that they concocted fantastic, but fruitless schemes to seize the team from the man who refused to take action to win pennants.

In addition to the ostensible William Wrigley, Jr., deathbed vow not to sell the Cubs, perhaps there was some influence within the Wrigley household to retain team ownership. Helen Wrigley apparently liked the family heirloom.

"Mrs. Wrigley got to like the Cubs very much and I think it was because of her that he would not dispose of the Cubs," George Halas theorized in 1977.

"Mrs. Wrigley was a bigger fan than her husband," Phil Cavarretta said.

Besides all the eager rich guys who could have owned the Cubs, put their heart and soul into the tradition-dripping franchise, the fans ended up drawing the short straw with Phil Wrigley. Part of him had the attitude of ultimate privilege. Another part of him didn't mind getting down and dirty, tinkering with engines, dodging spilled beer cups incognito in Wrigley Field. Either part on its own should have brought the Cubs a winner.

Maybe 100,000 to one against a man with Phil Wrigley's resources not bringing at least one pennant to the North Side between 1946 and 1976? A lot of factors go into compiling million to one odds. The modest man who wanted to live in a cave could claim a lion's share of the credit. What a legacy.

Educating Wrigley:
The Failed Experiment of
the College of Coaches

Andrew Hazucha

On December 20, 1960, Chicago Cubs owner Philip K. Wrigley shocked the baseball world by announcing that the Cubs would begin the 1961 season without a manager, employing instead a system of rotating coaches, each of whom would take turns managing the team from one week to the next. Citing the high rate of manager turnover in professional baseball, a phenomenon that meant most teams were continually changing entire coaching staffs and

A young Phil Wrigley, owner of the Cubs from 1932 to 1977 (courtesy Baseball Hall of Fame).

style of play, Wrigley declared that his experiment would standardize the coaching provided to the players and regulate the uneven performance of a Cubs team that had finished 60–94 the previous year under the combined managerial stints of Charlie Grimm and Lou Boudreau. If the project was daring in its conception, it turned out to be an abject failure in execution, as the '61–'62 Cubs went 64–90 and 59–103 respectively before Wrigley abandoned his plan after the second year and hired Bob Kennedy to manage the club without interruption in 1963 and 1964.[1] The managerial confusion caused by Wrigley's experiment led to frequent in-fighting among the eight coaches on the Cubs' staff and, perhaps more damagingly, a lineup that continually changed depending on which coach happened to make it out on any given day. Rather than providing stability in the mentoring process of players, the "College of Coaches," as Chicago sportswriters mockingly began calling it, ensured that each player in need of coaching — especially young, undeveloped players such as Lou Brock — received conflicting advice from a variety of tutors rather one coherent message. The result was that Brock and other talented rookies flunked out of the College that Wrigley founded, eventually moving on to more stable environments where they graduated with honors into the ranks of stardom.

Although Wrigley's project was fatally flawed in practice, in its original conception it had some currency with evolving managerial practices among other major league baseball teams. Wrigley and his top advisors met repeatedly in the fall of 1960 to discuss how to make the Cubs a more competitive ballclub, and they decided that their first course of action would be to expand dramatically the Cubs' three-man coaching staff and keep all coaches on the job year round rather than employing them from spring training until the end of the regular season. As long-time Cubs coach and Wrigley favorite Elvin Tappe tells it, he first convinced Wrigley in a private conversation that the Cubs' owner needed to systematize his team's coaching situation by retaining the same corps of coaches no matter who took the manager's position. Tappe told the Cubs' owner that if he fired a manager the existing coaching staff should remain in place, thereby offering some consistent, stable direction to the players over a period of many years (Phalen 125). Wrigley agreed, and he and the Cubs' brass immediately launched a plan to hire eight coaches to start the 1961 campaign, with the option of adding more if the need arose. Since many teams already had expanded their coaching staffs in a like manner and were even rotating some of these coaches in and out of their farm systems, Wrigley and his advisors were merely mimicking the strategies of the competition with their plan to use multiple coaches who would spend part of their time visiting the Cubs' minor league affiliates (Angle 127). What was truly radical, however, was Wrigley's insistence (much to Tappe's surprise and alarm) that no particular coach emerge as the unequivocal, undisputed manager — that several coaches, in fact, rotate in as manager of the parent club at some point during the year but that no one coach would remain in the position for any appreciable length of time. The Cubs would be, in effect, a team managed by committee.

If Wrigley was expecting the Chicago press to applaud this revolutionary maneuver and celebrate his genius, he badly misread his audience. Dick Hackenberg, a reporter for the *Chicago Sun-Times*, wrote a piece that was emblematic of the abuse Wrigley was getting from local newspapers. Using the persona of a fictitious bartender named Dennis Graham, Hackenberg has him say, "I been waiting for a call from Mr. Wrigley to manage his club; now I got eight times the chance I thought I had. Imagine, eight coaches! Why not nine? They could play the second game of doubleheaders!" (qtd. in Angle 128). John P. Carmichael of the *Chicago Daily News* wrote, "The day may come, if it hasn't already, when the Cubs set a baseball pattern of operating entirely with coaches and vice presidents and no players" (128). Ed Prell of the *Chicago Tribune* wryly remarked that Vedie Himsl, the man Wrigley designated to start the 1961 season as head coach, would be "long remembered as the first baseball coach who was appointed and given a two-weeks' notice at the same time" ("Himsl's Selection" 5: 3). And the *Chicago American* wrote a biting story the day after Wrigley's announcement under the satirical headline, "Wrigley Has Stocking Hung, Wants It Full of Coaches," inducing Wrigley three days later to buy two columns of space in the *American* so that he could write a rejoinder and chide the writer, Charles Chamberlain, for his "smart-aleck story" (Angle 129).[2] The passage of time has not softened the ridicule directed at Wrigley, as long-time Chicago sportscaster Chet Coppock has pronounced the College of Coaches "The dumbest single coaching situation in history of modern sports" (qtd. in Castle 73), and a 1985 book entitled *The Baseball Hall of Shame* has enshrined Wrigley's experiment in a chapter called "The Rear End of the Front Office: The Most Disgraceful Actions by Owners." The book's authors, Bruce Nash and Allan Zullo, deride Wrigley for his "typical loser logic" and conclude that the Cubs' management only "wanted eight flavors of jello" (38).

Although the Chicago press delighted in tweaking Wrigley whenever they had the chance, outside of his hometown the Cubs' owner was getting a slightly more positive reception — that is, his plan was met with an almost unanimous polite skepticism rather than outright mockery. Members of the baseball establishment weighed in one at a time, collectively creating the impression that the Cubs' eccentric owner was, say, a kind of latter-day Shakespearean pantaloon, a slightly crazy older uncle who needed patronizing rather than derision. National League President Warren Giles, for example, allowed Wrigley the benefit of a faintly off-kilter judgment, saying, "Certainly, Mr. Wrigley knows what he wants to do. [...] But I've never heard of a team without a manager" (qtd. in Holtzman and Vass 126). When a reporter asked Giles if he thought that Wrigley's experiment was a good one, Giles replied curtly, "I'd rather not be quoted on that" (126). American League President Joe Cronin was equally civil but as incredulous as Giles, declaring, "I'd feel a lot better with one chief and more Indians" (126). Less judgmental in his opinion was Commissioner Ford Frick, who intoned, "If Mr. Wrigley wants eight coaches and no manager that is strictly his business" (126). When Bill Veeck, the colorful owner of the White Sox and arguably baseball's most innovative experimentalist ever, was asked if he would adopt Wrigley's new system of rotating coaches, he quipped, "No, I'll go along with tradition. I guess I'm just an old stick-in-the-mud" (126).

In all his years of owning the Cubs Wrigley prided himself on his ability to ignore his detractors and remain above the fray, but midway through spring training in 1961 he had reached his boiling point. As the sympathetic 1975 biography of Wrigley — rather fawningly subtitled *A Memoir of a Modest Man*— terms it, Wrigley was likely "disturbed by the fact that no one, literally no one, saw in the multiple-coach system a bold, imaginative, and unconventional effort to pull the Cubs out of the doldrums" (Angle 129). Wrigley's first response was to have his brain trust produce and release in March 1961 a twenty-one-page manuscript entitled *The Basic Thinking That Led to the New Baseball Set-Up of the Chicago National League Ball Club*. The principal assertion contained therein was that a crisis of talent had occurred when the formerly independent minor leagues, which once produced a regular pool of somewhat finished young ballplayers, had been replaced in favor of farm teams administered by the parent major league teams. These farm teams were not as successful in turning out the numbers of qualified young players that previously existed because the coaching was uneven at best, as former ballplayers were frequently hired on at low salaries to oversee the raw talent coming through the system. The Cubs' philosophy, then, was to hire on eight ostensibly qualified and well-tested coaches to rotate regularly through the Cubs' system, from farm club to parent club, giving all the players in the Cubs' system the benefit of their collective wisdom. The chorus of laughter that had originally greeted Wrigley's plan induced him to release the twenty-one-page explanatory document along with this pointed written message for his critics:

> We have started out under an extreme handicap because of all the ridicule and criticism from the press at daring to try something different in baseball. When the [Cubs] announced last fall that we planned to do things differently in 1961 and that we would operate without the term or title of manager and would build a staff of eight or more coaches, the sportswriters seemed to think [...] that we had gone out of our minds. [...]
>
> The writers started talking about the management team idea in a sarcastic and belittling way, using such terms as "brain trust," "college of coaches," "the enigmatic eight," "double-domed thinkers," etc., in their tirades [...] yet those of them with children of school age would undoubtedly be heartily in favor of any and all efforts that might be made to provide more and better instruction in the schools which their children are attending [130–31].

Notwithstanding Wrigley's flawed logic in assuming that parents of a middle-school child would applaud the notion of eight rotating homeroom teachers — or laying that metaphor

aside, the same parents several years later endorsing a team-taught college freshman composition course employing eight instructors, each with different expectations for expository writing — he also betrayed his real obsession with his reference to the Cubs' "management team
idea." In short, Wrigley wanted to run his ballclub like he ran his chewing gum empire.

An August 1962 *Sports Illustrated* article by Robert H. Boyle offers perhaps the most
insightful commentary on the College of Coaches ever written, drawing its thesis from a public pronouncement by Wrigley that the Cubs were not so much a ballclub as "a corporation
organized for profit" (45). According to Boyle, the bizarre coaching system of the Cubs was
merely a reflection of the owner's steadfast commitment to applying business models to the
game of baseball. The Cubs, argues Boyle, were the only team in 1962 to use an IBM machine
to sift through all manner of data and predict success on the field. So instead of employing
human statisticians, Wrigley was relying on his IBM machine, or early-era computer, to systematically track fly balls, ground balls, weather conditions, field conditions, and lefty/righty
hitting and pitching percentages. In effect his computerized data collection could provide
"instantaneous information on all players on National League rosters" (Prell, "Cubs to Use" 3:
1). Boyle further posits that far from being disorganized, the Cubs had become, in his words,
"organized to the nth degree." They were, he concludes, "organization men in the truest sense
of the term; indeed, it would be more accurate to call them the Orgs instead of the Cubs" (45).

Boyle's observation that the Cubs had become baseball's first truly corporate entity is
supported by additional evidence that had come out of the Cubs' organization during the
1962 season. A devotee of managerial pamphlets and instructional manuals, Wrigley had a
booklet printed and privately distributed to his vice-presidents and field generals that enu-
merated all the changes the Cubs had enacted to their coaching system during its inaugural
run during the 1961 campaign. Entitled *Duties and Functions of the Management Team*, the
booklet went through more than eleven editions and used such business jargon as "associated
teams" to refer to the Cubs' minor league clubs (Boyle 45). One of the Cubs' coaches who
read the booklet and rotated into the manager's spot for the entire second half of the 1962
season, Charlie Metro, was a quintessential organization man who used to extol the power of
positive thinking. As Boyle reports it, Metro announced that he was reading two books by
Claude Bristol that encapsulated his philosophy of Panglossian optimism then in vogue in
the business world: *Magic of Believing*, and *TNT: The Power Within You* (45). Metro, it should
be noted, finished the 1962 season with a record of 43–68, refused to be rotated out of the
manager's spot at season's end, and was promptly fired by Cubs' vice-president John Holland
(Holtzman and Vass 128).

Despite Wrigley's determination to run his club like a business, the model seemed to
lack both the personnel and the internal discipline that would make for a successful practical
application. In his autobiography Metro chides the Cubs' organization for its lack of inten-
sity and focus, saying that when he arrived for spring training in 1962 the "Cubs situation
[...] was like a country club" (Metro and Altherr 252). Metro's estimation of his fellow College faculty is that they lacked professionalism; of fellow coach Elvin Tappe, for instance,
Metro opines, "He didn't know how to manage" (261). Veteran Cubs relief pitcher Don Elston,
who played with the team from 1957 to 1964, is even more critical of the coaches who Wrigley
recruited for his project, saying, "If you look at that list, there is not one decent major league
manager in the group. Not one" (qtd. in Golenbock 371). Elston includes Metro in his indictment, noting that Metro, like the other rotating coaches, was generally trying to sabotage the
others when he was not the one at the helm. According to Elston, while Elvin Tappe and Lou
Klein were taking turns managing the club during the first half of the 1962 season, Metro was
frequently in the outfield before games hitting fungoes and ground balls to his son, neglect-

ing his responsibility to assist the manager in coaching the Cubs players (372). "I never felt," says Elston, "that I was learning anything from any of the coaches. [...] I didn't see much teaching going on" (370).

If the Cubs were failing as a "corporation organized for profit," it was not for lack of coaches, however ineffective or embattled, who tried to make the corporate model work. The Cubs employed no fewer than eleven coaches over the course of their two-year experiment, the faculty of the College consisting of, at various times, Rip Collins, Vedie Himsl, Fred Martin, Harry Craft, Elvin Tappe, Gordie Holt, Charlie Grimm, Verlon Walker, Bobby Adams, Lou Klein, and Charlie Metro. Although only five of these men — Himsl, Craft, Tappe, Klein, and Metro — ever rotated into the manager's position, the continual changing of the guard at the manager's post made for many disgruntled players in addition to Elston. The Cubs traded one such unhappy veteran, third baseman Don Zimmer, who when interviewed decades later said of the experiment, "It was crazy. How could anything like that work? [...] You lose 100 games and they say it worked. The whole thing didn't make sense. If anybody told you any different, some of them would have to be lying, I think" (Muskat 66). One of the few notable exceptions was Ernie Banks, who had nothing but praise for Wrigley's College even though during the 1961 season he played three separate positions — shortstop, left field, and first base — depending on who was managing the day he arrived at the ballpark (Castle 76). As Banks phrased it in an interview several years after his playing days as a Cub were over, "we had several systems of managers here that didn't [negatively] affect me at all because I was just listening to them talk about things and philosophies" (Muskat 40).[3] Ever the company man, Banks always deferred to authority publicly and never criticized Wrigley, for whom he had a real fondness. A year later, as the Cubs were in the process of cruising to a 59–103 finish, their worst record since 1901, Banks said after the All-Star break, "I still think we have a chance to finish in the first division" (qtd. in Boyle 45).

At twenty-one years of age and having just finished his rookie season when Wrigley instituted the College of Colleges, Banks's teammate Ron Santo was considerably younger and more vulnerable to managerial instability than the veteran players when the experiment started. Team captain Don Zimmer, who mentored Santo at third base during the 1961 season, noted how the system frustrated Santo's ability to concentrate on the game:

> I can remember as this started, Santo was a young third baseman, a kid. One head coach, "Move back a little bit." Another one, "You got to move over a little bit." Another guy is telling him to come in. Finally, he said, "Let me play ball." He's got five guys telling him five different things. It was comical [Muskat 64].

In an interview in the early 1990s, Santo was asked to recall what it was like to begin his career under Wrigley's scheme of rotating coaches. "Well," he said, "it was kind of ridiculous. [...] Every two weeks you were having a new head coach and they all had different thoughts and different ways they wanted you to play that position and the way they wanted you to hit. So, it was very confusing as a young player" (Phalen 161). In his 1993 autobiography Santo explains his problems under the College in more detail, emphasizing how his survival as a player depended upon his putting aside much of the conflicting advice he was getting from the various Cubs coaches:

> Players often confide in their coaches rather than their managers — who could we confide in? It was a very difficult situation for everyone. One head coach would come aboard and tell me what was expected of me; two weeks later, the next coach would tell me something different. I would listen to everyone; if it didn't make sense, it went in one ear and out the other. After awhile, it was all I could do to keep my balance. I wasn't insubordinate; I just tried to get along and not get messed up at the plate or in the field [Santo and Minkoff 42].

Santo's performance during the '61 and '62 campaigns suggest that, rather than improving his game as he became increasingly comfortable with the system, Wrigley's rotating coaches were becoming a source of ever-growing frustration for him.[4] His offensive production plummeted over the course of the experiment along with the team's fortunes, and even Wrigley had to agree by the end of 1962 that the instability his coaching system had created was counterproductive. The Cubs' owner abandoned his project after the season, an indication that the talent on the Cubs' roster was not responding as he had expected. For Santo, the experiment was particularly damaging for the young prospects on the team who were just breaking in during the two years it was in place. Reminiscing about its effects on the other Cubs players, Santo said, "If our coaching system was confusing to the veterans, it was downright perplexing to rookies" (43).

Perhaps the best example of how young players coming through the Cubs' system fared under the College of Coaches was Lou Brock, who made his major league debut during the last month of the 1961 season (Castle 76). During Brock's rookie campaign the following year, Wrigley pointed to him and two other prospects as evidence that the coaching experiment was beginning to return dividends. "I think," said Wrigley, "that what we started out to do has been highly successful, and that is to develop young ballplayers. We have Cal Koonce, the pitcher, and we have Ken Hubbs (at second) and Lou Brock (in center field). They've jumped several classifications, and they're outstanding ballplayers. [...] And if you look at the system, you'll have to admit that it's working" (qtd. in Boyle 45). Santo recognized Brock's rare talents but saw his development much differently. According to Santo, by Brock's second year "his head was so filled with conflicting opinions he didn't know where he was" (Santo and Minkoff 43). While reflecting on his brief stint with the Cubs thirty years later, Brock said that the College of Coaches stunted his development as a player and created a leadership vacuum that hurt the Cubs on every level. "Players," said Brock, "are great followers of rules and regulations of one manager. When you have 14 coaches, who do you follow?" (qtd. in Castle 76). Having played mostly night games as a minor leaguer, Brock was regularly losing fly balls in the sun in right field, where the Cubs finally stationed him. But none of the Cubs' coaches ever taught him how to flip down his sunglasses while a ball was in play, and they were equally inattentive in instructing him how to approach left-handed pitchers, who seemed to own him. The coaching faculty also never turned him loose on the base paths, though he was timed going from home to first in an astonishing 3.6 seconds (77). The end result was that the Cubs stayed with their promising outfielder for just two full seasons before trading him to St. Louis on June 15, 1964 while he was hitting just .251. The Cubs received sore-armed pitcher Ernie Broglio from the Cardinals in return; he was out of baseball two years later. And Brock? He went on to finish out the 1964 season by hitting .348 for the Cardinals, who won the World Series that year (84). Brock, who went on to play fifteen more major league seasons and landed in the Hall of Fame, was characteristically diplomatic when speaking of the Cubs' mishandling of him as a young prospect. Of the College of Coaches Brock remarked, "I probably came along at the wrong time in the Cubs organization. [...] To shoot from Class C to the majors in one year had to do with the lack of talent in the organization. I didn't start to learn to play the game until I got there" (78).[5]

If one juxtaposes Brock's comments with Wrigley's, one sees that the two of them were viewing the same phenomenon but drawing two very different conclusions from their observations. Whereas Wrigley seemed to think that the tutelage provided by the rotating coaches permeated from top to bottom in the hierarchy and developed raw talent more efficiently and quickly than a traditional system, Brock only saw gaping holes in his education as each individual coach, busily trying to curry favor with Cubs management, often neglected his on-the-field duties and assumed that the others were providing basic instruction to their charges. And since there was no central command (to use modern military parlance) in the Cubs' dugout, a player who needed help could turn to one coach for advice, which often would be contradicted by another coach who came along a moment later. This scenario became a constant affliction for Brock while he was a Cub, as one coach tried to develop him into a power hitter while another demanded that he perfect the drag bunt to prepare himself for being a leadoff hitter (78). The ultimate effect of all this competing and oppositional instruction on Brock was a delay in his development, leading the Cubs' management to give up on him just as he was on the cusp of stardom.[6]

From 1947 to 1960 the Cubs changed managers seven times and finished in the second division of the National League fourteen consecutive seasons. During that time span they never finished higher than fifth (Enright 21). After Wrigley instituted the College of Coaches in an effort to change his team's fortunes, the 1961 Cubs finished seventh while the 1962 squad finished ninth, 42½ games back of first place and notching its fewest wins since the 1901 Cubs went 53–86. When Wrigley announced his plan to go to a system of rotating coaches in December of 1960, he made it clear that the last thing he wanted was an autocratic manager who would rule the team with an iron will. As Cubs vice-president John Holland phrased it at the time, "We couldn't hire a Durocher or a Stanky, although they're good baseball men. We didn't want the type of guy who wants it done his way or else" (qtd. in Bingham 48). By the end of the 1965 season Wrigley Field attendance was down 35 percent and the Cubs had lost $1,237,015 on their baseball operations (Angle 163). Having already abandoned the College of Coaches two years earlier, and now desperate for a way to end his team's dysfunction, Wrigley hired Leo Durocher to be his manager for the 1966 season. Coaching by committee was gone. As Durocher said in his first press conference, "I'm the manager. I'm not a head coach. [...] There can only be one boss" (164).

NOTES

1. That the Cubs only won 59 games during the 1962 season is all the more appalling given the extraordinary talent in the lineup. Ernie Banks, who hit 37 home runs that year, was at first base. Second baseman Kenny Hubbs won both the 1962 NL Rookie of the Year Award and a Gold Glove, going 78 consecutive games without an error. The left side of the infield had a young Ron Santo at third and a dependable Andre Rogers at short. The outfield consisted of George Altman, Lou Brock, and Billy Williams. Dick Bertell, the starting catcher, hit over .300 that year, and the starting rotation had Bob Buhl, Dick Ellsworth, Don Cardwell, Cal Koonce, and Glen Hobbie. As Cubs reliever Don Elston recalls, "That was *not* a bad team" (Golenbock 372).

2. The derisive laughter that greeted Wrigley after he announced his experiment to the press unnerved him, making him even more of a recluse in his own stadium. By 1960 he had largely stopped attending Cubs home games, and, on the rare occasion when he did attend, he sat incognito in the back of the grandstands, leaving his box seat vacant (Angle 124).

3. In his autobiography Banks is more forthcoming about his discomfort with having to play three different positions during the 1961 season. "Only a duck out of water could have shared my loneliness in left field," he writes. "How I managed to escape with just one error in twenty-three games is a mystery" (Banks and Enright 129).

4. In 1961, the inaugural year of the College of Coaches and Santo's sophomore season, he hit a respectable .284 with 23 home runs and 83 RBI's. The following year he tailed off to a .227 batting average with 17 home runs and 83 RBI's. In 1963 Wrigley hired Bob Kennedy to manage the Cubs, effectively ending the coaching experiment, and Santo rebounded to have his best year at the plate, with an average of .297, 25 home runs, and 99 RBI's. 1964 would be Santo's breakout year, as he hit .312 with 30 home runs and 114 RBI's, nearly winning the National League Most Valuable Player Award.

5. Don Elston said much the same thing about learning how to pitch *after* having arrived in the major

leagues. According to Elston, the pitching coaches in the Cubs' organization were all "PK Wrigley cronies" who knew very little about teaching the art of pitching. The result, said Elston, is that he was forced to learn how to pitch "from the mound after [getting] to the major leagues" (Golenbock 370).

6. Ron Santo is convinced that Wrigley's scheme of rotating coaches allowed the Cubs' brain trust to overlook Brock's formidable talents and stymie his development. "You knew this guy would be great," said Santo. "The system hurt Lou" (Golenbock 375).

Works Cited

Angle, Paul M. *Philip K. Wrigley: A Memoir of a Modest Man.* Chicago: Rand McNally, 1975.
Banks, Ernie, and Jim Enright. *"Mr. Cub."* Chicago: Follet, 1971.
Bingham, Walter. "The Cubs and All Their Coaches." *Sports Illustrated* 10 Apr. 1961: 46–49.
Boyle, Robert H. "Off Year for the Chicago Orgs." *Sports Illustrated* 6 Aug. 1962: 44–45.
Castle, George. *The Million-to-One Team: Why the Chicago Cubs Haven't Won a Pennant Since 1945.* South Bend, IN: Diamond, 2000.
Enright, James. "Wrigley Mum on '61 Lineup of Cub Chiefs." *The Sporting News* 28 Sept. 1960: 21+.
Golenbock, Peter. *Wrigleyville: A Magical History Tour of the Chicago Cubs.* New York: St. Martin's, 1999.
Holtzman, Jerome, and George Vass. *Baseball, Chicago Style.* Chicago: Bonus, 2001.
Metro, Charlie, and Tom Altherr. *Safe by a Mile.* Lincoln: U of Nebraska P, 2002.
Meyers, Doug. *Essential Cubs.* Chicago: Contemporary, 1999.
Muskat, Carrie, comp. *Banks to Sandberg to Grace.* Chicago: Contemporary, 2002.
Nash, Bruce, and Allan Zullo. *The Baseball Hall of Shame.* New York: Pocket, 1985.
Phalen, Rick. *Our Chicago Cubs.* South Bend, IN: Diamond, 1992.
Prell, Edward. "Himsl's Selection Wins O.K. of Cub Associates." *Chicago Daily Tribune* 8 Apr. 1961, sec. 5: 3.
_____. "Cubs to Use 8 Coaches Next Season!" *Chicago Daily Tribune* 21 Dec. 1960, sec. 3: 1+.
Santo, Ron, and Randy Minkoff. *Ron Santo: For Love of Ivy.* Chicago: Bonus, 1993.

PART II

RACE, ETHNICITY, AND THE CUBS

Making It Home:
Cap Anson, Fleet Walker, and the
Romance of the National Pastime

Steve Andrews

"Home is the place where, when you have to go there,
They have to take you in."
"I should have called it
Something you somehow haven't to deserve."
— Robert Frost, "The Death of the Hired Man"

By way of an anthem

On Memorial Day of 1897, Booker T. Washington was among the luminaries who addressed the crowd gathered in Boston's Music Hall for the dedication of Augustus Saint-Gaudens' memorial to Colonel Robert Shaw and the all-black Fifty-fourth Regiment of Massachusetts Volunteers. Rather than focus on the "beauty and magnificence" of the memorial, however, Washington shifted attention to what he called "the greater monument" of life among "the lowly in the South" who were in the process of being uplifted "[b]y the way of the school, the well-cultivated field, the skilled hand, [and] the Christian home." Such a living monument, Washington urged, would "justify all that has been done and suffered" on behalf of freedom for all ("Boston Honors" 4). The *Boston Transcript,* which Washington cites in his autobiography, stated that the "superb speech" was "the climax of the emotion of the day and the hour" (Washington 176). If so, William James, whose younger brother Wilky had fought with the 54th, helped set up that climax in an address just prior to Washington's that pointed out the "horrible self-contradiction" between this "land of freedom" and the "human slavery enthroned at the heart of it" that had driven the country to civil war (James, *Memories* 42).

Americans, according to James, were true believers in a "religion" whose basic tenets declare that a "man requires no master to take care of him, and that common people can work out their salvation well enough together if left free to try" (43). After lauding the exploits of Shaw and the 54th at Fort Wagner, James concluded that the "Democracy" for which they fought and died "is still upon its trial." The possibility of moving forward toward ever more democratic vistas can be preserved only if we maintain what James called an "inner mystery" (60) consisting of two "habits so homely that they lend themselves to no rhetorical expression, yet habits more precious, perhaps, than any that the human race has gained" (61). "One of them," James went on to say, "is the habit of trained and disciplined good temper towards the opposite party when it fairly wins its innings. It was by breaking away from this habit that the Slave States nearly wrecked our Nation. The other is that of fierce and merciless resentment toward every man or set of men who break the public peace. By holding to this habit the free States saved her life" (61). James underscored the symbolic value of what had been "saved" by concluding with an image of "the city of the promise" that would "lie forever foursquare under Heaven, and the ways of all the nations be lit up by its light" (61). With its "homely" habit of innings played out over a foursquare plat, James's conclusion seems to owe as much, at least figuratively, to Alexander Cartwright as it does to John Winthrop. The diamond platted out in Elysian Fields in 1846 becomes one more avatar of the city on a hill devoutly wished in 1630 and invoked by James in 1897 as the luminous destiny of the American nation-state.

Meanwhile, down at South End Grounds, the Boston Beaneaters, currently in fourth place but slated to win the championship in 1897, had the first game of their doubleheader with the St. Louis Browns rained out. As if to make up in one what they might have done in two, the Beaneaters took the afternoon game 25–5, as "the slippery grounds made good fielding almost impossible." Indeed, of the 25 Boston runs, only 14 were earned. Across the country, in Chicago's West Side Park, the hometown Colts (who would go on to finish in ninth place, exactly 34 games behind the Beaneaters) lost the first game of a twin bill from the league-leading Baltimore Orioles, 6–4, and then had to settle for a 6–6 thriller in the afternoon, the game being called in the ninth to "allow the teams to catch their trains" ("Other League" 8). Unbeknownst to Adrian "Cap" Anson, the player-manager of the Colts, this would be the final season of arguably the greatest career in major professional baseball up to that point.[1]

What is the point of this Memorial Day convergence? What does the "American Game *par excellence*," as Albert Goodwill Spalding once defined baseball (5), have to do with issues pertaining to the speeches delivered by two of the most significant cultural figures of the latter half of the nineteenth century? The simple answer, if one buys the notion that baseball aspires to the condition of democratic speech by other means, is that each has a deep investment in the idea of making America home. The more complicated answer, given a social context in which being white or black matters so much that segregation "in all things social" became the law of the land, is that each must come to terms in significant ways with the relational tension between home and homelessness.

As Washington had made clear in his Atlanta Exposition address of 1895, and as he had reiterated in his dedication speech, home for black folk would begin and end with the economic stability wrought by manual labor and by education in the manual arts. In light of that, and with a wary eye toward European immigration into the South, Washington mollified white institutional power — bankers, corporate investors, and political brokers — with the notion that "in all things purely social we can be as separate as the fingers, yet one as the hand in all things essential to mutual progress" (Washington 154). For some leaders, such as James's former student and Washington's frequent nemesis, W.E.B. Du Bois, the political franchise was the most important thing that a man could exercise, and they thus viewed Washington's speech as tantamount to a deft five-fingered discount of those rights guaranteed by the 14th and 15th Amendments, rights for which the 54th Massachusetts had fought so fiercely in its courageous charge on Fort Wagner on July 18, 1863. "So far as Mr. Washington preaches Thrift, Patience, and Industrial Training for the masses, we must hold up his hands and strive with him," wrote Du Bois in his 1903 landmark, *The Souls of Black Folk*. "But so far as Mr. Washington apologizes for injustice [...] does not rightly value the privilege and duty of voting, belittles the emasculating effects of caste distinctions, and opposes the higher training and ambition of our brightest minds [...] we must unceasingly and firmly oppose" him (50). To be fair, Washington had to figure out how best to create and maintain livelihoods for freedmen in the South during a socially repressive post-bellum period when black codes, with their anti-vagrancy laws designed to ensure cheap labor, made a mockery of the concept of "home" for African Americans. What could "home" mean in Louisiana, for instance, if to be homeless or vagrant meant being "'hired' at public outcry to the highest bidder for the period of one year" (Foraker 348)? How productive could it be to agitate on behalf of full and equal participation in local politics when lynching seemed to have more authority than the law? The Atlanta Compromise, as Washington's famous speech came to be known, was, from his perspective, a necessary five-fingered exercise, with a back-beat that left the better part of valor for another time when black folk might have the economic and educational wherewithal to demand more. To those who had for so long been homeless, even a separate but equal home seemed better than none at all.

Meanwhile, from the Civil War on, the numbers of actual homeless persons had risen to such an extent that real tramps, extravagant to metaphors of epistemological vagrancy, became cause for social panic.[2] "Freedom," according to that latter-day tramp, Bobbie McGee, "is just another word for nothing left to lose," and by the end of the nineteenth century tramps with little to lose were roaming free, and black folk who were nominally free could go nowhere without risking everything. Excluded from much that made the '90s gilded, gay, and naughty, both sets of marginalized citizens embodied homelessness, but only black folk were systematically excluded from playing in the major leagues of the one sport that seemed to embody the exquisite tensions of home and homelessness.

Taking the field

To use an athletic game as an index of democratic access surely threatens to trivialize the struggle for freedom and dignity waged by African Americans during the era of Jim Crow. Why, then, should it matter that blacks were excluded from major league baseball? Simply put, the rhetoric of "home" is the very marrow of the game and its tradition, and so to exclude someone from "America's pastime" is to exclude them, at least symbolically, from making America home. No one has articulated the homeliness of baseball better than the late A. Bartlett Giamatti, for whom baseball is "the story of going home after having left home, the story of how difficult it is to find the origins one so deeply needs to find. It is the literary mode called Romance" (90). "Romance," Giamatti goes on to say, "is about putting things aright after some tragedy has put them asunder. It is about restoration of the right relations among things — and going home is where that restoration occurs because that is where it matters most" (92). Baseball, Giamatti concludes a bit later, "is the Romance Epic of homecoming America sings to itself" (95). A Renaissance scholar long before he became the President of Yale or the Commissioner of Baseball, Giamatti knew a thing or two about Romance, and if you look up the official rules for baseball, as Giamatti did, baseball itself seems to understand that everything does, indeed, radiate from home:

> When location of home base is determined, with a steel tape measure 127 feet, 3⅜ inches in desired direction to establish second base. From home base, measure 90 feet toward first base; from second base, measure 90 feet toward first base; the intersection of these lines establishes first base. From home base, measure 90 feet toward third base; from second base, measure 90 feet toward third base; the intersection of these lines establishes third base. The distance between first

and third base is 127 feet, 3⅜ inches. All measurements from home base shall be taken from the point where the first and third base lines intersect ["The Playing Field," par. 1.04].

Nothing can happen — no exile and so no joyous return — until that imperative to determine the location of home plate has been realized; then everything is possible, even a confrontation between Adrian Constantine "Cap" Anson and Moses Fleetwood "Fleet" Walker.

Born in Mt. Pleasant, Ohio, in 1857 to "mulatto" parents, Walker would become the first African American to play major professional baseball before Jackie Robinson in 1947.[3] For the twenty-first century fan, the social significance of Cap Anson leans less on the extraordinary skills that so captivated his nineteenth-century admirers than on the significant role he played in the exclusion of African Americans, and Walker in particular, from the major leagues. Thus the interplay

Adrian "Cap" Anson, a great player and manager whose legacy is tainted by his aggressive racism (courtesy Baseball Hall of Fame).

between Anson, first baseman and manager for the Chicago White Stockings (a precursor to the Cubs, who did not integrate until 1953), and Walker, a catcher for the Toledo Blue Stockings, exposes the pathos of home and homelessness at the symbolic heart of baseball as it, too, came to terms with the vexed problem of race in post–Reconstruction America.

Between them, Anson and Walker offer up baseball not as Romance Epic, as Giamatti would have it, but as *Romance à la Twain*. While it is always the better part of literary valor to let Twain tell what you mean, allow me, by way of setting up the context, to briefly state that in the next few lines Twain is talking about the generic difficulties inherent in presenting the tale of *Pudd'nhead Wilson* (1894), a critique of, among other things, the incoherence of racial identity and the slipperiness of the legal grounds on which the doctrine of "separate but equal" would be settled. "I had a sufficiently hard time with that tale, because it changed itself from a farce to a tragedy while I was going along with it — a most embarrassing circumstance," he writes in prefatory comments to "Those Extraordinary Twins." "But what was a great deal worse was," he continues, "that it was not one story, but two stories tangled together; and they obstructed and interrupted each other at every turn and created no end of confusion and annoyance" (229). Twain explains by way of conclusion that he "pulled out the farce ['Those Extraordinary Twins'] and left the tragedy. *This left the original team in, but only as mere names, not as characters*" (233, emphasis added). Originally twinned, then separate and unequal, the box scores for Anson and Walker tell an equally unmanageable Romance of farce and tragedy.[4] In this, they reflect their larger culture, for if the Memorial Day dedication was a reminder to one and all that the Civil War had been a tragic necessity, the tragedy was undercut, and old wounds reopened, by the more recent recollection that Reconstruction had been a farce without parallel. "Democracy," as James had warned his post–*Plessy* audience, "is still on its trial." As for the game that Spalding claimed was "spread throughout the country by the soldiers returning to their homes after the Civil War" (539), a game that he also insisted was as "democratic" as "the genius of our institutions" (6) — it turns out that baseball had bribed the judge and rigged the jury. However, that didn't stop Spalding from imagining that America's game was "pure" of "soul" (535), or so he claimed as late as 1911. By then the souls of black folk had been squeezed out of the majors for more than a quarter century.

The romance of home and homelessness shared by Anson and Walker will be examined by way of their own writings. A chapter entitled "Home, Sweet Home" in Anson's ghost-written autobiography, *A Ball Player's Career* (1900),[5] detailing a round-the-world baseball tour that culminates in a hero's welcome, will be read against Walker's bitterly rational polemic of racial repatriation entitled *Our Home Colony: A Treatise on The Past, Present and Future of the Negro Race in America* (1908). According to Walker's biographer, David Zang, Walker had four exhibition "encounters" with Anson that were "symbolic of the increasingly tense race relations in baseball" (38). I shall briefly outline the contours of the first, in 1883, when Toledo was still considered a minor league team, and the second, in 1884, when Toledo was a member of the upstart major league American Association. The first was racially overheated, with racism on the part of Anson and his teammates boiling over onto the playing field, and the second, coolly calculated, was an agreement on the nature of race relations in baseball that took place, among gentlemen, behind the scenes.

In 1883, Anson and the Chicago White Stockings were coming off a pennant-winning season. Not only were they the biggest draw in baseball, but they were also its most profitable team (Fleitz 107). During the season, as their schedule permitted, they would line up exhibition games with minor league teams. On Friday, August 10, 1883, the White Stockings stopped on the way to Detroit from Buffalo for a game with the Toledo Blue Stockings, who were considered the class of the minor Northwest League. Upon being apprised that Anson "objected" to taking the field against black players, Toledo's management was originally willing to "oblige" (Fleitz 111). "Oblige" seems a stretch, since their catcher, Walker, the focus of Anson's objection, was nursing a sore hand and wasn't slated to play anyway. According to a contemporary account in the Toledo *Blade,* the visitors exacerbated the situation by repeating the demand in the most derogatory terms, insisting they would not take the field with "no damned nigger" (112). Anson apparently broadcast his objections to one and all upon entering the park, thus angering Charles Morton, the Toledo manager, who gave the order to put Walker in the lineup in right field. As expected, the Chicago team refused to take the field, and the Toledo manager upped the ante by threatening to withhold Chicago's share of the receipts, at which point Anson relented. "We'll play this here game," the *Blade* reported him as saying, "but won't play never no more with the nigger in" (Zang 39; Fleitz 112). If the syntactic accumulation of negatives is any indication, Anson, having lost the battle, wasn't about to lose the war. Although out-hit by Toledo sixteen to ten, Chicago won 7–6 in ten innings, with Anson getting a double and a single. Walker went hitless (the lone Blue Stocking to do so) but played errorless ball and managed to score a run (Fleitz 112).

The next scheduled encounter between Anson and Walker's Toledo team was to have occurred in July of 1884, the year when Toledo joined the American Association. Formed as a new major league that advocated Sunday baseball so that working class fans could attend, the Association slashed ticket prices from the National League's 50 cents to 25, sold beer at ballparks, had strict drinking policies for its ballplayers, and tried to attract more female fans (Zang 40). Walker's and Anson's biographers are at odds as to whether this particular exhibition game was ever actually played, but all agree that the machinations behind the scenes on the part of Chicago and Toledo management as early as April of that year ensured that on July 25th Walker would not have been allowed to take the field as a major leaguer with Cap Anson.[6]

But Walker was, indeed, a major league player. On May 1 of 1884, in a game against the Louisville Eclipse, Walker became the first African American to play major professional baseball. He played in 42 games that season, batting .263 (Nemec 238), but it was his prowess behind the plate for which he was chiefly admired. Tony Mullane, the ace of the Toledo staff, recalled years later that Walker "was the best catcher [he] ever worked with." Mullane had stone-cold evidence for such a bold statement. Admitting that he "disliked a Negro," Mullane's racial antipathy had been so strong in those days that when Walker caught him, he wouldn't even allow him the basic protocol of managing the game by way of calling the pitches. Instead Mullane would "pitch anything [he] wanted without looking at his signals." During one game, having been crossed up once too often, Walker walked out to the mound and told Mullane flat-out, "I'll catch you without signals, but I won't catch you if you are going to cross me when I give you signals." According to Mullane, Walker caught him the rest of the year "and caught anything [he] pitched without knowing what was coming" (Zang 43).

Given such overt racism on the part of Anson, Mullane, and others, and a host of injuries that curtailed his play, Walker didn't need his Oberlin and Michigan Law School educations (he never finished his degree at either place) to figure out what was coming. As expected, Toledo released him in October, thereby giving him the dubious distinction of being the *last* African American in major professional baseball until Jackie Robinson in 1947. Zang and Rosenberg are careful to spread the blame for the segregation of baseball beyond the local and particular "tenacity of Anson's racism" (Zang 55) to a larger social context in which segregation was well on its way to being legitimized by *Plessy* (Rosenberg 437). Fleitz, however, seems more willing to put the burden squarely on Anson. Citing a *Sporting Life* column, written three years after the second of the exhibitions with Toledo, which claimed that this was "the first time in baseball history that the color line had been drawn," Fleitz exposes what he perceives to be the active agent behind the passive construction by insisting that "Cap Anson, more than anyone else, was the man who wielded the infamous pen" (119).

"Home, Sweet Home"

Born April 17, 1852, in Marshalltown, Iowa, a town that his father had founded the previous year, Anson has the distinction of being "the first white child" born in Marshall County (Fleitz 6). The distinction is important for Fleitz, as he traces Anson's racism to boyhood encounters with the local "Pottawattamie" Indians, invariably described as "friendly" or "peaceful," in which "teasing" became a "favorite pastime" (8–9). An incident from Anson's boyhood, given some prominence in his autobiography, suggests not only the extent to which teasing may have been closer to torment but also makes symbolically visible the various links between white settlement and Indian removal that underscored nineteenth-century notions of the social function of baseball as "the moral equivalent of the frontier" (Reiss 8).[7]

One day Anson and several other boys from Marshalltown were spectators at a "war dance" the Pottawattamies were performing in Marietta, several miles up river from Marshalltown. The boys, as Anson describes it in his autobiography, "enjoyed themselves immensely." All would have gone smoothly, meaning the boys would have continued on in decorous spectatorship, if "two drunken Indians riding on a single pony" hadn't come into view. The temptation apparently being too much, "someone in the party [...] hit the pony and started him to bucking." "Angrier Indians," wrote Anson, "were never seen." A chase ensued, which, by the turn of the century would have had all the earmarks of a stock scene from a wild-west melodrama. "I ran every foot of the way back to Marshalltown," writes Anson, "nor did I stop until I was safe, as I thought, in my father's house." The presumption of being safe was shattered in the course of the night when he "started from sleep and saw those two Indians, one standing at the head and one at the foot of the bed, and each of them armed with a tomahawk." Initially paralyzed by fear to the point of being unable to scream, Anson describes himself as being "powerless as a baby." As soon as he begins to move, however, the Indians "vanish through the open door-way and disappear in the darkness" (Anson 11). The next day, Anson tells his father about the incident, "but the old man only laughed and declared that [he] had been dreaming" (12). While leaving open the possibility that the old man was right, the younger Anson nonetheless insists that he saw what he saw: "I saw those two Indians as they stood at the head and foot of my bed just as plainly as I ever saw a base-ball, and I have had my eye on the ball a good many times since I first began to play the game. I saw both their painted faces and the tomahawks that they held in their sinewy hands" (12).

Whether this tale is told in earnest or, as is more likely, with tongue planted firmly in cheek, the equivalence Anson sets up between seeing the Indians and seeing a baseball underscores the symbolic equivalence between baseball and frontier. The structure of the narrative that Anson describes takes on aspects of Richard Slotkin's structural analysis of the myth of the frontier, wherein separation (going from Marshalltown to Marietta) and regression (adapting "Indian" ways—in this case, watching a "war dance") leads the frontiersman to regeneration by way of violence (confrontation with, and victory over, Indians).[8] Anson's narrative also resonates with Henry Chadwick's "theory" of baseball which states that "the pitcher delivers the ball to the batsman, who endeavors to send it out of the reach of the fielders and far enough out on the field to enable him to run round the bases, and if he reaches the home-base—his starting point—without being put out, he scores a run" (36). However unsettling the experience, having run into and out of Indian territory without being "put out" made Anson safe at home, where he would continue to score enough runs for the local team to attract the attention of scouts. Those good eyes with which he vouchsafed the presence of tomahawk-wielding Indians would eventually be his ticket out of Marshalltown. He would sign first with the Rockford Forest Cities in 1871 (where he met Albert Goodwill Spalding, an ace pitcher who would go on to build a fortune in sporting goods as well as own controlling interest in the Chicago White Stockings), and then later that summer with the Philadelphia Athletics, for whom he would play four seasons beginning in 1872, and where he would meet his future wife, Virginia Fiegal. In 1876, as the nation celebrated its centennial and mourned the news from Little Big Horn, Anson signed with Chicago, and, from 1879 on, managed the team as well until his release in 1897.

From October of 1888 to April of 1889, Anson toured with ten other Chicago players and a handpicked team of "All-Americans" from other National League cities for what was essentially a barnstorming tour around the world on behalf of spreading the gospel of base-ball. In fact Spalding, who was chiefly responsible for organizing the tour, referred to it in his own account as a "Base Ball missionary effort" (Spalding 521). While that sounded good enough on the surface to elicit a sizable investment from Anson, the trip was really designed to spread the gospel of "the sporting goods business" of A. G. Spalding and Brothers into Australia and New Zealand, "their business being greatly benefited by the tour."[9]

While in Omaha on their westward swing out of the United States, Anson's entourage met Clarence Duval, who had been signed by Anson to be mascot for Chicago that past sum-mer. According to Anson, "Clarence was a little darkey that I had met some time before while in Philadelphia, a singer and dancer of no mean ability, and a little coon whose skill in han-dling the baton would have put to the blush many a bandmaster of national reputation. I had togged him out in a suit of navy blue with brass buttons, at my own expense, and had engaged him as a mascot" (148). Given that Anson never mentions his encounters with Walker in his autobiography, such explicitly racist moments as these in reference to Duval have become sub-stitute encounters that critics use to expose and underscore Anson's racism. Walker's biogra-pher reads Anson's descriptions of Duval as evidence of the nonchalance of the larger culture toward overt racism in a post–*Plessy* world. "When the retired Cap Anson published his auto-biography in 1900," Zang writes, "he referred with impunity and without fear of public rebuke to Clarence Duval, the White Stocking mascot of the 1880s, as a 'little coon,' 'little darky,' and 'no account nigger'" (91). Why would Anson fear retribution when, according to Spald-ing biographer Peter Levine, newspaper accounts of that period "unfailingly referred to [Duval] in ways that an American white public, bent on Jim Crow and segregation, could appreciate" (101)? Fleitz takes a more global approach to Anson's ethnocentrism based on the argument that since Anson "devoted nearly half of the autobiography" to the round-the-world trip, it must have been the "defining experience of his life." "However," Fleitz concludes, "it appears that the 36-year-old captain looked upon the opportunity to visit other lands not as a way to expand his horizons, but to ratify his existing opinions and prejudices. Anson's accounts are full of cringe-inducing references to Clarence Duval as a 'chocolate-colored coon,' and worse, he evinced little interest or sympathy for the 'beggars' and 'motley crowds' that he encountered in his travels" (186).[10]

As repulsive as Anson's attitudes were, it turns out that neither his racism nor his parochialism were particularly idiosyncratic in relation to the larger mission of the trip since spreading the gospel of baseball was hardly conceived as a reciprocal affair by the organizers. As the Australian edition of *Spalding's Official Baseball Guide* of 1889 reminded Spalding's potential Australian customers, in language directly cribbed from the editor Chadwick's *The Sports and Pastimes of American Boys* (1884), baseball nurtured "all those essentials of manli-ness, courage, nerve, pluck and endurance, characteristic of the Anglo-Saxon race" (Levine 103).[11] With such appeals to shared racial heritage, the tour, to put it as bluntly as Levine does, was "a less aggressive and more modest" version of a series of "late nineteenth century adventures in American imperialism" (99). Looked at from that perspective, the local and par-ticular was, indeed, going global. Baseball, as Spalding was wont to say, invariably "followed the flag" (14).

One incident stands out in terms of the potential link between Anson, Duval and the absent Walker. Described as "an adventure," it occurs in chapter XXVI, "From Ceylon to Egypt," and the setup involves a monkey—"as ugly-looking a specimen of his family" as Anson had ever seen—and Chicago pitcher Mark Baldwin. The monkey, tethered to the engine room by means of "a strap around his waist," was taken up on deck one morning by Baldwin without permission. Baldwin ran him around a bit, "treated him to beer and pretzels," and then, tiring of his gambols, returned the agitated monkey to the engine room. As Anson describes it, "the iron grating around the first cylinder enabled the monkey to get his head on a level with Mark's as he descended the stair and Mr. Monk flew at his throat with a shriek of rage. Mark luckily *had his eye on the brute* and protected his throat, but fell backwards with the animal on top of him, receiving a painful bite on the leg" (229–30, emphasis added). This particular scene winds up with the good-natured Baldwin injured but laughing uproariously, his sharp eye — shades of the Pottawattamie!— having saved him, or so Anson implies, from further life-threatening injury. Later, in the concluding paragraph of the chapter that will usher the entourage into the Valley of the Kings in the cradle of civilization, Anson presents his readers the punch-line: "Just as [sic] dusk we pulled into a little station some twenty miles from Cairo, and here Ryan [Jimmy Ryan, Chicago outfielder] started a panic among the natives by dressing Clarence Duval up in his drum-major suit of scarlet and gold lace, with a catcher's mask, [sic] over his face and a rope fastened around his waist, and turning him loose among the crowd that surrounded the carriages. To the minds of the unsophisticated natices [sic] the mascot appeared some gigantic ape that his keeper could with difficulty control, and both men and women fell over each other in their hurry to get out of the way" (232). According to reporters covering the tour, "one could hardly blame" the "natives" for running in "abject terror" at sight of what a "disciple of Darwin" would have admired as "a vision of the missing link" (Levine 104). The focus on the "unsophisticated" natives is a bit of misdirection, for the "missing link" here isn't just the black man as *Homo sapiens* manqué — it's also the catcher's mask. In an autobiography in which Walker and the segregation of baseball warrants no response from Anson, these two episodes — an actual monkey that literally threatens the livelihood of ballplayers and a masquerade of social Darwinism instigated by the ballplayers themselves — must suffice. The mascot, the "monkey" and the "rope fastened around his waist" narrate a farce whose central anxiety is tethered to white desire to control black masculinity by way of abject degradation — or lynching. The "thin disguise" of the catcher's mask (to borrow a phrase from Justice Harlan's dissent in *Plessy)* reminds us that what is farce for one is tragedy for another.

Just as the episode with the Pottawattamie can be viewed as a symbolic counterweight that helps equate Anson's exploits on the field of play with his father's settlement of the frontier — baseball as family romance — so now the "defining experience" of the round-the-world-trip enabled Anson to participate in the larger Romance of leaving home and returning as conquering hero. "All literary romance," according to Giamatti, "derives from the *Odyssey* and is about rejoining" (92). On April 6, 1889, the entourage steamed home into New York harbor on board the *Adriatic*.

In titling the last chapter of the trip "Home, Sweet Home," Anson left little doubt as to what he and the other Americans were rejoining. It was, he wrote, a "voyage back to God's country" (273), a phrase that thereby designated the tour a most excellent adventure in Baseball writ large. The returning players were feted to a lavish reception at Delmonico's, with Mark Twain in the lineup as "featured speaker" (Rosenberg 190). Speaking on behalf of the customs and mores of the "Sandwich Islands," that "far-off home of profound repose [...] where life is one long slumberless Sabbath," Twain feigned incredulity and marveled that the game had been played there at all and then proceeded to provide future critics with one of the most oft-cited quotes about baseball from the perspective of what he had dubbed the Gilded Age: "baseball, which is the very symbol, the outward and visible expression of the drive, and push, and rush and struggle of the raging, tearing, booming nineteenth century!" (Fatout 244). But what was clearly presented as satire threatened to devolve into farce, since, having disembarked in Honolulu on a Sunday, and Sunday blue laws being strictly enforced, *the tour had played no baseball in Hawaii at all* (Anson 176, 280). Apparently no one had the heart to tell Twain, who wrapped it all up with an imperial bow by drinking "long life to the boys who plowed a new equator round the globe stealing bases on their bellies" (Fatout 247).

"Our Home Colony"

Twain, we recall, had found that in trying to take out the farce and leave the tragedy he had "left the original team in, but only as mere names, not as characters." Bemoaning the loss of "character" reveals Twain to be a realist, the sort of writer that Albion Tourgee, former federal judge, practicing romance novelist, and chief legal strategist and advocate for the plaintiff in *Plessy v. Ferguson,* sneeringly labeled as being "devoted to anti-climax" and the "trivialities" of "chronic self-distrust" (406). Against this, Tourgee proffered Romance, with its antidote of "pathos," "agony," "the ills of fate, irreparable misfortune, [and] untoward but unavoidable destiny" (411). He said all these things, and more, in a short piece entitled "The South as a Field for Fiction," published about the time (December of 1888) the Spalding tour was busy trying to convince Australians that Australia was a field better suited to baseball than cricket. While blasting away at "the realists" Henry James and William Dean Howells, Tourgee insisted that "[t]he life of the Negro as a slave, freedman, and racial outcast offers undoubtedly the richest mine of romantic material that has opened to the English-speaking novelist since the Wizard of the North discovered and depicted the common life of Scotland" (410). Albeit a Northerner, Tourgee had nonetheless caught a wee bit of what Twain had dubbed "Sir Walter disease" (*Life* 418). But even though he clearly understood that the South, in terms of the literary prominence of Romance, was, as Henry James's older brother William might phrase it, "having its innings" in the post-bellum literary arena (Tourgee 405), Tourgee made it just as clear that the "original team" (to borrow Twain's phrase) of "dashing Confederate cavalier[s]" (408) would have to make room for Washington's "lowly" freedmen in their "well-cultivated fields." Tourgee's privileging of romance over realism notwithstanding, there is much that is socially progressive in his analysis of the literary potential of the freedman in a New South. Unfortunately, to borrow the title of his most famous novel, it was a "fool's errand," for the kind of romance novels that would dominate in the post–*Plessy* era were the kind written by people like Thomas Dixon, whose 1905 novel *The Clansman: An Historical Romance of the Ku Klux Klan* (the middle book of his Klan Trilogy) became the basis for D.W. Griffith's *Birth of a Nation* (1915). These novels, and film, were clearly more concerned with resurrecting the old regime at the sometimes gruesome expense of the approaching "New Negro." This is the context in which we return to Walker, circa 1908.

By this time in his life, Walker had been squeezed out of professional baseball for almost twenty years. He played his last game for the Syracuse Stars of the minor International League on August 23, 1889, and was the last African American in that league until Jackie Robinson (Zang 60–61). Much had happened during those years, including an indictment for and then acquittal of murder charges in Syracuse in 1891 (he had actually stabbed the man, who later died, but the jury found reason to acquit on self-defense) and a year in Federal prison for mail theft alleged during a stint as a railway clerk in his boyhood town of Steubenville in 1898. On a more positive note, there was the marriage to a second Oberlin sweetheart, Ednah Jane Mason in 1898. His first wife, Arabella, whom he met at Oberlin and then married while enrolled at Michigan in 1882, had died in 1895; the marriage had produced three children — a girl and two boys. In 1891 there was a successful patent for an "exploding artillery shell," but the much-hoped for development and production never materialized (Zang 68). He was awarded three more patents in 1920—an "alarm for motion-picture film reels," a "film end fastener for motion picture film reels," and a special film reel designed to accommodate the other two patents. The alarm made it easier for film projectionists by producing an audible signal when "all but a predetermined length of the film has been unwound from the reel" thereby enabling the projectionist to better synchronize the start of the next reel; and the film end fastener "provide[d] novel means for connecting the film end with the hub of the reel."[12] After a brief stint as a hotel proprietor in Steubenville beginning in 1900, Walker moved to Cadiz, Ohio, in 1904, where he and Ednah ran the Opera House, providing various forms of entertainment ranging from "opera, live drama, and motion pictures," and occasionally renting out the space for "graduation ceremonies, dances, vaudeville, and minstrel shows" (Zang 108). For a brief time at the "dawn" of the century whose most pressing problem would be, as Du Bois famously phrased it, "the problem of the color-line" (1), Walker and his brother, Welday, edited a "black issues-oriented newspaper" in Steubenville called *The Equator* (Zang 95). The ideas generated from their work with that newspaper would culminate in a treatise on race relations called *Our Home Colony*, published in 1908. It is to that endeavor that I now turn.

Positioning itself about as far from Booker T. Washington's program of accommodation and submission as is politically possible, *Our Home Colony* has no sentimental attachment to the idea of seeking "Christian homes" in a nation where, as Walker reminded his readers, a United States Senator had recently made a speech "in the Northern city of Chicago" in which he expressed the "sentiment" that "[t]his is a white man's country" (36). Instead, Walker advocated emigration back to Africa. This would be no hasty departure, however. Described by Zang as "certainly the most learned book that a professional athlete ever wrote" (95), Walker's treatise takes his reader back to Africa with due diligence and deliberation.

Our Home Colony maps out a trajectory of African-American history in terms that resonate, in part, with Du Bois's *The Souls of Black Folk* (a text from which Walker cites). For Walker, as with Du Bois, African-American history can be divided into three parts, the corresponding divisions being a "Dark Period" that covers the time from "the forcible bringing of the Negro to America up to the Emancipation Proclamation"; a "Colonial Period" that "includes the time from the Emancipation Proclamation to the present day"; and a "Destined Period" in which is "consider[ed] the future of the Negro race, together with the vexed Negro problem and its solution" (5). The "effects of slavery" as manifested in the lived experiences of blacks and whites become the bridge between the Dark and Colonial periods (14).[13]

Reconstruction (the Colonial period) was bound to fail, according to Walker, because the ideologies of superiority and submissiveness, thickened into explanatory narratives of blood and race, made political reconstruction on terms of equality guaranteed by the Civil War amendments a fantasy, if not an outright farce. "Now in theory," he writes, "there is no distinction to be made among the citizens of the United States in respect to race, color, or previous condition of servitude. All are supposed to be entitled to every right and privilege which the spirit of her institutions afford" (19). But as he well knew, the best intentions imbedded in the Fourteenth Amendment, the language of which he cites, were undercut by other language imbedded in legal decisions. "The first blow was struck by the repeal of the Civil Rights Bill in 1883," he had earlier reminded his readers (16). (In writing that portentous date, would Walker have recalled the encounter that same year in Buffalo with Anson?) Walker was referring, of course, to the Supreme Court's majority decision in the Civil Rights Cases, in which "civil rights, such as are guaranteed [*sic*] by the constitution against state aggression, cannot be impaired by the wrongful acts of individuals, unsupported by state authority in the shape of laws, customs, or judicial or executive proceedings" (Civil Rights). Alongside Wash-

ington's plea that "[e]ach race must be edu-
cated to see matters in a broad, high, generous, Christian spirit; we must bring the two
races together, not estrange them" (22),
Walker juxtaposes the brutal fact of lynching
that has "become so common as scarcely to
excite more than passing comment" (26).
Such was the sad "shape" of local "custom."
Given this volatile mix, it should come as no
surprise that Walker rejects inter-marriage as
a viable solution to the race problem (27).

The turn toward anti-miscegenation at
the end of the "Colony" period foreshadows
a more elaborate denunciation of what Walker
calls "white concubinage" in the section on
"Destiny." "We wish every thoughtful white
father and mother in the United States, and
every Negro interested in the welfare of his
race," Walker writes, "could fully appreciate
the wide prevalence of concubinage between
white men and Negro women all over the
land, but especially in the Southern States.
This crime needs earnest consideration
because its continuance and spread will ulti-

Fleetwood Walker, an early African-American
player who was driven from the major leagues by
Cap Anson (courtesy Baseball Hall of Fame).

mately sap all that is good from the American home" (43). On the surface, Walker's jeremiad
seems to be playing into the hands of white segregationists. But his focus on "the American
home" suggests that what he is really after is a sort of moral cleansing of the concept of, and
an opening up of political access to, the very idea of a home in America. Earlier, discussing
the "strong patriotism" that "the Negro has often been credited with possessing," Walker had
warned, "Let no one be deceived in respect to these patriotic feelings of the Negro. The love
of home and country is an original sentiment of the human soul. It lies in the class of affec-
tions, and is strengthened by national pride and association. It can be weakened when the
government ceases to protect his life, home and welfare" (35). What Walker ultimately desires
in *Our Home Colony* is moral and political reparation, or what he, in his concluding paragraph, calls "partial atonement." The return to Africa, as Walker plots it out, is preceded by
a concession on the part of an apostrophized Anglo-Saxon race that "[w]e have wronged your
race by forcing it from the Home where God placed it into an alien land, and there imposed
the yoke of slavery" (47). Recall now what Giamatti said about Romance, that it is "about
putting things aright after some tragedy has put them asunder. It is about restoration of the
right relations among things — and going home is where that restoration occurs because that
is where it matters most." *Our Home Colony*, devoted as it is to an upper-case ideal of "Home,"
desires not Africa so much as a right relation between the theory of equal protection guaranteed by the Fourteenth Amendment and the practice of it in neighborhoods across America.[14]
In that regard, its narrator manifests the complex black subjectivity on whose behalf Albion
Tourgee advocated in his romances and in his legal activities — not a black man "with the
curse of Cain yet upon him, but a man with hopes and aspirations, quick to suffer, patient
to endure, full of hot passion, fervid imagination, desirous of being equal to the best" (411).

And what of Anson? Having absolutely no qualifications for the position other than being a wildly popular ex-ballplayer, Anson was elected city clerk of Chicago in 1905, a significant political post that paid $5,000 per year ("Anson's Absentee's" 6). Running as a Democrat, Anson avoided providing any details about his fitness for the position and campaigned instead as a "foe of race suicide" ("Babies" 5). Apparently, this was to be a harbinger of how clear and decisive Anson would be about anything pertaining to his duties as clerk. His tenure was wracked by scandal, from a deputy clerk who had falsified records to three employees pulling down salaries without showing up for work. Exasperatingly reluctant to do anything about either case, and clearly in over his head politically, Anson nevertheless harbored hopes of running for Sheriff. It would be an uphill slog, if the *Tribune* had any say in the matter, as it did on May 21, 1906: "When an elective official's eagerness for some other elective office is of the sort which makes him a coward in his present office that cowardice is not a good qualification for another job" ("Anson's Absentee's" 6). Meanwhile, Walker was running the Opera House and contemplating a treatise on emigration in which the fact that black folk were systematically denied meaningful political access would be its organizing theme.

No persons ever actually returned to Africa under the direct guidance of the Walker brothers' emigration efforts (Zang 100). Walker himself continued to live in Cadiz, apparently making adjustments as needed. What adjustments, for instance, might he have made when D.W. Griffith's *Birth of a Nation* played in the Opera House in 1915? In 1992, Zang interviewed two people who lived in Cadiz during that period who claim to have watched it, or believe that it played there (119). Duly skeptical, Zang cannot be certain that the film actually played in Cadiz at all. He seems more certain that the young Clark Gable, born in Cadiz in 1901 but growing up in nearby Hopedale, "nurtured his aspirations to Hollywood glitter in Fleet Walker's Opera House" (121). Imagine, then, a pimply-faced young Gable watching the Klan ride to the rescue of white womanhood, revenge itself on the mulatto Gus, even as he dared hope that some producer might ride to *his* rescue, and so midwife his own rebirth, unaware, in that cavernous space, of the iconic status he would achieve as Rhett Butler in *Gone with the Wind* (1939), a film that reasserted the values imaged forth in *Birth,* but this time in sound and in glorious Technicolor. Cut to Walker in the projectionist's booth, hyper-attentive to the unspooling of Romance — the pathos, agony, and unavoidable destiny that *Birth* portends — framed reel after reel by the paradox of hating the product and desiring a better process. Surely, he muses, there must be a better way to run a 12-reeler! Such possibilities, tantalizing in their own right, would have been made all that much more ironic given one more turn of the Reconstruction-era reel.

In the middle of the Walker biography, there is a photograph of the block in downtown Cadiz where the Opera House is located. The view, Zang tells us, is "opposite the Court House...[circa] 1910. Fleet and Ednah Walker's Opera House is the second building from the left (the Court House statue appears to be almost touching it)." Zang does not mention whom the statue represents — a curious omission in a book so attentive to detail. The statue, as it turns out, is of John A. Bingham, who, as Republican Congressman from Ohio, was one of the chief architects of the Fourteenth Amendment. Bingham, who had retired to Cadiz, died in 1900, and the statue was dedicated in 1901, the year Clark Gable was born. At the dedication, the Hon. J.B. Foraker claimed that the Fourteenth Amendment "was, of itself, a great instrument second in importance and dignity to the Constitution itself" (345).

The first sentence of the Amendment states that "[a]ll persons born or naturalized in the United States, and subject to the jurisdiction thereof, are citizens of the United States and of the State wherein they reside." In his brief before the Supreme Court on behalf of Homer Plessy, Tourgee argued that "[t]his provision of Section I of the Fourteenth Amendment

creates a new citizenship of the United States embracing *new* rights, privileges and immuni-
ties, derivable in a *new* manner, controlled by *new* authority, having a *new* scope and extent,
depending on national authority for its existence and looking to national power for its preservation" (McPherson 24–5). As his accumulative stress on the *new* suggests, Tourgee's was a
renovation project all along, one that remodeled the very terms by which people could call
America home. And thus, as in a baseball game, we arrive at last where we started.

In Frost's "The Death of the Hired Man," wife Mary gets it just about right in her debate
with husband Warren on the nature of what home means and what their responsibility is
toward Silas, the hired man who has returned "home" to die. The Fourteenth Amendment
assumes, as does Mary, that if you were born here, as Walker and Anson were, making America "home" isn't something you "somehow" have to deserve. We arrive home, then, by way of
various genres — poems, speeches, autobiography, political tracts, romance and realist novels,
and the Constitution itself — a rag-tag mix of American writings of which, as Giamatti consistently emphasized, baseball, as narrative, is the paradigmatic form for two reasons: "The
first is that baseball, in all its dimensions, best mirrors the *condition of freedom* for Americans
that Americans ever guard and aspire to. The second [...] is that because baseball simulates
and stimulates the condition of freedom, Americans identify the game with the country" (83).
Would that it were always so.

When Anson died in 1922, *The Literary Digest* reported that he had wanted for an epitaph "Here lies a man that batted .300" ("Baseball's Grand" 62). Walker, who died in 1924,
would have settled for "Here lies a man."[15]

NOTES

1. Unless otherwise noted, all statistical information for any given year is taken from David Nemec's
The Great Encyclopedia of 19th-Century Major League Baseball (New York: David L. Fine Books, 1997).

2. For discussions of the impact of the Civil War and late nineteenth-century economic depressions on
the rise of tramps in America, see Kenneth Allsop, *Hard Travellin': The Hobo and His History* (London:
Hodder and Stoughton, 1967), pp. 110–34; Tim Cresswell, *The Tramp in America* (London: Reaktion
Books, 2001), pp. 34–47; and Kenneth Kusmer, *Down and Out, on the Road: The Homeless in American
History* (London: Oxford UP, 2002), pp. 35–56.

3. For Zang, Walker's "divided heart" is a function of being haunted by the ancestral "specters" of slavery and whiteness. Walker's parents were both free, and, in Zang's words, both "mulattos" (2). There were
also rumors that both parents had been slaves, and while Zang gives free range to speculations about these
hints (6), he does not confirm them.

4. History, ever corrosive of personal agendas, has consistently linked Anson with Walker, not unlike
the way Tony Curtis and Sydney Poitier are linked in Stanley Kramer's *The Defiant Ones.* Such structural
ironies aside, there may actually have been a twin in Walker's early life, thus adding one more layer of
sedimentation to his "divided heart." Zang explores this possibility based on the odd fact that in the
Steubenville census of 1860 a three-year old, Lizzie Walker, is counted in with the other members of the
Walker family, and is listed "right below the entry for the three-year-old Moses Fleetwood Walker." By
1870, she disappears from the family register (25).

5. The *Autobiography* was ghostwritten by Richard Cary, Jr., "a Chicago horse racing writer and poet
[...] who had the pen name of Hyder Ali" (Rosenberg 35).

6. Zang says that the game was "eventually cancelled" (42–3). Fleitz (119) and Howard Rosenberg (424)
have Walker sitting on the bench for that particular game. All three cite the same background source, an
April 11 letter from John A. Brown (Chicago's team secretary) to C. H. Morton (Toledo's manager), in
which Brown, dutifully washing management's hands of the affair, declares that "the management of the
Chicago Ball Club have no personal feelings about the matter," but "the players do most decisively object
and to preserve harmony in the club it is necessary that I have your assurance in writing that [Walker]
will not play any position in your nine July 25th. I have no doubt such is your meaning[;] only your letter does not express in full [sic]. I have no desire to replay the occurrence of last season and must have

your guarantee to that effect" (cited in Rosenberg, 424, with brackets in original). Initially refusing to play, Anson had to be coaxed by Spalding to do so.

7. Interestingly, Fleitz, for whom "[i]t appears that Adrian developed many of his attitudes toward minorities during his childhood through his contacts with the Indians" (9), does not mention this episode at all, while the more skeptical Rosenberg does. Rosenberg casts doubt on the impact of such encounters, however, since "[i]t is unlikely that Ady met many Indians growing up" [40]. I relate the episode less out of interest in its authenticity than in the symbolic value that Anson's early twentieth-century readers might be expected to glean from it.

8. For Slotkin, various versions of the myth of the frontier, from captivity narratives to Frederick Jackson Turner's frontier thesis, rely on a narrative which "represented [...] the redemption of American spirit or fortune as something to be achieved by playing a scenario of separation, temporary regression to a more primitive or 'natural' state, and *regeneration through violence*" (*Gunfighter Nation* 12). "The compleat 'American' of the Myth," according to Slotkin, "was one who had defeated and freed himself from both the 'savage' of the western wilderness and the metropolitan regime of authoritarian politics and class privilege" (11). Social critics, such as Steven Riess, would recognize the ludic version of the "compleat American" in the nineteenth-century professional baseball player. Baseball, says Riess, "was viewed as an edifying institution which taught traditional nineteenth century frontier qualities such as courage, honesty, individualism, patience, and temperance, as well as certain contemporary values, like teamwork" (*Touching Base* 13–14). Both Riess and Slotkin would understand that their respective versions of the "compleat American" necessarily merge aspects of populist and progressive ideologies, with populists, according to Slotkin, extolling the Jeffersonian vision of a nation of yeoman farmers, and progressives privileging the rise of a managerial class that mediated the growing tensions between capital and labor. Spalding implies this, and manifest destiny as well, when he notes that baseball "demands Brain and Brawn, and American manhood supplies these ingredients in quantity sufficient to spread over the entire continent" (*America's National Game* 5).

9. Anson figured he lost "about $1,500" (Anson 284–85).

10. Anson had previously toured England in 1874 with other members of the Boston Red Stockings and Philadelphia Athletics on a trip organized by Spalding and Harry Wright, star pitcher and manager, respectively, for the Red Stockings. That trip, which he enjoyed immensely, was the foundation for his friendship and professional relationship with Spalding. He also joined Spalding for a return trip to England in the fall of 1897, after the conclusion of what would be his final season with Chicago.

11. Note the similarity to the following from Chadwick's *The Sports and Pastimes of American Boys* (1884), where he delineates the many ways in which "baseball bears off the palm in all those features which are calculated to secure the popular favor of the American public." Among these, according to Chadwick, are "displays of *manly courage, pluck, and nerve*" (p. 35, emphasis added). Since the list of manly virtues is being exported nearly verbatim from America to Australia, the binding agent between Americans in 1884 and Australians in 1889 must be the added emphasis on the "Anglo-Saxon race." Spalding's imperial adventure is nothing if not a racial one.

12. The film end fastener, alarm, and film reel are patents 1,328,408; 1,348,609; and 1,345,813, respectively. The National Baseball Hall of Fame Library has copies of the patent letters filed under "Fleet Walker" in the Race and Ethnicity File, for which I am grateful for having had access.

13. Du Bois, in chapter VI of *The Souls of Black Folk*, "The Training of Black Men," likewise divides the emergence of America's racialized history into "three streams of thinking"—"human unity, even through conquest and slavery; the inferiority of black men, even if forced by fraud; [and] a shriek in the night for the freedom of men who themselves are not yet sure of their right to demand it"—loosely corresponding to Walker's Dark, Colonial, and Destined periods, respectively (74–75).

14. According to Brook Thomas, imagining there is a right relation the world ought to be restored to is one of the defining characteristics of romance; in works of realism, where the commitment to the contingencies of the world-as-we-know-it is greater than in romance, there is, as Thomas states, "no 'right reason' governing the world" (*American Literary Realism* 11–12).

15. Cap Anson was in the Chicago newspaper just the other day, and the news wasn't good. The most recent political scandal in Chicago concerns another city clerk, a gentleman by the name of James Laski. The *Chicago Sun-Times* for Wednesday, June 14, 2006 ran the following headline: "'I Have Thrown Everything Away For $48,000.' Ex-city clerk Laski gets 2 years in Hired Truck scandal." I turned to the story on page 8, and there he was, ol' Cap, in the inset under the caption "Crooked Clerks." In 1984, Fleet himself popped up in the "Odds and Ins" column of the *Chicago Tribune*'s sports pages as the correct answer to a "trick question" in Trivial Pursuit that asked "the name of the first black to play in the major

leagues" (March 14, 1984). Becoming a factoid in a board-game one hundred years after the historical event wasn't exactly the piece of the pie that Walker had been after while he was alive, but Walker's significance continues to grow as more and more people realize his status as a groundbreaking pioneer. Meanwhile, Anson seems the incredibly shrinking man, his reputation sagging, due in part, as Fleitz speculates, to increased "scrutiny" of "his role in the segregation of baseball" (310). His stats, likewise, have shrunk. Official Baseball no longer considers the National Association, for which Anson played five years, a major league. At one time Anson was credited with 3,500 hits, but that number has dropped precipitously in recent years. According to Fleitz, *The Baseball Encyclopedia* credits him with an even 3,000.

WORKS CITED

Anson, Constantine Adrian. *A Ball Player's Career*. Chicago: Era Publishing Company, 1900.

"Anson's Absentee's." *Chicago Daily Tribune* 21 May 1906: 6.

"Babies in His Platform." *Chicago Daily Tribune* 18 Mar. 1905: 5.

"Baseball's Grand Old Man." *The Literary Digest* 6 May 1922: 62–65.

"Boston Honors Col. Shaw." *New York Times* 1 June 1897: 4.

Chadwick, Henry. *The Sports and Pastimes of American Boys*. New York: 1884.

Civil Rights Cases. 109 U.S. 3 (1883). <http://www.tourolaw.edu/PATCH/Civil/>.

Du Bois, W.E.B. *The Souls of Black Folk*. New York: Penguin, 1989.

Fatout, Paul, ed. *Mark Twain Speaking*. Iowa City: U of Iowa P, 1976.

Fleitz, L. David. *Cap Anson: The Grand Old Man of Baseball*. Jefferson, NC: McFarland & Company, Inc., 2005.

Foraker, John B. "Address of Hon. J.B. Foraker on the Occasion of the Unveiling of Monument in Honor of Hon. John A. Bingham, at Cadiz, Ohio, October 5, 1901." *Ohio Archaeological and Historical Publications* v. 10 (331–51).

Frost, Robert. "The Death of the Hired Man." *North of Boston*. 1914. New York: Henry Holt and Co., 1927.

Giamatti, A. Bartlett. *Take Time for Paradise: Americans and Their Games*. New York: Summit Books, 1990.

James, William. *Pragmatism and the Meaning of Truth*. Cambridge, MA: Harvard UP, 1978.

_____. *The Principles of Psychology* v. 1. 1890. New York: Dover, 1918.

_____. "Robert Gould Shaw." *Memories and Studies*. New York: Longmans, 1911.

Korecki, Natasha. "Laski Gets 2 Years in Prison." *Chicago Sun-Times* 14 June 2006. Late Sports Ed.: 8.

Levine, Peter. *A.G. Spalding and the Rise of Baseball: The Promise of American Sport*. New York: Oxford UP, 1985.

McPherson, James Alan. "On Becoming an American Writer." *A Region Not Home: Reflections from Exile*. New York: Touchstone Books/Simon and Schuster, 2001.

Myslenski, Skip, and Linda Kay. "Sports Day: Odds & Ins." *Chicago Tribune* 14 Mar. 1984: C2.

Nemec, David. *The Great Encyclopedia of 19th-Century Major League Baseball*. New York: Donald Fine, 1997.

"Other League Games." *New York Times* 1 June 1897: 8.

"The Playing Field." "Official Info: Official Rules 1.00: Objectives of the Game." *MLB.com*. 22 Mar. 2005. <http://mlb.mlb.com/mlb/official_info/official_rules/objectives_1.jsp>.

Riess, Steven A. *Touching Base: Professional Baseball and American Culture in the Progressive Era*. Westport, CT: Greenwood Press, 1980.

Rosenberg, Howard W. *Cap Anson 4: Bigger than Babe Ruth — Captain Anson of Chicago*. Arlington, VA: Tile Books, 2006.

Slotkin, Richard. *Gunfighter Nation: The Myth of the Frontier in Twentieth-Century America*. New York: Atheneum, 1992.

Spalding, Albert Goodwill. *America's National Game*. New York: American Sports Publishing Company, 1911.

Thomas, Brook. *American Literary Realism and the Failed Promise of Contract*. Berkeley: U of California P, 1997.

Tourgee, Albion W. "The South as a Field for Fiction." *Forum* 6 (1888): 404–13.

Twain, Mark. *Life on the Mississippi*. London, 1883.

_____. *Pudd'nhead Wilson*. New York: Penguin Classics, 1986.

Walker, Moses Fleetwood. Alarm for Motion-Picture-Film Reels. Patent 1,348,609. 3 Aug. 1920.

_____. Film-End Fastener for Motion-Picture-Film Reel. Patent 1,328,408. 20 Jan. 1920.

_____. Motion-Picture-Film Reel. Patent 1,345,813. 6 July 1920.

_____. *Our Home Colony*. Steubenville: The Herald Printing, Co., 1908.

Washington, Booker T. *Up from Slavery*. New York: Signet Classics/Penguin, 2000.

Zang, David. *Fleet Walker's Divided Heart: The Life of Baseball's First Black Major Leaguer*. Lincoln: U of Nebraska P, 1995.

Mediocrity Under Pressure:
The Integration of the Cubs as
Covered by the *Chicago Defender*

Brian Carroll

If what Branch Rickey and Jackie Robinson accomplished in 1947 ranks historically as something on the order of discovering the New World, then what Philip Wrigley and his Cubs did in 1953 in signing the organization's first black ballplayers might be on par with, say, DeSoto's stumbling upon the Mississippi River. By the time the Cubs turned to the Negro leagues, Rickey had raided them for four rookies of the year.[1] The Cubs' integration, in other words, was inevitable, albeit belated, and it was seen as such by the black press, which covered the player additions of Ernie Banks and Gene Baker in September 1953 in its back pages.[2]

Chicago's leading black newspaper in the early 1950s was the *Chicago Defender*, which also was once the nation's largest black newspaper.[3] The paper covered the integration of the Cubs, the continuing desegregation of the national pastime in the early 1950s, and the Negro American League, the last surviving black professional league, which had been in decline since Robinson's first season in Brooklyn.

Sandwiched as it is between Robinson's courageous 1947 season and the U.S. Supreme Court decision in *Brown v. Board of Education* in 1954, the integration of the Cubs provides a key point in history at which to examine the values and priorities of Chicago's black community prior to the civil rights movement, which began in earnest in 1955 with the brutal killing of Emmett Till in Mississippi and the Montgomery, AL, bus boycotts of late 1955 and 1956. The period is an important one in Chicago's history of race relations. An expressway built in Chicago in the 1950s, for example, further divided white and black neighborhoods and served as a symbol of a government-supported racism, as did the high-rise public housing complexes that, as Arnold Hirsch described, "literally lined State Street for miles" in creating a kind of vertical ghetto (10).

The daring of Rickey and Robinson contrasts with the desperation of Wrigley and his field manager, Phil Cavarretta. While Rickey orchestrated high drama, issuing a one-sentence press release just prior to the 1947 season to announce Robinson's new status as a Dodger, the Cubs quietly added Banks and Baker late in an increasingly meaningless 1953 campaign.[4] Former Negro leaguers Robinson, Roy Campanella, Don Newcombe, and Joe Black meant that for the Dodgers, sellout crowds, even on the road, and postseason play would be *de rigueur*.[5] Banks and Baker, meanwhile, came too late to brighten another dark Cubs season. Chicago's attendance dropped by more than a quarter-million in 1953, and the team lost $500,000.

1952: Black and White

The key variable in the *Defender*'s baseball coverage in the early 1950s not surprisingly was race, of which even a cursory examination reveals as having been even more of a determining factor than proximity to a team. Anticipating the 1952 season, for example, *Defender* sports editor Russ J. Cowans spent spring training with the Cleveland Indians rather than with either the Cubs or Sox. Cleveland had Larry Doby, Luke Easter, and thirty-nine-year-old Quincy Trouppe, while the Cubs still were all white. The Sox had Orestes "Minnie" Minoso, a Cuban signed in May the year before.[6]

The Cubs in 1951 were nonexistent, at least in terms of *Defender* coverage, and the only mention of the team in 1952 appeared in a Cowans-written season preview in March ("Cavaretta Job" 12). In the *Defender* there is little record of the Cubs having even played the 1951 or 1952 seasons, and the Minoso trade further differentiated the North Side Cubs from the South Side Sox. In a letter to the editor published by the *Defender*, a reader noted the "coincidence" of the reversal of fortunes for the Sox and the arrival of Minoso. "Attention you cellar-hanging Cubs," he wrote. "You can't play ball with prejudice, and expect to reach first base" (Crowder 6).

The *Defender*'s interest in the White Sox only began in 1951 with Minoso's arrival. The "Cuban Flash," who had played for the New York Cubans and the Homestead Grays, came to the Sox that season from the Cleveland Indians as part of a complex seven-player, three-team trade. The *Defender* published sixty-five stories on the Sox during Minoso's first season, 1951, including a three-part feature series on Minoso written by Cowans. The sports editor's support of Sox management also is telling. Cowans defended general manager Frank Lane and field manager Paul Richards against charges that they were holding back two exciting black prospects, for example, calling the accusations "hogwash" ("Russ' Corner" 16).[7]

Chicago's black community was predisposed to embrace the Sox, an "interracial team" credited by the *Defender* with no less than changing "the racial climate in Chicago" ("Fabulous White Sox" 6). The newspaper in 1951 declared that "Win or lose, the White Sox have got the citizens by their hearts" and noted that Richards was "not only a southerner, but a Texan to boot" (6). The unbylined writer described the blacks and whites commingling at Comiskey as "the greatest lesson in interracial cooperation that the city has ever seen. [...] We take delight in saluting the fabulous White Sox" (6).

Comiskey Park was, after all, "in the middle of the teeming Southside," the editorial writer noted, "perhaps the largest Negro community in the world" (6). Locality explains much of the newfound loyalty. Sox ownership had a long-standing relationship with the Negro leagues reaching back to the Negro National's formation in 1920, a business relationship that enabled Comiskey Park's selection as host of the Negro leagues' all-star game, the East-West Classic, beginning with the inaugural game in 1933. Held each year for two decades at Comiskey, the all-star game routinely outdrew the major league version, which began in 1933, one month *after* the black event.[8]

Ironically, the same large crowds that made the East-West a success, the same ticket and concessions money that filled the coffers of the Comiskey family, provided convincing evidence for the black press and, eventually, for major league team owners that integration was in everyone's best business interests. For the black newspapers, this case was especially strong since Major League Baseball publicly lamented its sagging attendance and lack of profits (Washington 4). The Negro League all-stars bolstered this case with play on the field the equal to that offered by any major league team.

The Comiskey family's long and profitable business relationship with black baseball's ruling officials began with Andrew "Rube" Foster, the driving force behind the founding of the first Negro professional league of substance, the Negro National. Foster's perennial powerhouse Chicago American Giants played home games at Schorling Park, so named because it was owned and run by Charles Comiskey's son-in-law, John Schorling. Comiskey essentially bequeathed the field to Schorling, who was possibly an investor in the American Giants. Schorling used it to, among other things, generate rents from black teams of between $945 and $1,346 per month (Foster 3).

It was natural — and practical — for South Side blacks to transfer loyalty and patronage from Negro League teams like the American Giants and Clowns to the White Sox, particularly in the 1950s, a period during which the Negro leagues were increasingly seen as sources of shame, emblematic as they were of decades of separation and degradation. Although an important black economic and cultural institution was dying, for many blacks, especially young blacks, Negro League baseball was an unwanted relic of a segregated past. Cultural critic Gerald Early has argued that "baseball lost its cultural resonance with the black masses in the 1950s" when integration killed black baseball (Early, "Baseball" 413).

In April 1952, Minoso and new third baseman Hector Rodriguez, also a Cuban, took the field for the White Sox for an exhibition game in New Orleans in defiance of a state ban on integrated play. Attracting the largest crowd in Pelican Park's history, the game against the Pirates earned favor for Frank Lane, who Cowans credited with "cracking the racial intolerance in New Orleans" ("Russ' Corner" 12). The two Cubans did have to dress and shower in separate facilities, but "it was a grand ball game," Cowans quoted Lane as saying in a page-one story. "When Minoso left the field after five innings, everyone in the park cheered. After that I was proud to be an American," Lane told the *Defender* (Cowans, "Minoso, Roddy Set" 2).

The minor leagues, too, were desegregating, and in increasing numbers. In June, Mickey Stubblefield, a twenty-four-year-old pitcher for the Pirates, integrated the Class D "Kitty" league ("Pirates Farm Negro" 12). Six of the American Association's eight teams had at least one black player, the holdouts not surprisingly being Columbus and Louisville. The Texas, Sooner State, and Coastal Plain leagues all dropped restrictions on race. Even the eight-team Class B Florida International league integrated in 1952 without incident, a development that caught the attention of the establishment *Sporting News* weekly ("Four Florida Teams" 12). The movement gave large cities such as Dallas, Houston, Miami, and Tampa their first integrated minor league contests, and by the end of the year the trend had 104 non-white players on minor league rosters (Adelson 47).

In the big leagues, the 1952 World Series showcased Robinson, Campanella, and newcomer Joe Black, who pitched the Dodgers to two of their three victories, including game one in only his third major league start. During the Series, Robinson turned up the heat on major league teams that had not yet integrated by lashing out at the Yankees, accusing the organization of being prejudiced against blacks. The Yankees subsequently leaked to the *Defender* that the club was "racing" the Red Sox to sign pitcher Bill Greason and that the scout who had discovered Mickey Mantle, Tom Greenwade, had been assigned to do it ("Yankees Race" 1). The unidentified source of the leak assured the paper that New York had "several Negroes in its farm system," though in reality the Yankees did not. The notion of a "race" between the Yankees and Red Sox for a little-known independent Texas league player is far fetched, particularly since both clubs would wait years to integrate, the Yankees until 1955 with Elston Howard and the Red Sox in June 1959 for the ignominy of being last.[9]

It is probable that the Cubs also were feeling pressure to sign Negro Leaguers, but mostly from their South Side rivals. A losing franchise since 1943, the "Go-Go" Sox turned it around in 1951 under the leadership of Lane, who joined the club in 1949. Acquisitions Nellie Fox and Billy Pierce helped the team win 81 games in 1951, then, in subsequent seasons, 81, 89, and 94 victories. Lane and Richards teamed to transform a cellar dweller into one of the American League's elite teams, and the fans followed. With both white and black fans adopting the Sox, the team set attendance records at a time when overall attendance at major league games was in decline. Between 1952 and 1958, the team averaged 1.2 million fans (Rossi 88).

1953: Mediocrity Under Pressure

Thurgood Marshall, Ernie Banks, and Henry Aaron made 1953 a significant year in ending discrimination in the United States, Marshall as legal counsel for the National Association for the Advancement of Colored People, Banks in Chicago by becoming a Cub, and Aaron and four black teammates in Florida by integrating the South Atlantic "Sally" League, a fifty-year-old aggregation of mostly Old South cities (Adelson 87).[10] "We have nearly ended discrimination in dining cars," Marshall told the *Defender*, about his effort to erase the 1896 Supreme Court decision in *Plessy v. Ferguson*. "We are now working on coach cars" ("NAACP in Attack" 1). Marshall also was guiding the NAACP in its fight against separate schools in several states, an effort that culminated in the *Brown v. Board of Education* ruling the next year.

In Kansas City, a twenty-two-year-old the *Defender* called a "gangling 6-footer" dazzled Monarchs fans with "spectacular play" at shortstop and power at the plate ("Ernie Banks Plugs" 26). That shortstop, Ernie Banks, played for forty-one-year-old Buck O'Neil, who retired from playing in 1953 but continued as manager of the Negro American League Monarchs, his sixth season as pilot.[11] Ernie Banks had been a Monarch for the 1950 season before he went to Korea with the Army in 1951 and, according to the *Defender*, had in 1953 upon his return "all the attributes to make the majors" (O'Neil 200).

If in 1953 Banks's dynamic play with the Kansas City Monarchs was helping to keep the entire Negro League afloat, even in its dying hour, the bulk of newspaper space in the *Defender* once devoted to black baseball games went to the White Sox. The *Defender* covered the team from January through December, with most of the attention going to Minoso. When Rodriguez lost his third base job to Rocky Krsnich in January, the *Defender* led its baseball coverage with the story ("Rodriguez Loses" 12). The paper placed on page one the benching of Minoso in Memphis for a pre-season game between the Sox and Cardinals because of a local Jim Crow ordinance ("Racial Bias" 1).[12] And a story on the late-season call-ups of former Negro Leaguers Bob Boyd and Connie Johnson featured a three-column photo of the new Sox ("Sox Rookies" 16).

The Indians and Larry Doby, and, of course, Robinson and the Dodgers were covered wire-to-wire. But until September, the Cubs were largely irrelevant. In the *Defender*'s 1953 baseball coverage, the beginnings of a campaign to get Gene Baker promoted to the parent club is in evidence.[13] The *Defender* noted in March when Baker, a former Monarch, was not promoted and instead was reassigned to the minor league Los Angeles Angels, but the short article offered no criticism of the parent team ("Baker Returned" 25).[14] With the Cubs faltering, however, Fay Young in July argued that the team "didn't give a fair break" to Baker in spring training ("Fay Says" 28). Cowans joined Young in August, writing that the North Siders, "up to their individual and collective necks in the barrel of trouble," could use Baker, who Cowans called a better shortstop than Cubs starter Roy Smalley" ("Russ' Corner" 38).

Gene Baker, a pioneer African American in the Cubs' farm system, and mentor to Ernie Banks (courtesy Baseball Hall of Fame).

When the Cubs finally promoted Baker from the Angels and signed Banks and Bill Dickey from the Monarchs in September 1953, the *Defender* framed the decisions as coming from a team succumbing to pressure rather than from one proactively making roster moves: "Under extreme pressure from both the fans and newspapers in their respective cities, the Detroit Tigers and the Chicago Cubs have finally signed Negro ball players," wrote an un-bylined writer — most likely Cowans. The article specifically cited "a number of daily newspapers" that had been campaigning for the addition of Baker to bolster a Cubs defense that "fell apart" during the 1953 season ("Cubs To Bring" 16).[15]

Chicago's big move was treated as a trivial piece of news by the *Defender*, which announced Baker's buyout on page sixteen. There were no columns celebrating the move. No credit was claimed by the paper, which historically passed up very few such opportunities. In fact, far more attention was paid Robinson's Dodgers, who were gearing up for another World Series against the Yankees. Robinson, called one of Brooklyn's "Old Men," was playing at his fourth position for the Dodgers during the 1953 season at thirty-four years old, putting the Cubs' recalcitrance into some historical perspective ("Old Men" 19).

In the opinions of the *Defender*'s sports writers, the Cubs were late and, therefore, deserved little credit among readers. By contrast, the newspaper hailed St. Louis Browns' owner Bill Veeck and supported him in his fight to keep the team in St. Louis. Fay Young characterized major league baseball's decision to move the Browns to Baltimore as punishing Veeck for integrating the American League with the signings of Doby and Satchel Paige in 1948 ("Fay Says" 33).[16] That Veeck's '48 Cleveland Indians made it to the World Series added insult to injury, or, in this case, injury to insult.

1954: Turning Point

The year 1954 was predicted by the *Defender* to be "the turning point when baseball truly could [not] ignore racial prejudice," and the newspaper in part was correct. Banks and Baker would play a full season in Wrigley. Minoso again appeared with the Sox in Memphis to play the Cardinals, this time defying that city's racial ban by playing ("Minos [sic] And Boyd" 18). Cincinnati, Pittsburgh, St. Louis, and Washington would add their first African Americans, leaving only the Phillies, Tigers, Red Sox, and Yankees without a "tan" player (Overbea 13). Five more minor league circuits would integrate, including the Southern Association and Georgia State League.[17] And May 17 would become "Decision Day," as it was called in the black press, the day the Supreme Court outlawed "separate but equal" in public schools in its landmark decision, *Brown v. Board of Education.*

Previewing the baseball season in March, the *Defender* in 1954 covered the spring training camps of the Cubs, Indians, Sox, Giants, and Dodgers. The teams were treated equally, in both tone and in the amount of column inches devoted. The Cubs finally were in the club, relevant, and of interest to Chicago's black community. The Sox, however, clearly were South Side blacks' team of choice, as a page-one season preview story headlined, "Pennant Fever Hits Chicago Again as Fans Await Sox Opener Tuesday," demonstrated (Cowans 1).[18] Judging by *Defender* coverage, there were no black fans awaiting the Cubs' opener.

The newspaper's coverage of the Cardinals' integration, however, offers an interesting contrast. While the Cubs' owner, chewing gum magnate Philip K. Wrigley, is not mentioned by the *Defender* throughout the early 1950s and, therefore, is not seen as a sympathetic figure, Cardinals' owner August Busch, to whom the paper refers as "Gussie," received entirely favorable coverage.[19] Whereas the Cubs promoted Baker "under pressure," Busch a season later was characterized as "spear-heading the drive" to integrate the Cardinals organization in acquiring San Diego Padre Tom Alston (Cowans 29).[20]

One possible reason for the deferential treatment was Alston's high cost to the Cardinals, who gave the Padres more than $100,000 and four players. An astronomical price for a minor leaguer at that time, it easily was the most paid for a former Negro Leaguer. The *Defender* gave Busch credit for "personally negotiating" the deal and described him as "tickled pink" in acquiring the first baseman ("Tom Impresses" 10). The "Gussie" nickname and colorful descriptions indicate an access to and intimacy with Busch that Cowans and the *Defender* possibly enjoyed, a closeness clearly absent in dealings with Wrigley.

By June, the Cubs were irrelevant again, but for purely competitive reasons. Mired in seventh place, the North Siders lacked pitching and power. Banks's explosive, record-setting slugging was a year away. Fay Young wrote in mid–July a twenty-inch column on the "Cubs Woes," the longest *Defender* story on the team during the first half of the 1950s. Young expressed a lament that contemporary Cubs fans might find depressingly familiar: "Mr. Wrigley has the money. [...] Why don't [sic] he go out and buy players and give us a pennant? [...] Headaches and headaches, and fans yelling 'bloody murder'" (Young 17). In contrast to the deference paid to Busch, Young faults Wrigley for overlooking Willie Mays and Junior Gilliam, both of whom played regularly in Chicago in Comiskey Park when their teams — the Black Barons and Baltimore Elite Giants, respectively — came to town to play the American Giants.

The Cubs suffered another ignominious season, finishing second to last with just 64 wins in 154 games. But Chicago's season proved a picnic compared to that of the Negro American League. Despite all evidence, all odds, and even common sense, league president J.B. Martin predicted "a good season" for the four-team circuit. "In fact, I'm convinced it will be the best season since the war" ("League Head" 28). It was not. That the newspaper did not question Martin's improbable prediction signaled again the conflicted goals of its sports coverage, namely, to advance integration while at the same time trying to preserve a black institution.

The Indianapolis Clowns, Kansas City Monarchs, and Satchel Paige provided case studies of the sad state of black baseball. Paige signed to play with the Harlem Globetrotters, a traveling squad on the model of the famous basketballers of the same name. The Monarchs made Toni Stone their highest paid player. And the Clowns added two more female players — Connie Morgan and Mamie "Peanut" Johnson, promising "unmatched comedy" ("Clowns To Bring" 12). All that remained for black baseball was barnstorming. Young, who had covered the first black professional league, the Negro National beginning in 1920, had witnessed and covered several ebbs and flows of the sport as a black-run enterprise; he knew 1954 marked a low point: "We, who have spent more than half a life time following and helping to create an interest in the game 'are of no use to the game now,' [...] so why worry about it," he wrote ("Fay Says" 16).

An examination of the *Defender*'s baseball coverage during the years 1951–1954, a period during which Chicago's two major league franchises integrated, suggests that the newspaper's perceptions of the various teams' and owners' commitments to racial equality determined coverage, both in terms of frequency and nature of coverage. To the extent a team was perceived as committed to integration the organization was covered by the city's leading black newspaper. It is perhaps this variable that explains why generally the Cubs were not positively treated during the period while teams further from the newspaper's primary market, such as the Indians, Dodgers, and Cardinals, received more coverage and more favorable treatment.

Judging by the coverage, the Cardinals' commitment to racial equality was demonstrated in the high price club owner Busch was willing to pay and by the degree of personal involvement by Busch in brokering the deal that landed Alston. The newspaper gave the leaders in major league baseball's desegregation, the Dodgers and Indians, deferential treatment throughout the period. Not only were the two organizations first in integrating their respective leagues, but the Dodgers and Indians consistently acquired and developed black talent through the 1940s and 1950s.

By contrast, the Cubs were criticized for holding Gene Baker back, keeping him in the minor leagues while the player Baker likely would replace, shortstop Roy Smalley, and the rest of the Cubs struggled on the field. For the same reason, the Yankees were harshly criticized in 1954 by the *Defender*, which even scolded New York's first black player, Elston Howard, calling him a "boot-licker" for so passively accepting minor league assignments from the parent team instead of demanding advancement or a trade (Young 19).

The White Sox received mostly positive coverage. By trading for Minoso early, particularly by American League measures of progress, and then consistently giving black players opportunities, and because the team played at home in the heart of Chicago's black community, the newspaper's treatment of the "Pale Hose" is not surprising, nor is the fact that the club was the only major league team that had its upcoming games promoted in the newspaper.

Finally, this study exposes at least a few of the complexities for the newspaper in covering and promoting a diminishing product, black baseball. The mutually exclusive goals of pushing for greater integration in baseball and promoting the Negro American League, particularly after major league clubs diluted black baseball's talent base, are in evidence as the newspaper increasingly published what were essentially press releases. The absence of bylines and the uncritical coverage suggest this.

When viewed as a whole, the *Defender*'s baseball coverage shows how one-sided integration has been. The expectation that blacks had to move into the mainstream was not challenged in the coverage; the cost to the black community in terms of its own cultural institutions was not calculated. In the case of baseball in general and, more specifically, the Cubs, integration benefited white owners at the expense of the black-owned, black-run Negro leagues. The Cubs got Banks and O'Neil from the Monarchs, a team already so diluted of talent that it had to barnstorm to survive. It has been said that Cubs fans are the best because they have to be. The sluggishness with which the team integrated perhaps is another reason why. The Cubs' record in addressing the sport's systemic discrimination is lacking, and it was seen as such by the *Chicago Defender*.

NOTES

1. The Rookie of the Year Award winners were Robinson, Don Newcombe, Joe Black, and Junior Gilliam; these four were the only Brooklyn Dodgers ever to win the award.

2. The term "integration" is problematic. For the sake of simplicity, it is used here to refer to a team or institution opening itself for membership by blacks. Obviously, true integration as a social ideal is a complex process, or what cultural critic Gerald Early has described as a "tangled loom" ("Understanding Integration" 52). One player obviously does not "integrate" a team, and one player alone cannot change the norms, policies, and practices of an institution.

3. By 1925 the *Chicago Defender* had a circulation of 250,000, which set a new standard for black newspapers. With a pass-around readership of between four and five people, the true number of readers perhaps numbered more than a million (Pride and Wilson 137). The *Defender* had no real competition in the city in the early 1950s since the *Chicago Bee* closed down in 1946. Chicago's black community in the 1950s was served by *Muhammad Speaks*, the leading newspaper for black Muslims, but sports beat coverage was not a component of the publication. The *Defender* still was one of the nation's largest black weeklies in the period studied, and it acquired the oldest Negro newspaper still in business in May 1952 when it bought the *New York Age*.

4. Brooklyn finished way out front with 105 wins. Milwaukee was a distant second with 92 victories, while the Cubs managed only 65 wins under Cavarretta to place second to last. Rickey's press release, distributed on April 10, 1947 said only that the Dodgers had "purchased the contract of Jack Roosevelt Robinson from Montreal" (Anderson 1).

5. For Rickey black America presented an untapped market. A July 14, 1948, exhibition game between Robinson's Dodgers and Doby's Indians drew 64,877, a figure that included an estimated 26,000

blacks, which means that roughly one of every six blacks in Cleveland attended that game (Moffi and Kronstadt 8).

6. That Minoso is Cuban points to the reality that race in fact was not the issue for major league baseball and, by extension, American society. It was skin color. Light-skinned Cubans had played in the major leagues at least as far back as 1911 (Armando Masans, for the Cincinnati Reds). At least some in the Sox organization wanted to integrate as early as 1942. The *Daily Worker* quoted Sox manager Jimmy Dykes in 1942 as saying to Jackie Robinson, "I'd love to have you on my team and so would all the other big league managers. But it's not up to us. Get after Landis" (qtd. in Smith).

7. Cowans had spent six days with the Sox during spring training, interviewing Lane, Richards, and the two prospects, Bob Boyd and Sam Hairston. Boyd was promoted in 1953.

8. The East-West Classic in July 1943 produced Comiskey Park's second largest crowd in its history, 51,723 (Lester 212). The 1944 East-West drew 46,000 fans despite 98-degree heat, more than attended any major league game that same day (Lanctot ix).

9. The Red Sox, who gave Robinson a tryout in April 1945 and, therefore, could have been first, were the last to integrate when they inserted Elijah "Pumpsie" Green as a pinch runner on 21 July 1959. He was not on the roster for the 1960 season. By this time, the Dodgers were in Los Angeles and Robinson was as an executive with the Chock Full O' Nuts coffee company.

10. Aaron helped Jacksonville win the pennant and double its home attendance. His .362 average led the league. He also scored 150 runs, knocked in 125, and totaled 206 hits — a monster year.

11. O'Neil, who introduced the Cubs to Banks, was signed as a full-time scout by the Cubs in 1956. He scouted mostly historically black colleges and universities and predominantly black high schools (O'Neil 200). Among the players O'Neil signed for Chicago, in addition to Banks and Baker, are Hall-of-Famers Lou Brock and Joe Carter, Lee Smith, and Oscar Gamble. In 1962, the Cubs made O'Neil the first African-American coach in major league history. He was 50 years old.

12. The next day the Sox, with Minoso on the field, played in Nashville. Minoso's homer beat the all-white Philadelphia Athletics 4–3.

13. Baker was signed by the Cubs in 1950, putting him in the Cubs organization long before Ernie Banks. In subsequent seasons, Baker played for Des Moines of the Western League and Los Angeles of the Pacific Coast League. In 1963 Baker became the first black to manage a minor league club, piloting Batavia in the Pirates' system.

14. Baker's patience is remarkable. On Aug. 4, 1952, he set a team record with Los Angeles for most consecutive games played, 394, underlining for how long he had to toil in the minor leagues before being given the chance at the highest level (Newton 16).

15. Baker began the year with the Cubs in spring training in Mesa, AZ, but was sent down to Los Angeles because "at that time it was stated he needed more experience." The Tigers integrated by signing Claude Agee. Dickey, a pitcher, was assigned by the Cubs to their Cedar Rapids, Iowa, farm team. He was not promoted to the major league club. When Baker and Banks took the field in mid–September for the Cubs, they became the first black "keystone combination" (shortstop and second baseman) in major league history.

16. The NAACP also sided with Veeck, citing Baltimore's "rigid pattern of segregation," but to no avail ("Baltimore Blasted" 32).

17. The other minor leagues desegregating in 1954 were the Tri-State League (Tennessee, South Carolina, and North Carolina), Evangeline League (Texas and Louisiana), and Cotton States League, the last of which was in 1952–53 the subject of a series of court cases and public referenda on laws and ordinances enforcing racial segregation. The Birmingham City Council, for example, passed in September 1950 an ordinance that made it "unlawful for a negro and a white person to play together or in company with each other in any games," including baseball (Birmingham Segregation Laws, Section 597). The Southern Association integrated when the Atlanta Crackers played Nat Peeples, who had played for both the Monarchs and Clowns.

18. Flush from their three consecutive successful seasons, the Sox renovated Comiskey Park for the 1954 season at a cost of $250,000.

19. At least a partial explanation for the absence of Wrigley as a subject or source in the *Defender* was Wrigley's low opinion of newspapermen in general (see Paul M. Angle, "Mr. Wrigley's Cubs." *Chicago History* 5.2 [1975]: 105–15).

20. The Padres in 1954 were a minor league team in the Pacific Coast League. The glow in coverage of the Cardinals also could be partially explained by Busch's rescue of the team the previous year. The

team was almost sold and moved to either Milwaukee or Houston before Busch acquired it and kept it in St. Louis.

WORKS CITED

Adelson, Bruce. *Brushing Back Jim Crow*. Charlottesville: U of Virginia P, 1999.
Anderson, Dave. "The Days That Brought the Barrier Down." *New York Times* 30 Mar. 1997, late ed., sec.8: 1.
Angle, Paul M. "Mr. Wrigley's Cubs." *Chicago History* 5.2 (1975): 105–15.
"Baker Returned to Los Angeles." *Chicago Defender* 28 Mar. 1953: 25.
"Baltimore Blasted by the NAACP." *Chicago Defender* 1 Oct. 1953: 32.
"Cavaretta [sic] Job Not Easy One, Russ Reports." *Chicago Defender* 12 Mar. 1952: 12.
"Clowns to Bring Lot of Comedy." *Chicago Defender* 26 June 1954: 12.
Cowans, Russ. "Russ' Corner." *Chicago Defender* 21 Apr. 1951: 16.
_____. "Russ' Corner: Minoso, Roddy Set to 'Go.'" *Chicago Defender* 12 Apr. 1952: 2.
_____. "Russ' Corner." *Chicago Defender* 19 Apr. 1952: 12.
_____. "Russ' Corner." *Chicago Defender* 6 Aug.1953: 38.
_____. "Busch Fulfills Promise." *Chicago Defender* 6 Feb. 1954: 29.
_____. "Pennant Fever Hits Chicago Again As Fans Await Sox Opener Tuesday." *Chicago Defender* 10 Apr. 1954: 1.
Crowder, David Lloyd. "Those Sizzling Sox." Letter. *Chicago Defender* 9 June 1951: 6.
"Cubs to Bring Gene Baker Up." *Chicago Defender* 3 Sept. 1954: 16.
Early, Gerald. "Baseball and African American Life." *Baseball: An Illustrated History*. Narr. Geoffrey C. Ward. Pref. Ken Burns and Lynn Novick. New York: Knopf, 1994. 412–17.
_____. "Understanding Integration: Why Blacks and Whites Must Come Together as Americans." *Civilization* 3.5 (1996): 51–59.
"Ernie Banks Plugs Hole for Kaycees." *Chicago Defender* 2 May 1953: 26.
"The Fabulous White Sox." *Chicago Defender* 16 June 1951: 6.
Foster, Andrew Rube. "Rube Foster Has a Word to Say to the Baseball Fans." *Chicago Defender* 5 Jan. 1924, sec. 2: 3.
"Four Florida Teams Playing Negro Players." *Chicago Defender* 31 May 1952: 12.
Hirsch, Arnold. *Making the Second Ghetto*. Cambridge, UK: Cambridge UP, 1983.
Lanctot, Neil. *Negro League Baseball*. Philadelphia: U of Pennsylvania P, 2004.
"League Head Sees a Good '54 Season." *Chicago Defender* 15 May 1954: 28.
Lester, Larry. *Black Baseball's National Showcase*. Lincoln: U of Nebraska P, 2001.
"Minos [sic] and Boyd Play in Games." *Chicago Defender* 10 Apr. 1954: 18.
Moffi, Larry, and Jonathan Kronstadt. *Crossing the Line: Black Major Leaguers, 1947–1959*. Jefferson, NC: McFarland, 1994.
"NAACP in Attack on Segregation." *Chicago Defender* 28 June 1952: 1.
Newton, Burt F. "Angel Record Set by Baker for Durability." *Chicago Defender* 30 Aug. 1952.
"Old Men on Dodgers Win Praise." *Chicago Defender* 27 Aug. 1953: 19.
O'Neil, Buck. *I Was Right on Time*. New York: Fireside, 1996.
Overbea, Lui Virgil. "Large Crop of Negroes in Majors." *Chicago Defender* 16 Jan. 1954: 13.
"Pirates Farm Negro to Kitty." *Chicago Defender* 5 July 1952: 12.
Pride, Armistead S., and Clint C. Wilson. *A History of the Black Press*. Washington, D.C.: Howard UP, 1997.
"Racial Bias Bars Minny and Others." *Chicago Defender* 11 Apr. 1953: 1.
"Rodriguez Loses Third Base Post." *Chicago Defender* 17 Jan. 1953: 12.
Rossi, John P. *A Whole New Game: Off the Field Changes in Baseball, 1946–1960*. Jefferson, NC: McFarland, 1999.
Smith, Ronald A. "The Paul Robeson-Jackie Robinson Saga and a Political Collision." *Journal of Sport History* 6.2 (1979): 5–27.
"Sox Rookies." *Chicago Defender* 3 Sept. 1953: 16.
"Tom Impresses Manager Stanky." *Chicago Defender* 20 Mar. 1954: 10.
Washington, Chester. "Sez Ches." *Pittsburgh Courier* 2 Sept. 1933, sec. 2: 4.
"Yankees Race to Ink Negro." *Chicago Defender* 6 Dec. 1952: 1.

Young, Fay. "Fay Says." *Chicago Defender* 2 July 1953: 28.
_____. "Fay Says." *Chicago Defender* 8 Oct. 1953: 33.
_____. "Fay Says." *Chicago Defender* 1 May 1954: 19.
_____. "Fay Says." *Chicago Defender* 17 July 1954: 17.
_____. "Fay Says." *Chicago Defender* 7 Aug. 1954: 16.

Let's Play Two ... in Black and White: Ernie Banks and Race Relations in Chicago

Gerald C. Wood

The 1984 John Sayles film *Brother from Another Planet* takes a few minutes from the main plot (in which a black alien falls to earth and comically deals with his estrangement) to study two white boys lost in Harlem. Looking for directions to a subway that will get them to their meeting place, they duck into an African-American bar. Not recognizing that their companion at the bar is the alien, they drink heavily and drift, a bit defensively, into a discussion of their affection for Ernie Banks, their favorite baseball player:

> Visitor #1: I mean, I didn't want to be like Ernie Banks. I wanted to be Ernie Banks.
> Visitor #2: Mr. Cub.
> #1: And it never really dawned on me that he was black, you know.
> #2: Wrist hitter.
> #1: I was, you know — what? — seven years old. He was just Ernie Banks. He was my hero.
> #2: All in the wrists.
> #1: There weren't any black people in my town. At least I don't think there were.
> #2: Mr. Cub.

The brief scene reveals the innocence of Midwesterners, the racism that inevitably follows from their ignorance and narcissism. But, like the best of humor, it resonates with cultural significance beyond the boys' sweetness, implied fear, and silly assumptions about their drinking companion.

In my experience as a young Cubs fan from a white bread suburb of South Bend, Indiana, these words are truer than true. In the chilliest years of the Cold War, often squeezed under our school desks sheltering ourselves from imagined nuclear attacks, claustrophobic from thoughts of being buried by Nikita Khrushchev and his comrades, we looked to strong male figures. Especially if we had any anxiety that our fathers might be shown weak in the face of creeping momism, as James Dean's was in *Rebel Without a Cause*, we wanted to find male strength that would be exhibited with grace and resilience in the face of any danger, any failure. We liked Ike for all those reasons.

If we were Cubs fans, we weren't *like* the boys in *Brother from Another Planet*. We *were* those boys. As Chet Coppock explains in *For Cubs Fans Only*, we "just fell in love [...] with Ernie Banks, and it became almost a religion. [...] [we] would run home every day [...] dying to see Ernie Banks swing the bat hoping that he was going to hit a walk-off home run" (102). For us, America was still innocent and threats were always foreign, never domestic. When the Cubs bought the contract of Ernest Banks from the Kansas City Monarchs of the Negro League in 1953, the civil rights movement was a year from being declared a national priority. Like us, the new Cubs shortstop was respectful of authority; he embodied the assumption that we all, white and black, would be rewarded for patience and loyalty. In Ernie's own words, "Gene [Baker] and I didn't talk very much about things when we arrived here [Chicago]. We just introduced ourselves and then introduced ourselves to other players. We just came out on the field and went about our business and started taking ground balls. Talking was not a big part of our lives when I first came here" (Banks 39).[1]

As Banks explains, he learned the key, focused listening, from Jackie Robinson: "First time I walked on the field, he came across over to third base, and he said, 'I'm glad to see you here, and I know you can make it. You've got a lot of ability. Just listen.' And that's what I did." Such advice was particularly helpful with personal questions, some of which were embarrassing to Banks, that reporters inevitably asked him during interviews (Banks 40). Especially well suited to the Neighborhood of Baseball, which believed to the core that Wrigley Field embodied cultural and racial diversity, Banks considered his home field "a university" where he could learn "about different kinds of people, different cultures, different philosophies" (42). A black man, he nevertheless expressed white America's best-foot-forward attitude of never meeting a person he disliked and learning from "embarrassment and unkind things" lessons which "really can make us better — better people, better individuals" (41, 44).

He believed what we wanted to believe, that empathy was the key to peace and happiness. Sounding more like a Midwesterner than a native of Dallas, Texas, he says, "What I always thought of when I walked out of this ballpark when I was playing was that one day I might have to ask this little boy or girl for a job. I always thought of that. I don't know why. My children would say, 'Dad, we got to go.' And I'd be signing autographs, looking at faces, I thought, gosh, I might ask you for a job someday or you might have to save my life. I always thought of that. I can't explain it. I always had empathy for people who came to Wrigley Field" (Banks 45). It was an empathy that extended to those in authority, even to Leo Durocher during Banks's final years as a player.

That story is now central to the lore of Ernie Banks and the Chicago Cubs. Late in Banks's career, Durocher, an old time, hard-nosed, explosive manager from the days before integration, not only benched the veteran player. He verbally abused Banks for what Durocher considered lack of effort, told his supporters to "Cut out his Mr. Cub garbage," took him out of the starting lineup, "and suggested broadly he should quit" (Libby 91).[2] But, by his own description, Banks always respected the authority of his boss, even under such duress, and thus he reminds those who would find personal and racial implications in his relationship with Durocher that he attended Durocher's wedding and spent time with the Cubs' skipper in California and at an all-star game in Denver. Typical of his persona, Banks is sweetly philosophical: "I believe in forgive and forget, and keep your mouth shut and listen to whatever somebody is trying to tell you and you can learn something.[...] But it was just misinterpreted that Leo disliked me. He made my life better, he made me a better player" (Banks 41–43).

Banks was able to give such a kind and balanced approach to Durocher because he has always taken a non-confrontational, personalist view of race. For example, in his memoir, *"Mr. Cub,"* he explains,

> My philosophy about race relations is that I'm the man and I'll set my own patterns in life. I don't rely on anyone else's opinions. I look at a man as a human being; I don't care about his color.

Ernie Banks, Mr. Cub (courtesy Baseball Hall of Fame).

Some people feel that because you are black you will never be treated fairly, and that you should voice your opinions, be militant about them. I don't feel this way. You can't convince a fool against his will. He is still going to hold to his opinions, so why should I tell him, "Look, you are prejudiced. You don't like me because I'm black." If a man doesn't like me because I'm black, that's fine. I'll just go elsewhere, but I'm not going to let him change my life [84].

Consequently, during the 60s, he shunned protest, visited Vietnam in support of the troops, and spoke only of his gratitude and willingness to serve as a role model:

This country, including whites, has been very good to me. I have always been treated well. I'm well aware this has not been so for all blacks. I've been one of the fortunate ones. I care deeply about my people. I'd like to work to make things better for them. But I have to find work I want to do. Right now, I just try to live decently and be cheerful and get through the days. Right now, I just try to set a good example [Libby 111].

His philosophy on race, as on all things: be kind, keep to yourself, understand others, be thankful, lead by example.

His attitude toward compensation was just as flexible, he assures his fans. To those later players who complain about salaries — or, by implication his, in retrospect — Banks responds, "I didn't listen to them because playing here [in Wrigley Field] if you can get the feeling in your own heart of playing for the love of it — then your life is better. That's the way it is here. Playing for the love of it, then your life will be better and your career will be better. [...] The friendships you make while you're here are much greater than all the money you will make in your life" (Banks 48). Character is more important, Banks gently reminds us, if you are a Cubs fan. Winning, whether on the field or in the accountant's office, is secondary.

Equally tinged with potential injustice, financial and racial, are the conditions under which Banks left the Cubs' organization. For two years after his retirement, he coached for the team. Because of his high profile, he was retained in Wrigleyville as a promoter and guest speaker, after playing and coaching, as he pursued outside interests. Then, in 1983, in the midst of cutbacks, the team eliminated his position. This time, while Banks maintained his public profile of amicability, his representatives described him as "hurt" over lack of proper compensation and overbooking which caused him to lose his full-time job at the Bank of Ravenswood in Chicago. Whatever the reality, Banks was certainly overextended; he was also in the midst of divorce proceedings and was continuing his promotions for Heileman's Old Style beer (Goddard 7).

As such dramas began to build in such a mild-mannered man, Banks experienced panic attacks. As he later explained, "There were times, especially in restaurants when everyone wanted autographs, that I felt I had to leave, run away from everything and be a fugitive from myself. I felt trapped. No one looked at me as a human being. I couldn't get on with my life" (Kiersh 69). With the help of a psychologist, he came to believe "I had a fear of failure in doing something outside of sports, like a lot of athletes do. And people don't help, because they keep talking to you about your past. They are trying to be nice, but they don't understand the problems an athlete has in adjusting to a new career." The answer, in the words of the therapist, was "You can't change what you were, and you can't change the way people look at you. So why don't you just enjoy it?" Banks dedicated himself to that reality (Berkow D23).

By then a gap between the public image of Banks and the later realities of his life began to widen. Once he retired from baseball, he did, from time to time, focus more on racial concerns, emphasizing that he was African American as well as all–American. In an interview conducted while he was still with the Ravenswood Bank, he acknowledged that "It's going to be a while before I get to play for this team. Blacks aren't exactly in the mainstream of banking." Then, before sounding negative and undercutting the traditional public image of Ernie Banks, he quickly resumed his usual optimistic tone: "I'm especially interested in new business development, rising nations, the Third World. Tapping an oil well in Nigeria or developing farms in Saudi Arabia, that's what I want to do" (Kiersh 70). Nevertheless, Banks was acknowledging imbalances, especially financial ones, which he needed to address, at home and abroad.

Not coincidentally, by 1988 reporters had discovered that Ernie Banks, not Frank Robinson, had been the first black manager. Sensitive as never before to Banks as a representative of his race, the media remembered that on May 8, 1973, the second-year coach of the Cubs had replaced Whitey Lockman, the ejected manager, in a game against the Padres. So, technically, when the Cubs went on to win the game in the 12th inning on a double by Joe Pepitone, Banks had become the first bench leader of color. Better yet, he left baseball with a perfect managing record: 1–0. Typical of the new image of himself as both Mr. Cub and black man aware of racial injustice, Banks's words on the topic are both shy and proud: "I was aware but I was kinda like 'Let me enjoy this alone.' It was a private thing that I never talked about too much. I didn't want to flaunt it. If it got by without anybody knowing about it, then wonderful" (Cholakis 9).

But not all of his actions are so flattering, even when bolstered by male reporters anxious to rediscover sweet Ernie. For example, because of his image as a kind, non-aggressive person, journalists asked readers to feel sympathy for Banks when some of his sports memorabilia, including a sterling silver bat and the ball he hit for his 500th home run, were "sold without my consent." In fact, he had no claims to the merchandise because they were objects from a divorce settlement and Banks conceivably could have purchased them himself ("Banks Says" 48).

Fans, of course, might easily link this story with many others reporting that Ernie Banks never received more than $65,000 for any year he played major league baseball. But, by his own calculation, Banks invested (under the advice of P. K. Wrigley, the owner of the Cubs) fifty percent of all his earnings, which were worth four million dollars by the time he was 55, and allowed him to become "The first black Ford dealer in the United States," he claims.[3] His resume also includes two years with the Equitable Life Insurance Company and ten years with New World Van Lines. In his words, he replaced his passion for baseball with "A passion for money" ("Ernie Banks talks" pars. 4, 6, 11, 24–25). While the press tried to portray Banks as the victim of mercenary forces, those same forces had, in fact, supported and enriched him.

Now even the "Let's play two" story needs deconstructing. For the record, Banks played more than sixteen years without saying such a thing. He spoke those words in the Cubs' locker room before a game to be played in 100-degree heat during July of 1969. It was his way of encouraging his teammates to enjoy the game despite the conditions, and Jimmy Enright made good copy of the situation (Banks 46). That interpretation more than continued; it came to define all of Banks's days, even the early years, when he was shy, quiet, and retiring. In his laudatory description of baseball stars, Maury Allen is typical in his encapsulation of Banks's career:

> With a twinkle in his eye, a smile on his face, a warm handshake, and a high-pitched, warm voice, Ernie Banks would move close to a visiting sportswriter and laugh, "What a great day for baseball. Let's play two."
>   The rain might be beating on the top of the dugout roof at Wrigley Field or the clouds might be a dark, ominous gray or the world might be threatened with a nuclear holocaust, but Ernie Banks would still offer in his cheery way: Let's play two. Sometimes three [165].

So goes the legend.

Ernie Banks is more than one of the greatest power-hitting shortstops. He is more than technically the first black major league manager. He is a Chicago icon, a man who mirrors the city's history, ideals, and myths. There is no better evidence of this confluence of ballplayer and urban iconography than a series of events from 1967. That was the year that Chicago erected a 50-foot statue, an enlargement of a commissioned work by Pablo Picasso, an artist of some repute, though he was reported to be unable to either field or hit. Once unveiled in front of the city's civic center (where it stands today), the sculpture became almost as unpopular as the trade of Lou Brock for Ernie Broglio. And then Alderman Joe Hoellen, for whom history has recorded no batting average, gained his own fifteen minutes of fame by declaring the artwork "Picasso's fiasco" and, with the earnestness reserved for Midwesterners, asked the city to replace it with a five-story image of Ernie Banks, whom Hoellen declared "a living symbol of a vibrant city" (Rushin 53).

Ernie Banks is less influential as a political force in race relations (he lost his campaign for alderman of the South Side's 8th Ward) than an image of popular cultural history.[4] In part this is a natural extension of his personality; as a player he was what Jim Murray summarized as "up front and available and affable [...] the most perpetually sunny individual I ever saw in uniform" (1).[5] Such "a cheery personality" in a "gentle, charming" and "lovely man" was expressed on the field in his "easy, effortless" style of play (Allen 165–66). Such modesty led Stan Hack, one of his managers, to remark that "After he hits a homer, he comes back to the dugout as if he has done something wrong" ("From Banks to Baker" 100).[6] The result was a persona of a black man both innocent and regal, kind and majestic. He was not only the Sidney Poitier of baseball; he was, in the minds of white boys in Chicagoland, Fred Astaire. He could be simultaneously in this world and not of it, expressing a calm grace that is less the reality of American culture than its ideal.

The ideality of "Mr. Cub" is most clearly revealed when Banks is compared with Jackie Robinson, his most influential mentor after Gene Baker. Banks is tall, slim, light-skinned, and angular like a Gary Cooper or Jimmy Stewart, quiet and unassuming, waiting patiently for the appropriate moment for his calm self-assertion. Robinson was a bit squat, muscular and powerful. And while he had a similarly calm surface, he seemed always coiled, nervous, secretly aggressive. His beauty had more to do with the moments of abandon that he longed to express. Jackie Robinson would knock you down, steal your base, take both what was rightfully his and possibly what was yours as well. If Banks was Fred Astaire, Robinson was Gene Kelly, dogged by the need to overcome all deficiencies, to right all imbalances by the sheer force of his physicality and will. You could like him if you wanted, but you best respect him or trouble might start.[7]

There is no question that Ernie Banks was a great baseball player. He hit 512 home runs, most of them as a shortstop, including five seasons of forty or more and thirteen of twenty or more. He won two National League titles for home runs, two for runs batted in, one for slugging percentage, and he was MVP back-to-back in 1958 and 1959. He also batted over .300 three times. But his reputation as Mr. Cub and citizen of Chicago is more complicated than his clear and obvious achievements on the field. His quiet nature, affability, and accommodating lifestyle made him, in the short run, quickly accepted by the predominantly white fans on the North Side. Because of his beneficent ways, reporters and fans have too easily considered Banks the victim of social, economic, and racial forces. Actually, after his career as a ballplayer, Banks transformed himself, with varying degrees of success, into an entrepreneur, a spokesman for positive thinking, and a proponent of both global economic expansion and world peace. And so, in the long run, Jackie Robinson remains the hero of racial integration on April 15th, even in Chicago. Because Ernie Banks so easily wore the mantle of the happy, respectful ballplayer, he cast an unintended shadow over players like the late Gene Baker, the first black man to play for the Chicago Cubs' organization, the man whose gracious move from short to second, the *Chicago Defender* and *Ebony* magazine remind us, made room for Ernie Banks to play his first game on September 17, 1953, and become in the folklore of baseball "Mr. Cub" ("Cubs Pay" 24; "From Banks to Baker" 103).

NOTES

1. As Banks explained in his memoir *"Mr. Cub,"* written with Jim Enright, in more private times Gene Baker was Ernie's mentor on race relations, introducing him to prejudice with wit and sarcasm. For example, when they were denied entrance to a movie in St. Louis, Baker said, "I hope you enjoyed the show we aren't going to see at this theater." After Banks was run out of a store where he wanted to buy candy and a paper, followed by obscenities and threats, Baker said, "I see you just learned the facts of life about southern hospitality" (81–82).

2. In 1967 Durocher replaced Banks at first with John Boccabella and Clarence Jones, but Banks regained his form over the next two years, forcing Durocher to admit that he had put Mr. Cub out to pasture prematurely (Libby 100).

3. Banks received $15,000 from the Chicago Transit Authority in 1969 for serving on its board and took correspondence courses in banks, working initially for the Seaway National Bank. He went into partnership with Don Nelson in Nelson/Banks Ford on South Stony Island Boulevard (Libby 107–8).

4. According to Bill Libby, in 1962 Banks ran for Alderman in the eighth ward (three miles from Comiskey Park), finishing third of four candidates while running as an independent Republican who supported Richard Nixon. Banks campaigned "for lower taxes, more recreation for youngsters, more libraries, safer streets, better garbage service" under the slogan "Put a Slugger into City Hall" (*Ernie Banks* 114).

5. Jim Enright, in his piece "A Beautiful Man," in *"Mr. Cub,"* calls Banks a "Texas-born gentleman" with "a disposition as warm as a summer sun in Arizona and an outlook as bright as a brand-new full moon" (15).

6. George Castle explains this public image as a continuing creation of the Cubs' management, especially John Holland, who became GM in 1956:

> Erring on the side of caution, Holland demanded his African-American players be out of a narrow, conservative mold in their personalities and personal lives.
>
> "The three most prominent black players we had — Ernie Banks, Billy Williams, and Fergie Jenkins — had low-key or happy-go-lucky personalities. Fergie was Canadian. He was good in the Cubs' organization starting out because he was a black player who didn't know he was black. George Altman was laid-back and not tempermental [sic]. There were no 'angry young men' types."
>
> The model African-American Cub, of course, was Banks. Famed for his "Let's play two" proclamations and in the wake of his astounding 1950s slugging feats, he became Phil Wrigley's favorite player [121].

7. James T. Farrell noted this image of Jackie Robinson in his *My Baseball Diary*: "Robinson was a menacing, threatening ball player. Pitchers on opposing teams have admitted that when he got on base, they became nervous. He was at least reminiscent of Ty Cobb on the base paths. He was daring, alert and demonstrably out to beat the other team. He took baseball as a challenge, and in the challenge he accepted was flung at the opposing teams like a gauntlet" (251).

WORKS CITED

Allen, Maury. *Baseball's 100: A Personal Ranking of the Best Players in Baseball History.* New York: Galahad Books, 1981.

Banks, Ernie. "Ernie Banks." *Banks to Sandberg to Grace: Five Decades of Love and Frustration with the Chicago Cubs.* Comp. Carrie Muskat. Chicago: Contemporary Books, 2001. 39–48.

"Banks Says Loss of Memorabilia 'Hurts.'" *Jet* 13 Sept. 1993: 48.

Banks, Ernie, and Jim Enright. *"Mr. Cub."* Chicago: Rutledge, 1971.

Berkow, Ira. "'Cub Family' Minus Banks." *New York Times.* 14 June 1983: D19+.

Castle, George. "Race and the Cubs." *The Million-to-One Team: Why the Chicago Cubs Haven't Won a Pennant Since 1945.* South Bend, IN: Diamond Communications, 2000. 112–31.

Cholakis, James. "Forgotten First: Earliest Black Manager." *Sport* May 1988: 9.

Coppock, Chet. "The Best in the Business." *For Cubs Fans Only: There's No Expiration Date on Dreams.* Ed. Rich Wolfe. Phoenix, AZ: Lone Wolfe Press, 2003. 101–6.

"Cubs Pay 15 Gs For Banks: Must Battle Gene Baker For Post." *Chicago Defender* 19 Sept. 1953: 24.

"Ernie Banks Talks Baseball and Business." 25 Sept. 2000. <http://dir.salon.com/business/green/2000/09/25/banks/index.html?pn=2>. 3 Apr. 2004.

Farrell, James T. *My Baseball Diary.* New York: A. S. Barnes, 1957.

"From Banks to Baker to Fame." *Ebony* 11.7 (May 1956): 100+.

Goddard, Joe. "Ernie Banks is Out of a Job as No. 1 Cubs Fan." *Los Angeles Times* 13 June 1983: Sec. 3: 7.

Kiersh, Edward. "For Six Boys of Summer Grown Older, the Game Has Ended, But There Is Life after Baseball." *People Weekly* 11 Apr. 1983: 67–73.

Libby, Bill. *Ernie Banks: Mr. Cub.* New York: Putnam's Sons, 1971.

Murray, Jim. "Cubs Rob Game of a Ray of Sunshine." *Los Angeles Times* 14 June 1983: sec. 3: 1.

Rushin, Steve. "Living Legends." *Sports Illustrated* 30 July 2001: 53.

For Ken Holtzman:
Wherever I May Find Him

Terry Barr

"One morning, your name is Steve Bartman, a good Jewish Cubs fan. The next morning Cubs fans the world over are blaming the Jews not only for prevention of world peace, but also [for] maintaining 'the curse.' Only now do you feel ready to come out of hiding in order to submit this list to BangitOut.com."
— Shlomo Hubscher, "Top Ten Signs You Are a Jewish Cubs Fan" (#10)

When it gets down to it, I really have no credentials to write a piece on the Jewish culture of the Chicago Cubs. I've been to Chicago only once, actually driving past Wrigley Field (it was June, but the Cubs were out of town), and it never occurred to me to seek out Comiskey Park (US Cellular Field). The first little league team I played for was the Cubs — in small town Bessemer, Alabama — but even then our most hated rival for the two years I was on the team was the Cardinals. (In my first year, we tied them 4–4 in the last game of the season. After a crowding-the-plate walk and two awkwardly butt-first-sliding stolen bases, I was left stranded on third base as the game ended.)

Working against my credentials are the facts that I am a lifelong Yankees fan (though I, too, curse Bartman, being convinced the Yanks would have pasted the Cubs in '03 instead of suffering that great indignity, losing to the Marlins); while growing up in 1960s-era Alabama I saw Mickey Mantle play almost every Saturday on Dizzy Dean and Pee Wee Reese's national Game of the Week. Then, there's the fact that I'm only half–Jewish, meaning that I am not Bar Mitzvah, nor do I actually belong to a Jewish congregation, though I teach and have written about a variety of Jewish literary and film subjects at Presbyterian College, where for too many years I wasn't even supposed to be outspokenly Half-Jewish, much less the real thing. Finally, Philip Roth does happen to be my favorite Jewish author, which as far as American Jewish Literature of great cities goes alienates me from Chicago, but then Bellow just doesn't have that great baseball novel to his credit.

Still, because I was a Cubs fan for at least those two years of my little league youth, something stuck, and so in 1969, especially given just how badly the Yankees stunk then, I avidly rooted for the Cubbies. Like everyone else, I thought they were a shoo-in for the pennant. I was especially taken by their young, would-be lefty ace Ken Holtzman, following every box score in my afternoon daily to see how the Cubs and especially Holtzman, when he pitched, fared. I didn't know then, and would have cared less, that Holtzman was Jewish, and to be honest, it only mildly panged me when the Cubs collapsed to the Mets that fall (at least it wasn't the Cardinals, who finished first in my little league). I didn't think of curses then, or that Cubs manager Leo Durocher called his players ethnic slur-names. Life, and Ken Holtzman, moved on, and over the next few years, as is well chronicled, Holtzman, at least, won three world championships with the Oakland A's (my second little league team was, in fact, the A's) whose double-A farm team was in Birmingham, fifteen miles from Bessemer, and thus allowed me to see and root for Joe Rudi, Dave Duncan, Vida Blue, and yes, Reggie Jackson in their prelude-to-greatness days. I was glad for Holtzman, but he was just another cog in A's glory, and I still didn't know he was Jewish and still wouldn't have cared given that in the predominantly redneck Bessemer culture, my own ethnicity was as much an embarrassment as anything else.

Then Holtzman became a Yankee, which I thought was great, though it didn't work out too well for him. Billy Martin may or may not have called Holtzman a "kike," but what we do know is that he kept Holtzman on the bench during the Yanks' championship run in '77, after which Holtzman was traded back to the Cubs where he ended his career and fell off my personal radar. And I've never found him again — literally — which is an important aspect of this story.

Since the late 1980s, I have, in my own mind at least, become fully Jewish, sharing with my own Jewish father the rituals of circumcision, corned beef, a relative belief in one deity — and that Jewish of all sports, baseball.

As I have examined American Jewish culture and history, I've run across many interesting, if not disturbing facets of it. I've discovered, for example, that Henry Ford was an anti–Semite (perhaps explaining why Dad was a GM man). So as I was researching this article, I discovered this thesis from a 1921 edition of Ford's self-financed journal, *The Dearborn Independent*:

> If fans wish to know the trouble with American baseball, they have it in three words — too much Jew. Gentiles may rant out their parrot-like pro–Jewish propaganda, the fact is that the sport is clean and helpful until it begins to attract Jewish investors and exploiters and then it goes bad. [...]
>
> When you contrast the grandstands full of Americans supposing they are witnessing 'the only clean sport,' with the sinister groups playing with the players and managers to introduce a serpent's trail of unnecessary crookedness, you get a contrast that is rather startling. And the sinister influence is Jewish. [...] American baseball has passed into the hands of the Jews. If it is to be saved, it must be taken out of their hands [Ford, pars. 58–59, 61].

Although this diatribe was influenced mainly by the Black Sox scandal of 1919, the Cubs were nevertheless indicted as well, as, according to the *Independent*, in 1920, as the Cubs and Phillies were set to play a game, Cubs management got word that "several well-known Jews" had laid heavy bets on the Phillies. And though Chicago decided to use Grover Cleveland Alexander, who was not originally scheduled to pitch, to "save the game," Alexander's valiant effort came to no avail, and thus his effort to "thwart the Jewish gamblers" failed as well (Ford, pars. 19–20).

I wondered after collecting this information: is the curse on the Cubs — especially in its most recent manifestation, the infamous Bartman foul — a true conspiracy, aligned with the anti–Semitic "Protocols of the Learned Elders of Zion," the notorious forgery Henry Ford also published to the admiration of Hitler and Goebbels? This would be funny were it not for the reality that *The Dearborn Independent* was thought by many to be respectable; that Ford has a generally positive legacy; that there are those out there who associate curses with Jews, so God only knows what such people think or see when images of 1969, 2003, Ken Holtzman, or Steve Bartman pop up. So, in effect, does it really pay to be a Jewish Cub, or Jewish Cubs fan?

There is, of course, a real history of Jewish Chicago and the Cubs. And it seemed logical to me that in telling it, I would want to talk to the most famous Jewish Cub. How many people today actually remember Holtzman, know that he is Jewish, or care? I know that many in America do not associate sports and Jews at all. I discovered Holtzman's Jewish identity myself only in the last two years, as it was reported to me by a good friend, and then later affirmed by one of the editors of this volume when he suggested that I write this article. Through my research, then, I also discovered that

> Ken Holtzman is very serious about his Jewish background. He is very open and forthright about his pride in his people and his sincerity in his faith. While traveling with his team, he kept Jewish laws as best he could. He never pitched on a Jewish holiday. The Holtzmans maintain a Kosher home [Horvitz and Horvitz 88].

To be invited to that home, to eat a Kosher meal with Holtzman and his family, to talk baseball and Jewish culture: that became my dream. How hard could it be to realize this dream since Holtzman is, reportedly, so "open and forthright" about being Jewish?

As I was conducting more general research about the Cubs and their other Jewish players and history, I began seeking Holtzman's contact information. My editor suggested trying the Jewish Community Center of greater St. Louis because it was thought that Holtzman had retired to that rival area. So I called and e-mailed Jewish St. Louis. No response. Absolutely none. Messages on machine unresponsive. But as I was courteously awaiting some sign that they heard me in the Gateway city, I learned more about Chicago's Jewish history.

According to the historian Steven Riess, "The first Jews who settled in Chicago migrated from southwest Germany in the 1840s" (147). Nine years after Chicago was incorporated as a city, on October 3, 1846, fifteen Jews formed the first Jewish congregation in the city, Kehilat Anshe Maarav. During the Civil War there were enough Jewish Chicagoans to form a complete company and join the 82nd Illinois Volunteers ("Jewish Community of Chicago," pars. 1–2). These Ashkenazi Jews also set up hospitals, fraternal organizations, synagogues, and cemeteries. Their "interaction" with non–Jewish German-Americans was generally cordial and smooth, and some of the German Jews attained civic prominence quite early, most notably Henry Greenbaum, who was president of the German National Bank as well as Sixth Ward Alderman. Excluded from "native clubs," Chicago's Jews "formed their own Standard Club [...] that became one of the city's most prominent commercial fraternities" (147).

Throughout the 1880s and 90s Eastern European Jewish immigrants settled in Chicago, starting the city's first orthodox synagogues but also leading to segregated communities of Jews along denominational lines; the wealthier German Jews resided "in a northwestern corridor along Milwaukee Av. and south." Adopting "many of the values" of non–Jewish Chicagoans, these German Jews defied their "cerebral rather than athletic" stereotypes and "adopted" baseball as one of their favorite pastimes (Riess 147).

Once the orthodox Jews from Russia and Poland became the dominant Jewish community in Chicago in the 1890s, an all-too-common reaction set in. It is always with a sad sense of irony that it usually takes virulent forms of anti–Semitism to unite disparate groups of Jews, and thus it was in Chicago, as the Jews who settled there in the last decade of the nineteenth century "were viewed as part of an international financial conspiracy" (Riess 148). "Americanization" programs attempted to assimilate Jews and other minorities into mainstream culture, but since many of those programs were underwritten with a "Christian flavor," Chicago's Jews decided to institute their own parallel social, cultural, and charitable organizations. One, the Maxwell St. settlement, established in 1893, offered a "weekly physical culture class" for any of the 80,000 Jews who now lived in Chicago. In 1908, Jewish leaders, recognizing the importance and attraction of sports to all the city's youth, used the auspices of the Chicago Hebrew Institute (1903) to organize "indoor baseball games to attract young men and boys." The CHI's own athletic department was formed a year later with a mission of "promoting assimilation and respect for Jews [... and] featuring American sports" such as baseball, track, gymnastics, tennis, and handball. By 1910 the weekly attendance for these activities climbed to over 11,000. CHI physical director Harry Beckman was "crucial to forging [...] alliances" among all the divergent ethnic groups in Chicago, a major step for a young man whose early goal was to "overcome the anti–Semitic stereotype of Jews as bookworms who neglected physical development" (150–51).

By 1913, CHI instructor Harry Berg asserted that since its beginnings, the CHI athletic program "had decreased prejudice and dispelled the notion of Jewish cowardice [...] working-class ethnic youths began to perceive sport as a means to greater socioeconomic status, and many Jewish boys received their first formal athletic training at the Jewish settlements" (Riess 154). These achievements, it seemed, flew by *The Dearborn Independent*.

In 1921 the CHI changed its name to the Jewish People's Institute, spreading its message of "Jewish physicality beyond the local community." In that same year, the YMHA started a "traveling baseball team, while the JPI formed a city women's basketball team" (Riess 157). However, by the 1930s the JPI, after "accomplishing its goals of earning respect and bringing the Eastern Europeans closer to the mainstream American culture" (again with the athletic program proving pivotal), saw its influence begin to wane, ironically, because of its success:

> The Americanization programs taught independence, and athletes learned that they could rely on their physical abilities to make money, even during the hard times of the depression. Although the JPI still filled a transitional role for immigrants, Jewish American youths no longer needed its leadership and were reluctant to pay for its services. They preferred to frequent the public parks or neighborhood baseball clubs where the street culture persisted. Gambling on athletic contests proved more attractive than the adult-supervised programs at the institute [158].

So like many Americans, Jewish Chicagoans both identified with yet wanted to assimilate past their ethnicity; they liked the freedom of American life, including the freedom to place a few bets when they wanted. They were truly becoming mainstreamed and were thriving in Chicago as the Jewish population there grew from 10,000 in the 1880s to over 225,000 by the 1920s ("Jewish Community of Chicago," par. 4).

But this relative success for Chicago's Jews, according to Riess, would continue to "haunt Jews, for it is just such advancement in all areas of American life that poses a threat to the hegemony of non–Jews, suggesting that the process is not yet complete" (159). Can assimilation ever be "complete," though? Clearly, as *The Dearborn Independent* showed, there was opposition to this process, and while the *Independent* was finally discredited by history, its promulgation of stereotypes, unfortunately, lived on.

Chicago's Jewish history, however, is only a backdrop and context for the Cubs' Jewish history, and as I await word now from the University of Illinois Sports Hall of Fame, of which Ken Holtzman is a member, as to whether or not they have an address or number for him (they, too, never returned my repeated calls), I start the process of determining just who else could properly be considered a Jewish Cub.

"Properly" is intentional since, as I learned, like so many other things Jewish, there is disputed territory here.

According to Harold and Meir Ribalow's *Jewish Baseball Stars*, one of the earliest Jewish Cubs players was Johnny Kling, who was born Johnny Kline in Kansas City, 1875. Kling was a "born ball player," or so say the Ribalows: "There has never been a better catcher" than

Kling/Kline (15). In 1901 he became a Cub after earlier playing for Houston in the Texas League under his "Jewish name of Kline." Kling played in the 1906 World Series against the White Sox, but he did his "best work" against Ty Cobb's Detroit Tigers in the '07 Series (16–17).

However, Peter and Joachim Horvitz, another father-son Jewish writing team, contradict the Ribalows by asserting that "neither Kling nor [Big Ed] Reulbach [...] who pitched a shutout double-header [for the Cubs], the only player in major league history to do so [...] were Jewish" (Horvitz & Horvitz 9). The Horvitzes establish that in their pantheon of Jewish baseball stars they have included "[...] players with a Jewish parent and those who converted to Judaism, whether before or after their baseball careers [...]. But [...they] do not include someone with a Jewish spouse and never converted, nor someone with proverbial Jewish lineage who joins Jews for Jesus" (9).

I suppose we must trust the Horvitzes on Kling and Reulbach, for though they offer no proof of their claim, no one to my knowledge has come forth to challenge them since. Erwin Lynn, some fifteen years prior to the Horvitzes in his *The Jewish Baseball Hall of Fame*, listed both Kling and Reulbach as Jews, noting that Reulbach was a Cub from 1905–1913, with a pitching record of 19–4 in 1906, 17–4 in 1907, and 24–7 in 1908 (Lynn 269, 271). While both the Ribalows and Lynn acknowledge sources, neither of them footnotes his statistics or history, so the story of the earliest Jewish Cub is apparently still to be determined or, again, "not yet complete." Or maybe it's just that after *The Dearborn Independent* article, Kling and Reulbach decided that nothing good could come of being Jewish. There is precedent. As another Cubs historian explains, Johnny Kling's widow was Jewish and that fact might have caused the misunderstanding about Kling's ethnicity. It was surely what disqualified him from inclusion in the Horvitzes' Jewish-Cub pantheon (Weisberger 58).

Yet, as Kling historian Gil Bogen has amply documented, Kling's wife Lillian may have lied about his Protestant heritage, perhaps because she imagined that it was the perception of his being Jewish that kept Johnny from being elected to the Baseball Hall of Fame. In interviews conducted twenty years apart, Mrs. Kling changed Johnny's denomination from Baptist to Lutheran, though her efforts to have him elected to the Hall were unsuccessful. Lillian's manipulations, Bogen insists, are why Harold Ribalow's *The Jew in American Sports* no longer lists Kling as Jewish.

Bogen has done a thorough job in using circumstantial evidence found in Kling's family marriage, immigration, and burial records — as well as discussing aspects of Jewish law — that would cause most objective observers to conclude that Kling was likely "the Jew" that earlier baseball historians, including his own teammates, believed he was. And since Kling's children all married within the Jewish faith, when you get down to it, whether he was technically Jewish, he should be considered a de facto Jew (Bogen 221–42).

What the Horvitzes are certain of is that in 1906 a Jew by the name of Franklin P. Adams, while in the stands for a Cubs-NY Giants game, composed the following lament for his conquered heroes, the Giants:

> Baseball's Sad Lexicon
> These are the saddest of possible words:
> "Tinker to Evers to Chance."
> Trio of bear cubs and fleeter than birds,
> Tinker and Evers and Chance.
> Ruthlessly pricking our gonfalon bubble,
> Making a Giant hit into a double —
> Words that are heavy with nothing but trouble:
> "Tinker to Evers to Chance" [Horvitz & Horvitz 243–44].

So once upon a time it was the Cubbies themselves who could inflict curses. For the record, however, the other, "legitimate" Jewish Cubs, in alphabetical order, are:

Cy Block (1942–45). Block appeared in the 1945 World Series (the Cubs' last) against the Tigers for one game as a pinch runner. The Cubs won that game, at least (Horvitz & Horvitz 33–34).

Hy Cohen (1955). Cohen pitched in seven games for the Cubs in '55. He might have made the team earlier, but Army service in Korea interrupted his career. Stan Musial once credited Cohen with helping Musial end a prolonged hitting slump, and Cohen also contracted to have his image produced on a Topps trading card. But his career ended before any little boy could collect such a memento (Horvitz & Horvitz 47–48).

Ed Mayer (1957–8). Mayer was a pitcher who gave up one of the 660 home run balls hit by Willie Mays. His lifetime major league record was 2–2 (Horvitz & Horvitz 113–14).

Art Shamsky (1972). Shamsky played in fifteen games for the Cubs, batting .125 before being dealt that same year to Oakland. The two singles he hit for the Cubbies were the last two major league hits he ever had. Shamsky had earlier been a member of the '69 Mets! (Horvitz & Horvitz 169).

Steve Stone (1974–6). Later a broadcaster for Cubs' station WGN, Stone had "one of the best records" on the 1975 Cubs' staff, but before the '76 season, he was asked to take a pay cut. Management also asked him to undergo an operation for his shoulder, but Stone refused, declining also to take a recommended cortisone shot. Subsequently he became a free agent, signing with the crosstown White Sox and notching a 15–12 record the following year (1977). In 1979, after being traded to the Orioles, Stone won eleven games and then in 1980 went 25–7 and won the Cy Young award (Horvitz & Horvitz 181–82).

After reviewing Stone's story and resurrected career, I am at least willing to discuss bad timing as regards a cursed franchise. But as I'm contemplating such superstition, a potential Ken Holtzman source comes through. The Major League Baseball Players Alumni Association tells me that if I will fax to them my complete request for Holtzman info and my purpose for wanting it, they will help me contact Kenny. And so, on official Presbyterian College English Department letterhead stationary, I send in my request. A day or so later, I even get a return call. The pleasant young man on the phone informs me that he's sure Holtzman still exists, but that, unfortunately, when he tried the home number he had for him, he was met with the "That number is no longer in service" recording, with no forwarding number.

"My e-mails are bouncing back, too," he tells me sadly, with a "Recipient Server Unknown" message. "That's about all I can do," he explains.

And it begins to dawn on me that maybe Ken Holtzman doesn't want to be found. Fortunately, by now I have collected many books on the Cubs and Jews, with Holtzman abounding in them. While at this point I haven't officially given up hope of finding Holtzman, I am glad that I didn't formally apply for that travel grant from my college that I had hoped to use to celebrate Chanukah with the Holtzmans. My books then tell me that Holtzman lives, variously, in Buffalo Grove, IL, or somewhere near Skokie, IL, or north suburban Chicago, or near his family home in St. Louis, or close to the University of Illinois where he went to college. Or are these really the same place? But there is no Holtzman listed in Buffalo Grove, near Skokie, or anywhere else in Illinois or Missouri that I can find.

Focusing on Ken Holtzman now, I turn to a reference from my own collection, Peter Levine's *Ellis Island to Ebbets Field: Sport and the American Jewish Experience.* Sure enough, the index tells me that Ken Holtzman will be found on page 243. I look for him there, in a chapter on Jewish baseball players. On this page I see mention of Sandy Koufax, Steve Stone, and Hank Greenberg, but no Ken Holtzman. I read the twenty pages surrounding page 243; no Holtzman. I turn to page 143, then page 43; no Holtzman. There is no page 343, so that's it. My first foray into Holtzman history, and not even a blip! Should I be taking this personally?

Over the next few weeks I do find plenty of statistical, referential, and anecdotal citations of Ken Holtzman achievements. Holtzman was born in St. Louis and became a high school baseball star there, having been selected as MVP on his state championship team. He matriculated to the University of Illinois, although he "wasn't at all certain that he would go into baseball professionally." After his junior year in college, however, he did sign with the Cubs for an estimated $70,000 (Ribalow & Ribalow 241–42). In 1965 Holtzman earned a tryout with the "big club," but against his very first batter, the Giants' Jim Ray Hart, Holtzman saw his first pitch launched into the outfield seats. He threw in three other games that year and managed to keep his ERA to a very respectable 2.25. Starting for the Cubs in 1966, Holtzman wound up the season with an 11–16 record, one of his wins coming against Don Drysdale and the Dodgers (Horvitz & Horvitz 86). His most impressive win that year, however, came against that "other" Dodger ace, Sandy Koufax. As Koufax historian Jane Leavy describes,

> Kenny Holtzman faced Koufax at Wrigley Field [...] the day after Yom Kippur. They had moved their scheduled starts back a day so they could attend services. There had even been some discussion, Holtzman recalls, about going to synagogue together. A TV producer at WGN took Holtzman's family to his temple, where Kenny prayed he would beat the sonofabitch the next day. His mother prayed for guidance about whom to root for: "He was every Jewish mother's idol and now he's pitching against her son," Holtzman said. "Clearly, she didn't want anyone to lose. I said, 'But Mother, one of us has to lose.' She said, 'Maybe you can get a no-decision.'"
>
> [...] The next day, Holtzman's mother and his girlfriend, and her best friend, president of the Sandy Koufax Fan Club at the University of Illinois-Champaign, were in the stands watching as Kenny held the Dodgers hitless for eight innings. Mrs. Holtzman's son won; her hero lost. She told Kenny she had decided to root for him to be just like Koufax [Leavy 170–71].

Holtzman's two-hitter preserved the 2–1 win, with Koufax giving up only four hits. While Holtzman was hailed as a "new Koufax," Koufax described him as "the first Kenny Holtzman" (Horvitz & Horvitz 86–87).

In 1967, while spending much of that summer with the National Guard, Holtzman still compiled a 9–0 record, which set the National League mark then for most wins in an undefeated season. His ERA was 2.52 (Horvitz & Horvitz 87). While his 1968 record fell to 11–14, in 1969 it jumped back to 17–13. In that year, though of course the ending was tragic for the Cubbies, Holtzman completed his first no-hitter—a 3–0 decision with no strikeouts—on August 19 against the Atlanta Braves (Ribalow and Ribalow 243, 245). Then in 1970 he completed a 17–11 season with an almost no-hitter, while in 1971, his last season with the Cubs, he won but nine games, one of which was his second-ever no-hitter on June 3 against Cincinnati (Ribalow & Ribalow 246).

Clearly Holtzman's tenure with the Cubs was successful despite the team's failure to win a pennant or division. The Cubs had great potential as evidenced by a partial list of their stars from that era: Ernie Banks, Ron Santo, Billy Williams, Ferguson Jenkins, Don Kessinger, Randy Hundley, and Jim Hickman. With Jenkins and Holtzman, their pitching staff also included Bill Hands, Dick Selma, and relievers Phil Regan, Ted Abernathy, and Hank Aguirre (Golenbock 404). The chronicle of what went wrong with this Cubs era, particularly the collapse to the "Amazin'" Mets in 1969, has been painfully recounted elsewhere. But what of Holtzman's years and ultimate exit from this team? Was there potential for a title had he stayed? And did it really matter that he was the next Jewish prince of baseball? And how

Leo Durocher, the winning Cubs manager who was also known for his ethnic insensitivity (courtesy Baseball Hall of Fame).

comfortable was this Jewish ace in the Chicago ethnic climate? What was the Jewish makeup of Chicago during the Holtzman years?

Shortly before Holtzman hit the big leagues, in 1961, there were forty-three orthodox synagogues, twenty-five conservative synagogues, sixteen reform temples, and five "traditional" congregations in greater Chicagoland. In 1969, it was estimated that about fifteen percent of the Chicago Jewish community was foreign-born, and about five percent still used Yiddish as their vernacular. About three to five percent were strict Sabbath observers, but synagogue affiliation was less than fifty percent in the city and about sixty percent in the suburbs. Also in 1969, West Rogers Park and suburban Skokie were the largest Jewish communities, each with a population of 50,000, constituting about seventy percent of the total population in those areas. And by 1999, the Jewish population of the greater Chicago area (including all of Cook and DuPage Counties and portions of Lake County) was 261,000, the fourth largest Jewish center in America ("Jewish Community of Chicago," pars. 5–6).

While the strength of Chicago's Jewish community laid a foundation for the relative comfort of individual Chicago Jews, the late 1960s in America, and particularly 1968 in Chicago itself, were a turbulent and traumatic era. Urban riots, political assassinations, war protests, and Mayor Daley's handling of the '68 Democratic National Convention were discomfiting reminders that all was not home, apple pie, Mom, and baseball in our nation. Though baseball had in its history a record of leading the charge in America against some forms of social inequality, in the late '60s baseball teams could also be a microcosm for the internal conflicts faced by the country at large.

Perhaps the most popular television series of this era was the 1970s hit *All in the Family*. Foreshadowing the in-your-face ethnic slurring emanating from character Archie Bunker's mouth, the Cubs of 1969 were led by manager Leo Durocher. Maybe the country was ready to hear Archie's racial epithets, but were the Cubs ready for Durocher's brand of motivation and admonishment? While Ken Holtzman wasn't the only Cub to be targeted by Durocher's ire, in many ways he did become the team's scapegoat.

Holtzman maintained that regarding his comparison to Sandy Koufax, he "didn't feel any pressure to try to emulate" the Dodger ace and that he had "nothing but respect for [Koufax....]" Still, he "wasn't going to alter [his] style" to become more like Koufax, especially in trying to become a strikeout pitcher (Talley 60). One wonders, however, to what extent the comparison did affect Holtzman's Cubs years, especially when the Cubs folded in 1969. Indeed, Holtzman was "the first star of 1969 to walk away from the Cubs." As Holtzman recalls it, "I was frustrated with losing. [...] I really didn't think I'd be part of a winner with the Cubs, so I asked to be traded. It was a tough decision, especially since I had come up through the Cub farm system and felt so close to all the guys. It was traumatic" (qtd. in Talley 54). One teammate who did not take kindly to Holtzman's trade demands was third baseman Ron Santo, who asked Holtzman directly about his stance. Holtzman responded that if he remained with the club he wouldn't "help himself. It's going to get worse with Leo, and I've got to think of my future. I've got to go where I can pitch and feel appreciated" (54).

So what, then, was the beef with Leo? Many have speculated that Holtzman grew weary of and angry at his manager calling him "kike" on a regular basis. When asked directly whether Durocher once called him a "gutless Jew," Holtzman "laughed" and then said,

> I don't remember, but he could have. He called everybody everything. But I had my day. Remember a couple of years later when Leo and Santo went at it in the clubhouse? That's the day Ronnie ran up into Leo's office and grabbed him by the throat. Leo's tongue was sticking out six inches before we pulled Santo off him. [...] Anyway, that's when Leo came back into the clubhouse and announced he was quitting and John Holland came down to address the team [... telling us] how we can't let the manager quit and how it's not his fault [...] and all of a sudden I shout: "Let the son of a bitch go!" I think that's when Holland decided he would honor my request to be traded. But [...] I still don't blame Leo for what happened to us. I never did and never will" [qtd. in Talley 63–64].

Nevertheless, the stormy relationship between Cubs players and Durocher had to have factored into the players' moods and emotions, perhaps even carrying over to their performance on the field. As Ribalow and Ribalow have observed, Durocher frequently used ethnic and racial epithets to refer to many of the Cubs players, including calling Ron Santo "wop" and Don Kessinger "dumb hillbilly" (243). Apparently, though, the "gutless" tag was one that Holtzman, at least, felt Durocher attached to him after he once admitted to his manager at a conference on the mound that he was "tired." Thereafter, Durocher would yank Holtzman at the first sign of fatigue until Holtzman began lying to Durocher about his tiredness:

> When Durocher learned of this ploy, he threatened to fine anybody $500 who lied to him about being tired. At that point, the only thing that counted was that Durocher was no longer in contact with his young pitcher. A world had come between them [in '69] and for the rest of that season, Holtzman went 1–5. Ferguson Jenkins added that during this stretch, Durocher "started calling Kenny's pitches from the bench. Kenny resented this. [...] [F]rom 1969 on Leo was always picking on Kenny, who was on the defensive all the time" [Ribalow & Ribalow 244–45].

Holtzman's batterymate in 1969, Randy Hundley, offered a more nuanced version of the Holtzman-Durocher controversy:

> [...] Holtzman had a lot of ability, and he learned to be real tough mentally, too. In the beginning he and Leo had a love-hate relationship. Leo absolutely loved Kenny. Leo started to call him Hebe and called him everything you can imagine, and Kenny absolutely loved it. And to this day, Ken Holtzman to all of us is Hebe. We don't know him any other way. If I were to say "Hey Kenny," he would think, "Something is wrong" [Golenbock 408].

Maybe Hundley is right about their affection, for according to another account, Holtzman and Durocher did double date on one occasion, though Leo was two-timing his wife in the process (Talley 57–58). And Holtzman does assert that it wasn't Durocher who cost them the '69 pennant but rather their own losing attitude and inability to intimidate their opposition (Talley 55–56).

Ferguson Jenkins, however, did not see a healthy relationship between the two. Jenkins believes that one of the reasons Holtzman didn't like Durocher was that, as he puts it,

> Kenny was a real competitor. Kenny and Leo played hearts against one another, and Leo was the type of guy, he didn't care who you were, he called you your ethnic background. Kike or Spook [....] That's the way Leo was. He always called you Stupid. Guys would take it because he was Skip. Kenny disliked him. I don't know the real reason. Ask Kenny [Golenbock 40].

After Holtzman was traded in 1971 to Oakland, he commented to reporters that "he knew six or seven Cubs who didn't want to play for Leo." Responding to Holtzman, former Cubs coach Peanuts Lowrey stated that these Cubs were "primadonnas" and that "Holtzman had been the worst of them all [... to which] Ron Santo said simply, 'I'm going to keep my mouth shut and play ball'" (Langford 163).

It's a strange Cubs picture, this Holtzman-Durocher ethnic squabble. And maybe it wasn't an ethnic thing but was just part of a climate, era, and culture in America when human beings in general were not so willing to bow down reverentially to any authority, much less a paternalistic one.

Even more strange is that the team Holtzman migrated to — the Oakland A's — was a motley assortment of mustachioed bandito-rebels whose relationship with owner Charles O. Finley was, shall we say, a bit acrimonious. And then from Oakland Holtzman wound up with Billy Martin's Yankees, winning World Series in both cities but still suffering from owners and managers who weren't exactly models of patience and open-mindedness. Still, this is a Cubs story, and while Holtzman ended his career back with the Cubbies in 1978–79, obviously there was no championship in Holtzman-era Chicago. Perhaps Holtzman was correct in his analysis that the Cubs of '69 were intimidated by other teams. Or they may simply have not had that winning attitude, or the right personnel, or enough money. And the '69 Mets were pretty good.

Or, there could be a curse, and it could be linked to the Jews, because what if Holtzman had not been on that '69 team and they had won? What if he had left the previous year, been traded for another pitcher, Catfish Hunter, say, and the Cubs had held off the "Amazins" that year? Lose a scapegoat, gain a World Series banner?

I guess even a half-Jew can wallow in ethnic self-pity.

I would love to follow Fergie Jenkins's advice, though, and ask Kenny Holtzman these questions. Believe me, I tried.

My last-ditch step was to consult a white pages internet search engine, and I found several leads to my man. To verify that one or any of these leads could be confirmed as the Kenneth D. Holtzman I truly wanted, however, I would need to charge my American Express the $14.95 finder's fee that the service required. Hoping for the best (e-mail address, phone number), I knew I'd settle for anything. And what I got was a snail-mail address. (It wasn't even one of the cities I've already mentioned, and I'm NOT sharing it since anyone reading this is as capable of spending $14.95 as I am.) I again broke out the Presbyterian College letterhead and scrupulously wrote my request for an interview (by phone, e-mail, in person, ANYTHING) to Mr. Holtzman. I unabashedly included such personal information as having had his baseball card and keeping up with his box scores. I confessed my half–Jewishness and explained my feelings on receiving what I often believe are latent, half–anti–Semitic gestures at me from the more reactionary elements of my institution.

I put the letter in the mail, and immediately began waiting for a reply.

One and a half years later, I am still waiting.

I then discovered that there is a website for the Society for American Baseball Research. I entered its domain and made a request for current communications info for Kenneth D. Holtzman. Their prompt response was that they would gladly help me in my endeavor, that is, if I were willing to fork over the $65 subscription fee which would then entitle me to all the rights and privileges of other true believers ... er, members. And I confess that I did have my credit card in hand; the boxes on the internet form all-but-completely filled in; the "submit information" button one mouse-click away, when I simply pulled back from the screen. No more.

Ken Holtzman, it seemed to me then, was trying extremely hard not to be found by me or maybe anyone else ever again. Except maybe by those who know him as "Hebe." It is his right, after all, not to be found, and even had I contacted him successfully, what would I have discovered from his story that I hadn't already gleaned from all the others? I can see the meeting: a haunted figure, hounded by his own demons and curse, peering out at me:

And you are...?
Ken Holtzman.
And you have come home to Chicago?
Yes.
And you are Jewish?
Yes.
And Leo Durocher called you "Hebe" and "Kike."
Well, it was Martin who said "Kike."
OK, OK ... I just want to know because it's hard for my non–Jewish, or non–Cubbie fans to understand. It's something that we haven't got.... So why do you hate the Cubs?
I don't hate them. I DON'T HATE THEM! I DON'T. I DON'T. I DON'T HATE THEM!

OK, so I just finished teaching Faulkner and got carried away. But I do wonder if Ken Holtzman was simply "too Jewish" for the Cubs. After all, he once claimed that "Family, home and religion" were "very important" to him and that he "believe[d] in Jewish values and [...] religion," keeping kosher at home and ordering kosher food on plane trips to away games (Ribalow & Ribalow 262).

Timing is everything, and as I consider the climate of the late 60s in Chicago, and of the Cubs' own brand of ethnic turmoil, I wonder if, at this point in his career, there was simply too much attention paid to things that were peripheral to the game for Holtzman. Clearly, the move to a lower-profile media market like Oakland, despite its own controversies, was a good one for Kenny.

Such is the fate of the Cubs. The Dodgers had the Jewish pitcher who refused to take the mound on Yom Kippur, but he also propelled them to the World Series title in 1963 and '65. Ken Holtzman revered his Jewish identity and also won three World Series rings with the A's, and another with the Yankees. The Cubs, meanwhile, were left with ... well, actually, after 1971 I didn't much keep up with the Cubbies. I know that they almost got to the World Series in 1984, losing to the Padres, and then made the playoffs in 1989 and '98. And then, of course, came 2003 and Steve Bartman, which brings us to:

> The Kosher Top Ten's top three signs that you are a Jewish Chicago Cubs Fan:
> 3. You and your people have long wandered the desert, believing with steadfast faith, that you will reach the promised land one day.
> 2. Despite years of trials and tribulations, of mockery and persecution from your enemies, Yemach Sheman (Yankee Fans), you nonetheless remain identified and affiliated.
> 1. Mesilat Yesharim teaches us to view this life as but a vestibule To the World to Come, to cope with the difficulties and challenges of this world, for all the sweeter will it be when we arrive at the World to Come. So too, as Cubs fans, we must see these last 96 years of exile, of being in the baseball Diaspora, as a necessary prelude, so that we are zocheh the sweetness that will be the World Championship [Hubscher, pars. 8–10].

Maybe it will happen "next year," in Israel, or Wrigley. I can't help but feel that if the Jewish people could wait over 2000 years to attain their most cherished dream, then the Cubs can endure a few more "next years." It's too bad, though, that Jewish singer-songwriter Steve Goodman couldn't live to see it happen. But at least he made his love known in his 1981 ballad "A Dying Cub Fan's Last Request." One day Goodman's spirit will be at peace about his favorite team. In the meantime, author Byron L. Sherwin has a more proactive idea. Released on April 1, 2006, just in time for Passover and the season's first pitch, his latest novel, *The Cubs and the Kabbalist: How a Kabbalah-Master Helped the Chicago Cubs Win Their First World Series Since 1908*, describes how a rabbi employs the ancient Jewish mystical tradition of Kabbalah to help the Cubs to their first World Series title in nearly one hundred years.

Now that's kosher.

Clearly, "the Jews" don't control baseball, the arts, the economy, or international banking, as some people in the 1920s (and in other eras) thought. And I'll say it here: there is no curse on the Cubs, just like there wasn't on the Red Sox. Just like Jews don't wear horns on their head or cork their bats (oops!). To be sure, to be a Jewish Cubs fan is to know adversity, but whether players are Jewish or not—whether they are called "kike" or not—the fabric of Jewish ethnicity, the city of Chicago, baseball, and American culture is multi-cultural and textural. And really, would we have it any other way?

Goodbye Mr. Holtzman, wherever you are.

Addendum: A recent sighting: Ken Holtzman was managing the Ra'anana Express of the newly developed Israel Baseball League in its inaugural season. Ra'anana opened that season on June 25, 2007, against the Tel Aviv Lightning. Other luminary managers include

Ken Holtzman, Chicago Cubs ace and Jewish role model (courtesy Baseball Hall of Fame).

Art Shamsky and Ron Blomberg. Tickets are available online. I'm out of funds for this season, and so it's "Wait Until Next Year" ... in Jerusalem, for me and Ken.

WORKS CITED

Bogen, Gil. *Johnny Kling*. Jefferson, NC: McFarland, 2006.

Ford, Henry. "Jewish Gamblers Corrupt American Baseball." *The International Jew — The World's Foremost Problem*. 3 Sept. 1921. *The Dearborn Independent*. JR's Rare Books and Commentary. 10 Jan. 2006. <http://www.jrbooksonline.com>.

Golenbock, Peter. *Wrigleyville: A Magical History Tour of the Chicago Cubs*. New York: St. Martin's Griffen, 1999.

Horvitz, Peter S., and Joachim Horvitz. *The Big Book of Jewish Baseball: An Illustrated Encyclopedia & Anecdotal History*. New York: SPI Books, 2001.

Hubscher, Shlomo. "Top Ten Signs You Are a Jewish Cubs Fan." *Kosher Top 10*. Bangitout: Kosher Comedy for the Circumcised. 22 July 2006. <http://www.bangitout.com>.

"Jewish Community of Chicago." Museum of the Jewish People Online. <http://www.bh.org.il>. 18 Jan. 2006.

Langford, Jim. *The Game Is Never Over*. South Bend, IN: Icarus, 1980.

Leavy, Jane. *Sandy Koufax: A Lefty's Legacy*. New York: Harper Perennial, 2002.

Levine, Peter. *From Ellis Island to Ebbets Field: Sport and the American Jewish Experience*. New York: Oxford UP, 1992.

Lynn, Erwin. *The Jewish Baseball Hall of Fame*. New York: A Shapolsky Book, 1986.

Ribalow, Harold U., and Meir Z. Ribalow. *Jewish Baseball Stars*. New York: Hippocrene Books, 1984.

Riess, Steven A., ed. *Sports and the American Jew*. Syracuse, NY: Syracuse UP, 1998.

Talley, Rick. *The Cubs of '69: Recollections of the Team That Should Have Been*. Chicago: Contemporary Books, 1989.

Weisberger, Bernard A. *When Chicago Ruled Baseball: The Cubs-White Sox World Series of 1906*. New York: William Morrow, 2006.

PART III

THE SOCIOLOGY OF CUBDOM

"I'm a Cub fan. I cannot be bought": Onstage Fandom in *Bleacher Bums*

James Davis

In early August 1977, as the real live Chicago Cubs were in the thick of a three-way race for the NL East with the Phillies and Pirates, a play about the exploits of the right-field denizens opened at the Organic Theatre. The show, appropriately titled *Bleacher Bums*, ran in the Organic's Clark Street theatre and regularly played to sold-out houses, an unusual phenomenon for an original script featuring unknown actors (Houlihan 28). The Organic Theatre was at the center of Chicago's theatrical boom in the late 1970s. Beyond *Bleacher Bums*, the Organic produced the world premiere of David Mamet's *Sexual Perversity in Chicago*, as well as the theatrical version of *E/R*, which was rough inspiration for the television series of the same name ("Organic Theatre," par. 1). Following its successful run in Chicago, *Bleacher Bums* moved to what some might consider hostile territory for a six-month engagement in New York City and ultimately settled in Los Angeles for an open-ended run at the Burbage Theatre that lasted thirteen years (Zwecker 29).

The initial idea for *Bleacher Bums* came from Organic company member Joe Mantegna, a Chicago native and longtime Cubs fan. Mantegna, who would later win a Tony award for his work in the original Broadway production of Mamet's *Glengarry Glen Ross* and receive much acclaim for his stage and film work, "came up with the idea of creating a play based on characters who live the baseball season in the bleacher seats" (Houlihan 28). In a 2004 interview with the *Chicago Sun-Times*'s Bill Zwecker, Mantegna explained *Bleacher Bums'* genesis:

> I was sitting there in the bleachers every day, disappointed at what was happening down there on the field, but it made me wonder what it was that brought out these other 35,000 people every day to follow a team that's at best mediocre [Zwecker 29].

This type of process wasn't unusual in the 1970s Chicago theatre community. A great deal of the work created by local Chicago artists had been influenced by Viola Spolin's use of games to generate theatre pieces, and the Second City, a company noted for its improvisational performance style as well as its famous alumni (Harold Ramis, Amy Sedaris, Stephen Colbert, and almost anyone who has ever been funny on *SNL*). Generally speaking, this type of theatre usually results in scripts that place focus on the development of an ensemble of characters instead of a traditional, linear plot.

As these productions influenced the Organic's creative *modus operandi* at the time, the *Bleacher Bums* script evolved through a series of improvisations. In this instance, the actors made regular field trips to the Friendly Confines and then returned to the theatre in an attempt to recreate the characters and situations they had just seen. Eventually the script began to take shape, and by opening night each original cast-member received a co-author credit (Houlihan 28). Of course, as the Cubs' personnel and fortunes have changed in the nearly thirty years since *Bleacher Bums* was originally produced, the script has received numerous revisions in order to keep it current (Zwecker 29). For example, in the 1977 production, when the character Zig is asked about his relationship with his wife, he responds that he "wouldn't trade her for [shortstop Ivan] DeJesus" (Rapoport 127). In 1998, Zig continues to refuse a trade, but this time for outfielder Lance Johnson (Mantegna 75).

In production, *Bleacher Bums* creates challenges for actors and scenic designers. For example, the script only calls for one set piece, a section of bleachers that faces the audience. When the characters aren't interacting with one another, they ostensibly watch the action on the field in front of them, that is, in the audience. In order for this set to look at all convincing, whenever there is a bit of action or dialogue that refers to action on the field, like everyone's, "Oh no! Awww!" reaction to Henry Rodriguez being thrown out at first, the actors have to coordinate their physical movements to give the appearance of watching the game (Mantegna 26).

Another challenge *Bleacher Bums* presents, perhaps due to its improvisational roots, is its seeming lack of traditional dramatic action. The script features little in the way of traditional story and focuses instead on interaction between characters. The plot, as it is, concerns Decker (played by Mantegna in the original production), a businessman and "lead bum"; Zig, Decker's foul-mouthed foil and gambling partner; Greg, a blind man who listens to the game on a portable transistor radio; Richie, a junior member of the group who serves as Decker's scorekeeper; and Marvin, whose allegiance to the Cubs is questionable (Houlihan 28). These right-field regulars are joined by Melody, an attractive young woman who is more interested in sunbathing than following the action on the field; Rose, Zig's wife, whose baseball knowledge surprises everyone; and the Cheerleader, an overly enthusiastic left-field fan whose visits become increasingly annoying.

As the play opens, Greg sits alone in the bleachers, listening to the broadcast of the starting lineup on his transistor radio. He is quickly joined by Melody — who immediately lays out her towel and strips to a bikini — Decker, Richie, and Zig, all of whom enter just in time to jeer the Cardinals' line-up (Delino DeShields is "Delino DeShits," Todd Stottlemyre "ain't worth squatlemyre") and praise the Cubs (Kevin Orie is "bound for glory") (Mantegna 9–11). The action on the field starts, which kicks off a flurry of betting that hits a snag when Zig and Decker both refuse to wager against the Cubs. Marvin enters and volunteers to help them out, demonstrating a lack of ethical problems betting against the hometown team. He explains to Richie, "Today I'm a St. Louis fan. Tomorrow I'm a Pittsburgh fan and next week I'm a Philadelphia fan" (Mantegna 14).

In his article entitled, "Should Cubs Fans be Committed? What Bleacher Bums Have to Teach Us about the Nature of Faith," Thomas D. Senor writes, "when you are a genuine fan of a team, you make a commitment. You like them win or lose. A person who roots for whichever club happens to be winning is a true fan of no team" (38). This is particularly true of Cubs fans, who have had very little opportunity in the last century to cheer for the "club that happens to be winning" and whose status as "tortured souls" is often at the heart of their identity (Senor 39). Marvin is immediately put at odds with the rest of the group not only because he rejects the Cubs but because he puts his financial well-being ahead of his fandom. As the action of the play progresses, he reveals his motives to Decker, saying, "Listen, the only reason why I'm here bettin' with these assholes is because I can't lose. Otherwise I'd be out at the track" (Mantegna 24).

While he was an outsider before this statement, Marvin instantly becomes the play's antagonist, as his belief system contravenes the key tenet of the Cubs fans: he lacks unwavering devotion to the team. Marvin places his winnings ahead of his love for the team and would rather be anywhere besides Wrigley Field on a beautiful summer day. The Bums, of course, find this both alien and blasphemous.

As the action progresses, more bets are made, ballpark mythology is discussed — Zig is convinced that the scoreboard operator has "broads up there" — and Richie starts to doubt his devotion to the Cubs and the culture of the bleacher fans as he sees Marvin win more bets and bring in more cash (Mantegna 18).

Eventually, Rose, Zig's wife, appears and informs him that she's not pleased with his gambling, the Cubs' pitching starts to fall apart, and Richie's faith begins to crumble as he is seduced by the diabolical Marvin, who involves him in a bet that the Cardinals will come back from a three-run deficit. Immediately, the Cards load the bases with two outs in their half of the ninth inning and hit a grand slam into the right-field bleachers. Richie catches it and commits the most egregious sin in all of Cubdom. He refuses to throw back a home run ball, a ball hit by a Cardinal, no less:

RICHIE: I caught the Grand Slam Ball!
MELODY: Throw it back! Throw it back!
ALL: Throw it back! Throw it back!
RICHIE: You're crazy! We just won [the bet] cause of this. I'm not gonna throw it back! It's mine [Mantegna 73].

Of all the canonical traditions that exist in the bleachers, throwing back an opposing team's home run ball is probably the most sacrosanct. Any true, hardcore Cubs fan would throw the ball back reflexively — especially one hit by the Cardinals — but Richie's refusal to do so signifies his break from the Cubs. By keeping the ball to celebrate winning his bet, he actively alienates his former friends and accepts the embrace of the dark side.

Richie's excitement is short-lived, however, when he turns to Marvin to celebrate their win and Marvin barks, "Will you get your hands off me? You stupid moron! You little toad! [...] We won a couple of bets, that doesn't make us buddies" (Mantegna 73). Appalled by his treatment of Richie, the others increase the amount of money they bet with Marvin so they can clean him out if they win. Unfortunately, art imitates life, and the Cubs go down swinging, which leads to a big payday for Marvin, who tells his marks that they lose because they "bet with their heart, not with [their] head" (Mantegna 76). As Marvin starts collecting his winnings, Richie realizes that he doesn't have enough cash to cover his bet. He's rescued by Decker:

DECKER: Hey Marvin, is my marker good with you?
MARVIN: What are y —
DECKER: Is my marker any good? Yes or no?
MARVIN: I'll take your marker [...] you're gonna cover his bet?
DECKER: It's an investment, Marvin [Mantegna 77].

Richie, the prodigal fan, is welcomed back into the fold after a brief crisis of faith. After all, Cubs fans are nothing if not tolerant and forgiving. Marvin attempts to lead him astray one last time, however, offering him $150 for the grand slam ball he caught. Richie considers the offer for a moment, but he throws it back onto the field, redeeming himself, as he and Decker walk off together.

While Marvin wins the bets, the bums have scored the moral victory. Even though they may have lost their money, their community remains intact. Before his final exit, Greg informs Marvin that if he's smart, he'll bet on the Cubs tomorrow because "they're gonna win. Cause they're mad now. And when they get mad they get up and go, huh? As a matter of fact they're not only gonna win tomorrow, but they're gonna take the rest of the series!" He continues, explaining to Marvin that the Cubs are going to win their division, then the National League championship, then go to the World Series, at which point "they're gonna bring Ernie Banks out of retirement and he's gonna hit a homerun right into my lap [and] they [will] win!" (Mantegna 78). Despite being on the losing end of the score this time, the Cubs and their fans will be back, united in the hope that they'll win it all another day.

While it has been adapted for film twice, in 1979 and 2002, *Bleacher Bums* is primarily known as a piece of theatre.[1] At first glance this may seem unusual, given the number of successful baseball films, as well as the inherent limitations of theatre; however, for a number of reasons, theatre is an entirely appropriate medium to replicate the experience of sitting in the bleachers at Wrigley Field. Theatrical performances, like a trip to the Friendly Confines, are largely dependent on the liveness of the event and the way that live experiences affect audience members.

In his book *Liveness*, Phil Auslander writes that "live performance has a worth that both transcends and resists market value. In this view, the value of live performance resides in its very resistance to the market and the media, the dominant culture they represent, and the regime of cultural production that supports them" (7). In this sense, a performance of *Bleacher Bums* offers up a subtextual correlation between the live experience of watching a game from the bleachers and attending a play.

As Auslander has posited, much of the cultural capital of attending a live performance, be it theatrical, musical, sporting, or whatever, "resides in its very resistance to the market and the media," and it would be difficult to imagine a physical location that has a more resistant image than Wrigley Field (7). Despite the creeping commercialization that has entered the Friendly Confines — ads have appeared on the garage doors along the outfield walls and inside the dugout, a capitalist invasion that represents a significant change from the once-solitary Torco Oil sign that sat across Sheffield for over 25 years ("At Play," par. 3) — the Cubs organization still goes to great lengths to position the park as a citadel of iconoclasm amongst the domed stadiums and "Ball Malls" of the world.

The rejection of technology and media is one of the elemental building blocks of theatre, particularly in twenty-first century America. People attend theatre because it's a change from the commercialized, mediatized material that they encounter on a daily basis. David McGimpsey argues that attending a play/ballgame/concert rejects the "official," mediatized version and "allow[s] the fan to contemplate the shape of the games at [her] personal leisure" (91). By attending an event, audience members are able to interpret it in whatever way they see fit, essentially co-creating their own meaning of the event. It's no secret that, to many fans, watching the game is only a small part of the "Wrigley Experience." This is roughly analogous to the Manhattan visitor who attends whatever Broadway musical he can get tickets to from the TKTS booth. He isn't there as much to watch a specific team/production as he is to accumulate some of Auslander's "cultural capital" through attendance. Interestingly, the element that attracts many of these fans is the event's scenography. Whether it's attending a game in an "historic stadium" or watching a crashing chandelier, visual spectacle is at the forefront of the attraction to the experience.

Ultimately the bleacher denizen and the theatre fan are after the same thing: to reject technology in order to have a more "authentic" experience where they can participate to some extent in the event. Auslander writes that attendance at a live performance "places us in the living presence of the performers, other human beings with whom we desire unity" (57). Whether it's sublime, as in knowing that an actor is feeling and responding to the energy created by an enthusiastic audience, or ridiculous, like Zig and Decker jeering the Cardinals' starting lineup, it is a phenomenon that can't be replicated and must be experienced firsthand. While one can certainly look at the modern "Bleacher Experience" critically, it's difficult to compare the bleachers evoked in the script to what have been christened, thanks to the corporate generosity of a St. Louis brewery, the "Budweiser Bleachers"; the Cubs organization and the media continue to imbue them with the cachet of "authenticity."

Perhaps the best way to interpret *Bleacher Bums* is by seeing it as a period piece — a play that represents a time when the ivy was greener, the beer was colder, and the Cubs were just one pitcher away from having a roster that would allow them to catch up to the Cards. The world of the bleachers depicted in *Bleacher Bums* is the idyllic, pastoral baseball of American's popular, collective memory. However, as is often the case with nostalgia, it creates a longing for a time that may have never really existed. But really, who wants to see a play about the real bleachers? Much like the way *The Sound of Music* makes its Nazis almost lovable and *Les Misérables* makes the French Revolution seem like a rollicking good time, *Bleacher Bums* forgoes presenting the reality of having some drunk from Kenosha spill his beer down your shirt in order to create a piece of true escapism that illustrates a uniquely American event: catching a day game at Wrigley.

At the dawn of the twenty-first century in the United States, sports are a "core culture industry" in that they play a central role in the development and expression of a civic identity (Spirou and Bennett 17). While one can certainly argue whether or not a trip to the modern Wrigley Field is an "authentic" ballpark experience, it is undeniable that, to paraphrase the Deadheads, there is nothing like a ballgame at Wrigley Field. Despite the fact that the world of the play is often in direct contrast to the current Tribune-owned state-of-the-Cubs, the spirits of the two are in synch. This is where a trip to Wrigley and a trip to the theatre converge — they are both uniquely live events that often inspire devoted fandom and, in the case of the Cubs, a unique quest for tomorrow's win.

NOTES

1. It is worth noting that the 2002 film version — originally produced for the Showtime cable network — did not receive the blessing of the Cubs or MLB, so the Bums in this film spend their time in an unnamed ballpark rooting for the Chicago Bruins.

WORKS CITED

"At Play in the Fields of Chicago: Wrigley: Chicago's Field of Dreams." 16 July 2007. <http://centerstage. net/stumped/Articles/wrigley.shtml>.

Auslander, Philip. *Liveness: Performance in a Mediatized Culture.* New York: Routledge, 1999.

Houlihan, Mary. "The 'Bums' of Summer." *Chicago Sun-Times* 16 Apr. 2004: 28.

Mantegna, Joe, et. al. *Bleacher Bums: Revised 1998 Version.* New York: Samuel French, Inc., 1999.

McGimpsey, David. *Imagining Baseball: America's Pastime and Popular Culture.* Bloomington, IN: Indiana UP, 2000.

"Organic Theater." 16 July 2007. <http://centerstage.net/theatre/whoswho/OrganicTheater.html>.

Rapoport, Ron. "Bleacher Bums Revival Remains True to History." *Chicago Sun-Times* 22 Apr. 2004: 127.

Senor, Thomas D. "Should Cubs Fans Be Committed? What Bleacher Bums Have to Teach Us about the Nature of Faith." *Baseball and Philosophy: Thinking Outside the Batter's Box.* Ed. Eric Thompson. Chicago: Open Court Publishing, 2004. 37–55.

Spirou, Costas, and Larry Bennett. *It's Hardly Sportin': Stadiums, Neighborhoods and the New Chicago.* DeKalb, IL: Northern Illinois UP, 2003.

Zwecker, Bill. "Play's Success Still Amazes Mantegna." *Chicago Sun-Times* 16 Apr. 2004: 29.

The Friendly Confines of Prose:
Chicago Cubs in Fiction

Tim Morris

The most notable thing about Chicago Cubs fiction is that there isn't much of it, and what there is isn't especially good. The Cubs are the oldest surviving professional baseball team (founded in 1876). They play in a storied, picturesque ballpark in one of the nation's largest and most literary cities. The Cubs can match most franchises for their past glory of sixteen pennants, though with the last of them coming in 1945, their glory is in the ever-remoter past. And especially now that recent championships for the Boston Red Sox and Chicago White Sox have redeemed those hapless clubs, the Cubs can beat any franchise for bittersweet despair. Such a history of remarkable highs and lows ought to have engendered a noble literary heritage.

Yet fiction writers simply haven't done the Cubs justice. Major league franchises best served by novelists include the Red Sox (Jerome Charyn's *Seventh Babe*, Henry Garfield's *Tartabull's Throw*), the Brooklyn Dodgers (Ring Lardner's *Lose with a Smile*, Donald Honig's *Plot to Kill Jackie Robinson*, John R. Tunis's juvenile series), and the New York Giants (Eric Rolfe Greenberg's *Celebrant*, Darryl Brock's *Havana Heat*). There is even some very good fiction about the Minnesota Twins, including Mick Cochrane's novel *Sport* and W.P. Kinsella's story "Diehard." The ranks of Cubs fiction provide nothing to rival any of these works.

The most celebrated of all big-league teams in prose fiction has certainly been the Chicago White Sox. Sox fans would probably be just as glad to surrender that distinction since so much of this fiction is about the 1919 team that threw the World Series to Cincinnati. But even aside from excellent Black Sox novels (including Brendan Boyd's *Blue Ruin*, Harry Stein's *Hoopla*, Peter Rutkoff's *Shadow Ball*, and Kinsella's *Shoeless Joe*), the White Sox literary tradition runs deep. Lardner's great Jack Keefe stories, collected in *You Know Me Al*, are set among the pre–1919 White Sox. John Manderino's *Man Who Once Played Catch with Nellie Fox* and James McManus's *Chin Music* are about the Sox of later seasons. James T. Farrell's *Baseball Diary* follows the Sox. Stuart Dybek, heir to Farrell as a chronicler of the South Side in short fiction, is a Sox fan and works Sox references into his stories.

It's bad enough that the far-younger White Sox have now won more world championships than the Cubs and that they beat the Cubs in their only head-to-head World Series. That the Sox have also completely dominated the City Series of Literature adds insult to injury.

Yet if we try to count up Cubs novels, we're forced to conclude that in quality and quantity alike, they come nowhere near Sox novels. The canon of Cubs novels includes two mediocre general novels. *Out at Home* (1985) by Gary Pomeranz is a pleasant but forgettable story of the 1950s Chicago demimonde, incidentally involving some Cubs. *About 80 Percent Luck* (2001) by Gene Wojciechowski is a strained farce about a journalist sentenced to the Cubs beat. There are three Cubs crime novels: two series novels, *Murder at Wrigley Field* (1996) by Troy Soos and *Murder in Wrigley Field* (1991) by Crabbe Evers, and a stand-alone: *Suicide Squeeze* (1991) by David Everson. There's also one Christian novel by an author of the *Left Behind* series: *Rookie* (1991) by Jerry B. Jenkins, in which a youth ballplayer becomes a Cubs star at the age of thirteen with help from the Lord. And ... and that's about it.

One would think that the Cubs would appear in more juvenile fiction than they do, as well, but the annals of children's books are oddly devoid of Cubs. One title worth brief mention is Fred Bowen's 1997 novel *Playoff Dreams*, which features a star player for an inept youth-league team called the Cubs. Young Brendan is despondent till his uncle Jack tells him about the career of Ernie Banks and suggests analogies to Brendan's own situation. Brendan starts clamoring to "play two today," which helps console him when he drops the fly ball that eliminates his Cubs from the playoffs. It's a curiously downbeat juvenile, but perhaps appropriate in its Cubness.

I don't want to discuss any of those novels further; the exercise would be purely academic. The best of them is Soos's *Murder at Wrigley Field*, but even that novel (like Evers's *Murder in*) uses Chicago merely as a convenient stop on its tour of major-league killing fields. The Great Cubs novel has yet to be written. What am I saying is that the *OK* Cubs novel has yet to be written.

Yet it is interesting, and might offer some hope to the faithful of the North Side, that the Chicago Cubs figure in some of the most highly regarded baseball novels. The Cubs get a reference in Bernard Malamud's archetypal novel *The Natural* (1952) and are summoned up supernaturally in Kinsella's *Shoeless Joe* (1982). They serve an important function in Greenberg's *Celebrant* (1983), and they show up for the biggest of Big Games in Kinsella's *Iowa Baseball Confederacy* (1986).

Roy Hobbs begins *The Natural* with the earnest assertion: "I'm going to Chicago, where the Cubs are" (5). Of course, he never gets there. He gets as far as the Stevens Hotel, with his Cubs tryout scheduled for the next day. And then Harriet Bird shoots him, sending Roy into the annals of Grail myth rather than into the pages of the Cubs press guide.

But it's a *mention*, at least. And the Cubs get significantly more than a mention in *The Celebrant*, Greenberg's evocation of Christy Mathewson and the early twentieth-century New York Giants. For much of Mathewson's career, the Cubs were an important league rival of the Giants. Their turn in *The Celebrant* comes largely in a single episode from the 1908 season, the infamous Merkle game. When young Giants baserunner Fred Merkle neglected to reach second base after the winning hit, the Cubs appealed the play. Merkle was called out and the game ruled a tie. The Cubs won the replay and the pennant.

Greenberg's depiction of the Merkle game is one of the finest episodes in baseball literature, but of course the Cubs figure in it only as the other guys. *The Celebrant* is as much a recreation of New York City as it is of baseball. The Cubs just happen to have been the Giants' historical opponent in the 1908 stretch drive. There's no particular "Cubness" to the Merkle game; Pirates or Dodgers would have worked equally well had they fit the historical facts.

(The Cubs as opponents of a more famous team figure also in Gordon McAlpine's underrated novel *Joy in Mudville*, published in 1989. The central conceit of McAlpine's book is that Babe Ruth's "called shot" home run in the 1932 World Series leaves Wrigley Field and fails to return to earth, crossing the continent in a westward path, followed by acolytes much as the Magi followed the Star of Bethlehem. *Joy in Mudville* is only an honorary Cubs novel, though it is a good one.)

The Cubs loom larger in the fiction of W.P. Kinsella. A Canadian writer long associated with Iowa, Kinsella writes about sandlot and minor-league teams, Canadian and Caribbean teams, Pirates and Yankees and Twins and Mariners. Yet his adoptive Midwesternness leads Kinsella to feature the Black Sox in *Shoeless Joe* and the Cubs in *The Iowa Baseball Confederacy*. In the latter novel, at last, the choice of Cubs is not entirely arbitrary. They provide more than a mere touchstone, if something less than a central theme.

In *The Iowa Baseball Confederacy*, the Cubs are still opponents, not protagonists. The title league assembles an all-star team to play the 1908 Cubs in a Fourth of July exhibition game in Big Inning, Iowa. The game lasts forty days and takes up half the novel, so the Cubs get plenty of time onstage.

The game between the Cubs and the Confederacy is embedded in the larger narrative of Gideon Clarke, who tells the story in the year 1978. Gideon is the only surviving person who knows anything about the Iowa Baseball Confederacy. Until killed by a foul ball at a Milwaukee Braves game, Gideon's father Matthew Clarke had been the only person with knowledge of the Confederacy; Matthew's death transferred that knowledge into Gideon's mind. Obsessed with proving that the Confederacy existed, Gideon finds a rift in time and travels back to 1908, where he serves as mascot and occasional sacrificial pinch-hitter for the Confederacy stars as they battle Chicago to a tie for 2,614 innings.

Why the Cubs? They are relatively local. Kinsella includes the Cubs because they are near Iowa, not the other way round. Why 1908? It was a great season. The Cubs had won their first World Series in 1907, and would win their last in 1908, after tying the Merkle game. (The Merkle game, as noted in *The Celebrant*, is arguably still going on, since the final out was never actually made. The parallel to the Confederacy game, which threatens to become unending as well, is appropriate.)

The Cubs had been even better in 1906, compiling one of the greatest won-lost records of all time (116–36), but Kinsella avoids the 1906 season for two reasons: first, it would place the novel's "present"—carefully spaced three-score-and-ten years after the date of its Big Game—in the bicentennial year of 1976, risking symbolic overload. Second, 1906 was the year the Cubs lost the World Series to the White Sox.

The 1908 Chicago Cubs featured Joe Tinker, Johnny Evers, and Frank Chance, the double-play combination immortalized in doggerel by Franklin P. Adams. In a nod to Adams, Kinsella describes a double play that the trio turn on the tenth day of play: "Evers's foot brushes the bag softly, like a bird landing on a bush without disturbing the foliage, and, launching himself in the air, Evers fires to first ..." (*Iowa* 213–14). That's the most elaborate description of Evers in *The Iowa Baseball Confederacy*. Joe Tinker gets a little more exposure. He chats with Gideon at one point, extolling the meritocracy of baseball: "The Bigs are one of the only places where an uneducated farm boy can be a hero, win praise from tens of thousands of people" (*Iowa* 228). The fictional Tinker's observation is interesting, but generic.

The most fully realized Cub in Kinsella's *Iowa* is manager Frank Chance. When the game against the Confederacy stars is tied at the end of seven innings, Iowa captain Arsenic O'Reilly is happy to call it a draw. "Like hell," growls Chance. "Game ain't decided. We play extra innings" (*Iowa* 158). In real life, Frank Chance was one of the more combative managers in the major leagues. In *The Iowa Baseball Confederacy*, his obduracy quickly goes beyond realism to become figurally fraught. Chance alone speaks for the Cubs—they have no other voice, and none of them dream of demurring. After a couple of days, Chance sends the Cubs reserves home to play out the National League schedule while the famous starting nine stay in Iowa, playing the game that will not end.

When Cubs management orders Chance back to Chicago in a flurry of importunate messages, Chance matches them telegram for telegram. "WILL STAY UNTIL GAME DECIDED STOP CHANCE," he wires, and then again "WILL STAY UNTIL GAME DECIDED STOP DO YOUR WORST STOP CHANCE" *(Iowa* 205). Kinsella plays with the manager's accidental name. Neither the Iowa team nor the umpires initially want the game to continue into magical-realist interminability. Undaunted, Chance alone insists that the game continue, and, increasingly stripped of his given name and his human attributes, he keeps the game in motion. The Cubs immortal is condensed into one-note symbolism, verging on intolerable allegory.

As the Iowa Confederacy game goes on and on, giving the 1908 Chicago Cubs their longest exposure on the field of baseball literature, they are reduced to a sketch of Tinker, a suggestion of Evers, and the insistent, fortuitous surname of Chance. These are still the "real" '08 Cubs; Kinsella presents them accurately in every selected detail. But on one level it doesn't matter who they are historically or culturally. It only matters that the Cubs provide an appropriate foil for the elaborate signifying structures that Kinsella weaves around Iowa, Gideon's trumpet, the enormous spectral Indian Drifting Away, Theodore Roosevelt, and Leonardo da Vinci in a hot-air balloon.

Moreover, Kinsella does not give us the 1908 Cubs in Chicago. We never see Wrigley Field, of course, because it would not be built for another six years, but we never see the West Side Grounds, the Cubs' 1908 home park, either. We never see Chicago in the novel, which is set entirely in its parallel Iowan universes. And when you come right down to it, as much as Kinsella loves Iowa, he loves unreality even more.

It is fitting, then, that Kinsella's most memorable Cub is Eddie Scissons. "The Oldest Living Chicago Cub," Scissons is the title character of his own chapter in *Shoeless Joe.* Eddie features in the plot of *Shoeless Joe* as the character who sells Ray Kinsella the farm on which Ray will build his spectral ballfield. In addition to this inciting event, Eddie comes during the novel's second half to embody its most important themes. Ultimately Eddie Scissons is the most important character in *Shoeless Joe* aside from Ray himself. That would make Eddie the most important Chicago Cub in literature, except of course that Eddie never played for the Cubs.

Eddie Scissons is omitted from the film *Field of Dreams* (1989) because his complicated story parallels that of Moonlight Graham, another long-retired player whose motives are simpler. Graham, an actual player who barely took the field as a member of the 1905 New York Giants, is drawn to Ray's haven for ghostly ballplayers so that he can finally take his unrealized first big-league at-bat. Eddie Scissons also gets to play in Ray's converted cornfield, but in Eddie's case this is the culmination not of a long-deferred opportunity but of a lifelong fabrication.

The first time that Ray Kinsella meets Eddie Scissons on the street in Iowa City, he asks Ray the time, and then out of the blue says, "I used to play for the Chicago Cubs, you know?" *(Shoeless* 116). Eddie claims to be an obscure, little-used relief pitcher for the great Cubs teams of the 1908–10 era.

Eddie's claim finds a willing listener. Ray is enchanted with the notion that he has met and befriended "the oldest living Chicago Cub." As soon as Ray (not Eddie himself) introduces that phrase *(Shoeless* 117), it's apparent that the Cubs have at last found a distinctive place in the fiction of baseball. This scene is both difficult to unpack and emotionally unerring; it's very moving for Ray (and the reader) to meet the oldest living Chicago Cub. It might not be moving or even interesting to meet the oldest living Boston Brave or Philadelphia Philly.

It's even more appropriate that Eddie is not the oldest living Cub after all. Though he claims to belong to a rich community of former Cubs, to keep in touch with the son of Heinie Zimmerman and the grandson of Wildfire Schulte (*Shoeless* 125), Eddie is not the oldest Cub; he is at best the oldest veteran of a Class D league in Montana. Ray, though he takes Eddie's story to heart, never believes it with his head. Like any good fan, he immediately looks for Eddie's record in a baseball encyclopedia and finds it non-existent. Ray does not tell the reader about his discovery for 100 pages, but in any event, the reader has the same recourse. Moonlight Graham is in all the real-life encyclopedias; Eddie Scissons is in none of them.

The cryptic nature of Eddie Scissons presents some intriguing metafictional issues. Moonlight Graham is as "real" as J.D. Salinger or Eddie Cicotte, even though Kinsella's Graham is a fantasia on the bare facts of the real Graham's biography. With the novelist's license to create reality from whole cloth, Kinsella could just as easily invent a "real" oldest living Cub as he has invented the "real" Ray and Annie Kinsella. Indeed, readers who look up Eddie midway through *Shoeless Joe* might assume that Kinsella has done just that. Instead, Kinsella uses fictional license to create a "real" fraud.

Eddie looms larger in *Shoeless Joe* than Moonlight Graham does because the process of weaving a fictional world is more important to W.P. Kinsella than the process of chronicling the real one. Eddie is not humiliated in the novel, though Ray's brother-in-law Mark, one of the story's blocking characters, tries to humiliate him by unmasking Eddie's fraudulence (*Shoeless* 216). Precisely because Eddie is revealed as a fraud, though, he then gets a chance to pitch for the 1908 Cubs against the 1919 White Sox on Ray's otherworldly field. The Sox air out his pitches, but he achieves his dream: "It takes more than an infinite ERA to shake my faith" (*Shoeless* 230).

Eddie Scissons dies shortly after pitching against the White Sox. At his funeral, Ray has

> the feeling that if I were to go to Iowa City tomorrow, go to the public library or the university library, find the reference section, and pick up a copy of the *Baseball Encyclopedia* and turn to page 2006, I would find right at the bottom of the page [...] the details of Eddie's three seasons as a relief pitcher for the Cubs: his won-and-lost record, number of innings pitched, ERA, strikeouts, bases on balls, and batting record. I have the feeling. I have the feeling [*Shoeless* 237].

Eddie Scissons has lived a lie, not passively but flamboyantly. His one attempt to pitch against major-league competition is a disaster, even with a great lineup behind him. Yet in *Shoeless Joe*, Eddie emerges triumphant. Because of his fervent, self-deluding belief, he is redeemed.

Kinsella's world is hardly without moral compass. There are clear villains in Iowa, especially brother-in-law Mark and his predatory accomplice Bluestein, who keep trying to muscle in on Ray's farm and his ballfield. But their crimes are crimes of disbelief, crimes of which Eddie and Ray are innocent. It's an easy step from the patient will to believe in *Shoeless Joe*, exemplified by Eddie Scissons, to the legendary patience of Cubs fans.

Or, one might say, for Kinsella as for the denizens of Wrigleyville, ignoring reality is the paramount virtue. A subsequent short story by Kinsella, "The Eddie Scissons Syndrome," explores the phenomenon, prevalent as well in real life, of people, usually older men, who claim to have played professional ball (or worked at other glamorous occupations) in their youth. The Syndrome afflicted Democratic Presidential hopeful Bill Richardson in 2005, when Richardson was forced to admit that, contrary to his own publicity materials, he had never been drafted by the Kansas City Athletics. Within baseball, the malady claimed Toronto manager Tim Johnson, who had undeniably played in the major leagues but felt compelled to fabricate a past as a Vietnam War hero as well.

Such duplicity is routinely savaged in real-life media. In *Shoeless Joe*, however, Eddie Scissons syndrome in its type specimen is equivalent to baseball sainthood. Belief is everything. Believe strongly enough and you will be vindicated, precisely because you have resisted the power of fact so tenaciously.

I suspect that Cubs fans would still rather see another pennant fly over Sheffield Avenue than be buried in uniform after pitching an imaginary inning in Iowa. But W.P. Kinsella catches a wryness in the Cubs fan experience that rings true. If, as in the title of one of his minor short stories, the next pennant that the Cubs win will be "The Last Pennant Before Armageddon," the secular despair of such a promise is amply offset by a chiliastic faith in an era of bliss to follow. The Cubs are battered in Eddie Scissons's outing. They eventually lose the Confederacy game in Big Inning. But as Bob Dylan noted, the loser now will be later to win.

No writer distilled more pleasure from the exasperations of Cubness than Chicago journalist Mike Royko. While not a novelist or short-story writer, Royko created several quasi-fictional personae in over thirty years of columns for the Chicago *Daily News*, *Sun-Times*, and *Tribune*. His garrulous drinking buddy Slats Grobnik was the best-known Royko creation, but no less intriguing a fictional device was Royko himself, frequently appearing as a depressive Cubs fan. More than anyone else in the late twentieth century, Royko personified to the city and the nation an acid-etched facetiousness which came to be the semi-official identity of Cubdom.

Royko reports becoming a Cubs fan at the age of six, on Opening Day in 1939, when his father took him to Wrigley Field: "I couldn't believe anything could be that big and magnificent. To this day, I still have a trace of that awe whenever I see it. Of course the awe dissipates when I see the players ("A Pitch for Opening Day" 57). Unlike Kinsella, whose occasional bleakness is always subordinate to the sublime in baseball, Royko carefully undermines any tendency toward sublimity. Such a rhetorical stance allows Royko to rhapsodize while disowning his own rhapsody.

In Royko's world there are two constants: the Cubs will flounder and their fans will suffer. In fact, it seems to matter little to Royko whether the Cubs are actually occasionally good or not. Unlike the Boston Red Sox, who have made a habit of excruciating near-misses, the Cubs for most of Royko's lifetime were outright bad, and for Royko that badness becomes their quintessence, even when they win a division title here and there.

Royko popularized Boston writer Ron Berler's theory of the ex-Cub Factor, which states that a team fielding three former Cubs is incapable of winning the World Series. In modified form, the principle simply says that the team with fewer ex-Cubs is destined to win a play-off series. In Royko's Chicago, players arrive on the Cubs roster and become imbrued with a stain of underachievement:

Royko traces the roots of Cub futility to the postwar strategy of owner Philip K. Wrigley:

In 1945, with World War II still raging, the Cubs won a pennant with a team made up of some 4-Fs. When the war ended, P.K. Wrigley, the Cub owner, apparently reasoned that the way to win a championship was with 4-Fs. So while other teams began putting healthy athletes on the field, Wrigley continued hiring players who walked funny and had strange physical infirmities ["A Pitch for Opening Day" 58].

That's Royko writing in 1979. He would retell the story of Wrigley's 4-Fs in a 1988 column on the installation of lights at Wrigley Field ("Cubs Park Wasn't Always Like This" 197). In fact, the last column that Royko wrote, in 1997, blames Wrigley for hiring "older and more enfeebled" players in the 1940s and then for being slow to integrate the club in the 1950s, dooming it to more futility ("It Was Wrigley, Not Some Goat, Who Cursed the Cubs" 274–75). Another famous Royko column expresses his youthful anguish at seeing Jackie Robinson spiked by a Cub in the great Dodger's first appearance at Wrigley Field ("Jackie's Debut a Unique Day" 70).

For Royko, as for many Chicagoans, the Cubs' home field is always "Cubs Park." He sniffs that "true fans seldom called it Wrigley Field" ("Cubs Park" 196), not just because it had been known briefly by that name before Wrigley's acquisition of the team but probably too because of Royko's animus against Wrigley. It isn't hard to see the deep-seated disillusion of Royko's youth in his continual slating of Wrigley's ownership. Royko was thirteen years old on Opening Day in 1946, ready to watch the defending National League Champion Cubs win the pennant and redeem themselves from their 1945 World Series loss. He would go to his grave without seeing the Cubs in another Series.

Royko's bitterness and nostalgia are perhaps best balanced in his August 1988 column on the inaugural night games at Cubs Park. He starts the piece by remembering a game-day ritual from the 1940s:

> The kid brother and I would leave the family flat at about 8 o'clock in the morning and start walking the five miles from Milwaukee Avenue and Armitage to Cubs Park. [...] We always got there early enough so that we'd be up front and chosen by The Man. [...] Then we'd start work. It was an easy enough job. In those days, the box seats had folding chairs that had to be set up and put in place. That was our job. And our pay was free admission to the ballpark, with our choice of grandstand seats ["Cubs Park" 196–97].

The actual Cubs of the era, Royko remembers, were of course not much good: Eddie Waitkus, Johnny Schmitz, and Roy Smalley, whom Royko once recalled as "the only shortstop in baseball who had a deformed hand" ("A Pitch" 58). But a session of unfolding chairs bought a batting-practice glimpse of visiting heroes like Johnny Mize, Stan Musial, or Jackie Robinson.

Most precious of all was a sense that the park and the team and the day belonged to a small band of believers. "I remember being in the ballpark when there were only about 800 people, including the vendors," says Royko ("Cubs Park" 198). In 1988, by contrast, Royko scarcely recognizes the old yard, and not just because of the lights. The Cubs are now selling out (in both senses).[1] Tickets to the Cubs' home night debut are being scalped for $1,000 apiece, "the same seats that I used to sit in for unfolding a few chairs" ("Cubs Park" 197). Royko's column ends in a bath of venom:

> Yes, it is a new era. The only thing that remains the same is that the team stunk then and the team stinks now. And the biggest difference isn't the lights. It's that in those bygone days, nobody was stupid enough to pay a grand to watch a bunch of losers ["Cubs Park" 198].

The close of this column could be dismissed as the rant of an aging cynic, except that the experience of getting into the park as the wages for unfolding the box-seat chairs was not presented, earlier in the piece, as a cynical assessment of the value of seeing the 1947 Cubs. In fact, the persona of Royko as embittered curmudgeon is held in suspension with the persona of Royko as a spellbound kid. They're two aspects of the same person; the writing gains its power from melding both together.

In the works of Royko and Kinsella, the two best writers to attempt extended prose reflection on the nature of Cubs and their fandom, we see frustration as the inevitable alter ego of enchantment. We see humiliating failure redeemed as magical success. For Cubs fans, there's no other way to love the team and retain one's peace of mind at the same time.

NOTE

1. In point of fact, the late-1980s Cubs averaged only about 25,000 fans per game, and the postwar Cubs about 17,000; the difference is greatly magnified in Royko's memory. The great trough in Cubs attendance occurred in the truly hopeless years of the late 1950s and early 60s, and the current phenomenal packing of Wrigley Field postdates Sammy Sosa's great year in 1998. See "Chicago Cubs Attendance" at Baseball-Reference.

WORKS CITED

Bowen, Fred. *Playoff Dreams*. Illus. by Ann Barrow. Atlanta: Peachtree, 1997.

"Chicago Cubs Attendance, Stadiums and Park Factors." Baseball-Reference. 22 Mar. 2006. <http://www.baseball-reference.com/teams/CHC/attend.shtml>.

Kinsella, W.P. *The Iowa Baseball Confederacy*. 1986. Boston: Houghton Mifflin, 2003.

_____. *Shoeless Joe*. 1982. Boston: Houghton Mifflin, 1999.

Malamud, Bernard. *The Natural*. New York: Farrar, 1952.

Royko, Mike. "Cubs Park Wasn't Always Like This." *Chicago Tribune* 9 Aug. 1988. Rptd. *One More Time*. Chicago: U of Chicago P, 1999. 96–198.

_____. "It Was Wrigley, Not Some Goat, Who Cursed the Cubs." *Chicago Tribune* 21 Mar. 1997. Rptd. *One More Time*. Chicago: U of Chicago P, 1999. 273–75.

_____. "Jackie's Debut a Unique Day." *Chicago Daily News* 25 Oct. 1972. Rprtd. *One More Time*. Chicago: U of Chicago P, 1999. 68–70.

_____. "A Pitch for Opening Day." *Chicago Sun-Times* 5 Apr. 1979. Rptd. *Like I Was Sayin'....* New York: Dutton, 1984. 56–59.

The Voices of Cubs Broadcasters

Curt Smith

Radio baseball began August 5, 1921, over America's first station, KDKA Pittsburgh (Smith, *Voices of Game* 6). Its real cradle, though, was the town that won't let you down — especially its teddy bear of a north side park. Chicago's first radio game was April 13, 1924 — Cubs 12, Cardinals 1 — on WMAQ, the first outlet to do a whole big-league home schedule (12). Team owner Philip Wrigley had wanted a jock-turned-Voice. "When Solly Hoffman bombed, I volunteered," said Hal Totten. "What a great way to see games free" (Newman 10C). And Totten, a stringer for the Chicago *Journal* and *Daily News*, painted the homey picture for his audiences: Wrigley Field's bleachers, nearby L tracks, drop-dead closeness, and animal-cracker size. In 1926, Totten added the White Sox, who even then were Avis to the Cubbies' Hertz (*Who's Who in Major League Baseball* 514).

In those days stations eyed listeners, not rights. "Forget sponsors," Totten said. "Nobody paid to carry games" ("Hal Totten" 54). By 1929, five outlets aired the Cubs and Sox, including WJKS's Johnny O'Hara, WGN's Bob Elson and Quin Ryan, and WBBM's Pat Flanagan and Truman Bradley. "Phil Wrigley made Chicago radio baseball's Mecca. 'With enough stations, we'll own the city,'" Totten asserted (Smith, *Voices of Game* 14). But he was a bit late; already Wrigley had control. Papa Cub lowered the field, built a hand-operated scoreboard, and double-decked the grandstand: ergo, the Friendly Confines. Even friendlier were four flags from 1929–38. Not so the White Sox. As Totten remembered, the Sox had the appropriate name; in Hal's words, the *Pale* in Pale Hose was "a synonym for their fans. They didn't expect notice, and didn't get it" (Smith, *Voices of Summer* 11).

But they did get the first All-Star Game at Comiskey Park in 1933. And Totten was there to interview its apotheosis — Babe Ruth. "We're ducking pre-game fouls, and Babe's getting the raspberry from Sox fans, who hated his Yanks," Totten explained to his listeners. Once the game began, Ruth homered, made a diving catch, and led a 4–2 A.L. victory. But the Cubs fans could quickly take solace in the words of Hal Totten. Next day, back at Addison and Clark, Totten orally etched how the fielder crouched, batter cocked, and pitcher draped against the stands — above all, surety that there was no place on earth that you would rather be. In 1934, the two teams dealt WMAQ for NBC's "Blue Network," WCFL. "It was a stronger station," Totten said. "I could do road trips and hire a No. 2. Before I'd done it by myself — no relief or sponsor" (Newman 10C).

On all the stations, the audiences liked the voice, high and gentle, signing off "g'bye now," and hearing Totten's "foot on the slab" and "funny little hop." He was a "pretty husky fellow," said fellow broadcaster Bob Elson, "not flashy, just baseball like it was" (Smith, *Voices of Summer* 11). Ultimately, Totten aired twelve network Series, tying Elson and Graham

McNamee, then generally considered the greatest Voice in the Republic. In 1944, the Federal Communications Commission made NBC sell a network ("Blue" became ABC) and WCFL, kicking Totten off the air — and sending the Cubs to WIND.

Next year Bing Crosby played Father Flanagan in the film *Boys Town* (Smith, *Voices of Summer* 13). By then that surname was well known to Cubs fans, for they had been putting their faith in Pat Flanagan from 1929–43. "One of those unique gifts," Charles Carroll Flanagan called the nickname "Pat" (13). Other gifts included a breezy voice, can-do knack, and blueprint of a mind. Pat Flanagan grew up in Iowa, fought in World War I, practiced chiropractic at Palmer School in Davenport, and taught philosophy on its station. Arriving in Chicago, he found only home games broadcast. "Stations didn't do the road because line charges were expensive" (Wilson 20). Problem: How to air baseball without *being* at the park? Answer: Western Union's Simplex telegraphy machine, "[giving] play-by-play," wrote *The Sporting News*, "within three seconds of the time it occurs" (qtd. in Wilson 20). An operator sent Morse code to the station. B1L meant ball one, low. Eureka! A Voice could etch play he never saw. Flanagan used Simplex for a Cubs game from Cincinnati and petitioned his listeners, "If you want these out-of-town games regularly, write and tell us," he said (Smith, *Voices of Summer* 13). Next day 9,000 listeners responded in the affirmative.

In Flanagan's first-year the Wrigleys won the 1929 pennant. On the radio the Series pitted CBS's Flanagan versus NBC's McNamee. Up 2 games to 1, Chicago led game four by a score of 8–0. "In the seventh, the [Philadelphia] A's suddenly score ten runs," said Flanagan (Smith, *Voices of Summer* 13). For Cubs fans that half-inning lives in infamy through the words of Pat Flanagan. When Mule Haas flew to center, Hack Wilson felt the drive was a can of corn. "He's over, getting under it," said Flanagan. "Wait, it looks like Hack's lost it [in the sun]! He has ... the ball falls! [Joe] Boley scores, and Max Bishop! And here comes Haas. An inside-the-park homer!" The inning whipsawed the fall classic, Philly winning that day 10–8. The result was even sadder, as Flanagan explained, because Chicago had come to *expect* a National League flag every third year: "an itch," said Flanagan, "like clockwork" (13).

In 1938 Flanagan salved his last three-year itch. On September 28, Chicago trailed Pittsburgh by half a game. Inning nine began tied. "It's dusk, Wrigley had no lights," said Flanagan. "The ump said game's over if no one scores this inning." The Bucs and the first two Cubs went meekly. Gabby Hartnett faced Mace Brown. "This is it. The Cubs have to score. A long drive to deep left-center! Gone! Gone! Cubs win!" (Smith, *Voices of Summer* 14). Such was the "Homer in the Gloamin'" as described by Pat Flanagan. Clinching October 1, The City of Big Shoulders then shouldered another blow. Like 1932, the Yankees swept the Series. Flanagan spoke about 30,000 words in a typical nine-inning game. On an admirer's "word-meter" that's 240 words per minute (Wilson 20). But even with Pat Flanagan's magical, rapid-fire descriptions, the Cubs' regular clock stopped after 1929–32–35–38.

By 1935, four Des Moines outlets aired the Cubs. "Most did games live from Wrigley," said WHO's Ronald Reagan. "Through re-creations, I could do them from hundreds of miles away" (Boswell 1). One day the wire stopped. Reagan considered returning to the station but then "thought, no, if we put music on people'll turn to another station doing it in person." What to do? Make a big to-do (Broeg 11). "Fouls don't make the box score, so for seven minutes I had Billy Jurges set a record." Cardinals pitcher Dizzy Dean mopped his brow, tied a shoe, used the resin bag. Rain neared. A fight began. "It was fake, but at home seemed real." The wire finally revived. "Jurges popped out on first ball pitched" (Smith, *Storied Stadiums* 165). In 1937, Reagan left for Hollywood.

Today, devoted Cubs fans recall other early Cubs announcers. From 1927–33, Johnny O'Hara did Chicago's N.L. and A.L. teams and daily 5:00 P.M. talk show. "Al Capone gets paid by the bullet," he told an audience. "How come I can't get paid by the word?" ("Johnny O'Hara" 24). Before Jimmy Dudley called the 1948–67 Indians, Hal Totten used him as a gopher during the 1930s. Another master of the re-creation, Russ Hodges called Cubs baseball, boxing, and Big Ten football. As he remembered, "Re-creations! For three years I didn't see a park" (Smith, *Voices of Summer* 61). And then there was Bob Elson. Once a member of Chicago's famed Paulist Chorister Choir at nine years of age, Bob's entry into broadcasting was remarkable. While visiting pool whiz Willie Hoppe in 1928, Elson, then in his early 20s, was staying at St. Louis' Chase Hotel (Spink 24). Its top floor housed KWK, which Elson toured past, finding hopefuls in line. "You're the last today [for an audition]," a woman misinterpreted. Elson's career took a carom shot (Condon, "Elson a Celebrity" 1).

Elson read a script, was picked by listeners, and was contacted next day by wowed WGN executives. At the station he did everything from news to organ music. But he also become the seminal personality in pre-war baseball radio, covering both the Cubs and White Sox between 1929–41 and later the Sox from 1946–70 (Sons 112). Reminiscing about his early career, Elson said, "I was close to [Commissioner] Kenesaw Landis, who made assignments. He'd bellow, 'Don't mention any movie stars attending the World Series even if they slide into second base'" (Craig 40). Elson's first Series was 1930, the same year he quizzed Connie Mack in the "[f]irst interview on the field. Judge Landis said it was OK to run a wire from the booth. At first players were antsy. Before long they got the swing" (40). Elson also covered the 1932 series when Babe Ruth did/did not prophesy his homer. And in 1935 he joined Quin Ryan and Red Barber at Mutual Broadcasting's first fall classic. In 1939 multiple coverage came to an end when the Gillette Company gave the World Series exclusive coverage to Barber and the soon-to-be The Old Commander (a name Elson was given for his attachment to the U.S. Great Lakes Naval Training Center between 1942 and 1945).

"There was an excitement to him," Jack Brickhouse said. "His voice cut through the air." Brickhouse reddened. "If Bob had lived in New York, he'd have been the first inducted into the Hall of Fame [Ford C. Frick Award for broadcast excellence]." Elson was actually

Bob Elson, the voice of the Cubs (and White Sox) on pre–World War II Chicago radio (courtesy Baseball Hall of Fame).

third, in 1979. Brickhouse asked a recount, even then (Condon, "Bob Elson" 1). "You're like shit," Ralph Houk once told Howard Cosell. "You're everywhere." Neither Cosell nor shit, Elson was nevertheless everywhere. He read ads, hyped bands, and interviewed actors, singers, and politicos from the Chicago Theater, the Pump Room (Ambassador East Hotel), and "Twentieth Century Limited" (LaSalle Street Station) (Smith, *Voices of Summer* 18).

In 1946, Elson returned from war to find a WINDer blowing for the Cubs. Born in Ohio, Bert Wilson moved to Cedar Rapids, played the trumpet, and entered the University of Iowa. At 20, he junked engineering for commercial radio (Smith, *Voices of Game* 89). By 1943, Wilson, 32, did hockey, hoops, roller derby, Iowa football, Indianapolis 500, and Double-A baseball. When Pat Flanagan needed an aide, an ex-sponsor suggested that Wilson audition. "Despite laryngitis," WIND gusted, "he managed to talk his way in." Daily Bert Wilson watched charters deposit pilgrims from the outposts to Wrigleyville. Ivy cloaked the outfield wall. The scoreboard boasted line scores, lineups, and yardarm flags of N.L. cities and standings. Said Wilson: "I don't care *who* wins as long as it's the Cubs!" (90).

To Brickhouse, Wilson "was a souped-up Elson." The Midwest Cheering School of Milo Hamilton, Jack Quinlan, Harry Caray, and Vince Lloyd, among others, began with Bert Wilson's call letters: IDCW2ALAITC. When, in his first year, the Cubs began 1–13, Wilson said he "almost went back to my trumpet" (Smith, *Voices of Summer* 54). Instead, in 1945, MVP Phil Cavarretta hit a league-high .355, Andy Pafko had 110 RBI, and the Cubs won a pennant. "At the team victory party," James Enright wrote, "[manager] Charlie Grimm had a pair of shears. Everybody who had a necktie on contributed. He had a quilt made" (54). Soon its fabric, like Grimm's Fairy Tale, tore. "It was just a tease," a writer dubbed the '45 World Series versus Detroit. "You knew we'd lose Game Seven." When the team lost consistently for the next decade, Bert Wilson vowed, "We'll light a candle, not curse the dark" (55).

His eternal flame wafted from the Kansas City Monarchs: Ernie Banks, homering for the first time on September 20, 1953. The Cubs' future two-time MVP hit 290 of his 512 homers at Wrigley. "He's the real McCoy," Wilson correctly predicted in 1954 (Smith, *Voices of Summer* 55). But his enthusiasm for the Cubs also gave Wilson benign illusions: "I've had a good chance to see all the promising young rookies who'll be fighting for a job this summer, and believe me, they look great," he claimed one day the following March (55). Then he gushed, "The Cubs' infield [...] is recognized as one of the best in the big leagues already, and there are several outfielders who look like real major leaguers [....] The catching department was given a big boost when Harry Chiti [who would hit .231], a fellow built like Gabby Hartnett [and played like Gabby Hayes], came back from the service. Yes, it looks like a very interesting season for the Chicago Cubs this year" (Smith, *Voices of Game* 94). This "one of the best [...] real major leaguers [...] very interesting" team finished 72–81. It also was the last year for the man business manager Jim Gallagher termed "the biggest Cubs fan I've ever known" (94–95). Bert Wilson's heart stopped beating on November 5, 1955. IDCW2ALAITC was 44 years old.

That January Brickhouse turned 39. As a teenager Brickhouse had played basketball, was a newspaper boy, and "tried to cover a lack of sports knowledge with slang." At 18, he "got a [local broadcast] job as a $17-a-week spare announcer" (Smith, *Voices of Summer* 81). Off-duty, Brickhouse tuned to the master of the day. "Elson got us identifying with baseball," he explained (Smith, *Voices of Game* 171). Brickhouse did the news, called the Three-I League, and got a 1940 telegram: "Expect call from WGN as a staff announcer and sports assistant. Remember, if asked, you know all about baseball. Best of luck, Bob Elson." Hired, he introduced Les Brown's band, became Kay Kyser's Voice, and "had to fight the urge to imitate Bob" (172). In 1942, it was Jack Brickhouse who replaced the Navy-bound Commander.

"I didn't like that sophisticated approach of New York," he mused. "People call me gee-whiz! I've never seen a mirror that doesn't smile back if you smile first" (Smith, *Voices of Summer* 81). But he couldn't have been smiling when, unforeseen by Cubs fans, WGN axed baseball after 1943: "Mutual was the parent, and day games killed profitable kiddie shows" (81). So Brickhouse moved to WJJD, where he darned the 1944 White Sox. A year later he would have knit a sweater to call the Cubs when they returned to the World Series against the Tigers. "The last weekend Bert's berserk, and I'm doing the Sox by ticker tape," said Brickhouse (Smith, *Voices of Game* 173). In 1946, when the Commander returned, Brickhouse was booted temporarily to New York. But the next year he returned to Chicago, the home of 1 in 10 U.S. TV sets. Two years later pioneering WGN Channel 9 contracted to telecast each Sox and Cubs home game, *live*. "It worked," said Brickhouse, "because they weren't home at the same time." Daytime helped the Cubs, he remembered: "Wrigley had no lights, so kids got home from school, had a sandwich, and turned TV on," making many of them "life-long kids" who supported the Cubs (173).

Like Elson, Brickhouse was, it seemed, everywhere. And he was involved in many firsts at the station: TV daily Voice (180 games yearly); WGN mikeman (boxing, Chicago Stadium); and center-field camera shot (1951). As he explains for historians of Wrigley and television,

"A guy at a schoolboy game saw the scoreboard and thought, 'A camera there'd show the hitter and pitcher'" (Smith, *Voices of Summer* 82). Everyone envied Hey-Hey!'s energy. He did fires, conventions, inaugural parades, a one-on-one with seven U.S. Presidents, sports from golf to football, four World Series, five All-Star Games, and an audience with Leo Durocher and Pope Paul VI—alas, a writer said, not simultaneously. "Name it, I did it," Jack quipped; he was too busy to be tired (82). Above all, Brickhouse understood the Cubs fan, who he correctly identified as "born so that he can suffer."

In 1942, Lou Novikoff—a.k.a. "The Mad Russian"—hit to right-center field. A runner rounded third base, held up, and returned. Head down, Novikoff slid into third. "Where the hell ya' going?" said now-coach Grimm. "Back to second," said Lou, rising, "if I can make it" (Smith, *Storied*

Jack Brickhouse, the voice of the Cubs on early WGN-TV (courtesy Baseball Hall of Fame).

Stadiums 168). Postscript on May 6, 1960: "I want you to make a trade," said Wrigley. "[Cubs 1958–90 radio analyst Lou] Boudreau for [again-manager] Grimm." "Boudreau for Grimm?" Brickhouse said. "Yes," Wrigley replied. "Charlie's worrying himself sick over the team, out walking the streets when he should be resting. If the Cubs don't kill him his sore feet will" (169). Grimm moved to radio. Lou replaced him on the field. "A manager for a broadcaster," said Brickhouse (Smith, *Voices of Summer* 83). Dying is easy. Cubs comedy is hard.

How could the White Sox match the Cubs' TV, park, and slapstick? In 1968, Sox owner Arthur Allyn had a thought: he would dump WGN for Chicago's first UHF (ultra-high frequency) outlet (Smith, *Voices of Game* 181). WFLD aired each game, in Comiskey Park or away. "Until now," said Brickhouse, "neither team televised away with the other at home" (181). Livid, Wrigley began each-game coverage, flaunting "[Brickhouse's] enthusiasm that nothing could shake," said producer Jack Rosenberg. "Didn't matter whether the team was in first or last" (181). The next April 8, Willie Smith pinch-homered on opening day, a ninth-inning, 7–6, euphoria-inducing victory. By mid–August, the Cubs held a 9½ game lead. Who guessed that the benign-as-Benji Mets would finish 38–11? Depressed, Brickhouse did not despair. The following spring Ernie Banks faced Pat Jarvis on May 12, 1970. "He swings and a drive — a liner, left field! It is — there it is! Mr. Banks has just hit his five hundredth career homer! He is getting a standing ovation! [....] Waves to the fans as he jogs into that dugout! They are standing here at Wrigley Field and giving Ernie an ovation!" (Smith, *Voices of Summer* 85). Mr. Cub retired a year later. In 1981, the Tribune Company bought the club. For five decades, "Back, back, back! That's it! Hey-Hey!" for a homer roused each side of the Windy City. A reporter mused that even if Brickhouse didn't make Cooperstown, his suitcase would. "Fortunately," said Brickhouse, "we arrived together" in 1983 (Smith, *Voices of Game* 170). He broadcast his final game September 27. He died August 6, 1998, at 82, of a stroke after brain surgery, having penned his own epitaph: "Here lies the guy who could do the best soft-shoe anywhere for 'Tea for Two'" (Smith, *Voices of Summer* 85).

Seven of Cooperstown's 30 Frick honorees have aired the Cubs. The newest member (2006) is Gene Elston (1954–57). But the most famous made it in 1989. A half-century as Voice of the Cardinals, A's, White Sox, and 1982–97 Cubs, Harry Caray was born in 1920, orphaned at age three, and raised by an aunt. Selling papers, he used three cents to borrow books from a library. "I'd buy a sundae at a soda fountain and get halfway through the book" (Smith, *The Storytellers* 37). Next day he finished his reading — and bought another sundae. By 1942, Harry auditioned at St. Louis's KMOX. "I'm given a script about Puccini! *Puccini*? Who's he? I stink, but get another try," Caray remembered (Smith, *Voices of Summer* 156). In 1945, he began Redbirds radio. For the next quarter century, Caray became a Roland in Webster, Iowa, and Cleveland, Tennessee, and Lawton, Oklahoma. Axed in 1969 for an affair with Cardinals owner August Busch's daughter-in-law, he joined the White Sox, doing at least 64 free TV games a year. In late 1981, new Sox owners Jerry Reinsdorf and Eddie Einhorn shifted largely to pay television on cable. "I kept thinking of their less than 50,000 Greater Chicago homes — I'd be Harry Who," Caray worried (Smith, *Voices of Game* 473). So one day he picked up the phone and dialed Wrigley Field.

WGN flung the old warhorse into every corner of the city: "Bars, homes, my guys!" he said, shocking fans by the simple fact of his presence (Smith, *Voices of Game* 475). Ultimately, Channel 9 became a superstation. "Once the Cubs belonged to the North Side," a columnist said. "Now even North America isn't big enough" (Smith, *Voices of Game* 475). The 1984 Cubs won a division. Then, in 1987, Caray had a major stroke. For three months Bill Murray, Bill Moyers, and George Will, among others, did play-by-play till Harry, a long-playing record loved for his exceedingly long wear, rediscovered the booth. The Cubs hoped to forget the

Harry Caray: Cub fan, Bud man, 1982–1997 (courtesy Baseball Hall of Fame).

last century. Caray was looking forward to the next one. But he fell while dancing, on Valentine's Day 1998, had a heart attack, and died on February 18. When asked if Broadway had been good to her, Ethel Merman replied, "Yes, but I've been good to Broadway" (Smith, *Voices of Summer* 161). And the same is true of Harry Caray. Baseball was good to the man who quaffed sundaes as a child. But he was good to it as well.

One person who didn't have all positive memories of the Cubs, and especially Harry, was Milo Hamilton. Another Iowan, Hamilton was fired by the Cardinals and Cubs in 1955 and 1958, respectively. Hamilton went on to air the White Sox, Braves, and Pirates, and, in September 1981, he got the chance to retrieve his past. "Anybody in my place would jump at the opportunity," he said after being called by Cubs radio. Included in the return offer was a WGN promise of television by 1982. "*Promised?* It was *announced*. Brickhouse'd be retiring," he recalled. And Hey-Hey even named him "The Voice of the Cubs for years to come" (Smith, *Voices of Game* 364). Then, on November 16, a station exec phoned at 7:30 A.M.: "Can you come to the office? We need to tell you in person." At 10 o'clock that day Caray snatched Cubs TV from Hamilton. "WGN spent an hour praising me, then said, 'But the bottom line is that Harry doesn't like you, and he's more important.' Talk about history repeating itself," said Hamilton, though not in the way he expected, or hoped (364–65). In 1955, Harry had dumped Milo Hamilton for Joe Garagiola. Hamilton was left with the bad taste of gall in his mouth, remembering Caray's "bragging on the air, 'Today I mailed alimony checks to all my ex-wives,'" said Hamilton. "No wonder we never got along" (Smith, *Voices of Summer* 180). In late 1984, Hamilton moved to Houston and became the voice of the Astros.

And there were other great announcers, though they were less known outside the Chicago area. After graduating from Notre Dame, Jack Quinlan made Chicago at 28 years old, in the mid–1950s. "His voice possessed the firmness of a heavy handshake," said WGN sports editor Jack Rosenberg. "The resonance of a finely tuned harp, the clarity of a starry night. The quality of a prayer" (Smith, *Voices of Summer* 247). Unfortunately, in March 1965, their radio Voice was killed when his car skidded nearly 200 feet into a truck during spring training in Arizona. Brickhouse likened his death to losing a younger brother. He was followed by Vince Lloyd, the man with a cloud-nine voice which defined the Confines for a generation of Cubs fans, and who had telecast the 1950 and 1954–64 Cubs beside Jack Brickhouse. "Lou Boudreau was my best friend," said Lloyd. "He said he'd quit if I didn't take Quinlan's job" (247). Lloyd joined that best friend on radio, where they aired the Cubs through 1986. DeWayne Staats called the 1989 division title. In 1998, Pat Hughes etched a "record-assaulting, home run-blasting summer," which *Sports Illustrated* termed the Sammy Sosa-Mark McGwire marathon. If the Great Race would have stirred any teams, the Cubs-Cardinals matchup made it sing (364).

Like Bogart and Bergman in *Casablanca*, who always had Paris, the Cubs fans will always have radio/television to bring Wrigleyville to life. But TV, as actor Fred Allen knew, sometimes can be flat, "a collection of passport photos" (Smith, *Storied Stadiums* 88). Radio is more involving; it demands imagination from its audiences. Prince Hal. The Old Commander and The Gipper. Hey-Hey! Holy Cow! Cubs announcers have been up, down, warm, cold, intentionally funny, inadvertently comic, humane, and above all, human — toddling, like the town. As Caray said, the link, going deep, is that "You can't beat fun at the ol' ballpark," especially when it's vividly recreated by such talented broadcasters (Smith, *Voices of Game* 483).

WORKS CITED

Boswell, Thomas. "Cooperstown Comes to the White House." *The Washington Post* 28 Mar. 1981: 1+.

Broeg, Bob. "Reagan Reminiscences with Famers." *The Sporting News* 11 Apr. 1981: 11.

Condon, David. "Bob Elson, 76, Long-time Cubs, Sox' Voice, Dies." *Chicago Tribune* 11 Mar. 1981: 1.

_____. "Elson a Celebrity Who Kept Common Touch." *Chicago Tribune* 12 Mar. 1981: 1.

Craig, Jack. "Elson Is Dean of Baseball Announcers." *The Sporting News* 13 June 1970: 40.

"Hal Totten New Prexy of Southern." *The Sporting News* 13 Apr. 1960: 36+.

"Johnny O'Hara Named Game's Outstanding Air Reporter of the Year." *The Sporting News* 16 Dec. 1943: 24.

Newman, Zipp. "Broadcasting Pioneer Totten Reminisces." *The Birmingham News* 5 Aug. 1973: 10C+.

Smith, Curt. *Storied Stadiums*. New York: Carroll & Graf, 2001.

_____. *The Storytellers*. New York: Macmillan, 1995.

_____. *Voices of Summer*. New York: Carroll & Graf, 2005.

_____. *Voices of the Game*. New York: Simon and Schuster, 1992.

Sons, Ray. "Elson Voice the Style of a Generation." *Chicago Sun-Times* 12 Mar. 1981: 112.

Spink, J.G. Taylor. "From Chorister to Crack Aircaster." *The Sporting News* 10 Oct. 1940: 24.

Who's Who in Major League Baseball. New York: Buxton Publishing Co., 1933.

Wilson, Darrell. "This Man Invented Re-created Baseball." *San Francisco Chronicle* 5 Sept. 1953: 20.

Paradise Lost:
Cubs Fans, the Tribune Company, and the Unfriendly Confines

Ron Kates

"In the early 70s," *Chicago Sun-Times* writer Lloyd Sachs lamented, "it cost five bucks to get into the bleachers. Here's what years of hiking the price [...] has done: it has squeezed out true Cubby-blue regulars who know what the score was in favor of 'fans' who ask whether there are 'assigned' seats, are more likely to press their ears to cell phones than transistor radios and yell 'C'mon Sammy!' when Fred McGriff is up. It has converted what was the greatest bargain in sports into an outdoor boutique where cappuccino — half caf and skim, if you please — would go over better than beer" (1).

The Chicago Cubs have rewarded their fans with four trips to the postseason since 1984, but in doing so, the club's ownership, the Tribune Company, has succeeded in changing the Wrigley Field culture and Cubs fan image in subtle, yet dramatic ways. While the Tribune has begrudgingly and sporadically pumped money into the club, this expenditure comes with a cost for the fans who have supported the team through decades, generations, and across parts of three centuries. No longer can a thirteen year old catch a ride or a bus to the "L" station, ride to the Addison stop, walk to the Wrigley box office, plunk down a few dollars for a ticket, and enjoy a day of playing hooky from school. Of course, the parental fear of seeing one's child on a billboard, milk carton, or direct mail flyer labeled "Missing Child" has tempered the likelihood of such an odyssey, but the team has played a role as well. Yes, fans can still purchase a ticket from the box office for as little as $10 a game, but only for "value dates," six weekday games in April and May. If a fan wants to purchase the same ticket for a weekend game, she can expect the cost of the ticket nearly to triple. The point here is not to lament how the economics of the game has negatively affected the young, casual, or die-hard fan but rather to demonstrate a culture change that has seeped from the Tribune front office to the Wrigley box office, and eventually to the Cubs crowds themselves. Indeed, as native Chicagoan Studs Terkel notes, "many Cubs fans today are from the suburbs, brought in by busses. It's like going to an air show or *Cats*— something tourists do. After the game, you ask them: 'Who did the Cubs play? What was the score?' They shake their heads. It's not about baseball, it's about having been to a place to be" (A25).

When the Tribune Company bought the Cubs in 1981— to much ridicule in financial circles — they did so to ensure the success of WGN, which had broadcast Cubs games since

1948. While the on-field results remained the same until the 1984 breakthrough to the play-offs, the corporate machinations began almost immediately. As one writer noted, "the Cubs were transformed overnight from a loveable knockabout lap dog of a ball team, the cute Chicago losers playing on a daytime field with one of the last manual scoreboards outside a baseball museum, into a corporate investment" (Randolph C1). In 1984, after the Tribune had spent significant money overhauling the on-field product and front office, some Chicagoans wondered if this expenditure meant "that the Cubs, like other sports teams, [would] lose the folksiness that made them national favorites" (C1). And even though Wrigley Field still maintains the "Friendly Confines" moniker more than twenty years later, not only have the stadium's inhabitants changed but also the perceptions of these contemporary fans. As *Chicago Sun-Times* writer Carol Slezak mused in 1998, the games themselves "were incidental. [...] For the last decade or so, anyway. Ever since Wrigleyville became yuppified, homogenized, and stultified and the new breed of Cubs fans took over Wrigley" (BB9). To Slezak, the growing fan support during the 80s and 90s "ensured that [the] Tribune Co. would never try to field a winner. Maybe a player here and there to keep [fans] interested," but ultimately "the bottom line never has been about winning" (BB9).

With the exception of those thirty-two companies and/or entities fortunate enough to own a National Football League team, professional sports ownership in America has become a risky, multi-faceted proposition. Rather than simply worry about putting a competitive product on the field, court, or rink, owners also have to pay particular attention to the new breed of fan who requires entertainment above and beyond the game itself. Fans demand value for their hard-earned and easily-spent dollars, and increasingly the perception of value comes not from team or individual achievements during the game itself, but rather the peripheral accoutrements that make a day at the ballpark like a miniature trip to Disney World. As one commentator has aptly stated, "[a]s underdogs go, nobody beats the Cubs. Nobody does futility better. No other team in the majors can hang with the Cubs' history of heartbreak. With the quaint park, their rabid fans and all that pent-up underdogness, the Cubs are the type of team that a fan — a non-biased, baseball-loving fan — can root for" (Donovan, par. 1). This truth affirms an observation *Minneapolis Star-Tribune* columnist Patrick Reusse offered seven years earlier: "The Cubs are the only major league team that actually uses ineptitude as a marketing tool. Come to baseball's great antic. Sit almost on top of the players in the Cozy Confines. Have a couple of beers. Sing during the seventh-inning stretch. Laugh at the Cubs" (4C).

Time and again in newspaper and magazine articles over the past twenty-two years, the dichotomies of the Cubs fan emerge: die-hard but uncaring, knowledgeable but coming to Wrigley largely for the off-field entertainment, griping about management's spending habits and missteps but willingly (and proudly) carrying the banner of the "long-suffering Cubs fan." In short, Cubs fans have largely assumed the brand created for them by ownership, have embraced the ineptitude associated with the franchise, and have become, in essence, a national caricature. And as the desire has increased in fans of all interest levels to join this tribal experience, so too has the Tribune Company's tendency to up the ante for those seeking simply to enter the park and become part of the Cubs experience. In 2003 the Cubs began a ticket-reselling operation to distribute unsold game tickets through a private company, Wrigley Field Premium Ticket Services. During court proceedings (yes, the Cubs were sued by a group of their own fans), a judge ruled that although both are owned by the Tribune Company, the Cubs and Premium are separate entities, a decision that allows the Cubs to continue funneling unsold tickets to Premium to sell for markups ranging well into double-digit percentages. "Why," *Chicago Sun-Times* sportswriter Greg Couch asks, "not just price the ticket where they want it in the first place instead of sneaking around, luring fans in and never giving them a shot at the price they promise?" ("Shameless" 87). The most egregious example of the markup Couch points to occurred when the Yankees made their first trip to Wrigley in over fifty years, on June 6, 2003: "the Cubs advertised a top seat at $45, then never allowed Average Joe to buy it at that price. Instead they sold it to themselves, and Premium put it up for $1500. It's called bait-and-switch" ("By Hook" 108).

Perhaps the Tribune Company recognizes the marketability of the Wrigley Field aura, and has consequently created an air of exclusivity surrounding the Cubs game experience. Or maybe the Tribune has simply embraced perceptions of the fan base as reality. As longtime Cub Mark Grace once observed, "Wrigley Field is like a tourist trap [...] when people come to Chicago during the summer, they say, 'Yeah, let's go take in a game at Wrigley Field.' They don't say, 'Let's go watch the Cubs'" (qtd. in Hoynes 7C). Certainly the Tribune did not invent the concept of linking outside perception of the fans to the venue where the game takes place rather than to the action or the team on the field. While the new Red Sox ownership has revitalized Fenway Park, it did so largely without damaging the symbiotic relationship between the New England region and the Red Sox. According to one pundit, "Boston isn't America's best baseball city because of Fenway Park. A ballpark can't make people care about the sport" (Justice 1). And maybe this is where the Tribune brass has erred — the thinking that any group of fans drawn into the magic cauldron of Wrigley Field will automatically embrace the passion of the true long-term, die-hard fans. In marketing ineptitude, the Tribune and the Cubs have willingly embraced the "'I went to the game last night, and I had seven beers, and I met a real hottie, but don't ask me who won' fan" (Roeper 11), often at the expense of those wanting to attend a game with scorecard, pencil, and transistor radio in hand. With Red Sox fans, on the contrary,

> It's not about Fenway Park. It's about caring. It's about fathers taking sons. It's about granddads and college students and all the others. They're not there because it's the place to be, but because they want to be there. They watch, too. They cheer at the right moment. [...] They pore over the sports pages and television reports. They discuss their Red Sox with the guys at work and the man who changes the oil on the car. They have the latest box score memorized by lunchtime. They do it because their fathers did it. And their grandfathers. They do it because they were raised to believe baseball mattered [Justice 1].

When screenwriters Lowell Ganz and Babaloo Mandel set about "Americanizing" Nick Hornby's *Fever Pitch*, the documentation of the author's fixation with all things Arsenal soccer, they debated which sport and which team should serve as the object of the main character's obsession. As movie buffs, sports fans, and those with an entertainment bent already know, the two writers chose the Boston Red Sox as the subject and co-stars of the 2004 movie, rewriting the ending with Jimmy Fallon and Drew Barrymore "embracing and celebrating among the Sox players at the actual World Series" (Graham N11). Ganz and Mandel discussed using the Chicago Cubs as the focal point of an Americanized *Fever Pitch*, but ultimately they "decided that Cubs fans looked too happy [... and] didn't seem to suffer enough" (McGrath 13). Director Bobby Farrelly admits, "'We did talk about the Cubs and Wrigley Field, but in the end it had to be the Red Sox and Fenway. [...] Yes, the Cubs fans have been through it longer, but I don't know that they've had the heartache. The Cubs are futile, but they don't have the charm of the Red Sox [who are] always good enough to get your hopes soaring" (qtd. in Graham N11).

In Hornby's *Fever Pitch*, he ruminates that "the big clubs seem to have tired of their fan-base, and in a way who can blame them? Young working-class and lower-middle-class males bring with them a complicated and occasionally distressing set of problems," leading team chairmen to argue that "middle-class families — the new target audience — will not only behave themselves, but pay much more to do so" (76). But Hornby points to what he considers a "fatal flaw in the reasoning," one which has striking parallels to the Cubs propagating — and profiting from — the "loveable losers" concept they sell to fans and the media. "Part of the pleasure to be had in large football stadia," Hornby insists, "is a mixture of the vicarious and the parasitical," since fans largely "rely on others to provide the atmosphere; and atmosphere is one of the crucial ingredients of the football experience. These huge ends are as vital to the clubs as their players, not only because their inhabitants are vocal in their support, not just because they provide clubs with large sums of money [...] but because without them nobody else would bother to come" (76–77). Yes, people pay to watch the match itself, Hornby argues, "but many of them — the people in the twenty pound seats — also pay to watch people watching [the players] (or to listen to people shouting at them)" (77).

To the point of having created a largely clichéd metaphor, sports broadcasters often invoke the phrase "dramatic" when describing the functions of a sporting event. In one sense, the events seem dramatic, almost scripted (two World Series home runs come to mind: Carlton Fisk's 1975 blast and Kirk Gibson's 1988 shot), yet would the drama exist without the fans as a backdrop? And more to the point here, have the Cubs and the Tribune Company created a long-running theatrical performance that largely inverts the roles of performer and audience? Is the game on the field as important to the audience as the peripheral elements occurring beyond the diamond: life in the bleachers, "Take Me Out to the Ballgame," and "enough Budweiser to float the Sears Tower off its pilings" (Kindred 60)? Moreover, does Hornby's "mixture of the vicarious and parasitical" accurately describe the Cubs fan's desire perhaps to observe less and participate more in the daily Wrigley drama?

In "(Caray)³: Baseball as Narrated on Television," Gerald Wood cites Ava Rose and James Friedman's "Television Sports as Mas(s)culine Cult of Distraction" to explain the cast roles the baseball broadcast team members play. "In a baseball commentary," writes Wood, "the play-by-play man tries to construct a reality and evoke a sense of immediacy that combines with the color man's perspective to make the viewer feel like he is watching the game with the guys in the booth. The goal, and illusion, of such combination is the dissolution of the boundary between those at the ballpark and the television viewer, absorbing the viewer into the actual" (125). In the process, Wood goes on to say, "the commentators [... narrate] a history and drama of expectation for their teams and opponents" (125).

While it's true that "the performance of a particular team influences initial audience interest in a game, broadcasters can influence the medium fans will choose to access the game, how long they'll stay tuned to that medium and even how they feel about product messages that accompany the broadcast" (Bonham and Hinchley 5C). Indeed, "possibly because there is less continuous action in baseball, its broadcasters seem to have the power to endear or alienate us more than announcers of other sports" (5C). From the 1950s through the 70s and into the 80s, Chicagoans could turn on their radios, spin the dial to 720-AM, and hear Jack Brickhouse, Vince Lloyd, and Lou Boudreau narrate the action with professionalism augmented by flair. As Wood reflects, "In the primitive, innocent period which included broadcasters like Jack Brickhouse, the game was the thing. The high point was an invisible speaker helping us to look through the screen to share the moment when Ernie Banks hit his 500th home run" (134). Harry Caray, Brickhouse's successor as lead announcer and a prolific broadcast figure in his own right, simply could not remain invisible in the broadcast booth. More than perhaps any other announcer of his era, save perhaps Vin Scully, Caray was ideally positioned for the time when "the game was not enough, and so the audience developed a taste for the cult of personality" (134). While Brickhouse and company had brought the Cubs to the WGN radio and television airwaves for longer than Caray's fifteen-year stretch, Caray's visage, style, and attitude have remained synonymous with the Cubs' aura and the Wrigley experience. In Caray, the Tribune found the ideal spokesperson for the branding of the Wrigley experience. And yet the Cubs took on Caray during the back nine of his illustrious forty-two-year broadcasting career, the majority of which he spent as the voice of the St. Louis Cardinals on KMOX. A year after hiring Caray, WGN paired him with recently retired pitcher Steve Stone. Only two years removed from his Cy Young performance for the Baltimore Orioles, Stone had spent 1974–1976 as part of the Cubs' rotation, and therefore he could blend his considerable knowledge of the game with an awareness of a pre–Tribune Cubs world.

Stone's knowledge of and love for the game quickly became a hallmark of his broadcasting style. Rather than calling attention to himself with self-aggrandizing quirkiness or boasting of his own mound exploits, Stone became Caray's foil, tempering the "Holy Cow" with careful game-based observations often punctuated by "for all you young fans watching out there." In a *Sports Illustrated* interview, Stone related the impact Caray had on his career: "'He said I should make sure, when I'm looking into that camera, that I'm telling the truth. You can't cover up for anybody; you can't soft peddle too many things'" (qtd. in Haskins, par. 12). As Stone mused in 1994, "'you can't take something that looks terrible and make it sound good [...]. I make my comments one day, and that's it. I forget them. I don't carry them over to the next game. I never hold any vendettas or grudges against players'" (qtd. in Cahill 119). The context of this particular statement holds some interest, shedding significant light on Stone's decision to step out of the Cubs' announcing booth following the 2004 season. Cahill later mentions that "Cubs reliever and player rep Randy Myers went out of his way to thank announcer Steve Stone for being kindly critical. 'He just told me that we've been fair about it,' Stone said. 'He said the players really appreciated it'" (119).

Flashing forward a decade, to the end of the frustrating 2004 season, Stone questioned a series of moves made by Cubs' manager Dusty Baker during a game against Cincinnati. As he recalls, "After the game I questioned Dusty about the ninth inning and he was quite upset with it" (qtd. in Haskins, par. 22). Baker's complaints to the print media and General Manager Jim Hendry's contention that Stone "had crossed a line" (qtd. in DeLuca, par. 20) made public an in-house issue that had festered throughout the season. Stone's broadcasting partner that year, Chip Caray, "acknowledged that the [2004] season was difficult for both he and Stone off the field, revealing that Cubs management met with and tried to chastise the several players who were at the core of contentious feelings with Stone. Reliever Kent Mercker was a vocal opponent of Stone's, confronting him on the team charter jet and in the team hotel'" (qtd. in DeLuca, par. 16). Other reports surfacing in the wake of Stone's resignation, however, claim that Cubs' management from President Andy MacPhail down to manager Dusty Baker took only minimal action to address the verbal abuse and physical threats directed at Stone throughout the 2004 season.

For a good number of fans, both die-hard and casual, in Chicago and around the globe, Stone's resignation and the subsequent reports regarding his decision represented a tipping point in their relationship with the Cubs. As the *Chicago Sun-Times*'s Jay Mariotti pondered in the wake of Stone's announcement, "Is it me, or were the Cubs much easier to stomach as loveable losers than hateable contenders? [...] Simply, the Tribsters are too arrogant to succeed, too pompous while counting the profits from their Wrigley cash cow, too quick to allow petulant finger pointing and not strong enough to stop nonsense when necessary" (114). Did Stone, the man who told the truth to Cubs fans for twenty-one years, have to leave because he continually pointed out what the fans could see for themselves but often would not totally believe? And while the Cubs' management and the Tribune Company might display a willingness to overlook a mediocre product on the field, mismanagement in the dugout and front office, and a shift in fan loyalty to (gasp!) the White Sox, who play a more engaging style of baseball and have not placed undue emphasis on at-the-park-but-off-the-field-entertainment, perhaps the Stone debacle paired with the 2005 Sox's success have caused the average Cubs fan to look in the mirror and ask, "Am I that person that everyone says I am?"

Prior to the 1989 postseason, *Washington Post* columnist Tony Kornheiser warned, "brace yourselves for the Swarm of the Designer Fans" (E1). In an article entitled "Instant Cubs Fans Glut Market," Kornheiser caricatures Cubs fans, saying,

> It's chic to be a Cubs fan now, to genuflect at the ivy in the outfield and caterwaul about the lights, as if Gibraltar would crumble because the Cubs have to play at night [...]. I'm not talking about the Bleacher Bums or any of the true believers, the ones who were there when times were tight; they're authentic fans, they'll drink beer from a cup and never complain they can't get Pinot Noir. I'm talking about those commodity traders, these arrivistes, these people who don't care much about baseball but like the Cubs as a concept, these people who act as if they should be able to order the Cubs from the *Sharper Image* catalogue [E1].

In *Drama and Reality,* Richard Hornby (no relation to Nick) suggests, "for the individual, theatre is a kind of identity laboratory, in which social roles can be examined vicariously. In a safe environment, detached from everyday reality, the audience member can forget his own identity for a while and identify with the characters he sees" (71). Kornheiser's extreme caricature aside, have Cubs fans willingly accepted the Kool-Aid offered them by the Tribune Company, embracing the "going to Wrigley" process in all its theatrical glory as opposed to going to see and (deeply, truly, achingly) caring about the game's result? Richard Hornby continues, "Just as the individual must revise his identity at crucial times throughout his lifetime, so too must a dynamic society frequently revise the way in which it wants its members to play roles" (71). The dynamic, ever-changing society that necessarily exists at any ballpark has changed at Wrigley in favor of blasé homogeneity. Yes, the die-hards exist in pockets and communities throughout the park, but the Tribsters, as Jay Mariotti derisively refers to them, prefer the fans with deep pockets who can satisfy their desires to consume buckets of Bud, purchase Cubs-related tchachkas (as my grandmother would say), and embrace the kitsch that makes the Wrigley experience increasingly more like a trip to see *The Rocky Horror Picture Show.*

But then again, can one blame Cubs fans for essentially emulating what has been modeled for them on WGN broadcasts over the past quarter century? Whereas slickly produced ESPN or Fox broadcasts maintain a professional detachment that focuses on the game itself and the statistical ennui the casual fan craves, the WGN Cubs broadcasts tend to include more of the audience itself. While this homey touch certainly brings back floods of memories to those Cubs fans who ran home from school to watch the last few innings, or those who kept the Cubs broadcast on as a constant companion in the house, bar, or nursing home, it also fulfills an agenda Hornby relates above: the ability to attract the right types of fans to Wrigley. Certainly the Cubs have not had to confront the fan violence that occurs at Arsenal and other football stadiums across Britain and the world, but a closer look at the fans attending games whose faces show up on television suggests that perhaps the Cubs would willingly embrace a stadium full of beer-swilling bleacherites and families appareled in layers of team-licensed accoutrements. The Cubs may market the image of the long-suffering fan having fun at the ballpark, but perhaps an underlying message exists alongside the smiling faces enjoying the Wrigley sunshine: You can come to the game and become part of the tribe, the experience, but you'll need to adapt to behavioral traits in certain areas of the park. And, oh yeah, it wouldn't hurt if you looked like the others around you.

The result? While the Cubs have played to near-capacity crowds over the past several years, the fear exists that the die-hard baseball fan is gradually being elbowed out not only by the casual baseball fan and theatre-goer who come to the park to see the game itself but also by those others in the audience who place greater primacy on the periphery than the on-field action. Thanks to rising ticket and concession prices, the Cubs fan going to Wrigley not only needs to parrot and project the image of the other fans but to plan on hitting the ATM machine before (and likely during) the game. The Cub Club is expensive, but its nine-inning advertisements aired on WGN are oh-so-enticing. Pure marketing on the part of the Tribune Company and the Cubs. Pure marketing.

Works Cited

Bonham, Dean, and Don Hinchley. "Bad Broadcaster on Your Team Can Cost You Fans." *Rocky Mountain News* [Denver] 28 Aug. 2004, final ed.: 5C.

Cahill, Dan. "Cubs' Broadcasters Awarded High Marks for Objectivity." *Chicago Sun-Times* 6 May 1994, late sports final ed.: 119.

Couch, Greg. "By Hook or Crook, Fans Scalped." *Chicago Sun-Times* 27 Feb. 2005: 108.

_____. "Shameless; Cubs no Longer Even Trying to Hide What They're Doing in Ticket Scheme." *Chicago Sun-Times* 31 July 2005: 87.

DeLuca, Chris. "End of Broadcast Era: Stone Resigns." *Chicago Sun-Times* 29 Oct. 2004. 27 pars. <http://www.suntimes.com/output/sports/cst-spt-stone29.html>.

Donovan, John. "Dogging It: These Cubs are More Insufferable than Loveable." *SI.com* 15 Aug. 2005. 13 pars. <http://sportsillustrated.cnn.com/2005/writers/john_donovan/08/15/cubsdebacle/index.html>.

Graham, Renee. "Finally! The Red Sox Got Their Win, and the Farrellys' *Fever Pitch* Got the Perfect Ending." *Boston Globe* 27 Mar. 2005, third ed.: N11.

Haskins, Maggie. "The Sorcerer Stone: Exiled Cubs Broadcaster Still the Best in the Business." *SI.com* 13 Aug. 2005. 26 pars. <http://sportsillustrated.cnn.com/2005/writers/maggie_haskins/08/12/stone.color/index.html>.

Hornby, Nick. *Fever Pitch*. New York: Penguin, 1992.

Hornby, Richard. *Drama, Metadrama, and Perception*. Lewisburg, PA: Bucknell UP, 1986.

Hoynes, Paul. "Losing Doesn't Matter — Wrigley Will Draw." *Plain Dealer* [Cleveland, OH] 6 Apr. 1997, final ed.: 7C.

Justice, Richard. "National Pastime; When you Get Right Down to it, the Ballpark or the Players Don't Forever Bond the Sport to a Town. It's the Insatiable Devotion of the Fan Base that Separates the Bostons from the Atlantas." *Houston Chronicle* 10 July 2005, star ed., Sports: 1.

Kindred, Dave. "Sox Fans Have Baseball: Cubs Fans Have Beer." *Sporting News* 4 Nov. 2005: 60.

Kornheiser, Tony. "Instant Cubs Fans Glut Market." *Washington Post* 3 Oct. 1989, final ed.: E1.

Mariotti, Jay. "Easy to Finger the Culprits: It's the Cubs; The Tribsters Are Too Arrogant to Succeed, Too Pompous While Counting Profits from the Wrigley Cash Cow." *Chicago Sun-Times* 30 Oct. 2004: 114.

McGrath, Charles. "Translating 'British Obsessive Male' Into American." *New York Times* 9 Apr. 2005, late ed., sec. B: 13.

Randolph, Eleanor. "The Trib's Winning Season: Owning the Cubs and Covering Them, Too." *Washington Post* 29 Sept. 1984, final ed.: C1.

Reusse, Patrick. "Competitive Play Ruins Cubs' Appeal." *Star Tribune* [Minneapolis] 7 June 1998, metro ed.: 4C.

Roeper, Richard. "Don't Be Blue Over Cubs Bias — Time to Focus on Men in Black." *Chicago Sun-Times* 4 Oct. 2005: 11.

Sachs, Lloyd. "Wrigley the Movie: 'Field of Greedy Dreams.'" *Chicago Sun-Times* 5 May 2002, Show: 1.

Slezak, Carol. "Cubs Fans Deserve Round of Applause." *Chicago Sun-Times* 4 Oct. 1998, late sports final ed.: BB9.

Terkel, Studs. "Nine Men In." *New York Times* 28 Oct. 2005: A25.

Wood, Gerald. "(Caray)³: Baseball as Narrated on Television." *Baseball/Literature/Culture: Essays, 2002–2003*. Ed. Peter Carino. Jefferson, NC: McFarland, 2004. 124–35.

Scoring at Home

Holly Swyers

"It's one big party in the bleachers," *The Sporting News* reporter, Tricia Garner, described in the column, "Buzzer Beaters: Things All Sports Fans Must Do before They Die." Her subject: a day game at Wrigley Field. In one sentence, she captured a sentiment widely echoed in Chicago, sometimes cheerfully, sometimes in disgust. Her tone was approving, but she noted, "If you're looking to focus on the game [...] the field boxes are your best bet" (Garner 13).

From a certain point of view, Garner is right. There is so much going on in the bleachers of Wrigley Field during any given game that it sometimes seems impossible anyone could be watching the game. The sun-drenched stands draw out winter-weary Chicagoans determined to soak up as much summer as possible. They attract large groups, drawn by a general admission policy that enables people to purchase tickets willy-nilly and still have a chance of sitting together. The crowd *mingles* in the bleachers, daily reinventing the scene of happy revelers broadcast (and arguably created) for over twenty years on television superstation WGN. Young, scantily clad twenty- and thirty-somethings buy one another beers and maitais, at their worst recreating the environment of a frat-house row block party.

It is not surprising, in such an environment, that Cubs fan detractors point to the bleachers and exclaim that fans are not even watching the game. In my own experience of the bleachers, I have had people ask me who we're playing, what the score is, and even which team is the Cubs. However, a person willing to push through the standing crowd into the seating area would quickly note that the game is not, in fact, ancillary to the action in the stands. To be sure, a fair number of people in the seats are doing more drinking and flirting than game watching. At the same time, on a 3–2 count with Cubs runners on base, there are ample people aware enough of the on-field action to rouse the crowd and start chants urging the home team to success. Even during slower parts of the games, an observant person will notice groups of fans passing an emptied beer cup stuffed with dollar bills, participating in any one of a number of games that connect winning the contents of the cup to the fortunes of the batter at the plate. Whoever is holding the cup during a given at-bat is always watching the field with keen interest.

With more time to study the crowd, a person might begin to pick up quieter kinds of attentiveness. She might observe parents leaning down to explain something to children, pointing to the field as they do so. She might see the earphones of the fans listening to the play-by-play on the radio as they follow the game unfolding before them. Ultimately, our observer might realize that among all these other activities, *there are people keeping score.*

There are a number of reasons this circumstance might be surprising, not the least of which is Tricia Garner's already cited opinion that the field boxes are the best bet for focusing on the game, and thus the place one would expect the scorekeepers to flock. Of course, field boxes are not cheap seats, running anywhere from $45 to $67 on most game days in 2007. However, the current bleachers are not particularly cheap — or easy — to come by, either. Mostly sold out before the season even began, the 2007 bleachers cost $32 to $42 a seat at the box office, and often much more on the street. To be sure, bleacher seats were a cheap day-of-game option as recently as the early 1980s, but savvy marketing by the Cubs has changed that. A fan truly looking for a bargain in 2007 would claim a high corner of the upper deck, would still be closer to the game than he would be in most parks, and would never pay more than $19 for the privilege.

With cost minimized as a factor, the question remains why a fan intent on tracking every play would sit in the section of the ballpark renowned for its distractions. It is a question the Cubs' management must have asked itself after receiving irate e-mails and phone calls for understocking scorecards in the bleachers. Who are the scorekeepers, and what are they doing out *there* of all places?

While I cannot answer for every scorekeeper in the bleachers, I can offer insights on many of them. I am one of them. I am also a member of the bleacher regulars, a loosely organized group of Cubs bleacher fans who can date the existence of their community to the end of World War II. The oldest members can describe the days when fans dressed up to go to the ballpark, when they sat in center field in seats now blocked off to create a better backdrop for the batter's eye. Many women in the group got hooked on the Cubs after coming to games for free on Ladies' Days during the 1960s and 1970s. A few regulars retain buttons from the 1980s that read "Working Cubs Fan," a response to then-Cubs' manager Lee Elia's famous rant against the day-game fans, whom he categorized as jobless, booing his team. They describe now-forgotten days, only thirty years in the past, when a fan could "count the house" at Wrigley Field, when the upper deck almost never opened and the bleachers were so thinly populated that some fans stretched out on benches to work on their tans.

I have spent the last several years talking to and writing about the regulars, arguing that by studying the regulars and their self-proclaimed community, we can gain insight into the ways in which communities work and develop in practice. Many of the bleacher scorekeepers are a subset of the regulars, and a snapshot of their activities and interactions not only gives a sense of the community they have formed but also begins to answer the question of why people might keep score.

The Regulars, and the Scorekeepers Among Them

The regulars are a group of Wrigley bleacher fans who readily describe themselves as a community, and some members have even gone so far as to claim that they are part of "the last true community in the United States." This assertion is overstated, but it reflects the pride regulars express in the world they have created for themselves from chance meetings at a ballpark. The group numbers roughly 200, and it subdivides into smaller, spatially defined knots in various corners of the bleachers. There is an even mix of male and female members, and their ages range from the children hauled out by their parents to retirees into their 80s, although I would put the average age of the most steadfast regulars at their mid–40s to 50s. Reflecting the demographics of Wrigley attendance in general, the regulars are predominantly white, but at present they include small numbers of Asian Americans, Native Americans, African Americans, and Latinos. Almost all of them share three specific traits: (a) a great love for baseball in general and the Cubs in particular, (b) a devotion to the Wrigley Field bleachers, and (c) a willingness to go to a ballgame alone.

This last trait is perhaps slightly less prevalent than their love for the Cubs or for the bleachers, but it is the trait that accounts for the formation of the community in the first place. Regulars generally became regulars by one of two routes. They either attended many games in the bleachers by themselves until they noticed and joined one of the subgroups of regulars who sat near them, or they met a regular in some other context and got adopted into the community through the connection.

Regardless of how a regular got enmeshed in the community, however, once a member, she buys solo tickets without a second thought. "I'll meet my friends there" is a common sentiment among regulars, and the general admission seating makes this kind of insouciance possible. Among each subgroup of regulars, there are a few people who arrive at the ballpark when the gates open two hours before game time. These regulars put down towels and blankets, holding sections of bench for people they know will be coming. Most regulars take a turn at seat saving if possible, although there are always a few people who are permanently deputized to the task. Any regular enjoys reasonable confidence that provided he arrives at the game before the lineups are announced, there will be friends holding a seat.

The subgroups among the regulars tend to identify themselves by field, and there are different degrees of consolidation among the fields. Left field is the home of the most centralized grouping of regulars, a situation initially made possible by the relative smallness of the left-field seating area and by the unifying influence of a group of fans, who, in the 1960s, dubbed themselves "The Bleacher Bums" (Shea 253, 261–62). Smaller subgroups of left-field regulars splinter off toward left-center, but most regulars concentrate in the left-field corner and maintain traditions of interacting with the players that go back to the Bleacher Bums. As an example, the left-field regulars open the bottom of the first inning with the "Fe Fi Fo Fum" chant. This chant, always led by a regular, begins by spelling out the opposing left fielder's last name in the classic, "Give me a ____" formula. When the name is spelled, the leader asks, "What's that spell?" The proper reply, regardless of the fielder: "BUM!" This routine is followed by the chant, represented here in the clean version used when regulars note children in the crowd: "Fe Fi Fo Fum, ____ is a stinkin' bum! And don't you forget it!" Opposing fielders are judged by how well they react to this opening volley and how willing they are to play off the regulars' various jibes throughout the game.

Center field, just to the right-field side of the batter's eye, is my bleacher home, and it includes two relatively large groups, one settled and one nomadic. The settled group claims the back two rows of the lower bleacher section, right in front of the concession stand and relatively far back from the field. Convenient to concessions and providing a good, if distant, view of the strike zone, these center-field seats also are sheltered from wind by the scoreboard. This location makes them the warmest seats in the ballpark on a sunny day, and in midsummer it gets blisteringly hot. The heat drives the nomadic group to the "summer seats," a section of the back rail one aisle over. The summer seats are at the top of one of the entrance ramps to the bleachers, and if there is any breeze to be had, it will be channeled up the ramp and cool that section of the stands. The same feature makes the same seats unbearably cold on April days and September evenings, prompting the nomadic center-field regulars to retreat to their "winter seats" by the other center-field subgroup. As with left field, smaller knots of regulars scatter throughout center field.

Finally, there are the right-field regulars, defined prior to 2006 as much by their lack of centralization as by any other single trait. When the bleachers were expanded at the start of the 2006 season, one right-field subgroup, unhappy with the loss of a short bench it claimed to have controlled since 1937 (the year the bleachers were built), moved over to a short bench at the back of the bleachers by the left-field foul pole. I mention this historical fact because it affects a generalization that used to be true: scorekeepers as a percentage of regulars increased from left field to right field. In left, a scattering of regulars kept score. In center, the proportion was and is about 50/50, and for years the regulars who did not keep score were gamblers who bet on every pitch. In right, scorekeeping was as much the glue that maintained groups as any other activity.

I am tempted to assign the scorekeeping spread among the regulars to different ideas of game participation. The regulars, as noted, share the trait of a love of baseball and of the bleachers. Their relationship to the bleachers is proprietary, and, by dint of long occupation, they can tell you things about the bleachers that members of the Cubs' front office might not know. They know that bees plague the bleachers in September, for instance, and that the top of the bleacher wall was made to angle sharply toward the ground to deter bleacher fans that took to walking along the top of the wall during games. Such knowledge gives the bleachers a reliable, home-like atmosphere for regulars, but no amount of specialized knowledge can offer regulars comfort of the fortunes of the team they love.

Regulars live and die by the Cubs. "I've been snapping at everyone lately, and I realized it's because of the Cubs," Bea from center field revealed in June of the 2006 season. At that point, the Cubs were in the middle of losing six in a row at home after a miserable May and were struggling to stay out of last place in the division. During the same stretch, more than one regular pointed out in consoling tones, "Well, we get to see each other, at least."

Between 1981 and 2005, the Cubs made the playoffs four times, but they also had seventeen seasons in which they lost over half their games. They managed to lose ninety or more games in six of those losing years — including two years in a row in 1999–2000. So many losing seasons give credence to the widely held belief that the Cubs are a cursed team, and there is precious little the regulars can do about it. They attend games religiously and engage in any variety of superstitious behavior, but all too often they find themselves watching another game frittered away in the late innings or sitting through lopsided losses without much to hope for in terms of a comeback. In the worst of this kind of season, when anger and frustration gives way to resignation, it is not unusual to hear a regular say, "We make our own fun."

Such "fun," however, has careful boundaries, because the regulars are adamant that they are different from the inattentive party crowd that has invaded "their" bleachers. Whatever fun behavior the regulars create during a slowly moving or hopelessly lost game must project a distinction between the revelers and the regulars. This may in part explain why gambling on every pitch, once a popular pastime among regulars in right and center fields, has died out with the older regulars who participated in it. The regulars' fun must show that they are *in* the game, even if the Cubs are not, and it must be obviously different from the party crowd's interactions with the team. The pitch-by-pitch bets reflected a knowledge of strategy and baseball smarts, but the cup game described earlier favors luck and, at its worst, encourages fans to root for *opposing* players to hit home runs. The popularity of the cup game with the party crowd and the difficulty of easily distinguishing between the two types of betting have cost at-the-park gambling some cachet.

Among the activities that persist to mark the regulars' social connection to the Cubs and the bleachers are clever heckling and creative chants, although a certain critical mass of participants is needed to give a chant any carrying power over the general buzz of crowd noise. The left-field regulars have such a critical mass, along with a carefully maintained tradition of chants and a large enough group to ensure a good reaction to a smart jeer. In addition, they sit close to the field — close enough to have conversations with left fielders for both teams. These activities help connect the regulars to the play on the field, even when the game is nothing to write home about.

In contrast, while both center- and right-field regulars will offer approval of a game-related insult, none of the subgroups are large enough to carry a chant by themselves. Nor do most of them sit close enough to the field to really engage with the players, although prior to Sammy Sosa's explosive popularity in the late 1990s, right field had more of a presence closer to the action. The arrival of the "Sammy groupies," defined by regulars as devotees of the home run ball with no apparent interest in the game as a contest between two teams, pushed many of the right-field regulars to the back rows of their sections. In these relatively smaller social groupings scorecards are much more visible, and, perhaps, more necessary. As Paul Dickson comments in *The Joy of Keeping Score*, "Scoring will always bring you closer to the game on the field" (1).

I say I am tempted to make this connection between social groupings and scoring behavior, but I may have the relationship backwards. Regulars gravitate toward the fields where they feel most comfortable, and the prevalence of scorecards in any given field may reflect the preferences a regular brought to the game. A regular already invested in scoring might be drawn to the small group social model of right field, while a fan who valued vocal participation would likely settle with the large group in left. These decisions would also be affected by personalities in each field and the various connections regulars develop during their time outside the ballpark. Most gather socially after they've met at Wrigley, and some become close enough friends to vacation together, mind one another's children, and, in a few instances, marry one another. The closer the friendship, the more likely two people are to sit in the same field.

Regardless of the connection between seating and scoring, the regulars who score at least know of one another, keeping track of where others sit in case a play gets missed or an argument emerges about how to score a particular play. In this way they form an important subnetwork among the regulars, one of several mechanisms that overcome the potential boundaries between fields and serve to unite the community. Further, the presence of scorecards, a widely acknowledged signal of baseball savvy, serves notice that party or no, there are serious fans in the bleachers, a message regulars are eager to promote.

The Social Life of a Bleacher Scorecard

The above discussion suggests the social function of the bleacher scorecard, or, to follow anthropologist Arjun Appadurai, I have traced the "social history" of scorecards in the bleachers. As Appadurai points out, "it is the social history of things, over large periods of time and at large social levels, that constrains the form, meaning, and structure of more short-term, specific, and intimate trajectories" (36). Scorecards may be, as Dickson explained above, a way of connecting to the game of baseball, and that may constrain some of the form and meaning that are imputed to them. At the same time, however, scorecards have a particular social life in the bleachers of Wrigley Field, serving as touchstones in interactions and working as props and signs that bring people together in response to particular pressures.

The first point of scoring for regulars is the acquisition of a scorecard. There are two options of scorecard for a regular: the official scorecards packaged with the *Scorecard Extra* and printed for each home stand, or a season scorebook purchased from any bookstore. The decision between these options tends to be driven in part by scoring preferences but also to some degree by cost. While most regulars who score used to buy the official scorecard when it was 75 cents, many switched to scorebooks in 2001 when the sixteen-page *Scorecard Extra* debuted for $1 and it became impossible to get a scorecard without the magazine. More regulars defected to scorebooks in 2005, when the price of the *Extra* increased to $2, and they rail against away stadiums where a scorecard can only be had in a $7 team publication. Even regulars who get the official scorecard are disdainful of the printed matter that comes with it, and they quickly discard the glossy pages. They retain only the scorecard, printed on heavy paper stock with the scoring grid, the team rosters, and the list of pitchers and umpires throughout Major League Baseball.

The decision to buy a scorecard at the ballpark or to bring a scorebook is one of several social distinctions that scorekeeping creates. This distinction, though, is one that brings regulars together around the sharing of information. The scorebook scorekeepers must be more attentive to the announcements over the PA and on the scoreboards in order to catch who has entered the game since they do not have a roster to compare to the numbers on the backs of the players. By working with the scorecard-buying regulars, they can offer information on game changes and get information on rosters. Interestingly, no regular to my knowledge purchases the unofficial scorecards available for $1 on game days outside the ballpark. The unofficial scorecards come bound in newsprint magazines, and they lack the virtue of a heavy card stock scorecard that can be ripped free and saved when the rest of the magazine is discarded.

The regulars who do purchase the official scorecards, still the majority of scorekeeping regulars, mark their status as regulars even at the point of purchase. The act of keeping score at a game already distinguishes a fan, but doing so every day creates a set of relationships with vendors as well as other fans. Every regular has particular vendors he frequents, whether to get a beer or a hotdog or a scorecard. The scorecard interactions, because they occur at every game the regular attends, have a particular texture. They begin with eye contact, often when several feet remain between the regular and the vendor. The regular has his two dollars in hand, and the vendor is ready with scorecard and pencil. The exchange is made seamlessly, often accompanied by casual conversation if the vendor is not busy. If the vendor *is* busy, the purchase takes on a more marked character, noteworthy because the transaction will occur regardless of what other business is being conducted. Scorecards are routinely kept on the counters of stands around the ballpark. When a long line has formed at a vendor's stand, a regular needing a scorecard will slip to the side of the line, claim a scorecard, and leave the money as near to the vendor as he can reach. A glance of confirmation ends the transaction, often without any disruption of the sale of other souvenirs. Regulars engaging in such purchases confirm their claim to the ballpark and the game and provide local color for first-time Wrigley visitors through their obvious seriousness about the game, signaled by the scorecard.

Once a scorecard or scorebook has been acquired, it passes out of the commodity stage of its existence and begins a new phase of its cultural biography, becoming firmly linked to the person and personality of the scorer who uses it (Appadurai 38). Every scorer makes different decisions about what information to record, when to record it, and how to record it. These decisions can be driven by any number of factors, including superstition. At Wrigley Field the starting lineups are announced and put on the scoreboards twenty minutes or so before the game. A regular taking a bathroom break during pre-game to avoid missing any part of the game itself might miss the lineups and thus have to crib the lineup from someone else or record the batters as they come up. If the Cubs win that game, it is likely that that regular will *deliberately* skip the announcement of lineups at the next game.

Once the game begins, the conversations between scorekeeping regulars are punctuated by confirmations of plays or queries about missed plays. Regulars who do not keep score generally know the conventions, and they will contribute — or willfully misinform — as the whim strikes them. One regular will routinely claim a missed play was a 6–3, regardless of what it was. Another regular delights in teaching a scorekeeper's daughter to make backwards K's on her mother's scorecard. Often non-scorers display prodigious feats of memory, asking for confirmation in the eighth inning, for instance, that Barrett had two doubles and a strikeout and getting that confirmation from the closest scorekeeper. "The scorekeeper is the captain of her row," Judy from center field announced one day, relating an article she had read, "and our row has enough captains for the whole section."

So many captains do not uniform scoring make, however. Each scorekeeper has her own style. Over time, for instance, I have learned that Judy's "3UA" is the same as my "U3" (an unassisted putout by the first baseman). These idiosyncrasies aside, regulars generally aim for accuracy in scoring and will retrace difficult plays together. "6–5–4–6?" someone will ask after a rundown, and another regular will attend to a radio while the rest of the group reconstructs the play.

More unusually, a play will leave all the scorers flabbergasted, either because they disagree with the official ruling or because it is something that no one has seen before. "K-2–3, E3? E3 for two bases?" a scorer will ask, trying to figure out how the batter got to third by striking out. The most unusual plays will prompt scorekeepers to make in-game visits to other sections and start conversations about rare or painfully comic plays: "So, how'd you score the ball that bounced off his head? E6?" At their most dramatic, plays might prompt a scorer to go back to old scorecards.

Not all regulars keep their scorecards, of course. Some abandon them before the game is over, either because the game is going poorly, or because the scorer made a mistake that he deems irrecoverable, or just because. Others throw scorecards away immediately after the game, or they take them home to accumulate on counter tops or tables for a few weeks before ending up in the trash. Most scorekeeping regulars, though, collect their scorecards in files by year (or keep a shelf for their scorebooks), and some take pains to make sure they are in chronological order. The most elaborate systems involve logbooks and box scores clipped from the next day's paper and filed with each scorecard.

On its simplest level, what a person does with a scorecard after she begins scoring a game is one of several topics of conversation that can while away rain delays and slow innings. Both the abandonment of a scorecard and the careful maintenance of one can be the source of good-natured ribbing among regulars, demonstrating social familiarity and acceptance. Such behaviors can also become evidence for or against someone's character during the occasional bleacher dispute. But the scorecard's social life does not end when it leaves Wrigley Field.

Sometimes, scorecards even return to the ballpark.

On August 28, 2005, the Cubs retired the number of the newly inducted Hall-of-Famer Ryne Sandberg. The long-time Cubs second baseman was voted into the Baseball Hall of Fame on his third time on the ballot, and Cubdom was thrilled. The regulars were at the ballpark in force, as they often are on special occasions, and a high percentage had arrived when the gates opened. During the usual rounds of pre-game visiting in which many regulars indulge, I wandered over to right field to find a knot of regulars assembled around Mike from right field. Mike's scorecards are works of art: tidily notated, aesthetically finished, carefully maintained. He had with him a collection of memorable moments from Ryne Sandberg's career, all preserved on scorecards he had kept for decades. I, like the others, reverently reconstructed Sandberg's first major league hit from his days with the Phillies, just one of the career moments Mike had witnessed and recorded. I traveled back twenty-one years to the "Ryne Sandberg game," a 12–11 extra-inning win against the Cardinals, a game I had only seen replayed on *ESPN Classic*. Seeing it on the scorecard made it more real than seeing it on TV. When I finally returned to my section, I sent other regulars to go see the treasures Mike had brought. Many went eagerly, appreciating the opportunity to remember concretely the history of a player and games that, as regulars, they shared.

There are undoubtedly similar markers of shared history at other ballparks. Regulars at other fields might or might not buy scorecards, depending on their cost and availability. They will have their own ways of engaging with the game, and even of deciding what part of the game is worth engaging. They will be affected by seating patterns and attendance histories that determine who knows whom and whether they share scorecard information or collect souvenir cups or tailgate. The memorabilia they keep might evoke the warmth of summer in Boston or the welcome breath of the cooling desert when the roof opens in Arizona, but in any case, they will have their memories, one of many things, that, when shared, can form the backbone of community. These memories, unique to place, will make each of these potential communities as distinct as the regulars.

Not every regular keeps score, and even those who do may be hard to spot in the party that characterizes the Wrigley Field bleachers. Ensconced in their usual seats, surrounded by their community, the scorers squint at the field, shield their scorecards from the occasional thrown beer, and yell, "Down in front!" in order to see the play. Why not sit in the field boxes? "The field looks funny from over there," will likely be the reply. "It's hard to judge fly balls. I mix up the fielders."

The real reason? The bleachers are home, and where else would one want to keep score?

Works Cited

Appadurai, Arjun. "Commodities and the Politics of Value." Introduction. *The Social Life of Things.* Ed. Arjun Appadurai. New York: Cambridge UP, 1988. 3–63.

Dickson, Paul. *The Joy of Keeping Score.* San Diego: Harcourt, 1996.

Garner, Tricia. "Buzzer Beaters: Things All Sports Fans Must Do before They Die: Fun in the Sun at Wrigley." *The Sporting News* 12 Aug. 2005: 12–13.

Shea, Stuart. *Wrigley Field: The Unauthorized Biography.* Washington, D.C.: Brassey's, 2004.

PART IV

PLAYERS AS ICONS

John Clarkson, the 34 Million Dollar Man

Shawn O'Hare

The greatest pitcher in the history of the Chicago Cubs is not Mordecai "Three Finger" Brown, or Ferguson Jenkins, or Bruce Sutter, or even Greg Maddux. In fact, according to Major League Baseball's Fantasy Baseball statistics, if the greatest Cubs pitcher of all-time were alive today, he'd earn $34 million a year. That's twice what Babe Ruth would make. According to the statistics, this oft-forgotten Cub produced three of the best fifteen seasons a pitcher has ever had in professional baseball since 1885. And, while he only played for Chicago for four years, righty John Clarkson certainly left his mark on the record books and history of the Chicago Cubs, then called the Chicago White Stockings.

Known for a curveball that was the best of his era, the 1963 Hall of Fame inductee posted a 327–177 career record, with 2,013 strikeouts and a 2.81 ERA over twelve years. That includes his marvelous 1885 season, when he won more than fifty games and led the White Stockings, then managed by Cap Anson and featuring King Kelly, to a World Series tie. In the somewhat controversial but always entertaining *The New Bill James Historical Baseball Abstract: The Classic—Completely Revised*, the famous numbers guru names Clarkson the best pitcher in 1885 and 1889 (40), as one of two pitchers on the "Major League All-Star Team, 1880–1889" (46), as one of two of the "Best-Looking Players" of the 1890s (59), and, most importantly, as the 42nd best pitcher in the history of professional baseball (873).

Born in Cambridge, MA, in 1861, Clarkson trained as a jeweler in his father's shop. He played for a number of elite amateur teams in the Boston area and developed a solid reputation as a pitcher. At this time in baseball, the pitcher was not permitted to release the ball above his waist and the batter was allowed to request a high or low pitch. Although he stood 5'10" and weighed only 155 lbs., Clarkson had long and strong fingers (Clarkson's teammate Billy Sunday claimed that Clarkson could spin a billiard ball in a complete circle around a billiard table) that allowed him to generate a great amount of torque and throw a very effective curveball. David L. Fleitz, in an essay about Clarkson in *Ghosts in the Gallery at Cooperstown*, notes that as a teenager, Clarkson played for a "gentlemanly amateur team, the Beacon nine" (109). In 1882, Clarkson moved up to the National League for three games with the Worchester Ruby Legs and went an undistinguished 1–2 with 49 hits given up and only three strikeouts in 24 innings pitched, with a 4.50 ERA because of a sore arm. The following year, 1883, Clarkson played for Saginaw in the Northwest League. In 1884, Clarkson went 34–9 for Saginaw before the league collapsed and he became a free agent (Fleitz, *Ghosts* 109–10).

After winning three NL pennants in a row—1880, 1881, 1882—the Chicago White Stock-

John Clarkson won 53 games in 1885 for the Chicago White Stockings, later renamed the Cubs (courtesy Baseball Hall of Fame).

ings and manager Cap Anson were looking to bounce back from a disappointing second place finish in 1883 and signed Clarkson in August 1884; he pitched fourteen games, winning ten and losing four. That performance earned Clarkson the second spot in the rotation, after Larry Corcoran, who finished with a 35–23 record, though the Chicagoans finished in fifth place (Fleitz, *Ghosts* 110). During the early and mid 1880s, the White Stockings were known for two things: winning baseball games and raising hell off the field. Clarkson was a "drinking man," and he fit right in with his wild new teammates led by the second-best player on the team (after Anson), King Kelly. As David L. Fleitz discusses throughout *Cap Anson: The Grand Old Man of Baseball*, Anson was constantly fining his players for drinking, being late for games, and getting in trouble with the law. Those teams made the 1986 New York Mets look like choirboys.

In 1885 Clarkson had one of the greatest years in the history of baseball. He pitched in 70 games, completed 68 of them, won 53, lost 16, gave up 497 hits in 623 innings pitched, walked 97, whiffed 318, tossed 10 shutouts (including three shutouts in five days in May and a no-hitter in July), and posted a 1.85 ERA. Fleitz argues that if there had been a Cy Young Award and Most Valuable Player during that time, "Clarkson probably would have won both of them unanimously" (*Ghosts* 111), an impressive feat for a 24-year-old hurler. Although he had a decent fastball, precision control and a sweeping curve were Clarkson's main strengths. In 1909, middle infielder Fred Pfeffer said, "John Clarkson never had a superior as a pitcher, and never will. I have stood behind him day after day and watched his magnificent control, as confident of his success, especially in tight places, as if he had the United States Army behind him" (qtd. in Fleitz, *Ghosts* 112). Jimmy Ryan, one of baseball's first power hitters and the man who later replaced Anson as Cubs' manager, said about Clarkson, "He was one man who was a star. The heaviest batter looked all alike to him. Clarkson was as resourceful and foxy as any pitcher who ever lived, and there have been few equal to him, none to surpass him, in later years" (112).

As successful as the 1885 season was for Clarkson, by the time the White Stockings challenged the St. Louis Browns of the American Association for the best of seven World Series, Clarkson's arm was worn out. He pitched the opening game of the series, which ended in a 5–5 tie when the game was called because of darkness. The White Stockings won the second game, as the umpire ruled a forfeit victory when the St. Louis manager took his team off the field after an argument with the umpire. Leading the Series 1–0–1, the White Stockings pitched Clarkson in Game 3, which he lost. Clarkson again pitched in Game 5, with Chicago winning 9–2, but that was his last game of the year. Chicago lost the next two games, and though the Series was tied 3–3–1, St. Louis declared themselves champions, ignoring the forfeited game (Fleitz, *Ghosts* 111).

Working to Clarkson's benefit during his remarkable 1885 season was a rule change in 1883 that turned the game from something like fast-pitch softball to baseball as we now know it, as the pitcher was allowed to "deliver a ball from above his waist," and starting in 1884, he could deliver the pitch any way he wanted. This pitcher's advantage was further enhanced by the fact that six balls constituted a base on balls. Clarkson's other advantage was a big shiny belt buckle that he wore in an effort to distract the batter by reflecting the sun off the buckle into the batter's box. Clarkson also was not averse to arguing with umpires. Indeed, this is a trait that he shared with skipper Anson, who even as a young manager earned a reputation as a "kicker."

Clarkson's temper, though, did not work in the positive fashion that Anson's did (think of Anson as a nineteenth-century John McEnroe: his frustration, indeed his angst about perceived injustices, actually made him a more focused and driven player). Clarkson had a reputation of being high strung, eccentric, and a bit of a loner. In his autobiography *A Ball Player's Career*, Anson writes that the pitcher had a "particular temperament" and that he needed encouragement to "keep him going." "Scold him, find fault with him and he could not pitch at all," Anson writes. "Praise him and he was unbeatable" (qtd. in Fleitz, *Cap* 127). "Black Jack" Clarkson, as some called him because of his irritability, also tended to coast if the White Stockings had a big lead, which in those pre-glove, error-filled days made his manager uncomfortable. Anson notes that he had to "keep spurring him along, otherwise he was apt to let up, this especially being the case when the club was ahead and he saw what he thought was a chance to save himself" (qtd. in Fleitz, *Cap* 127). Considering that Clarkson averaged 500 innings pitched per year during his four-year tenure with the White Stockings, pacing himself might have been a good idea.

Perhaps Clarkson's most famous run-in with an umpire happened one late afternoon when the pitcher complained that it was too dark to continue the game. The umpire disagreed and sent Clarkson to the pitcher's box. In the fading twilight, Clarkson fired a first-pitch called strike. Instead of throwing one of his trademark fall-off-a-table curveballs or sneaky fastballs, Clarkson had delivered a "lemon-ball." When the umpire saw the fruit in the catcher's hands, he quickly called the game due to darkness (Fleitz, *Ghosts* 113).

Along with his temper, Clarkson was also well known for his professional appearance, even having a reputation for being a bit of a dandy. An article in the *Detroit News*, following Clarkson's death, noted that he "was always a 'tidy' pitcher. His uniform was always immaculate, his linen always possessed that fresh-from-the-laundry touch, he was always smoothly shaven, his manners were always faultless." Clarkson was also known to carry a white silk handkerchief in his baseball uniform, though when Pittsburgh's Jake Stenzel once taunted him to "put away that society rag and pitch ball," Clarkson struck him out on three pitches, all curveballs, of course (Fleitz, *Ghosts* 112).

As well as pitching Chicago to a World Series championship in 1885 and posting those remarkable statistics, Clarkson helped stymie the defending champions, the Providence Grays, who completed the previous year with an 84–28 record and won the championship. Most remarkable about that team was Charles "Old Hoss" Radbourn, who pitched in 75 games and won 60, the major league record (Clarkson and Radbourn were later teammates on the Boston Beaneaters from 1888–1890). When Anson signed Clarkson in 1884, one of the things he had in mind was to find a pitcher who could compete against Radbourn, an inductee in the fourth Hall of Fame class in 1939. Clarkson was ready for the challenge, and in fact he asked for the ball every time the White Stockings matched up with Radbourn. Clarkson got the best of his future teammate, winning 10 of 12 starts against him, which included a no-hitter thrown in Providence on July 27, 1885.

After Clarkson pitched the White Stockings to back-to-back World Series appearances in 1885 and 1886,[1] team owner Albert Spalding decided to retool the club. His most controversial decision, which was supported by Anson, was to sell the team's star, King Kelly. Michael Joseph "King" Kelly from Troy, NY, was one of the best ballplayers of his day. In 1886, he hit .388 and stole 53 bases. Although he led the Chicago team to five pennants in seven seasons, Anson was tired of his drunken escapades, and when the Boston Beaneaters offered a then record $10,000 for him, Spalding accepted the richest deal in baseball history. Kelly was so well-loved in Chicago that fans sang a song about him called "Slide, Kelly, Slide" that lamented his leaving. In his first year in Boston, in 1887, Kelly hit .394, but his career started to fall apart after that. He died in 1894 at the age of 36, and in 1900 Anson wrote:

> He played good ball for a time, but his bad habits soon caused his downfall [...] for baseball and booze will not mix any better than will oil and water. The last time I ever saw him was at an Eastern hotel barroom, and during the brief space of time we conversed together he threw in enough whiskey to put an ordinary man under the table. [...] He died in New Jersey, a victim to fast living, and a warning to all ballplayers [qtd. in Leitner 165].

The spring after the Beaneaters bought Kelly — on April 3, 1888 — they again offered Chicago $10,000, this time for Clarkson. The White Stockings were in the midst of rebuilding — the year after they lost the World Series to the Browns they dropped to third place — and Clarkson was glad for the opportunity to get back to his native Massachusetts. The sale of Clarkson had two significant results: first, the National League "formally adopted a standard salary clas-sification for players in 1888. [...] players henceforth were to be divided into five fixed salary categories, which automatically would restrict their income as follows: A $2,500; B $2,250; C $2,000; D $1,750; E $1,500" (Leitner 166), and second, that salary structure eventually led to the Players League revolt in 1890 since, much like today's professional sports, the players wanted a larger cut of the owners' profits.

In *The Complete Chicago Cubs*, Derek Gentile calls Clarkson the Jim "Catfish" Hunter of the nineteenth century (462). It is a fitting comparison because, like Hunter, Clarkson welcomed the chance to pitch in the big games. Though he relied heavily on the breaking ball, Clarkson could mix up his pitches with an effective fastball and a change-up that has been described as "hellacious" (Gentile 462). During the course of his twelve years in the big leagues, Clarkson had to adapt not only to playing with four teams (Worchester, Chicago, Boston, and Cleveland) but also to a variety of rule changes. For the most part, the rule changes benefited the pitcher. In 1883 the pitcher could throw overhand. The following year, six balls was a walk. In 1887, the pitcher's box was trimmed to 4 feet by 5½ feet, batters no longer requested the location of pitches, five balls became a walk, and, in that season only, four strikes were needed for a strikeout and a base on balls counted as a hit for the batter. In 1889, four balls became a base on balls. The rule change that Clarkson could not overcome, however, was when the pitching distance went from 50 feet to 60'6" in 1893.

During the 1892 season, Clarkson was traded from Boston to the Cleveland Spiders, and, statistically, his last two years —1893 and 1894 — were his worst two years, as he went 24–27. Undoubtedly, the removal of the pitching box, the addition of a 12" × 4" pitching rubber, and having to throw the ball 20 percent further greatly affected Clarkson, who had built his career on angles and deception. In *The Physics of Baseball*, Robert Kemp Adair, a Yale profes-sor and official Physicist to the National League from 1987–1989 (a title bestowed on him by Commissioner A. Bartlett Giamatti), contends that on a 60'6" flight, the curveball moves 14.4 inches. This happens because excess force is applied to one side of the ball (from the way it is gripped and the movement of the wrist) and forces the ball to the low resistance side which makes it curve. This is known as Bernoulli's Principle, named for the eighteenth-cen-tury Swiss scientist (Adair also reminds us that a 23-year-old Isaac Newton studied the cur-vature of a tennis ball, the nineteenth-century mathematical physicist Lord Rayleigh examined the paths of spinning balls, and the Scottish physicist P. G. Trait wrote about the curve of golf balls. According to Adair, with a curveball, half of the movement happens in the last 15 feet) (Adair 25–27). Simply put, after years of throwing curveballs at 50 feet, the addition of another 10½ feet more than likely flattened out Clarkson's curveball. The rapid decline of Clarkson's career, despite his great number of innings pitched and his inevitable sore arm, probably has more to do with physics. In *Baseball-istics: The Basic Physics of Baseball*, Robert Froman underscores this role of physics in throwing a baseball by recalling two of Galileo's discoveries: (1) "Any body free to fall toward the earth will fall faster and faster the longer it keeps falling" and (2) "A body's horizontal speed has no effect on its rate of fall toward the earth" (68).

In short, if we apply Galileo's theories to Clarkson, it becomes apparent that even if Clark-son threw harder — and his curveball was more along the lines of a roundhouse than a nickel — it really would not make much of a difference. Years of muscle memory told Clarkson's body to throw a fifty-foot curve, and thus just after he turned 33, rather than report to the Balti-more Orioles, who had recently acquired him, John Clarkson retired as the all-time leader in wins in National League history. Sixty-one years later Clarkson finally was inducted into the Hall of Fame.

Following his retirement in 1894, Clarkson held a number of jobs, including owning a cigar shop in Bay City, Michigan. In 1906 he had a psychological breakdown, and he spent the final years of his life in and out of hospitals. He eventually moved back to Massachusetts to be closer to his family. In 1909, when he was in a hospital in Belmont, MA, Clarkson died from pneumonia. In the 1970s, however, Clarkson's name started to appear again in the media with rumors that in 1905 Clarkson murdered his wife. The rumor was even presented as a fact in a 1994 book. The rumors, however, were unsubstantiated, and Fleitz ably discredits them in *Ghosts in the Gallery at Cooperstown* (124). Still, the "Clarkson was a murderer" tale appears occasionally when arguments are made about the moral status of Hall of Famers, and in recent years allusions to the Clarkson rumor have been made to further the contention that Shoeless Joe Jackson and Pete Rose should be allowed into the Hall of Fame. Despite the innuendos and the tragedies of his personal life, John Clarkson's career statistics, his reputation as one of the game's great pitchers, and his place in the Hall of Fame mark him as the greatest pitcher in Chicago history.

NOTE

1. In 1886, in the tenth inning of the sixth game, Clarkson actually threw a wild pitch that lost the Series to the St. Louis Browns; the great King Kelly, however, called it a passed ball and said, "I signaled for Clarkson for a low ball on one side and when it came it was high up on the other. It struck my hand as I tried to get it, and I would say it was a passed ball. You can give it to me, if you want to. Clarkson told me that it slipped from his hands" (Sullivan 143).

WORKS CITED

Adair, Robert Kemp. *The Physics of Baseball*. New York: Harper & Row, 1990.

Fleitz, David L. *Cap Anson: The Grand Old Man of Baseball*. Jefferson, NC: McFarland, 2005.

_____. *Ghosts in the Gallery at Cooperstown*. Jefferson, NC: McFarland, 2004.

Froman, Robert. *Baseball-istics: The Basic Physics of Baseball*. New York: GP Putnam's Sons, 1967.

Gentile, Derek. *The Complete Chicago Cubs*. New York: Black Dog & Leventhal Publishers, 2004.

James, Bill. *The New Bill James Historical Baseball Abstract: The Classic—Completely Revised*. New York: Free Press, 2001.

Leitner, Irving A. *Baseball: Diamond in the Rough*. New York: Criterion Books, 1972.

Sullivan, Dean A., ed. *Early Innings: A Documentary History of Baseball, 1825–1908*. Lincoln, NE: U of Nebraska P, 1995.

Hack Wilson in Chicago

Bob Boone and Jerry Grunska

[Editors' Note: From rural western Pennsylvania, Hack Wilson worked his way through the minors, despite prejudice against his height, 5'6", and John McGraw's concern that "He ain't got no neck." After a brief stint with the Giants in 1923, he had a very successful year in 1924, batting .295 with 10 home runs in 107 games. But, typical of the roller-coaster ride of his career, 1925 didn't match his first full year, and he was demoted to the Toledo Mudhens. He was unprotected by McGraw and the Giants the next year, and the Cubs' new manager, Joe McCarthy, was quick to take Wilson for the $5,000 fee. The story below picks up at the beginning of the 1926 season.]

Hack eased into spring training in 1926 by averaging one hit per game, making several notable catches, stealing five bases, and winning one game with a long homer. This performance was good enough for him to be made cleanup batter, but not good enough to earn headlines. To Irving Vaughan of the *Chicago Tribune*, however, he was already "McCarthy's most valuable player."

When the Cubs began the regular season in Cincinnati, Wilson was in center field. He had a triple that day in four trips to the plate. The next day he went hitless, and in the last game of the series he had one more triple. The team moved on to St. Louis, where he began to hit with authority. In the third game of this series, he went three for four and scored the winning run. Chicago was the next stop.

It was a time when Chicago sports fans badly wanted an athletic hero. In an age of national figures like Ruth, Dempsey, Tunney, and Tilden, the city could claim few sports figures of its own. Sports in Chicago had been generally disappointing in recent years. The White Sox had done nothing to distinguish themselves except get caught fixing the 1919 World Series. In six of the last seven years the Cubs had finished in the second division. The 1925 team had finished last.

That opening day at home, 26,000 fans turned out to see if the team would be any better under a new manager. Many had read about Wilson, the new center fielder, who now was referred to in the papers as merely a "pleasant surprise." He was, in fact, about to begin a batting assault that in six weeks would take him to the very center of the Chicago sports scene.

His attack began that day in Chicago with a double that helped Grover Cleveland Alexander beat the Reds. Two days later he contributed to an 18–1 Cubs victory by going two for four. Two days after that, in a win over Pittsburgh, he went two for three and stole a base. On April 29 he had the game-winning hit against the Cardinals. The St. Louis pitcher had intended to walk him, but Wilson reached out and bashed one to right for a double. The

Cubs swept the St. Louis series, with Wilson going two for four in each of the remaining two games. After the final game, his picture appeared at the top of the *Tribune* sports page.

Within a week, newspaper writers began to reach for inflated language to describe Wilson. In a close game against the Giants, it was "Heroic Hack" who came to bat with the bases loaded. The crowd, according to a news report, was "mad with joy." That day he dribbled meekly to short.

But in two days he was once again performing up to the crowd's expectations. He went two for three that afternoon but ended the day in the arms of four teammates as they lugged him from the field with a badly twisted ankle. When the game ended, the outfield crowd descended on the dugout, not to congratulate the winning pitcher, Alexander, but to clamor around Wilson. After they were shooed away, Judge Landis approached to ask about the injury. "It's all right, Judge," beamed Wilson. "I'll be back in there in a few days."

He returned sooner than he promised. The next afternoon, May 9, he sat on the bench for the first eight innings watching his Cubs stay two runs behind the Giants. Then in the ninth inning, McCarthy called on him to start a rally. Swinging a load of bats, he limped from the dugout. At the plate he went through his ritual with the dust and then stepped in as 36,000 people watched. Knowing Wilson's propensity for hitting to right and well aware of his gimpiness, Giants manager McGraw moved the shortstop to the first base side of second. He also waved the outfielders around. Wilson rejected the first two pitches, stepped out for some dust and then, with uncharacteristic guile, bent one to left for a double. He stood on second with his hands on his hips. He panted and smiled until a pinch runner replaced him, and then he limped slowly back to the dugout. A fan recalled that this was "the first time I knew Hack Wilson was something special. It was not just that he was good, but that he knew when to be good."

Back in action one week later, he raised his average to .370 by going three for three. On May 23 he made the headlines for the sixth time that month after he hit a home run that bounced off the scoreboard outside the left center-field wall. This was the longest ball ever hit in Wrigley Field. The next time at bat he had to be restrained by four teammates after Braves hurler Bunny Hearn threw a fastball at his head.

That night after dinner, Wilson was invited upstairs to the apartment of Lottie and Michael Frain. Fifty neighborhood people were there; so were buckets of beer. For most of the night Wilson was surrounded by knots of well-wishers who wanted to hear all about the long homer. At 11:00 P.M. four Chicago policemen arrived to put a stop to the illegal drinking. Wilson tried to slip out the side door but was nabbed. While other arrests were being made, Mrs. Frain suddenly picked up a cupid-shaped bookend and fired it at a policeman. The bookend was followed by an ashtray. On his way out the door, Wilson and others who had been arrested first gave her a loud cheer.

The next day an article on the front page of the *Chicago Daily News* reported that Mrs. Frain had been fined $100. The others at the party, including Wilson, were fined $1, to be given to the Aged and Adult Charities.

A few days after this arrest, Wilson got into a shoving match with two policemen in a line waiting to buy food. He was charged with disorderly conduct, but at the station the captain, a loyal fan, dismissed the charges. He also ordered the officers to apologize.

By the end of May, even Wilson's baseball failures were being rewarded. On the 29th his only contribution was a weak trickler back to the mound, but that didn't stop a gang of men and boys from escorting him to his apartment, as they had been doing for the past several weeks. As the entourage moved noisily through the streets, people leaned out of windows to wave and shout.

When such groups left Wilson at his apartment, they may have thought he was getting ready for another night on the town. Actually, those who knew him well in those first Cubs years insist that he gained most of his pleasure from his profession and his family, not alcohol. Incidents like the one at the Frains were rare. More typical was a walk in the park, with Wilson, in suit and tie, pushing the baby carriage while his wife strolled alongside. At home at night, he and Virginia chatted about their home town of Martinsburg, WV, or quibbled about money. Often Wilson would drift off into a smiling snooze while Virginia sat on the couch, quietly knitting.

As the 1926 season moved to a close, the fans grew more fanatic. In August, after a timely homer by Wilson, a dozen people were waiting for him at the plate. Three days later when he was booted from a game for swearing at the umpire, the crowd set up an eerie howl that lasted for innings.

Newspapers continued to follow him assiduously, taking note even of his sweating. To Westbrook Pegler he was "Hack Wilson, that porous party of perspiration." Other writers observed that his sweating, red neck, dirty uniform, and stocky frame were perfect for such a character.

On September 14, his first year as a Cub ended abruptly. A pitch thrown by Philly hurler Hal Carlson struck him in the temple and dropped him to the ground, where he lay as if he were dead. He did haul himself up on his legs but then fell back once more with a grunt that could be heard throughout the suddenly silent ballpark.

He did not play again until the final game of that season, but he had done well enough before his injury to get 21 home runs and 109 RBIs to accompany a .321 batting average. In RBIs he was second in the league to "Sunny" Jim Bottomley. In slugging percentage he was also second. In bases on balls — an indication of the respect he had earned — he led the league with 69. His home run total topped the league.

Wilson's stunning rise in Chicago is attributed in part to McCarthy's leadership. McCarthy not only knew that Wilson should be allowed to swing when he wanted, but he also understood that his slugger had an unusual need for public approval. If the crowds failed to applaud, McCarthy would take their place. McCarthy also brought a toughness to the Cubs organization which fit Hack's volatile style.

Opening day of 1927 brought 42,000 people to Wrigley Field. Wilson went hitless, but each of his successive trips to the plate ignited a thunderous reaction. Two days later he won a game with a homer in the ninth. By the time he reached the plate, fans were scurrying around the field like crazed mice. The next day when he came to bat, the cheering could be heard at the lake two miles away.

One day in June of 1927 he became embroiled in a shouting match with the umpire, who had called him out on strikes. In the midst of the shouting, Reds catcher Val Picinich muttered an insult about fat people. Wilson turned on him, reached through his mask to twist his nose and then shoved him all the way to the box seats. A week later he pushed another umpire into Cubs first baseman Charlie Grimm, who fell down on his bat.

In a game on April 25, 1928, he threw a ball so far over the catcher's head that it lodged in a rain gutter. A few days later he saved a game for the Cubs by making a miraculous catch in the far corner of the outfield. On May 12, he chased after a pitcher who had thrown at his head. Early in July, after a swinging strike, he threw his bat in disgust all the way to the outfield. He sprinted out to retrieve it and then hit a home run on the next pitch.

As a hitter in 1928 he was particularly potent in the first half of the season. On July 7 he completed a week in which he batted .531. At that point in the season he was batting well over .300 and leading the league with 22 home runs. But suddenly he dropped into one of the worst slumps of his career. On July 14 he batted .182 for the week. By July 25 his weekly average had slipped to .136. By August 4, his season average dropped below .300. For the first time as a Cub he began to hear boos. He did not react to this criticism on the field, but at home he grew edgy. Twice during his slump he disappeared for long evenings on his own.

At last on August 7 he broke out of the slump by going three for four, and for the rest of the season he played up to his fans' expectations. His only absence from the lineup until the end of the season was due to a three-day suspension that followed another bat-throwing incident.

Wilson started the 1929 season with a predictable flourish. Early in May he made perhaps his greatest catch as he raced to the far reaches of the Polo Grounds to haul down a Mel Ott drive and save a game for Chicago. Two days later he sprained his ankle badly after a diving grab in short center field. Cameramen surrounded his wheelchair that night at the Boston train station.

The Cubs played well early in the season, but not well enough to lead. On June 17 they endured a 13–3 loss to the Cardinals, but they came back to win the remaining three games of the series. The *Tribune* took special satisfaction from this turn of events: "Those haughty Red-birds flew into town last Monday and trimmed our nine in the opener and limped out last night jabbering like Cockatoos." Businessmen joined the paper in promoting the Cubs' pennant drive. In July Hack was awarded a radio by the Grigsby and Grunow Company after he hit six home runs in four days.

But gradually the Cubs' power began to dominate. By the end of July, after winning nine in a row, Chicago had developed a lead of four and one-half games.

On August 25 the Cubs opened a series in Cincinnati that attracted interest because certain Reds had vowed to "get" Wilson for an attack he had made on Reds pitcher Ray Kolp earlier that year. The day before the series began, the president of the Reds urged spectators to be "ladylike," including those 2,000 who traveled from Chicago. As it turned out, nothing violent happened. Wilson chatted happily with fans in the outfield and even smiled in the third game after a pitch sailed past his ear. After dumping the Reds three out of four games, the Cubs left town 14½ games in the lead.

By the middle of September, the Cubs had clinched the pennant and eventually finished 10½ games ahead of Pittsburgh, 13½ over New York, and 20 over the Cardinals.

In the 1929 World Series against the Philadelphia Athletics, after losing games 1 and 2, the Cubs won game three 3–1 and were ahead 8–0 after six innings in game 4. Al Simmons began the seventh inning with a home run to left, making the score 8–1. Jimmy Foxx followed with a single. Bing Miller then hit a fly that became a single when Wilson lost it in the sun. Jimmy Dykes singled to left, Foxx scored, and Miller stopped at second. The score stood at 8–2 with no outs and two men on base. Joe Boley followed with a single, making the score 8–3. George Burns, batting for Eddie Rommell, made the first out of the seventh by popping to Woody English, but Max Bishop singled to center, scoring Dykes and making the score 8–4.

Art Nehf relieved Charlie Root and faced Mule Haas. With the count one and one and with Bishop on first and Boley on second, Haas sent a fly ball to center field. Wilson ran in, suddenly lost it in the sun, and tried to block it with his body, but it sailed over his head. By the time he returned the ball to the infield, Haas had rounded the bases for an inside-the-park home run, making the score 8–7. The Athletics scored two more runs in the inning and won 10–8.

Enraged, *Tribune* writer Ed Burns shared his feelings with readers the next day: "It remained for our beloved Cubs to furnish the greatest debacle, the most terrific flop in the history of the World Series and one of the worst in the history of baseball and games of all kinds." Burns fixed much of the blame on Wilson, not the sun. Wilson had made an error in the fifth and dropped a ball earlier in the seventh; therefore, "he had ample warning that his sun glasses were not adequate."

Tom Meany, in a 1932 article for the *New York World Telegram*, summed up the popular view of Wilson's reaction to the dropped fly:

> Hack took his humiliation heavily. He walked from the field with tears in his eyes, his round head hanging low on his chest, looking every inch a beaten man. Wilson knew how much winning the world series would have meant to his owner, the late William Wrigley, who had dealt so generously with him, and to Joe McCarthy, the man who had given Hack his second shot at the big time. The idol of Chicago's north side felt that he had betrayed his public, his president and his manager.

This account is fanciful. Wilson impressed people at Shibe Park by walking from the field with his eyes straight ahead. He did not hide in the corner of the clubhouse, and when the bus got back to the hotel, instead of running to his room he remained in the lobby, talking and smiling with acquaintances. Not until the next day did he start to criticize himself and to refuse his teammates' condolences.

In that day's *Tribune* appeared the "Wrigley Field Blues":

> The sun shone bright in our great Hack
> Wilson's eyes — Tis Sunday, the Mack men are gay —
>
> The third game's won, and Cub pitching's gone astray —
> As our series title fades far away.
>
> Weep no more, dear Cub fan,
> Oh weep no more today; for we'll
>
> Sing one song for the game and fighting Cubs,
> For the record whiffing Cubs far away.

The 1929 World Series ended quietly on October 14 in Philadelphia, no longer front-page news in the *Tribune*, when the A's scored three runs in the ninth to win 4–3. Wilson, wearing special six-ply glasses, went one for four. His first fielding chance since the seventh inning of game 4 came in the eighth inning. He ran back to where he thought the ball was going to land, appeared to lose sight of it, and then ran in to make the catch.

After the game, he tried to joke. "I don't suppose the Martinsburg chapter of the Elks will meet me in the station, but we'll have a great winter all the same." On the train back to Chicago, players were awakened by a drumming sound. Peering out from the curtains on the berths, they saw Wilson in the aisle on his knees, cursing and beating the floor.

Five hundred fans greeted the Cubs at Chicago's Union Station. Kind words fell upon Wilson as he moved slowly through the station. "They give me hell with their razzing when I'm going good and now when I deserve it, they give me cheers instead. You can't figure 'em," he said.

Perhaps the people in Chicago were kindly because they realized that Wilson did not entirely deserve the goat horns. His .470 batting average led both teams. In the first three games he had fielded brilliantly, saving several runs. Even if he had caught Haas's fly in the seventh inning of the fourth game, Philadelphia still would have won, assuming the other A's produced the same hits. The four errors of English and the .238 batting of Rogers Hornsby were as much responsible for the series loss as Wilson's dropped fly.[1]

During the 1929 season Wilson had two well-publicized fights that crystallized his reputation as a brawler. The first, which took place on July 4, was a two-round affair. Round one opened with Wilson on first base, being heckled from the Reds dugout. The opponents insulted his physique, his nightlife, and his style of play. A disparaging reference to his birth shouted out by Ray Kolp, a notorious bench jockey Wilson had frequently vowed he would silence, was the last straw. After the fourth "bastard" Hack called time out and rocketed toward the dugout, where he disappeared head first with his arms flailing. Police, ushers, players and a few courageous fans pried him loose. On his way to the showers, he twice broke free from his handlers, but in the end he was taken from the field.

Round two was fought that night at the train station where the Cubs and the Reds were both leaving on the same train. When Wilson arrived, he marched up to a group of Reds standing near the gate and demanded to see Kolp. His face was red and his voice shook.

Jake May of the Reds tried to mollify him. "He's back in the Pullman, Hack. Take it easy." The advice did not penetrate. Wilson vowed, "I'm going back in there and make him apologize for what he called me."

In the group was pitcher Pete Donohue, who stood practically a foot taller than Wilson. "You go in there and you'll never come out," Donohue suggested. Wilson turned on him. "Well, I may not come out, but I'm going in all the same. No one can call me that word and mean it."

Donohue followed with another sarcastic remark, and then mumbled that Kolp's word was the right one. "Get ready, you son of a bitch," Wilson warned as he pushed between two players and smashed Donohue in the face. The Reds pitcher had a mouthful of blood as he fell to the cement floor.

Wilson's suspension after this attack was loudly condemned by Cubs loyalists. An alderman told the newspaper what he felt about the fight: "Mr. Wilson is a fine young man, and I know that Mr. Donohue deserved to be struck in the mouth. Otherwise Mr. Wilson would not have struck him there."

John Heydler, president of the National League, apparently concurred. He examined all the facts and concluded that Wilson had not technically attacked Donohue since the Reds pitcher should have been prepared to defend himself.

That same season Wilson's name appeared in the headlines a second time for fighting. This time he vaulted into the stands to throttle an abusive fan named Young. As a result of the attack, Wilson was served with a $20,000 lawsuit. At the trial Young, a milkman, told the judge that he called Wilson nothing worse than a big tub. He asserted that Wilson lost control of himself, climbed into the grandstand, bent Young back over a seat, and fractured his lip with his fist.

Wilson's version was that a drunken Young had called him names far worse than 'big tub." He climbed into the stands intending to warn Young, but he slipped and the milkman jumped him. The judge agreed that Wilson was acting in self-defense and dismissed the suit.

The belligerent Art Shires, a White Sox first baseman who fancied himself a fighter, had his manager, James Mullins, send Wilson a telegram challenging him to a public bout. Wilson, smiling all the time, rose to his feet, paused, and then bellowed: "I accept. Wire him right away and tell him to name the place." Toward the end of the meeting a second telegram arrived from Shires: "Have decided I will fight any place but in the sun." A queasy silence followed.

The battle began with verbal exchanges in the newspapers. Wilson was quoted as saying:

Sure I'll fight. I'm in good shape from hunting and I'm going to start tomorrow strengthening my ring muscles. I'm going to get some of the best fighters in the East to help me brush up on boxing, and I'll give Art a good fight. Art Shires will be a mighty good man if he earns a victory over Lewis R. Wilson of Martinsburg, West Virginia.

The next day Shires fired back:

> Hack will lose sight of my gloves just as he lost sight of the ball in the World Series. But instead of looking at the sun, he'll be seeing more stars than there are in heaven. The fact that Hack Wilson belongs in the National League, which is really a minor league, does not prod my major league pride. The worst thing I have to say about Sunny Boy is that he is an outfielder and outfielders, for the most part, are a worthless lot.

A typical Wilson response was:

> Right here and now I want to tell Mr. Shires that I am one of those hearty mountaineers from West Virginia, the class of people who do things without bragging about them. Down here we knock poundage off each other, so if Mr. Shires has any superfluous flesh on his body, he won't need any training to get it off after we get together.

While boastful language bounced from West Virginia to Illinois and back again, Cubs president Bill Veeck tried to stop the fight. He called Hack and reminded him that he would be acting on his own if he fought Shires. An unawed Wilson broadly hinted that a $10,000 raise might change his mind. That afternoon Veeck called Virginia Wilson about the same time that Mullins, sensing the pressure on Wilson, increased Wilson's share of the prize money from $10,000 to $15,000. The newspapers made him a 7–5 favorite.

When the *Chicago Tribune* sent reporter Ed Burns to West Virginia, Wilson explained his dilemma: "$15,000 is a lot of bucks. I've been undergoing the most terrific struggle trying to be good and say no, but I just can't turn down that kind of dough." Out of respect for the Cubs, he did offer to fight under a different name. He chose "Battling Stouts."

At his home on John Street, Wilson talked to Burns about knockouts. He had no real fear, he explained, because getting knocked out was just like "seeing canaries and rainbows and pretty stars. Rather pleasant, in fact."

When Shires unexpectedly lost a preliminary fight to George "The Brute" Trafton, the center for the Chicago Bears, Wilson sent word that, as far as he was concerned, the fight was off. Earlier, intrigued by the prospect of the promised cash, he had gone to the local bank and fondled $15,000, first in bills and then in gold. But while the money intrigued him, his reaction to the abortive Shires match was different from that of the others involved. Shires posed and postured. Mullins poured out promises of dollars. The newspapers filled the normally dull holiday sport pages with news of the coming event. Wilson, on the other hand, took the fight quite seriously: "I had a feeling that I owed it to the quiet, dignified players of the major league to slap down this braggart, but Trafton took care of the matter."

In 1930 the Cubs got off to a sluggish start. By the end of May, the Cubs had a mediocre 19–19 record. In June they began to win more persistently, but after they finally fought their way into first place on June 30, they dropped right back into second. Writer Irving Vaughan used a culinary metaphor to tell this tale. "Our Cubs had a noon meal in first place, but when the supper bell rang they were right back in second," behind the Robins.

Hack had continued to act in the grand style. One day in June he faced his old nemesis, Dazzy Vance, an encounter milked by Vaughan:

> Vance's face beamed in smiles as Hack Wilson strode to the plate. Vance's merriment became contagious. Times almost innumerable in seasons past, Vance had sent the slugger trudging crestfallen back to the dugout after swinging blindly at three strikes. Six times in a row last year he had fanned the Cub slugger, and on numerous other occasions had caused him to tap meekly to the infield. Vance wound up and pitched. With lightning speed, the ball passed Hack and cracked in the glove of Deberry with the report of a pistol shot. Ball one! Another flash of white between the pitcher's box and the plate, and Hack swung, twisting completely around as he put all his

weight behind the blow. Again the crack in the glove, and the crowd laughed as the umpire's right hand flashed up to signal "strike one." There was a suspicion of sarcasm in Vance's smile as he tossed the next one outside for ball two, and it became more pronounced as he sent the next one zipping past Wilson and Hack half fell to the ground as he swung. The ripple of laughter from the stands this time grew into a roar in which "Boo-oo" was the dominant note. Again Vance wound up, again the ball flashed, and again Hack swung. Again there was the crack with the report of a pistol shot. But the crack was the impact of a ball, traveling with dazzling speed, against the bat swung with all the power and weight of Wilson's 200 pounds. Vance looked calmly upward as the ball rose over his head and straightened out toward center field. Wilson plodded toward first and English loped lightly toward the plate. The "boo" changed slowly into an "ah" and then to a "yeah" as Wilson rounded first. The smile on the face of Vance — Vance the dazzler — the conqueror of Chicago, the nemesis of Wilson, faded slowly and his jaw dropped as the ball landed high up against the scoreboard in deep center field and smacked with a crack faintly reminiscent of the crack in Deberry's glove. Wilson trotted briskly around the bases and planted his right foot firmly on the plate, turning to Vance with a grin. The ball game was over. [...] The rest of the game was just an encounter between eighteen men doing nothing in particular.

It is said that Wilson persuaded his teammates to read this passage aloud to enrich the long train rides east. Through the years, this was one article he supposedly kept nearby, even after he had lost everything else.

But just when it appeared that the Cubs would slug their way into another World Series, they ran out of muscle. On August 31 Chicago fell to the surging Cardinals. St. Louis pitcher Bill "Either you walk 'em or you fan 'em" Hallahan did not give Wilson a chance to hit, issuing him four intentional passes. The next day the Cubs dropped two more, collecting only eight hits all afternoon.

The difference between Wilson and other team members also appeared in performance, for, unlike his fellows, Wilson did not falter. On September 6 he whacked his 47th homer, but more consequential than that was RBI number 162. This established a new league mark. On the 15th of September he reached 50 home runs and went right on two days later to collect numbers 51 and 52. On the last day of the season he banged home numbers 55 and 56 and batted in his 190th runner. These statistics were accompanied by a .356 batting average.

At the beginning of the 1931 season, the Cubs struggled into a first-place tie with the Cardinals by the end of April. But Wilson didn't lift a home run until Saturday, May 2, in an 8–3 loss to the Cards at St. Louis.

The Cubs dropped to fourth by the middle of May. Rogers Hornsby, the new manager, was caught in a swirl of rumors that he planned to bench both Wilson and Gabby Hartnett for light hitting. After a month Wilson had had just two homers. However, Hornsby was no terror at bat himself, registering only .192 at this stage. By the end of May, Wilson had dropped from .281 to .273 and was finally benched.

Frustrated, one afternoon he vaulted from his dugout confinement to challenge the entire Cincinnati team. Teammates joined umpires to pull him back.

On June 4 he stood 80 points down from the previous June, 1930, average of .341 and had only 3 home runs, compared with 17 in 1930. Later in June he had a brief flurry of four homers in five games against the Braves and Robins. He hit another against the Giants on June 22, but by the end of the month he was riding the pines again. This time it was because "a clambake or lodge meeting" had captured his and Hartnett's attention past the curfew hour, according to the paper.

It was not published at the time, but reprimands for each of these misadventures lightened Wilson's billfold. His contract for 1931 was for a then-spectacular $33,000.

Up until midseason of 1931 Wilson's irregular social habits had been treated lightheartedly in the press. As long as he was producing timely hits, his escapades were reported as earned respites. Now that he was struggling at the plate, his appetites became a convenient target for finger-pointing.

After July 4 Wilson came to life again with a .406 average for a six-day span, which he climaxed with his 11th home run on the 11th. From then on, though, he was strictly a punch-and-judy hitter and was benched a third time by month's end. Hornsby suggested that the rest would improve his hitting.

The critical events that led to Wilson's suspension took place on the eastern swing the last two weeks in August. In the first doubleheader in New York on August 24, with Cubs president Bill Veeck and owner William Wrigley, Jr., in the stands, Wilson protested a called third strike in the sixth inning of the second game and was chased by umpire Reardon. But he refused to leave. Instead he took his place in the outfield and pantomimed insults to Reardon. Finally his own teammates had to pull him off the field so the game could go on. He went on a tear that night, and Hornsby vowed to suspend him right then. Wilson, contrite and desperate, stood before the whole team the next day and pledged to mend his ways, being careful to praise Hornsby's fair treatment of him.

Hornsby, though, apparently intended to have him hug the bench the rest of the season. On September 4, the day before the trip home from Cincinnati, the Cubs developed an outfield dilemma when Vince Barton had to fly to the funeral of a brother in Toronto. With Riggs Stephenson already out and Wilson benched, Hornsby chose to use pitcher Bud Teachout in the outfield, explaining, "Hack knows he is through as a Cub so it would hardly be fair to either himself or the team to play him."

Wilson's promise to behave himself dissolved after the sixth straight loss to Cincinnati on Saturday, September 5. Wilson and Pat Malone did the town again, and then they encountered two reporters at the train station while preparing to board for Chicago. The newsmen were Harold Johnson of the *Chicago American* and Wayne K. Otto of the *Herald-Examiner*. Malone had just been beaten the day before, 3–2 in ten innings. Johnson taunted him by saying, "I've just had a chat with Mordecai Brown. Did you ever hear of him, Pat? He was a great pitcher in his time." Malone responded by bouncing a right fist off Johnson's head. Otto leaped in and Malone turned his ferocity on him, pummeling him about the head and shoulders. Players rushed to pry them apart as Wilson stood by, apparently approving the assault.

Malone drew a $500 fine and a promise to be traded at season's end. But the trade did not materialize, and he remained a Cub for three more seasons. Wilson, however, was suspended for the remainder of the year, which meant he lost $3,500 in salary. He accepted it without a whimper, although claiming that his wallet had already been lightened that season by $1,800 for periodic infractions.

His apparent good grace made him seem oblivious to the implications of the punishment. He came to Wrigley Field as a spectator, vowing to return as a Cub. But he also talked of starting a comeback in the minors. He signed autographs, and he and his wife were photographed in the stands, smiling amiably. Mike Kreevich from Des Moines replaced him on the Chicago roster.

On the 22nd a parody of Oliver Wendell Holmes's "Old Ironsides" appeared in the *Chicago Tribune*. It was titled "Old Hack."

Freedom's price was indeed dear, and the lament became a fact on December 10, 1931, when he and Bud Treachout were traded to St. Louis for Burleigh Grimes. He enjoyed one more glory day in Chicago when the McKeesport, PA, team he played for in his late 30s journeyed to Chicago on August 21, 1938, for a doubleheader with another semipro team in Mills

Stadium on the west side. Entranced by his return, eight thousand people turned out to see the former Cubs slugger. But he produced only one single and retired from exhaustion in the fifth inning of the second game. The fans, though, applauded his every move, and rose to welcome him in his first appearance at the plate. When he left the game, they protested so vociferously that he finished the afternoon as coach at first base. The *Chicago Tribune* reported that he

> [...] spoke with longing of his days with the Cubs, the peak of his tempestuous career. His smile was as spontaneous as ever, but his eyes told the story. There were shadows there and one could gather without his saying it that his thoughts were even then in ornate Wrigley Field, where 40,000 fans, the same fans who had cheered him to the echo only eight years before, were inspiring the new north side idols to double victory over the Pirates.

The *Tribune* quoted Hack as saying,

> "Chicago. What a town it is for baseball! What I wouldn't give to come back here to stay in some capacity with a major league club. Cubs or Sox, it wouldn't matter — just so I could step out upon the field and know that my Chicago friends were watching me."

Then, the *Tribune* said, Wilson

> glanced proudly at the 8,000 who had jammed the wooden stands above him and overflowed into foul territory down either line. He narrowed his eyes and stood, for the moment, the swashbuckling little warrior who had faced the best pitchers in the game and made them give ground.

In the summer of 1939 Wilson was back in Chicago as master of ceremonies, assistant bartender, and aid to a dice girl in a place known as Hack Wilson's House of Seven Gables, on the southeast corner of Oakton and Milwaukee Avenue in suburban Niles.

At this time he also hired himself out as a stand-up attraction for functions where he could be used as a drawing card. Merino "Flip" Maestri, a semipro manager, hired him to officiate at a baseball game in Highwood, Illinois, in July 1939. Several thousand fans showed up on the fiercely hot day, but Wilson didn't. A couple of players raced over to the tavern on Milwaukee Avenue, where he lived in a back apartment. Finding him in a trancelike slumber, they roused him and hustled him off to the ballpark. Wilson waved vigorously to the crowd and took up a station behind shortstop. In the third inning, he toppled over and had to be revived.

When Hack Wilson died in a Baltimore hospital on November 23, 1948, the official cause of death was pulmonary edema, or water on the lungs, a common condition among alcoholics. The autopsy report also revealed that his liver was sclerotic.

But while his was a drinker's death, he did not die a drinker. A year before, he had found the strength to give up alcohol. He stopped showing up at the North Avenue bars and drank only an occasional beer at home. It is not clear what brought about this decision.

Wilson's death made him news all over again. Writers resurrected the figure from the public years. John Carmichael of the *Chicago Daily News* recalled the friendship with Malone: "They were a caution in those days of long ago. They punched sportswriters in the nose, staged marathon pillow fights, and set fire to customers' newspapers in hotel lobbies." Maurice Fisher, in a front-page *Daily News* article, told of the time that Wilson visited a youngster at Children's Memorial Hospital in Chicago. The boy, who had been severely injured in an accident, had requested a visit from his favorite player. All through their chat, Fisher explained, Wilson had to hold off tears because only he, the doctor, and the boy's parents knew that the youngster had lost a leg.

At a memorial service ten months later, on September 27, 1949, at Rosedale Cemetery in Martinsburg, West Virginia, Joe McCarthy stood before a sober crowd and said his last words about Hack Wilson: "I know you will say a fervent prayer for the great Hack. And may God rest his soul."

Standing near McCarthy on that gray afternoon were others from Wilson's baseball world. From the Cubs was Charlie Grimm. Next to him were other Chicago ballplayers, Kiki Cuyler and Johnny Schulte, who were Red Sox coaches that year. Nick Altrock stood off to one side. Bareheaded in the slight drizzle, McCarthy turned and pulled a cord to uncover a tapered granite block 30 inches square at the base and 10 feet high. On the top were crossed baseball bats and an inscription: "One of Baseball's Immortals Lewis R. (HACK) Wilson Rests Here."

NOTE

1. When he was out of baseball and in Chicago briefly some nine years later, Wilson visited the Michigan Avenue office of Dr. Stuyvesant Butler. He had heard of Butler's articles showing the relationship between migraine headaches and spots before the eyes. Wilson said that he suffered from headaches during the 1929 World Series and was uncertain of his eyesight. After testing him, Butler concluded that Wilson did suffer from migraines. He prescribed intravenous injections.

A version of this essay originally appeared in Robert S. Boone and Gerald Grunska, *Hack: The Meteoric Life of One of Baseball's First Superstars* (Highland Park, IL: Highland, 1978).

Gabby, Gangsters,
the Great Depression, and
the "Homer in the Gloamin'"
William F. McNeil

Charles Leo "Gabby" Hartnett was the Chicago Cubs' greatest catcher and possibly the greatest catcher in major league history. During his storied baseball career, which spanned the years 1922 to 1941, he was witness to some of the most momentous events in Chicago and American history, including the end of World War I, Prohibition, the Roaring Twenties and the Golden Age of Sports, the rise of gangsterism and racketeering, the Great Depression, the New Deal, and the beginning of World War II. These were nationwide events, but Chicago, the country's second largest city, had a ringside seat to most of them.

When World War I ended in 1918, Hartnett, a small-town boy from Millville, Massachusetts, population 1700, was attending a prep school, and when Prohibition went into effect in 1920, he was working in the local rubber shop and playing amateur baseball up and down the Blackstone Valley. The ratification of the 18th Amendment to the Constitution in 1919 had banned the manufacture and sale of alcoholic beverages in the United States, and although it became the law of the land on January 16, 1920, it didn't eliminate the alleged evils of drinking in the country. It only drove the sale of alcohol underground, to illegal drinking establishments known as speakeasies. It also contributed to the rise of gangsterism and racketeering in the country, as opportunistic criminals created an illegal booze industry that distilled illegal alcohol in isolated areas of the United States and smuggled other liquor into the country from Canada, Mexico, and the West Indies. Prohibition also proved to be a health hazard, as thousands of people died from drinking denatured alcohol. Perhaps not surprisingly, arrests for drunkenness and drunk driving increased in the years after the 18th Amendment was ratified.

Gabby Hartnett joined the professional baseball ranks in 1921, with the Worcester Boosters of the Eastern League, and the following year he became a member of the Chicago Cubs, where he was the backup catcher to Bob O'Farrell. But he quickly impressed Grover Cleveland Alexander with his catching expertise during spring training on Catalina Island and became Alexander's personal catcher during the season. Hartnett was a polished catcher when he arrived in Chicago thanks to the training he received from his father at an early age. But he had to wait for his opportunity before he could claim a regular job with the Cubs. When O'Farrell went down with an injury in 1924, Hartnett took over the backstopping duties, and he did so well that O'Farrell was traded to the St. Louis Cardinals the following year, where he sparked them to the World Championship in 1926. In his first full season as a regular player with the Cubs, Hartnett became the first catcher to hit twenty home runs in a season, and he would go on to become the first catcher in major league history to hit 200 career home runs (McNeil, *Gabby* 28, 63, 301).

Chicago, the second largest city in the United States, with a population of approximately 2,000,000 people, had become one of the centers of bootlegging and racketeering in the country by 1925. The city was divided into two distinct areas, the North Side and the South Side, and each area had its own distinct identity. Comiskey Park, home of the White Sox, was located on the South Side, while Wrigley Field was located on the North Side. Johnny Torrio, a local gangster who rose to become the head of the criminal element in the Windy City, had his headquarters on the South Side, while Dion O'Banion, another Chicago gangster, controlled bootlegging and racketeering on the North Side. Torrio and O'Banion agreed to divide the city between them in 1925, but it wasn't long before distrust overcame the two men and the two sides met on the field of battle. First O'Banion was assassinated. Then Torrio was gunned down outside his Clyde Avenue apartment, and although he survived the attempted assassination, he subsequently sailed for Italy after turning control of his empire over to a New York hoodlum named Al "Scarface" Capone. Capone, who quickly became the Czar of the South Side, ran his criminal operations from his armored office in the Hawthorne Hotel. The turf wars between the North and South Sides continued as he and O'Banion's successor, George "Bugs" Moran, were in constant conflict. Between 1925 and 1929, gang warfare became a popular diversion in Chicago, with more than 400 mobsters being assassinated before the St. Valentine's Day massacre brought the situation to the attention of federal authorities, who took immediate steps to curtail the violence (Sann 105–7; *This Fabulous Century* 3: 175).

Gabby Hartnett, like the majority of Americans, enjoyed a good beer now and then, and in the early 1920s he frequented the speakeasies in Chicago as well as those in other cities around the National League during the hot summer months when the Cubs were on the road. In 1925, however, that all came to an end. The pride of Millville met a Chicago girl by the name of Martha Marshall, and his bachelor life came to a screeching halt. He still visited the speakeasies around the National League during the summer, and he still put 'em away with the best of them on his hunting trips to South Dakota in the fall, but when he was home in Chicago, he was a teetotaler under the careful supervision of Martha. They did enjoy the Chicago nightlife, however, and often went to the Edgewater Beach Hotel for dinner and dancing on the terrace overlooking Lake Michigan. But it was always alcohol-free, with lemonade the beverage of choice (McNeil, *Gabby* 65, 83, 90).

The 1920s, known as the Roaring Twenties or the Jazz Age, was a decade of hedonism and self-gratification in the United States, as the youth of the country drank and danced the night away to the tune of "Eat, drink, and be merry, for tomorrow we die." This fatalistic attitude was brought about in part by the horrors of World War I, when thousands of families lost loved ones and thousands of other shell-shocked soldiers returned home with missing limbs or emotional problems.

The decade was also known as the Golden Age of Sports because of the preponderance of legendary athletes who strutted their stuff on the field of athletic endeavor. There was Babe Ruth, the "Sultan of Swat," in baseball; the "Four Horsemen" of Notre Dame and Red Grange, the "Galloping Ghost," in football; Bill Tilden and Helen Wills in tennis; Jack Dempsey, the "Manassa Mauler," in boxing; and Gertrude Ederle in swimming. Gabby Hartnett was an enthusiastic sports fan, and he followed the sports pages closely, but he seldom attended any of the big events. He was a participant who enjoyed playing baseball, basketball, bowling, and golf, and he was an avid hunter, but he was not a spectator. He was a big Notre Dame football fan, but there is no record that he ever attended a Notre Dame game. Later in his life he became a big fan of DePaul University basketball, and since DePaul was located near his home in Chicago, he did attend many of their games and became a good friend of the legendary DePaul coach Ray Meyer (McNeil, *Gabby* 52; Hornoff).

Yankee Stadium opened on April 18, 1923, and a raucous crowd of 74,200 people pushed its way through the turnstiles, with another 25,000 fans being turned away. Babe Ruth put his personal stamp on the opener by crashing a three-run homer in the bottom of the third inning off Howard Ehmke of the Boston Red Sox to pace the Yankees to a 4–1 victory. The same day the Cubs opened at home against the Pittsburgh Pirates, and their play was just as satisfying as they won 7–2 behind Grover Cleveland Alexander. Gabby Hartnett, Old Pete's personal catcher, was behind the plate for the opener, going one for four (Brown, Keylin, and Lundy 23–24).

On August 6, 1926, Gertrude Ederle, a courageous nineteen-year-old New York girl, became the first woman to swim the English Channel, accomplishing the feat in 14 hours, 31 minutes. She completed the crossing from Cape Gris-Nez, France, to Kingsdown, England, after an epic struggle with the wind, rain, and chilling air. She also broke the men's record by more than two hours and was rewarded with a huge ticker-tape parade down Fifth Avenue in New York on her return home (Brown, Keylin, and Lundy 33–34).

The year 1927 was filled with historic events, on and off the athletic field. At precisely 7:51 A.M. on May 20, American aviator Charles A. Lindbergh took off in a drizzling rain from Roosevelt Field, Long Island, on a solo, non-stop flight across the Atlantic Ocean, attempting to become the first person to accomplish the feat. He pointed his monoplane, the *Spirit of St. Louis*, toward the British Isles and the coast of Europe, and then sat back and relaxed, munching sandwiches and drinking hot coffee to keep awake. Finally, after 33 hours, 29 minutes, and 30 seconds, the twenty-five-year-old former airmail pilot landed at Le Bourget Field outside Paris, with a reported 100,000 people crowding the runway to welcome him to France. In appreciation of his monumental achievement he, like Gertrude Ederle before him, was greeted with a ticker-tape parade in New York City (Hoffman, no. 35: 2–3).

Four months later, on September 23, Gene Tunney defended the heavyweight title he had won from Jack Dempsey a year earlier by out-pointing the former champ over the fifteen-round distance in Soldiers Field, Chicago. The fight, controlled by Tunney for the majority of rounds, witnessed the famous long count in which Dempsey put Tunney on the canvas in the seventh round, but due to Dempsey's failure to go to a neutral corner, the start of the count was delayed, giving Tunney an extra six seconds to regain his senses. That knockdown has been controversial for over eighty years, but films of the fight seem to show an alert Tunney ready to get to his feet at any time. Hartnett did not attend the fight because he was on the road with the Cubs (Brown, Keylin, and Lundy 43–45).

One week after the fight, Babe Ruth hit his sixtieth home run of the season to establish a new major league record that would endure for thirty-four years. Number sixty was hit off southpaw Tom Zachary of the Washington Senators in New York on September 30 and paced the New York Yankees to a 4–2 victory. The Bambino accounted for all the runs, scoring three himself and bringing in Mark Koenig with his homer (Brown, Keylin, and Lundy 46).

Hartnett began to come into his own in 1927. He was already recognized as the best catcher in the National League, but his overly aggressive approach to the game caused him to lead the league in errors three times between 1924 and 1927. When he finally got his game under control in 1928, he topped the .300 mark in batting for the first time, finishing at .302, and he led the league in fielding average, assists, and caught-stealing percentage, allowing only thirty-nine stolen bases against a league average of eighty-seven. In head-to-head competition with his American League rivals, Mickey Cochrane and Bill Dickey, Hartnett outperformed them in most defensive categories year after year, while holding them to a draw on offense (McNeil, *Gabby* 124).

Hartnett and his long-time girlfriend, Martha Marshall, finally married in 1929 after five years of courtship. The wedding took place in St. Mary's of the Lake Roman Catholic Church on January 28; and, two weeks later, they left their 6200 N. Washtenaw apartment for their honeymoon on Catalina Island, where the Cubs had their spring training camp. The date was February 14, St. Valentine's Day, and just 2.6 miles from the Hartnetts' apartment, a beehive of activity was happening in the North Side garage of Bugs Moran, as preparations were being made for a meeting between Moran and his South Side counterpart, Al Capone. But Capone had no intention of attending a meeting. He had bigger plans. He sent four of his paid gorillas to assassinate the North Side leader. At precisely 10:30 A.M. a black limousine pulled up to the garage at 2212 N. Clark Street and four men got out, dressed as policemen. They went inside and, under the pretext of arresting the occupants, they lined the seven men up against the wall and chopped them down with Tommy guns, a bloody carnage that would forever be known as the St. Valentine's Day Massacre. The assassination attempt failed, as Bugs Moran was a no-show, but the furor caused by the carnage eventually led to Capone's downfall. The federal government convicted the Chicago gang leader of income tax evasion two years later and put him away, first in Atlanta and then in Alcatraz. He was released from prison in 1939, suffering from syphilis, his mind gone, and he spent his remaining eight years at his Miami estate, fishing quietly and staring into nothingness. Bugs Moran, on the other hand, kept a low profile after this attempt on his life, finally dying of natural causes in 1957 (Sann 204–15).

Although not a homegrown Chicago boy, John Dillinger said his final farewell in the Windy City. The so-called "gentleman bandit," perhaps the most romantic figure in criminal lore, often attended Cubs games when he was in town, in full view of the fans and police. He was considered a Robin Hood figure during the Depression years, robbing from the rich and giving to the poor, and the local law enforcement agencies ignored his presence, even refusing to notify federal agents of his whereabouts. But Dillinger's luck eventually ran out, and his end came in a violent burst of gunfire outside a Chicago theatre. He was gunned down by federal agents as he exited the Biograph Theatre with two women. One of the women — known as the "Woman in Red"— turned in Dillinger in exchange for a promise from the feds not to deport her on a prostitution offense (Caren 176–77).

Hartnett was never more than an interested spectator to the gangland wars that enveloped Chicago in the 1920s. He never met any of the local gangsters personally during his tour of duty in the Windy City, other than posing for a photo with Al Capone and his son Albert "Sonny" prior to a City Series game against the White Sox in Comiskey Park. It is doubtful that Capone ever attended a baseball game in Wrigley Field since that was O'Banion-Bugs Moran territory and off-limits to Capone. In fact, the only time Hartnett's name was ever mentioned in the same breath with one of the gangsters came during a family vacation in Spooner, Wisconsin. One evening, when the family was dining in a local restaurant, Martha noticed holes all over one of the walls, and when she asked the waiter about it, she was told they were bullet holes made during a shootout involving Bugs Moran (Hornoff).

The Chicago Cubs captured the National League pennant by a whopping 10½ games over the Pittsburgh Pirates in 1929, but Hartnett could only watch the action from the peace and quiet of the dugout. He missed most of the season with a mysterious arm ailment that his mother claimed was all in his head. She predicted his arm would return to normal after his wife gave birth to their first child in December. And curiously enough, that's exactly what happened. When the 1930 season opened, Hartnett was his old self, gunning down would-be base stealers with his usual aplomb, allowing only forty-seven stolen bases against a league average of sixty. But in '29, he could only sit and watch, and it was a painful sight. In the World Series against Connie Mack's Philadelphia Athletics, the Cubs fought back from a two-game deficit to take game three, and they were leading the A's 8–0 after 7½ innings in game four when their world crashed. In the most amazing comeback in World Series history, the powerful A's scored ten runs in the bottom of the seventh inning and went on to win the game 10–8. They wrapped up the title two days later, overcoming a 2–0 Cubs' lead with a three-run rally in the bottom of the ninth inning (Brown, Keylin, and Lundy 49–50).

The 1920s had been a boom decade for the American economy, as thousands of people bought items on credit with low down payments. Opportunistic investors became million-aires on the stock market by buying on margin, putting up only 10 percent and borrowing the rest. But the bubble burst on October 29, 1929, a day known as Black Tuesday, when the market crashed with more than sixteen million shares changing hands. The average market price plummeted from 311.9 on September 3 to 164 on November 13. The "paper million-aires" suddenly went bust when their loans were called and they were unable to come up with the money. Investors went broke by the thousands, and the small investors were wiped out. As reported in the history entitled *This Fabulous Century*, the president of Union Cigar, after watching his stock plummet from $113.50 a share to four dollars a share, jumped to his death from the ledge of a New York hotel. More suicides followed as the magnitude of the catas-trophe became known (3: 128).

Hartnett was luckier than most people during the Great Depression. He wasn't heavily invested in the stock market, and he had a steady job with a salary in the neighborhood of $20,000. He and Martha didn't forget the less fortunate people; they contributed many dol-lars to charities around the Chicago area, and Martha often passed food out the back door to people in need or fed them at the kitchen table. And every day, when Gabby arrived home from Wrigley Field, he had a trunk full of Wheaties and other Wrigley Field giveaways that he passed out to the neighborhood kids. His daughter Sheila said that the Hartnetts never had any boxes of Wheaties in the house. Her father had given them all away (Hornoff).

In 1932 the Cubs swept to the National League pennant, edging the Pittsburgh Pirates by four games. Charlie Grimm's cohorts won with a dominant pitching staff, a tight defense, and timely hitting. Hartnett had a good season, but not one of his best. He hit .271 with 12 home runs and 52 runs batted in, and he once again played solid defense. In the World Series that year the Cubs met the powerful New York Yankees — with Ruth, Gehrig, Dickey, and Lazzeri — and, not surprisingly, they were swept in four games, as the Bronx Bombers outscored them 37 to 19. The high point of the Series was Babe Ruth's legendary "called shot" home run. In the fifth inning of game three, with the score tied at four apiece, Ruth allegedly pointed to the center field stands before the pitch and then drove the ball to the exact spot he had pointed to, giving his team a lead they never relinquished. Witnesses to the event were evenly divided as to whether it actually happened. Hartnett, who was closest to the play, said, "I don't want to take anything from the Babe, because he's the reason we made good money, but he didn't call the shot. He held up the index finger of his left hand, looked at our dugout, not the outfield, and said, 'It only takes one to hit.'" Charlie Root of Chicago, who had a reputation as a mean pitcher who would knock down his mother if she crowded the plate, said, "He didn't point. If he had, I'd have knocked him on his fanny. I'd have loosened him up. I took my pitching too seriously to have anybody facing me do that" (Ahrens and Gold 116, 135).

Away from the playing field, Franklin Delano Roosevelt was elected as the thirty-second

President of the United States, running on a New Deal program that promised to aggressively attack the economic depression that had incapacitated the entire country for the past three years. During his first 100 days in office, Roosevelt, who had won a mandate with almost 60 percent of the popular vote, pushed numerous relief and recovery bills through Congress, including aid to farmers, unemployment relief, assistance to banks, and federally funded work programs such as the Works Projects Administration, or WPA, that put people to work again by building bridges, roads, and parks. By 1933 twelve million people, about one-fourth of the American work force, were unemployed, but thanks to President Roosevelt's decisive action, the unemployment ranks continued to shrink during the 1930s, and the American economy righted itself by the end of the decade. Roosevelt also launched the Social Security Act that provided retirement pensions to most workers (Hoffman, no. 36: 1; no. 37: 3–4).

The year 1933 was important for the citizens of the United States for another reason. The federal government, after years of struggling to enforce the 18th Amendment, finally capitulated and repealed it in 1933. The manufacture and sale of alcohol were once again legal, and the rumrunners and bootleggers were put out of business, as were the thousands of speakeasies across the country. And with alcohol now flowing freely once again, the price of a drink plummeted dramatically.

In the world of baseball, the year 1933 brought about another innovation to the national pastime. Arch Ward, the sports editor of the *Chicago Tribune,* suggested to league owners that an all-star game be played in Chicago during the city's World's Fair. The owners quickly endorsed the idea, and the first Major League All-Star game was played in Comiskey Park on July 6, 1933, matching the greatest players in the National League against the greatest players in the American League. The teams were managed by John McGraw and Connie Mack, two of baseball's legendary managers, with a total of sixty-nine years of managerial experience between them. Fittingly, the game belonged to the Sultan of Swat. Babe Ruth launched the first home run in All-Star history, a two-run shot in the third inning that put the Junior Circuit on the road to a 4–2 victory. Gabby Hartnett went 0-for-1 for the Nationals, striking out against Lefty Grove (McNeil, *Gabby* 181–82).

On April 13, 1934, Babe Ruth slugged his 700th career home run off right-hander Tommy Bridges in Detroit. The homer, a two-run shot in the third inning, traveled an estimated 480 feet over the right field wall, pacing the Yankees to a 4–2 victory (Brown, Keylin, and Lundy 66).

The Chicago Cubs were National League Champions once again in 1935, and it was Hartnett who sparked his team to the pennant, batting .344 with 13 home runs and 91 RBI. He also led the league in assists, caught-stealing percentage, and fielding percentage, and was rightly rewarded with the league's Most Valuable Player trophy. The Cubs met the Detroit Tigers, managed by Hartnett's friend and rival, Mickey Cochrane, in the World Series. Detroit captured the Series in six games, and Cochrane scored the winning run on a single by Goose Goslin. Cochrane hit .292 with one RBI in six games and tossed out two of three prospective base stealers. Hartnett hit an identical .292 with one home run and two RBI. He caught one of two men attempting to steal and picked Pete Fox off third base after the Tiger outfielder had tripled (Cohen and Neft 157–61).

Three years later, the Cubs were locked in another National League dogfight, this time with the Pittsburgh Pirates, and Hartnett was a part-time player and new Cubs' manager at the age of thirty-seven. The husky backstop had been given the managerial reigns by owner P.K. Wrigley on July 21, with the Cubs in third place, 5½ games behind the Pirates. For the next six weeks the team treaded water, but on September 14 they began their drive to the top, and on the 27th, when the Bucs visited Wrigley Field for a three-game series, only 1½ games separated the two adversaries with eight games left in the season. Dizzy Dean, the old warhorse, took the opener for the Cubs by the score of 2–1, pulling the Cubs within ½ game of first place. Game two was a tense struggle that was tied at 5–5 entering the ninth inning and, with darkness settling over the park, the umpires let it be known that it would be the last inning played. A tie game, which would necessitate a doubleheader the next day, would be welcomed by Pittsburgh, but not by the Cubs, whose pitching staff was decimated. With two men out and the bases empty, Hartnett strode to the plate. After getting two quick strikes on Hartnett with fastballs in the rapidly fading light, Pittsburgh pitcher Mace Brown inexplicably threw the big catcher a curve, and Hartnett promptly deposited it in the left field stands to win the game 6–5, as all hell broke loose in Wrigley Field. The dramatic home run propelled the Cubs into first place, and has come to be known as "The Homer in the Gloamin'." It also made Hartnett an instant legend. The Cubs went on from there to win the pennant by two games, but paired off against Joe McCarthy's mighty Bronx Bombers in the World Series, they were brought back to earth quickly, New York winning in four (McNeil, *Gabby* 248, 251, 254–8).

Having formulated a plan for European domination in the early 1930s, Germany began to put its plan in action in 1938 by gradually invading and annexing districts and eventually entire countries, beginning with Austria in 1938, followed by Czechoslovakia and Poland in 1939, and Norway and Denmark in 1940. England and France declared war on Germany on September 3, 1939, and the United States was dragged into the conflict when Japan, one of Germany's Axis allies along with Italy, bombed Pearl Harbor on December 7, 1941 (Hoffman, no. 38: 1–3).

Hartnett had played his last major league game just sixty-nine days before Pearl Harbor. On September 29, the New York Giants shut out the Philadelphia Phillies by the score of 2–0, and Hartnett, catching for the Giants, went one for four. In his last big league season, "Old Tomato Face," as he was affectionately called because of his ruddy complexion, batted .300 and fielded .994. He left many catching records behind, including leading the National League in fielding average six times, putouts four times, assists six times, and double plays six times. He had the highest career percentage of base runners caught stealing until Roy Campanella appeared on the scene, and his 53 percent caught-stealing percentage still ranks as number two all-time. His 238 career home runs were the most home runs hit by a catcher until both Yogi Berra and Roy Campanella topped him in 1957 (McNeil, *Gabby* 301).

Hartnett was often compared to the great American League backstops Mickey Cochrane and Bill Dickey, both of whom played during the same era in which Hartnett played. The American Leaguers seemed to attract most of the headlines, but the statistics clearly show that Hartnett outperformed the other two in almost every defensive category. Hartnett's caught-stealing percentage was twelve percentage points better than Dickey's and fifteen percentage points better than Cochrane's. He outgunned each of his rivals nine times in ten years. The master of the pickoff also had a comfortable advantage in adjusted assists over Cochrane, beating him seven times in ten years while holding Dickey to a five-five draw. He outfielded Dickey six times in ten years, but came in second to Cochrane, six to three with one even. On offense, the three men were closely matched, with Cochrane edging Hartnett for the top spot with Dickey close behind. Cochrane finished first in on-base percentage while Hartnett outslugged the other two (McNeil, *Backstop* 218).

A statistical analysis of all major league catchers, both offensively and defensively, identified Gabby Hartnett as one of the two greatest all-around catchers in major league history, along with Roy Campanella.

Works Cited

Ahrens, Art, and Eddie Gold. *The Golden Era Cubs, 1876–1940*. Chicago: Bonus, 1985.

Brown, Gene, Arleen Keylin, and Daniel Lundy, eds. *Sports of the Times: Great Moments in Sports History*. New York: Arno, 1982.

Caren, Eric C., comp. *Crime Extra: 300 Years of Crime in North America*. Ed. Julie Saffel. Edison, NJ: Castle, 2001.

Cohen, Richard, and David S. Neft. *The World Series*. New York: McMillan, 1986.

Hoffman, Robert M., ed. *News of the Nation: A Newspaper History of the United States*. Englewood Cliffs, NJ: Prentice-Hall, 1975.

Hornoff, Sheila Hartnett. Telephone interview. June 2006.

McNeil, William F. *Gabby Hartnett: The Life and Times of the Cubs' Greatest Catcher*. Jefferson, NC: McFarland, 2004.

_____. *Backstop: A History of the Catcher and Sabermetric Ranking of 50 All-time Greats*. Jefferson, NC: McFarland, 2005.

Sann, Paul. *The Lawless Decade*. New York: Crown, 1957.

This Fabulous Century: Sixty Years of American Life. Ed. Ezra Bowen, et al. 8 vols. New York: Time-Life Books, 1969–70.

Loving Ivy:
Ron Santo, Ryne Sandberg, and the Ideals of Cubs Nation
Gerald C. Wood

The term *nation* is a loose and trendy means of describing the fans of any team. It is most often associated in baseball history with the Boston Red Sox, indicating a passionate and even militant commitment to and belief in the team. These days it seems all teams call their supporters part of their nation, for public relations and marketing purposes. So I use the term advisedly. But in the case of the Cubs, and particularly Ron Santo, the term is more indicative than clichéd. It suggests that Santo, as player and broadcaster, has come to represent not just loyalty but a set of values that many Cubs supporters fear are endangered in both Chicago and the United States. They respect Ron Santo because he represents passion, ethnicity, and a sense of place — all increasingly rare in baseball and American culture in general. While Ryne Sandberg publicly supports these ideals, he is more problematic. Sandberg lacks the spontaneity and old-fashionedness of Santo. There is something programmed and mediated in the Hall of Fame second baseman that feels inauthentic.

Ron Santo seems genuinely humble in times of run-away egos and infectious arrogance. He says in the preface to his book *Few and Chosen*, written with Phil Pepe, "I consider myself very fortunate that I got to play most of my career with a team I love very much, the Chicago Cubs, and that I got to play home games in Wrigley Field. And I'm doubly fortunate that I'm still associated with the Cubs as a radio broadcaster" (xiii). Even though he was visibly disappointed at not being selected to the Hall of Fame, as recorded in his son's film *This Old Cub*, Santo is equally sincere when he declares to the fans that having his jersey number retired meant "more than the Hall of Fame." Faithful to the end, he says, "If I couldn't be in the World Series with the Cubs, I wouldn't want to be in the World Series."

But certainly Ernie Banks and Billy Williams, even Harray Caray and Steve Stone in their own ways, were loyal to the team, both the fans and franchise. Santo's loyalty appears driven by a passion for baseball's dramas, and for surviving his real struggles with serious health problems, unknown (at least in any demonstrative way) to Banks, Williams, or especially Ryne Sandberg. The various personalities interviewed in *This Old Cub* call it his "exuberance" (William Peterson), "spontaneous joy" (Bill Murray), "so much" love for "the game" (Brooks Robinson), and "great enthusiasm" (Ernie Banks). In his Introduction to *Few and Chosen*, Sandberg names it Santo's "enthusiasm, and his passion for the Cubs" (Santo xxx). He carries this energy and resilience, his supporters believe, into his struggles with diabetes, including amputations of both legs below the knees. As Pat Hughes says in the film, Santo is "not about sadness" but rather resilience, echoed by Jeff Santo, his son, who says his father's life's theme is "keep moving on."

In addition to his own courageous fight against diabetes and his effective support for the JDRF (Juvenile Diabetes Research Foundation), Santo is identified with the traditional sense of place valued by many Midwesterners. In his autobiography, written with Ron Minkoff, Santo explains the appeal of Wrigley Field: it "[is] special [because] it's a part of Chicago. You know looking at the OUTSIDE of Wrigley Field where you are and that you are a part of history" (*For Love of Ivy* 213). That past includes ethnicity, in Santo's case his Italian heritage; his father was born in Italy. At

Ron Santo, a Cubs player from 1960 to 1973, and current Cubs broadcaster on WGN radio (courtesy Baseball Hall of Fame).

one point Santo embraced his ethnic past to the point of endorsing the selling of pizza under his own name at Wrigley Field. Such identification made him, in the minds of people like actor Dennis Franz and former player and broadcaster Steve Stone, "blue collar." For the descendants of the original middle class and lower-middle-class inhabitants of the Lake View area, he "looked like us" (*This Old Cub*). Consequently, when Peter Golenbock asserts that "Ron Santo's play, as much as any player's, defined a ten-year period when the Cubs fought and scrapped and played exciting, aggressive baseball" (*Wrigleyville* 359), the assent of many Chicagoans has a class and ethnic flavor.[1]

For traditional Cubs fans such a class identification is equivalent to passing the test of character. As Barry Rozner explains in *This Old Cub*, Santo epitomized what it means to be a Cub because he was "not pretty, not flashy." Instead he had "substance." Especially because of his battles with diabetes and the health complications that followed, Santo is associated with what Andrew Hazucha calls the Midwestern "counter-myth to the American obsession with winning." It is focused on "a more authentic and ultimately more compassionate worldview, a perspective honed by tragedy and the lessons it teaches." Despite his sometimes inappropriateness on the air and weaknesses with American English, Santo is identified with what Chicago writers Nelson Algren and Mike Royko call "Man's ceaseless failure to overcome himself" and the "sensible and level-headed reminder" not to "expect the most and to be happy with small gifts" (qtd. in Hazucha 109). His resilient and ceaseless struggle against

Italian-American Ron Santo making pizza for fun and profit (courtesy Baseball Hall of Fame).

overwhelming odds, and acceptance of inevitable loss, is the key to why Cubs fans continue to support and respect Santo.

But, as civic religion would have it, there is also a mystique associated with Santo's becoming and remaining a Cub. In his behavior and spin, Santo himself created this bigger-than-life love story. In his preface to *Few and Chosen* he explains, "Call me crazy, but I signed with the Cubs for $20,000.00 and turned down the Reds' offer of $80,000. Something just told me this was the right situation for me. I can't explain it. It was the mystique of Wrigley

Field, day baseball, and Ernie Banks. And one more thing! When I was 12 years old, a buddy of mine from Seattle moved to Chicago and was there for two years. When he left, we were the same size, and when he returned, he was a foot taller than me, so I got to thinking they grow them big in Chicago, and that stayed with me" (xvi). Such a sense of transcendent purpose was, of course, capitalized on by WGN, when they advertised the television showing of *This Old Cub* on Saturday, July 16, 2005, 7:00 P.M. (C.S.T.) in Chicago: "Baseball was his love. Chicago was his destiny." Whether it was general or particular providence wasn't clarified.

Ryne Sandberg, Hall of Fame Cubs second baseman and present Peoria Cubs farm team manager (courtesy Baseball Hall of Fame).

Ryne Sandberg's fame is a different matter. He became a baseball star thanks to television. The deal was sealed by "the Sandberg game," nationally televised on June 23, 1984, in which — at age 24 — he hit home runs off future Hall of Famer Bruce Sutter to tie the score in both the 9th and 10th innings, while batting 6 for 7, with 7 RBIs. But there was always something unusual about Sandberg, even after he had become the speedy and powerful player affectionately known as Ryno. Many players are quiet, but Sandberg's silences suggested absence, emotional sluggishness. Other players kidded that his only words were "I've got it" or "You take it" on infield fly balls. And, if Glenn Beckert is correct, when Sandberg, now a Cubs icon, first joined the team, he "didn't know Ernie Banks's name" (Phalen 159). Even his interviews with smiling, worshipful broadcasters were uninspired, full of undeveloped responses, lacking in affect. As he accumulated Hall-worthy numbers, he seemed to lack passion, especially when the cameras, against the wills of their operators, caught Sandberg picking his nose or pairing his fingernails, apparently indifferent to the drama of the game. From the media's point of view, he was a "portrait in bland" created by the player's "inability to deliver a single usable quote in 16 major-league seasons with the Chicago Cubs" (Crasnick, par. 2).

After a brief retirement, Ryno returned to the Cubs for a second employment. Though not the dominating player of his first stint, and plagued by a maddening vulnerability to the low-and-outside slider, he was still a representative second baseman who often hit for power, though he had, as they say, lost a step or two. But off the field, his life was substantially different. He had endured a divorce, which required, for the shy and reclusive Sandberg, embarrassing public legal proceedings. But in the process he had become much more open and friendly, seemingly inspired by an extroverted, happy, and supportive second wife, whose brother now works in public relations for the Cubs. The press and WGN were quick to emphasize this new Ryne Sandberg, a Cubs hero awaiting induction to the Hall of Fame, as a spokesman for Old School baseball.

Sandberg didn't disappoint that segment of the media in his acceptance speech. His deference to other players and baseball tradition was obvious. He was, he said, "humbled," "grateful," "honored," and "in awe" (par. 1). The word that resonated throughout the speech was "respect"—"for the game," "for the team," "your opponent," "your team mates," "your organization," "your manager," even "your uniform" (pars. 2, 3, 4, 8). Behind all this iteration was the Ryne Sandberg II dictum: "the name on the front is a lot more important than the name on the back" (par. 8). He further explained that his fear of failure, his obsessive need to achieve, during his playing years had been fueled by his desire that he never let down such supportive, loyal father figures as Don Zimmer, Jim Frey, and Dallas Green. As a rookie he may have asked for uniform 14, oblivious that the number had been made immortal by Ernie Banks. But now, as a Hall of Fame inductee, Sandberg incanted the names of his favorite player heroes, collected from his childhood through his playing days: Willie Stargell, Johnny Bench, Luis Tiant, Yaz, Fisk, Pete Rose, Mike Schmidt, Steve Carlton, Manny Trillo, Rick Sutcliffe, Bob Dernier, Bill Buckner, Shawon Dunston, and Mark Grace, just to name a few (pars. 3, 4, 6, 9, 10, 13, 16, 17).

But the speech was not sweet in all its parts. As a disciple of Old School ethics, the inductee defended those values with a bit of sarcasm and a touch of anger. Sandberg ended one paragraph, for example, with "When did it become okay for someone to hit home runs and forget how to play the rest of the game?" (Sandberg, "Respect," par. 10). Since Sandberg only played for the Cubs, that comment seemed directed at Sammy Sosa, though he may also have had in mind Barry Bonds, famous for delaying his home run trot by self-indulgent pirouettes and short, slow steps around the bases, designed to congratulate himself and humiliate his opponents. Referring to the Hall of Famers behind him on the dais, Sandberg added, "These guys sitting up here did not pave the way for the rest of us so that players could swing for the fences every time up and forget how to move a runner over to third, it's disrespectful to them, to you, and to the game of baseball that we all played growing up" (par. 11). His induction into the Hall, according to Ryno, validates "that learning how to bunt and hit and run and turning two is more important than knowing where to find the little red light at the dug out camera" (par. 12). He continued, "the natural way [read: without steroids]" to play baseball is like Andre Dawson, who followed the correct, respectful path (par. 18).

As new as this Old School litany may have seemed on July 31, 2005, it was actually designed and articulated in 1994–1995 by Sandberg and Barry Rozner in the book *Second to Home: Ryne Sandberg Opens Up*. The reinvention began in the acknowledgement section of that book, where, even before the Foreword, Rozner dedicates his contribution to "Ryne Sandberg, who'd rather have his teeth drilled without Novocaine than talk about himself; for his patience, honesty and generosity; and for reminding us all that being a decent human being still has its rewards in this world" (viii). In the Foreword, Harry Caray echoes that Sandberg is "a good-hearted and affable man who never thought he was too important to speak with anyone. [...] a shy guy who minded his own business and asked people to do the same for him." In Caray's words, Sandberg "enjoyed playing the game," "was a true professional in every sense of the word, and a role model for adults and kids alike." Then Caray lays down the gauntlet by asserting, "The only people who ever said anything bad about him [...] were the ones who were jealous of him, because there was little or no room for criticism" (xi).

Sandberg begins Chapter One by asserting that his retiring from the game had nothing to do with the breakup of his marriage. His reason is simple. It was about the old-fashioned desire to play baseball the right way: "I lost the desire that got me ready to play on an everyday basis for so many years. [...] The adrenaline wasn't there. The nervousness wasn't there. [...] The competitive feelings that I counted on so heavily in my mental preparation were gone as well" (*Second to Home* 2). Furthermore, like a loving dad, he wanted to be involved in the raising of his children Lindsey and Justin, then six and eight (5). Within the Cubs organization, Sandberg was peeved at Larry Himes, the Cubs' general manager at the time, who disrespected Greg Maddux and Andre Dawson, trading "decent and loyal" players like Paul Assenmacher, and getting little in return for "Rick Sutcliffe, Joe Girardi, Dwight Smith, Bob Scanlan, Chuck McElroy and Doug Dascenzo." And then there was preferential treatment for Sosa. Himes, Sandberg writes, "didn't seem to have a relationship with anyone on the team except the players he brought in, like Sammy Sosa. It made for a very tense clubhouse because Himes would walk through and say hello to just one guy, Sammy, and walk right past everyone else. It seemed like he had a grudge against almost the whole team, even though almost the whole team was his" (6–7).

Most predictive of his future position is his repeated assertion that he lost enthusiasm because "many of the players today don't seem to respect the game or each other anymore." On the other hand, his respect and loyalty are indicated by returning the millions left on his contract, acknowledgement of "some great teammates, coaches, managers and friends in my 13 years," and gratitude "to Tribune Co. and the Cubs organization for all they did for me" (*Second to Home* 6, 10). By ignoring the complications and failures of the past, Sandberg is able to assert that he "missed my baseball generation by a decade or two. I would've loved playing in the days of Pete Rose [though not because of the chance to bet on baseball, we assume] and Willie Mays and Mickey Mantle. I would've loved those Cubs teams of the late '60s with Ron Santo and Ernie Banks and Billy Williams. Players from that era loved the game and gave everything they had to the game. They played for their teammates and because they were proud of their uniforms" (11). Like such peerless members of the sacred past, Ryno assures us that he "played for love of the game," "the enjoyment that came with winning," and the "substance and consistency" of "tradition," which is pure at the core (13).

Then in *Second to Home* he "opens up" about himself. You play the best baseball possible so that you will be rewarded with "pride and pleasure" (18). He was private because he "preferred to handle things on my own," an approach learned from his father, who used to say, "Keep your mouth shut and keep your eyes and ears open. You might learn something." He was not a more vocal, extroverted leader, especially early in his career, because "I had enough to do just worrying about myself, making sure I took care of myself and did my job, and I would've been uncomfortable forcing my help on someone else." Besides, he says, he was never as quiet as people said, only "around new people, in new situations, or when I was preparing for a game." His seeming lack of passion was really a way of controlling his anger, usually toward himself, and always out of "self respect and respecting your opponents and coaches and teammates." Even though he was never a good public speaker, he was "a closet practical joker" who kept trainer Tony Garofalo nervous by sneaking up behind him and yelling "look out" or stealing gloves and shoes from other players, usually Shawon Dunston, and depositing them in the freezer (18–22).

The remaining chapters of *Second to Home* establish the characteristics that we now associate with Yahoo Ryno. He didn't dawdle around the bases after a home run like Barry Bonds because "it just isn't right. You don't have to be disrespectful to have fun. [...] I'm amazed by what goes on in today's game, with the laziness and lack of work ethic and preparation, and just the way some players don't follow the rules" (95, 128). Such Sandbergian respect is traceable to his father's example. In Sandberg's words, as shaped by Rozner, "He taught us good values and respect and just plain common decency. I respect the way he raised his family and taught us a lot about life and took us to church every Sunday. He was a good human being and I don't think there's anything you can say about a person that means more than that" (107). And he avoided free agency, particularly in 1989, because he had learned loyalty: "I wanted to stay with the Cubs. I didn't want to leave Wrigley Field and the Cub fans. I didn't want to leave Chicago. Honestly, Cub fans are the most amazing group of people you could find anywhere. Such a thing does not exist anyplace else in sports" (123, 159).

What is new, then, in the Hall of Fame speech if it isn't the Old School rhetoric? It is the assumption of the persona of Ryne Sandberg, a public image built on his history with the press. Equal to his declarations of humility and respect are references to his own accomplishments and personality. For example, he kids his insider audience about his reticence, saying, "This will come as a shock I know, but I am almost speechless" ("Respect," par. 1). Then in a similar vein he directly addresses the Baseball Writers Association, naming his history as "a great interview" and his "many quotes you could wrap a story around" as the reasons for his selection by those members (par. 21). While maintaining a humble demeanor, he follows previous reporters in remembering Bob Dernier and himself as the "daily double" at the top of the Cubs' lineup and reminds listeners that he and Dunston and Grace were a double play combination for a full ten years (pars. 13, 17). While once again using irony to name himself a "great [...] public speaker," Sandberg ritually thanks everyone from his trainer and high school teammates to his "advisors, confidants and close friends," even the "great folks here at the Hall of Fame, as well as Barry Rozner, a "great writer and good friend" (pars. 24, 2023). Seizing the moment, he politics for Ron Santo and Andre Dawson being elected to the Hall of Fame.

This tone of false modesty, barely hiding self-aggrandizement, marks the public image of Sandberg since the Hall speech. Indicative of the lack of coherence in Sandberg's position is his declaration to Carrie Muskat that he calls the "Sandberg game" the Sutter game (par. 3). By doing so, Sandberg is trying to act humble and welcome Bruce Sutter into the Hall fraternity, but in a classic reversal of history, Sandberg names his own play "so special" because those "two home runs" came off "a Hall of Famer." Once time is put in its proper order, he is saying that the Hall's validation of Sutter's skill makes Sandberg's achievement even more remarkable, hardly the logic of a player who puts the game first. Similarly, in his column for *Yahoo! Sports*, while calling himself "kind of a traditionalist" and "a big believer in the history of the game," he supports Pete Rose's entry into the Hall of Fame because there can be no definitive proof that Rose's "gambling ever affected an outcome of a game that he played or managed." Pete "realizes his mistake," writes Sandberg, and, yes, "nobody loved the game more or played the game 'the right way' better" (7 June 2005; 17 June 2005; 4 Aug. 2005). He overlooks obvious character flaws to support his childhood idol.

He also waffles on steroids. He defends MLB against the Congress, saying that he is "confident it will work," the "hearings on Capitol Hill were nothing more than a PR power move on the part of Congress," and the "most important thing right now is to get information to young kids" (*Yahoo! Sports* 17 Mar. 2005 pars. 4, 6, 9). Within a week he praises Barry Bonds for not letting "off-the-field problems or distraction" affect "his on-the-field performance" (par. 5) and declares Bonds "the greatest player I've ever seen," overlooking the implications of Barry's alleged use of steroids (22 Mar. 2005 pars. 5, 6). Instead Sandberg returns to his usual complaint that while "baseball players are better athletes today" than they were, say, 20 years ago, they are too "focused on hitting home runs" and "lack technique in laying down a good bunt or bunting for a base hit or executing a hit-and-run" (21 Apr. 2005). His focus on the game itself quickly loses sight of the contexts for baseball.

In his weekly column for *Yahoo! Sports*, Sandberg plays the typical role of the opinionated analyst who picks his best and worst teams and players, makes predictions on teams that will rise and fall, and chooses his own MVP and Comeback Players, for example. Most of his positions seem canned, middle-of-the road, and based on information available to anyone who reads MLB.com at least semi-regularly. As expected, he supports the Cubs in Cubs Corner, and navigates (as he did in *Second to Home*) carefully, trying to be supportive of both the players and ownership. While using worshipful words like "incredible," "awesome," and "amazing" to define today's players and their accomplishments, he reminds his readers that in "the past 10 years" "individual athletes have become 'bigger than their team.' They've forgotten that it's the team that wins games, not individual players" (4 Aug. 2005), tabs their demands to be traded lack of loyalty (29 Dec. 2005), and agrees with George Steinbrenner's public dressing down of his players because they make so much money (19 Apr. 2005).[2] Overall, his favorite words seem to be "nice" and "wow," his favorite tone ambivalence, as when he argues that the White Sox were both "lucky and great" in the World Series (27 Oct. 2005).

Sandberg has always been an anomaly in Cubs lore in the second half of the twentieth century. Ernie Banks was controlled and graceful, rarely angry, respectful of those in authority. But Banks always seemed pleasant; his inveterate optimism made him approachable. In contrast, Sandberg was lumpish, restrained. Billy Williams, like both Banks and Sandberg, was graceful and balanced, but he clearly enjoyed his talent; he was one of the first professors of hitting, a man born to swing a bat. Best of all was the boyish exuberance and the puckish enthusiasm of Dunston, Santo, and (despite Sandberg's words) Sosa. They represented the resilience that you needed to survive all those years of loss, followed by equally sad ones of disappointment. Fergie Jenkins seemed troubled, Maddox had a short fuse and was self-absorbed, and Mark Grace was a bit artificial and above-it-all. But they had secret passion that Sandberg never seemed to express, even in the most dramatic of games. The others were, finally, articulate — one way or another — while Sandberg verged on being mute.

What we have in the place of revelation is an equally fascinating record of the role of the media in baseball. We only know that Ryne Sandberg was born in Spokane, Washington (to a mortician and a nurse), one older brother died in his early 40s, and Ryne's first marriage fell apart (he insists without any warning signs) ten days after his first retirement from baseball. There were also many rumors of his first wife's infidelities. Now he belongs to a blended family, inspired by his wife Margaret, who is described in his Hall of Fame address as "the best thing that's ever happened to me," "my best friend," "the love of my life," "my salvation," "my past, my present, my future," "my sun, my moon, my stars," and "everything that's good about life" (par. 28). But, with the help of Barry Rozner, the Cubs media department, and Yahoo Sports, Sandberg has also evolved from a poor interviewee to a spokesperson of the new nostalgia. To fans hungry for innocence, Sandberg articulates the myth of Old School Eden, a past with benign owners, insignificant labor strife, and no racism, abuse of drugs, or narcissism.[3] Cyber Ryno describes a nice place, where conflict is finally resolved by a respect for the game so profound that it will radiate naturally from pitcher to catcher, offense to defense, team to team, city to city, and the National to the American League. And millions of fans collaborate in his fantasy because, to borrow a line from Ernest Hemingway's *The Sun Also Rises*, it is "pretty to think so."

Both Ron Santo and Ryne Sandberg are near the center of Cubs lore because they represent the traditional ideals of their fans. Santo recalls the blue-collar ethic and the mixed ethnicity associated with the Wrigley Field area in the minds of older Northsiders. More than that, his loyalty to the team and passion for the Cubs, not just the game of baseball, are so deeply felt they carry him beyond the political correctness of modern broadcasting. When on

September 23, 1998, Brant Brown dropped a fly ball that forced the Cubs into a playoff game, and Santo followed with expletives, the listeners shared his feelings and forgave the breach of radio's conventions. The new Ryne Sandberg — on television, in the Hall of Fame, and from his 2005 Yahoo columns — also calls for a return to "the way the game should be played," cheerleads for his ex-teammates, and lives for the day the Cubs win the World Series. But his passion seems carefully crafted, sidestepping the implications of drugs and management decisions, as well as his own pain and anger. Even though both players came from the West Coast, Santo is the one who recalls the golden years between 50s loveable losing and today's yuppiedom. Sandberg has neither the edge nor the affect of Santo. Instead, Ryno serves WGN's national and international audiences, telecubbies encouraged to worship a recycled version of the old values, ones general enough, safe enough to be sold everywhere.

NOTES

1. The work ethic and family values of blue-collar life is also reflected in the preface to Santo's book *Few and Chosen*, where he says he liked baseball because it met the needs of family life and was "like a nine-to-five job" (xviii).

2. Certainly fundamentals are essential to winning, as Cubs teams have demonstrated all too often. And just as clearly, big money has increased the number of self-indulgent egos among the players. Some of the benign rituals of the game are, as Sandberg says, in decline. But there is danger in such an abstract approach to the game, especially among commentators; it can be misleading and sometimes discriminatory. For example, in the ceremony "Retiring Ryno," telecast on WGN, Sunday, August 28, 2005, Sandberg's deflecting attention away from himself and toward Gary Mathews was described as "Ryno Being Ryno," a reference to Red Sox fans forgiving Manny Ramirez's antics as "Manny Being Manny." The implication is clear: Cubs players and fans don't condone such displays in players like Ramirez or, by extension, Sammy Sosa, an ex-Cub who was indirectly criticized in Sandberg's Hall speech. At that point the subject takes on a racial and cultural dimension that is, whatever your position, highly problematic and, whether acknowledged or not, essentially political.

3. For example, one pretext for the establishment of the National League was the need to control gambling and the fixing of games which had become commonplace by the 1870s. So much for professional baseball as Eden.

WORKS CITED

Crasnick, Jerry. "Sandberg speaks his mind." *ESPN Insider*. 31 July 2005. <http://insider.espn.go.com?mlb.columns/story?columnist=crasnick_jerry&id=2121189&action=login&app>. 12 Feb. 2006.

Golenback, Peter. *Wrigleyville: A Magical History Tour of the Chicago Cubs*. New York: St. Martin's Griffin, 1999.

Hazucha, Andrew. "Historic Futility as Civic Virtue: The Singular Case of the Chicago Cubs. *Baseball/Literature/Culture: Essays, 2004–2005*. Ed. Peter Carino. Jefferson, NC: McFarland, 2006. 108–16.

Muskat, Carrie. "Sandberg Welcomes Sutter to Hall." <http://chicago.cubs/mlb.com/NASApp.mlb.content/printer_friendly/chc/y2006/m01/d11/cl>. 11 Jan. 2006.

Phalen, Rick. *Our Chicago Cubs: Inside the History and the Mystery of Baseball's Favorite Franchise*. South Bend, IN: Diamond Communications, 1992.

Sandberg, Ryne. "Respect the game." 1 Aug. 2005. <http://sports.yahoo.com/mlb/news? slug=rs-speech 080105&prov=yhoo&type=lgns>. 12 Feb. 2006.

_____. Column for *Yahoo! Sports*. <http://ca.sports.yahoo.com/mlb/news?slug=rs-mailbag090205&prov=yhoo&type=logns>.

Sandberg, Ryne, and Barry Rozner. *Second to Home: Ryne Sandberg Opens Up*. Chicago: Bonus, 1995.

Santo, Ron. *Few and Chosen: Defining Cubs Greatness Across the Eras*. With Phil Pepe. Fwd. Ernie Banks. Intro. Ryne Sandberg. Chicago: Triumph, 2005.

Santo, Ron, with Randy Minkoff. *Ron Santo: For Love of Ivy*. Chicago: Bonus, 1993.

This Old Cub. Prod. Tim Comstock and Jeff Santo. Dir. Jeff Santo. Emerging Pictures, 2004.

PART V

EPILOGUE

Why the Cubs Must Not Win the World Series ... Yet

Rick Moser

"Better to reign in Hell than serve in Heaven."
—John Milton, *Paradise Lost*

The consensus most important figure in baseball history is, of course, Babe Ruth, the icon whose name is synonymous with the game that he saved and remolded in its modern form. The debate over number two, however, is vigorous. Is it another great player—an Aaron or Mays? Is it a pioneer—Alexander Cartwright, the codifier; Al Spalding, the commercializer? Or is it a history-maker, such as Jackie Robinson, whose achievement stands so high above the statistics in which the legends of the game are written? The question is akin to asking which school of philosophy is most correct. The response says at least as much about the chooser as the choice.

To avoid this subjectivity in weighing a question of such moment, we must seek to reduce the subject to its most elemental terms. Baseball's significance towers above the implications of its parts—economic, sociological, demographic, or any other of the thousand lenses through which the game may be narrowly viewed. But, when seen in the proper light, when evaluated on the basis of what is most fundamental to its essence, the answer becomes as clear as a summer's day at Wrigley Field. The number two spot in baseball history can be filled by one person alone: Steve Bartman, the colossus who saved the game anew by helping the Chicago Cubs fulfill their destiny and blow the 2003 National League Championship Series against the Florida Marlins when victory lurked nearby. Far from being the hapless, security-salvaged nebbish he was misunderstood to be at the time—a twerp so clueless as to interfere with destiny for the sake of a souvenir foul—when placed in his proper context, Bartman emerges as a chosen agent of divine purpose.

While he shared the grim fate of his classical predecessor, Laocoön, Bartman differed by executing his suicide play successfully: his selfless act prevented a tragedy that his people were too blind to see. His heroic reach preserved the basic dialectic that sustains the game. In essence, all of baseball—not just its history but, more importantly, its meaning—boils down to the equipoise of just two teams: the New York Yankees and the Chicago Cubs.

The Yankees *are* winning. Their unrivalled success surmounts baseball itself, to become the all-purpose standard of sustained excellence in all things, as in "The New York Yankees of Fill-in-the-Blank." Winners, of course, require losers. Enter the Cubs, the most magnificently cursed losers of all time, whose haplessness, like the Yanks' glory, has risen to represent a dimension of humanity's experience far beyond the bounds of the simple game they play so poorly.

There have been other magnificent losers, of course. There have been the losers of barely unfulfilled excellence: the Brooklyn Dodgers who were cursed to be forever the bridesmaids during what was, perhaps, the Yankees' greatest era (the decade 1947–1956, in which the Yanks played in eight of ten World Series, and won seven times, five of them against Brooklyn), winning and winning and winning the National League Championship, only to be crushed by their cross-town tormentors (MLB.com).

In more recent times that role has been fulfilled to a more exaggerated, if less dramatic or poetic, extent by the Atlanta Braves, who managed to win their division an astonishing fourteen consecutive seasons (1991–2005, excluding strike-shortened 1994), while — more impressive still — earning only a single World Series title (MLB.com). But the Braves lacked a consistent foil to make more of their haplessness than a notable curiosity.

Ironically, the Yankees themselves have begun to suggest this same syndrome. Having won their ninth straight division title in 2006, they faded meekly that October to the unintimidated Tigers, exiting in the first round of the playoffs for the second time in a row. Of course, the three Series they won at the beginning of the streak rather mitigate the sting of the less-than-total success they have experienced in recent seasons.

Until their 2006 World Series victory, the recent vintage of the St. Louis Cardinals appeared to be making a place in this pantheon, after their posting the best record in baseball two years in a row (2004 and 2005) and exiting the postseason with scarcely a whimper (MLB.com). In 2006 they defaulted into the playoffs with the worst record of any postseason participant (including both wild card teams) thanks to playing in a division not only built on the solid basement of the Cubs but one with only one other team above .500 (Houston, whose late dash to catch the Cards raised them to a lofty .506).

But both the Cards' recent failures and success taste like their long-term legacy: bland. They've been the second most successful World Series team in history, winning ten titles to the Yanks' twenty-six — but who's noticed? Their impression on the game and the national psyche is remarkably faint compared to the substance of their accomplishments.

The Cards' analogue on the losing side is the Cleveland Indians, who, in their 106 years of existence, have, like the Cubs, won only two Series, the last one coming fifty-nine years ago (MLB.com). But because it lacks structure and resonance, the Tribe's losing tradition is undistinguished and uncelebrated. They're mere losers. The form and nature of their losing anchors them to their ignominy while the Cubs' allows them to rise above it. In the long yarn of baseball legend, even a team as consistently and enduringly excellent as the Cards, or one as consistently and enduringly poor as the Indians, are merely also-rans. There is only one winning and one losing: the Yankees and the Cubs. Everyone in between is a footnote. Baseball is about absolutes.

The next sub-type of hard-core loser is the team that has never been anything else: the Texas Rangers, who have not seen the inside of a World Series in their thirty-six seasons of existence; the Houston Astros, who took forty-four seasons to make their first Series, only to be swept; the Tampa Bay Devil Rays, whose tender years would have spared them the expectation of success if their downstate cousins, the Florida Marlins, hadn't managed a pair of championships in just their first eleven seasons (MLB.com).

And then, most importantly for a game with such a long and romantic memory, there are the chronic, historic losers. This was a small but singular fraternity, composed of only three of baseball's most venerable franchises — three that were around for the first World Series (indeed, including the one that won it); three that between them claimed four of the first five Series titles (and nine of the first fifteen); and three that had, between them, played 269 seasons without a championship: the Boston Red Sox, the Chicago White Sox and, with a nine-year lead over their nearest rival, the Cubs (MLB.com). With the Cubs and Red Sox tucked into their cozy old parks (the White Sox having annihilated their even older yard, Comiskey Park, with its long heritage, for a concrete bowl lyrically dubbed U.S. Cellular Field in honor of the highest bidder), this trio offered a wonderful kind of reassurance. Their losing was like one's grandparents — it had always been there; it gave one a past.

While the Cubs' streak was the longest of these three, it was certainly neither the most glorious nor the most dolorous. With few exceptions (the 1969 collapse to the Miracle Mets, the 1984 playoff grounder between Leon Durham's legs, that would have given him a spot on the All-Goat team had Bill Buckner not made the same gaffe in a still bigger game two years later), the Cubs' streak has been relatively uneventful. They've asserted their peculiar excellence after the fashion of Henry Aaron: doing it day in and day out, reliably, without a great deal of flair but to remarkable effect over time.

But the curse of the Billy Goat was a mild one compared to the caliber of disaster and suffering brought on by that of the Bambino. Fans of the Red Sox had to endure a fate similar to that of Brooklynites, extended an agonizing fifty years longer. While the Dodgers brought their suffering to an end in 1955 (before imposing a still more terrible fate upon their fans, turning mere losing into permanent Loss Angeles), the Red Sox stretched their excruciating Yankee complex into a new millennium (No, No, Aaron Boone), while having their hearts broken by others as random as the '76 Reds who mooted Carlton Fisk's thrill of victory and the '86 Mets who made poor Billy Buck synonymous with the agony of defeat (MLB.com).

Because they were so often competitive, even excellent, the Red Sox inflicted a much more exquisite variety of pain on their long-suffering fans than could the Cubs. The Cubs kept the superb and lovable Ernie Banks from even seeing a Series in his nineteen-year, Hall-of-Fame major league career, fitting him with the tragically appropriate mantle of "Mr. Cub." But the Red Sox managed to inflict an even more bitter fate upon their star-crossed immortal. The BoSox's curse was so severe that it allowed Ted Williams — The Natural, The Kid, Gil Gamesh — to breathe Series air but once in his twenty-one seasons and doused his fire-touched bat when he got there. In his single World Series, Teddy Ballgame batted a mere .200, 144 points below his career average; he slugged .200 as well, less than one-third the .634 average he amassed over his Olympian career, the second highest in history (Reichler 1594).

The greatest source of tribulation for the White Sox, meanwhile, was less their failure to win the Series (or to reach it, their own self-inflicted curse — brought on by the Black Sox scandal of 1919 — allowing them only a single Series appearance over the course of their drought, fewer even than the Cubs) than being relegated to second-class status in their home town, behind their consistently less talented cross-town rivals (MLB.com).

All of this came to an end, of course, with stunning symmetry and millennial inevitability over consecutive seasons. The Red Sox's memorable run of eight wins in a row *en route* to the 2004 title — including, more important still, their comeback from the brink of extinction in the ALCS at the hands of the inevitable Yankees — brought them their first taste of victory since 1918. The White Sox, who last won the Series the year before their crimson counterparts, reversed order and swept the series in 2005 (MLB.com). This left, then, only the Cubs in sole possession of the crown of thorns. Millennialists anticipated the completion of a redemption trifecta, with the Cubs following suit in short order, turning those thorns to Series laurels.

Thankfully, this did not happen. And, for the sake of baseball, this must not happen until they fulfill their destiny. Even if we are witnessing the results of some unprecedented astral alignment, the Cubs must not submit to this fate. They succeeded brilliantly in not winning in 2006, posting a .407 winning percentage. They must find the strength to lose in 2007 and 2008 as well to achieve a truly epochal consummation by completing a full century of abject failure. They must learn from the bitter fates of their former fellows and summon the grit and incompetence needed to get the job done and fail utterly. As we shall see, the alternative, mere victory, is far worse.

As *The New Yorker*'s David Denby noted after their 2004 victory, the Red Sox had passed from "the grandeur of eternal loss to the banality of success" (205). They went from membership in a club so exclusive that no one else would ever be able to join it to the company of so many Angels, Diamondbacks, and other hobbledehoy who'd managed to pull off a fleeting season of success. The Red Sox extended their tragedy by sinking weakly in the 2005 playoffs, as if remembering who they were. Their spiritual rout was completed when they lost the emblem of their brief happiness, Johnny Damon, to, of all possible insults, the Yankees, where he uncomplainingly shaved off the scruffy symbols of his Hub City defiance and adopted the clean-shaven countenance of the empire he'd once opposed: Luke Skywalker choosing the Dark Side, after all.

When, in '06, the Yankees reprised their 1978 "Boston Massacre" with a five-game sweep in Fenway, the Sox were broken. After having led through much of the back-and-forth campaign against the Yanks, they faded to third, eleven games back and out of the postseason altogether. The White Sox followed suit, receding to third in parallel after staying with the Tigers all year and being passed by the sprinting Twins, who took the AL Central on the last day of the season (MLB.com).

The Sox's descent into success provides the Cubs a cautionary example and the opportunity to accomplish something heroically pathetic, securing a place in history more unassailable than Dimaggio's consecutive-game hitting streak or Aaron's record of clean home runs. With their historical peers out of the picture, the only other organization on Earth that can compete with the Cubs' claim to enduring futility is the French army.

The question now is: "Do the Cubs have what it takes?" Can they understand the value of what they possess and what they are about to achieve, and can they commit to fulfilling their unique potential? The Cubs must open and train their minds to embrace a higher goal, one that confounds the one they're accustomed to pursuing. As Milton, a guy who knew a few things about loss, put it, "The mind is its own place, and in itself/Can make a Heav'n of Hell, a Hell of Heav'n" (*Paradise Lost*, 1.254–55). Can the Cubs recognize that the hell they believe they've been in can become heaven through an act of imagination and mythological understanding?

A century. One hundred years of splendid solitude, undisturbed by the vulgar din of fans celebrating victory. How many can achieve something of such iconic magnitude?

The greatest fear today for a Cubs — or baseball — fan with a sense of history is that the team may somehow blunder into victory now, before achieving this apotheosis. And what could be truer to the Cubs' record and essence than that? Going a full century without winning is a completely singular occurrence. There is neither precedent nor rival. The likelihood of this record being surpassed is vanishingly small.

Making it to one hundred years without a title would make for a wonderful baseball story. It's still a mind-boggling record of failure, reaching back to the adolescence of the national pastime and of the nation itself, with victory and absolution coming at last, upon the eve of the century. This would make for a satisfyingly tidy conclusion to a very long chapter.

But to win now, after just ninety-nine years of losing, would turn those years to injury and the win to insult. One hundred years (or more) without a championship would ennoble defeat, suggesting the activity of a higher power; one hundred years in the wilderness before returning to the promised land of the championship is a fable worthy of Parson Weems, brimming with meaning to be mined by pundits and schoolchildren alike. But *ninety-nine* years? That just means you sucked for a very long time. Then winning is not a relief and release, not a final pardon or soaring *denouement*. It becomes simply a matter of, "What took you so long?" Achieving the milestone justifies the years of ignominy that made it possible; anything short of that mark amplifies their horror. Winning now would make the Cubs losers; losing will make them immortal. This is what makes Bartman more important than the Billy Goat and his reach the pivotal act of Cubs history: his intervention came so near the mark with so much more at stake. Had the Cubs' streak halted at some earlier point — had they taken the 1945 Series, had Durham closed his legs, had Don Young caught that fly — their streak would have been notable, but not transcendental. Now every season brings us closer to the Rapture, and every threat of success is elevated from yellow alert to red.

Let us put the magnitude of the Cubs' achievement in perspective:

- The number of different franchises that have won the World Series since the Cubs last did, in 1908: twenty-one. The Braves have won for three different hometowns over this stretch (Boston, Milwaukee and Atlanta), the Athletics (Philadelphia and Oakland) and Dodgers (Brooklyn and L.A.) for two each (MLB.com).
- Since the Cubs last won, eight new, Series-winning franchises were created, taking fourteen titles between them (MLB.com).
- All of the Yankees' twenty-six World Series wins have come since the Cubs' last one, which came before the New York Highlanders even adopted the name "Yankees" (MLB.com).
- The Cubs, founded before the World Series even existed (in fact, before the National League came into existence in 1876), have won as many Series championships as the Florida Marlins, founded more than 120 years later, in 1993 (MLB.com).
- There are eight current major league teams that have never won a World Series: the Texas Rangers (founded in 1961 as the reincarnated Washington Senators, then relocated to Texas and renamed the Rangers in 1972); the Houston Astros (1962); the Milwaukee Brewers (*nee* Seattle Pilots), Washington Nationals (*nee* Montreal Expos) and San Diego Padres (all three founded in 1969); the Seattle Mariners (1977); the Colorado Rockies (1993); and the Tampa Bay Devil Rays (1998). These eight profoundly unaccomplished teams have not won a Series in the 258 collective seasons they have existed — a period that is, nonetheless, just two-and-one-half times the length of the Cubs' *solo* winless streak. And these teams include six of the eight clubs after the Cubs with the longest non–Series streaks in baseball. Only two legacy teams have been out of it longer than those six latter-day losers. The third-longest current streak without a championship belongs to the Giants, who haven't won the Series since moving to San Francisco in 1957 (though they've appeared three times since, and were just five outs from victory against the Angels in 2002). At number two are the Indians who, having last won in 1948, are still forty years behind the Cubs (MLB.com).
- And not only do the Cubs hold the record for the longest time between World Series victories but it's been longer since the Cubs were even *in* a Series, than any other team. Their last appearance was in 1945, three years before the last win of the Indians (who played in the Series as recently as 1997) and nine years before the Giants, who last won in 1954 (MLB.com).

The Cubs' is, almost certainly, baseball's truly unbreakable record, and one that is as likely to persist across all sports. The evolution and baseball maven Stephen Jay Gould theorized that Joe Dimaggio's record of fifty-six consecutive games with a hit is the baseball record least likely to have ever occurred, much less ever to be broken (Gould 466–67). We can't keep up with the eminent paleontologist's math, but it seems even less conceivable that a team can ever again do what the Cubs have done, not least because none would want to. Pete Rose's forty-four-game hitting streak came to only seventy-nine percent of Dimaggio's mark while the White Sox's eighty-seven consecutive winless seasons amount to eighty-nine percent of the Cubs' current ninety-eight. But the Cubs' total is still climbing. Dimaggio's record has stood for sixty-seven seasons, but would take only one to break, and that attempt can be made every year; but it will be another forty years until the team closest to the Cubs' record, the Indians, can even have a shot at the ninety-eight, much less at what dizzying low to which the mark may yet sink.

Achievements of this magnitude are not to be taken lightly. It is extremely doubtful that we'll see its like again. Such singularities — like eclipses, harmonic convergences and perfect games — must be appreciated in the brief time that we are able. We've had ninety-nine years to watch the Cubs lose. We'll have only a few in which to appreciate that losing as something extraordinary and greater than itself. Achievements (or, at least, events) of this magnitude give us occasions for pause and reflection. Like mountains or natural disasters, they confront us with something greater than ourselves, something in which we can find or create meaning.

What is the possible significance of such a dubious accomplishment as that before the Cubs? The meanings are multiple and of great import and nobility.

First, the Cubs allow us to enjoy baseball, the one sport with which our nation has a true spiritual connection, in a very pure and contemplative way, allowing us to cultivate salutary habits of mind while suppressing unruly tempers. The lack of interest in winning that the Cubs make possible — nay, necessary — allows for the purest breed of baseball fandom. P. K. Wrigley, the Cubs' longtime owner, sought to emphasize the baseball experience over winning in order to keep his turnstiles spinning, win or lose (Angle 63); ironically, his self-interested marketing strategy bred civic virtue over time. We don't go to Wrigley Field for the vicarious thrill of victory; we're there to celebrate every other aspect of the game, unencumbered by such selfish hopes. The Cubs' ineptitude brings to the fore the better angels of our baseball nature.

Second, and more important still, the Cubs are our perpetual *contemptus mundi*. Their Sisyphean failure reminds us, amidst too much plenty, that all life is sorrowful. We Americans savor the myth that we're the Cubs, the little guy striving, when, in fact, we're the Yankees, dominant and forever building, in ways that sometimes don't quite seem fair, on our dominance. The Cubs remind us not that sometimes the little guy can win too but that the big guy can't win all the time. We were thinking like Yankees when we blundered into Iraq. If we'd remembered the Cubs instead, history and our place in the world today would be very different indeed. As the emblematic Chicago columnist Mike Royko put it in a National Public Radio interview after another epochal Cubs failure — their passion play against the Philadelphia Phillies, May 17, 1979, which they heroically managed to lose 23–22 — their extensive experience of loss has made Chicago fans "philosophical and tolerant." Cubs fans know we shouldn't expect things to go our way. Like Shaw's reasonable man, we adapt ourselves to the world around us rather than expecting it to adapt to us. "The Yankees aren't real," said Royko. "Nobody goes around triumphing over everything [...] most people don't triumph over *any*thing. The Cubs help teach us that life is rough" (Royko). And, one might add, they teach us that the way to confront that adversity is not to create more of it for others when we don't win the game.

Baseball and the nation need the Cubs to reach the century mark. Just as the great milestones of the 1990s — Cal Ripken breaking Lou Gehrig's consecutive-games-played streak (1995) and Mark McGwire breaking the single-season home-run record (1998) — brought the game back from the attempted suicide of the strike-cancelled Series of 1994, the Cubs reaching their centenary will renew our collective soul in a time of great spiritual malaise: not only does a steroid cloud hang over the game itself (casting shadows even on the redemption we enjoyed with McGwire) but the concatenation of scandals in business and government, the lingering of New Orleans on minimal life support, and the pall cast by our squandering of the high ground after 9/11 have given us need for another great, redemptive symbolic event in the life of the nation.

The Cubs are competing with only themselves, now. This is more worrisome than it might seem; we know what happens when the Cubs try to compete. We now face the dilemma that confronted Al Tiller, the fictional manager of the Cubs in W. P. Kinsella's short story entitled "The Last Pennant Before Armageddon." Managing the Cubs toward their first Series appearance since '45 (not even forty seasons when the story was published in 1984), Tiller is faced with a Hobson's choice: to lose and let down legions of prayerful fans or to bring on the end of days that his apocalyptic dreams warn will commence should they actually take the National League Championship. The story ends with Tiller's choice unmade and the fate of the world unknown (Kinsella 21).

Because we stand similarly perched upon the razor's edge today, we need Bartman's protection now, more than ever. We implore the Cubs with a plaintive paraphrase of the old Ebbetts Field *cri de coeur*, when the Yanks had dealt the faithful yet another blow: wait until next year — please.

WORKS CITED

Angle, Paul M. *Philip K. Wrigley: A Memoir of a Modest Man.* Chicago: Rand McNally, 1975.

Denby, David. "Track and Field: 'Kontroll,' and 'Fever Pitch.'" *The New Yorker* 18 Apr. 2005: 202–5.

Gould, Stephen Jay. "The Streak of Streaks." *Bully for Brontosaurus: Reflections in Natural History.* New York: Norton, 1991. 463–73.

Kinsella, W. P. "The Last Pennant Before Armageddon." *The Thrill of the Grass.* Toronto: Penguin, 1984. 3–21.

Major League Baseball. *MLB.com.* 2001–2006 Advanced Media, L.P. Aug. 2006. <http://mlb.mlb.com/ NASApp//index.jsp>.

Milton, John. *Paradise Lost. John Milton: Complete Poems and Major Prose.* Ed. Merritt Y. Hughes. Indianapolis: Bobbs-Merrill, 1983. 207–467.

Reichler, Joseph L., ed. *The Baseball Encyclopedia.* 7th ed. New York: Macmillan, 1988.

Royko, Mike. Rebroadcast of 1979 interview with Alex Chadwick. *All Things Considered.* Natl. Public Radio. WBEZ, Chicago. 16 Oct. 2003. Transcript.

Selective Bibliography

Ahrens, Art. *Chicago Cubs, 1926–1940*. Charleston, SC: Arcadia, 2005.

_____. *How the Cubs Got Their Name*. Chicago: Chicago Historical Society, 1976.

_____, and Eddie Gold. *The Cubs: The Complete Record of Chicago Cubs Baseball*. New York: Collier Books, 1986.

_____, and Buck Peden. *Day by Day in Chicago Cubs History*. West Point, NY: Leisure, 1982.

Alibi Ike. Dir. Ray Enright. Prod. Edward Chodorov. Starring Joe E. Brown and Olivia de Havilland. Warner Bros., 1935.

Angell, Roger. "Takes: The Confines." *Game Time: A Baseball Companion*. New York: Harcourt, 2003. 312–18.

Angle, Paul M. *Mr. Wrigley's Cubs*. Chicago: Chicago Historical Society, 1976.

_____. *P. K. Wrigley: A Memoir of a Modest Man*. Skokie, IL: Rand McNally, 1975.

Anson, Adrian. *A Ball Player's Career*. Chicago: Era, 1900.

Banks, Ernie, and Jim Enright. *"Mr. Cub."* Chicago: Follett, 1971.

Barber, Ron. *Jack Quinlan: Forgotten Greatness*. RonJackCubs, 2005. [sound recording]

Bellamy, Robert V., and James R. Walker. "Baseball and Television Origins: The Case of the Cubs." *Nine* 10.1 (2001): 31–45.

Billington, Charles N., and Andy Pafko. *Wrigley Field's Last World Series: The Wartime Chicago Cubs and the Pennant of 1945*. Chicago: Lake Claremont P, 2005.

Bitman, Ronnie. "Rocking Wrigley: The Chicago Cubs' Off-field Struggle to Compete for Ticket Sales with Its Rooftop Neighbors." *Federal Communications Law Journal* 56.2 (Mar. 2004): 377–96.

Blaisdell, Lowell L. "Remembering the Babe: October 1, 1932." *Nine* 12.1 (2003): 180–84.

Bleacher Bums. Dir. Stuart Gordon. Starring Dennis Franz and Joe Mantegna. PBS-TV, 1979.

The Blue Brothers. Dir. John Landis. Prod. Robert K. Weiss. Starring John Belushi and Dan Aykroyd. Universal, 1980.

Bochner, Ben. *World's Greatest Fans! Or, How I Learned to Stop Worrying and Love the Chicago Cubs*. Eugene, OR: Blue Medium Video, 1999. [videotape]

Bogen, Gil. *Johnny Kling: A Baseball Biography*. Jefferson, NC: McFarland, 2006.

_____. *Tinker, Evers, and Chance: A Triple Biography*. Jefferson, NC: McFarland, 2003.

Boone, Bob, and Gerald Grunska. *Hack: The Meteoric Life of One of Baseball's First Superstars*. Highland Park, IL: Highland, 1978.

Brickhouse, Jack. *Jack Brickhouse Presents Great Moments in Cubs Baseball!* Chicago: Major Official Productions, 1971. [sound recording]

_____, and Harry Caray. *Within These Walls of Ivy the Cubs: Everybody's Team Since 1876*. Chicago: Odon Productions, 1986. [videotape]

Bristow, Dennis N., and Richard J. Sebastian. "Holy Cow! Wait 'Til Next Year! A Closer Look at the Brand Loyalty of Chicago Cubs Baseball Fans." *Journal of Consumer Marketing* 18.3 (2001): 256–75.

Brown, Warren. *The Chicago Cubs*. New York: Putnam, 1946. [Rprtd. Southern Illinois UP, Carbondale, 2001]

Campana, Dan. *The Fan-Friendly Guide to the Friendly Confines: A Wrigley Field Companion Book.* Bloomington, IN: Authorhouse, 2004.

Carino, Peter, ed. *Baseball/Literature/Culture: Essays, 2002–2003.* Jefferson, NC: McFarland, 2004.

_____. *Baseball/Literature/Culture: Essays, 2004–2005.* Jefferson, NC: McFarland, 2006.

Castle, George. *Baseball and the Media: How Fans Lose in Today's Coverage of the Game.* Lincoln: U of Nebraska P, 2007.

_____. *Cubs Diary.* Champaign, IL: Sports Publishing, 2007.

_____. *Entangled in Ivy.* Champaign, IL: Sports Publishing, 2007.

_____. *The Million-to-One Team: Why the Chicago Cubs Haven't Won a Pennant Since 1945.* South Bend, IN: Diamond Communications, 2000.

_____. *Where Have All Our Cubs Gone?* Dallas: Taylor, 2005.

Cava, Pete. *Tales from the Cubs Dugout.* Champaign, IL: Sports Publishing, 2000.

Chadwick, Bruce. *The Chicago Cubs Trivia Book.* New York: St. Martin's, 1994.

Claerbaut, David. *Durocher's Cubs: The Greatest Team That Didn't Win.* Dallas: Taylor, 2000.

Cohen, Rich. "Letter from Chicago — Down and Out at Wrigley Field — A Prayer for the Chicago Cubs." *Harper's* Aug. 2001: 55–62.

Coletti, Ned. *You Gotta Have Heart: Dallas Green's Rebuilding of the Cubs.* South Bend, IN: Diamond Communications, 1985.

Crepeau, Richard C. "Divine Wrath: The Goat and the Bambino." *Nine* 13.1 (2004): 109–13.

Cubs: A Video History from 1876. Chicago: Odon Productions, 1986. [videotape]

Disco, Matthew D., Felix Paulick, and Paul M. Sommers. "Some Differences Are Like Day and Night." *Journal of Recreational Mathematics* 24.2 (Summer 1992): 94–97.

Easter, Eric Richard Marvin. "Mass Media Spectation and the Social Identity Theory." Diss. U of Northern Colorado, 1999.

Ellis, George. *The Cubs Fan's Guide to Happiness.* Chicago: Triumph Books, 2007.

Elmer the Great. Dir. Mervyn LeRoy. Prod. Raymond Griffith. Starring Joe E. Brown and Patricia Ellis. Written by George M. Cohan, Ring Lardner, and Thomas J. Geraghty. First National, 1933.

Enright, Jim. *Chicago Cubs.* New York: Macmillan, 1975.

Eskenazi, Gerald. *Bill Veeck: A Baseball Legend.* New York: McGraw-Hill, 1988.

Evers, John J., and Hugh S. Fullerton. *Touching Second.* Jefferson, NC: McFarland, 2004. [rprt. of 1910 edition, published by Reilly and Britton]

Feldmann, Doug. *September Streak: The 1935 Chicago Cubs Chase the Pennant.* Jefferson, NC: McFarland, 2003.

_____, and Don Kessinger. *Miracle Collapse: The 1969 Chicago Cubs.* Lincoln: U of Nebraska P, 2006.

Ferris Bueller's Day Off. Dir. John Hughes. Prod. John Hughes and Tom Jacobson. Starring Matthew Broderick, Alan Ruck, and Mia Sara. Paramount, 1986.

Fleitz, David L. *Cap Anson: The Grand Old Man of Baseball.* Jefferson, NC: McFarland, 2005.

Forever Loyal: A Salute to Cubs Fans and Their Field. Dir. Bob Ray. Prod. Bob Ray and John Maloney. MPI Home Video, 2003.

Freedman, Lew. *Cubs Essential: Everything You Need to Know to Be a Real Fan.* Chicago: Triumph Books, 2006.

Fulk, David, and Dan Riley. *The Cubs Reader.* Boston: Houghton Mifflin, 1991.

Gatto, Steve. *Da Curse of the Billy Goat: The Chicago Cubs, Pennant Races, and Curses.* Lansing, MI: Protar House, 2004.

Gentile, Derek. *The Complete Chicago Cubs: The Total Encyclopedia for the Team.* New York: Black Dog and Leventhal, 2002.

_____, and Studs Terkel. *Chicago Baseball in the City.* San Diego: Thunder Bay P, 2006.

Gifford, Barry. *The Neighborhood of Baseball: A Personal History of the Chicago Cubs.* New York: Dutton, 1981.

Gillette, Gary. *Total Cubs.* Kingston, NY: Total Sports, 2000.

"Go Sox, Go Cubs." *The Christian Century* 122.24 (2005): 3–4.

Gold, Eddie. *Eddie Gold's White Sox and Cubs Trivia Book.* Chicago: Follett, 1981.

_____, and Art Ahrens. *The Golden Era Cubs, 1876–1940.* Chicago: Bonus Books, 1985.

_____, and _____. *The New Era Cubs, 1941–1985.* Chicago: Bonus Books, 1985.

_____, and _____. *The Renewal Era Cubs, 1985–1990*. Chicago: Bonus Books, 1990.

Golenbock, Peter. *Wrigleyville: A Magical History Tour of the Chicago Cubs*. New York: St. Martin's, 1996.

Goodman, Steve. *Live at the Earl of Old Town*. Nashville, TN: Red Pajamas Record, 1978. [sound recording]

Goss, David A. "September Streak: The 1935 Chicago Cubs Chase the Pennant." *Nine: A Journal of Baseball History and Culture* 13.2 (2005): 178–79.

Green, David. *101 Reasons to Love the Cubs*. New York: Stewart, Tabori and Chang, 2006.

Green, Stephen. *Wrigley Field: A Celebration of the Friendly Confines*. Chicago: Contemporary Books, 2003.

Hageman, William. *Baseball Between the Wars: A Pictorial Tribute to the Men Who Made the Game in Chicago from 1909–1947*. Chicago: Contemporary Books, 2001.

Hartel, William. *A Day at the Ballpark: In Celebration of Wrigley Field*. Rock Island, IL: Quality Sports Publications, 1994.

Hazucha, Andrew. "Historic Futility as Civic Virtue: The Singular Case of the Chicago Cubs." *Baseball/Literature/Culture, Essays, 2004–2005*. Ed. Peter Carino. Jefferson, NC: McFarland, 2006. 108–16.

_____. "Leo Durocher's Last Stand: Anti-Semitism, Racism, and the Cubs Player Rebellion of 1971." *Nine* 15.1 (Fall 2006): 1–12.

_____. "Nelson Algren's Chicago: The Black Sox Scandal, McCarthyism, and the Truth about Cubs Fans." *Baseball/Literature/Culture*. Ed. Peter Carino. Jefferson, NC: McFarland, 2004. 49–59.

Holtzman, Jerome, and George Vass. *Baseball, Chicago Style: A Tale of Two Teams, One City*. Chicago: Bonus Books, 2001.

_____, and _____. *The Chicago Cubs Encyclopedia*. Philadelphia: Temple UP, 1997.

Honig, Donald. *Baseball When the Grass Was Real*. New York: Coward-McCann, 1975.

_____. *The Chicago Cubs: An Illustrated History*. New York: Prentice-Hall, 1991.

Hornsby, Rogers, and Bill Surface. *My War with Baseball*. New York: Coward-McCann, 1962.

Hughes, Pat, and Ron Santo. *Chicago Cubs Greatest Hits, Volume 1*. New York: Alphabet City Sports Records, 1999. [sound recording]

"In an Effort to Make Up for Declining Ad Revenues from Televised Baseball Games, Tribune Broadcasting and the Chicago Cubs Took to the Air with an Hour-Long Home Shopping Show Featuring Cubs Memorabilia." *Broadcasting* 123.22 (31 May 1993): 58.

Jacob, Mark. *Wrigley Field: A Celebration of the Friendly Confines*. New York: McGraw-Hill, 2002.

Johnson, Steve. *Chicago Cubs Trivia Teasers*. Madison, WI: Trails Books, 2006.

Juffer, Jane. "Who's the Man? Sammy Sosa, Latinos, and Televisual Redefinitions of the 'American' Pastime." *Journal of Sport & Social Issues* 26.4 (2002): 337–59.

Kaduk, Kevin. *Wrigleyworld: A Season in Baseball's Best Neighborhood*. New York: New American Library, 2006.

Kaplan, Ron. "The Cubs: A Review Essay." *Nine* 10.2 (Spring 2002): 136–41.

Kinsella, W. P. *The Iowa Baseball Confederacy*. Boston: Houghton Mifflin, 1986.

_____. "The Last Pennant Before Armageddon." *The Thrill of the Grass*. New York: Penguin, 1985. 1–21.

Klein, Frederick C., and Mark Anderson. *For Love of the Cubs: An A to Z Primer for Cubs Fans of All Ages*. Chicago: Triumph Books, 2005.

Kogan, Rick, and Sam Sianis. *A Chicago Tavern: A Goat, a Curse, and the American Dream*. Chicago: Lake Claremont P, 2006.

Langford, Jim. *The Cub Fan's Book of Days: A Guide to Every Year*. South Bend, IN: Diamond Communications, 2000.

_____. *The Cub Fan's Guide to Life: The Ultimate Self-help Book*. Notre Dame, IN: Diamond Communications, 1984.

_____. *The Cubs Fan's Little Book of Wisdom: 101 Truths Learned the hard Way*. South Bend, IN: Diamond Communications, 1993.

_____. *The Game Is Never Over: An Appreciative History of the Chicago Cubs, 1948–1980*. South Bend, IN: Icarus, 1980.

Logan, Bob. *More Tales from the Cubs Dugout*. Champaign, IL: Sports Publishing, 2006.

_____. *So You Think You're a Die-hard Cub Fan.* Chicago: Contemporary Books, 1985.

Malone, J. C. *Sammy Sosa in 9 Innings.* Bronx, NY: Editorial Miglo, 2005.

Mausser, Wayne. *Chicago Cubs Facts and Trivia.* South Bend, IN: E. B. Houchin, 1996.

McNeil, William F. *Gabby Hartnett: The Life and Times of the Cubs' Greatest Catcher.* Jefferson, NC: McFarland, 2004.

Mitchell, Fred. *Cubs: Where Have You Gone?* Champaign, IL: Sports Publishing, 2004.

Muskat, Carrie, comp. *Banks to Sandberg to Grace: Five Decades of Love and Frustration With the Chicago Cubs.* Lincolnwood, IL: Contemporary Books, 2001.

Myers, Doug. *Essential Cubs: Chicago Cubs Facts, Feats, and Firsts — From the Batter's Box to the Bullpen to the Bleachers.* Lincolnwood, IL: Contemporary Books, 1999.

Nagel, David A. "A Study of the 1984 Chicago Cubs Baseball Team." M.S. Thesis: Illinois State U, 1996.

Names, Larry D. *Bury My Heart at Wrigley Field: The History of the Chicago Cubs (When the Cubs Were the White Sox).* Chicago: Sportsbook Publishing, 1990.

Nelson, Scott. "Best of Times, Worst of Times: Superlative & Dismal Ten-year Team Performances." *The Baseball Research Journal* 31 (2002): 51–54.

Out of the Blue: The Remarkable Story of the 2003 Chicago Cubs. [*Chicago Tribune* Special Commemorative Edition.] Chicago: Triumph Books, 2003.

Parker, Clifton Blue. *Fouled Away: The Baseball Tragedy of Hack Wilson.* Jefferson, NC: McFarland, 2000.

Peterson, Paul Michael. *Chicago's Wrigley Field (Images of Baseball).* Charleston, SC: Arcadia, 2005.

Phalen, Rick. *Our Chicago Cubs: Inside the History and the Mystery of Baseball's Favorite Franchise.* South Bend, IN: Diamond Communications, 1992.

Riess, Steven A. "Professional Baseball and Social Mobility." *Journal of Interdisciplinary History* 11.2 (Autumn 1980): 235–50.

Ritter, Lawrence S. *The Glory of Their Times.* New York: HarperCollins, 1992. [Orig. pub. Macmillan, New York, 1966]

Rookie of the Year. Dir. Daniel Stern. Prod. Robert Harper. Starring Thomas Ian Nicholas and Gary Busey. 20th Century–Fox, 1993.

Rosenberg, Howard W. *Cap Anson 4.* Arlington, VA: Tile Books, 2006.

Ross, Alan. *Cubs Pride: For the Love of Ernie, Fergie & Wrigley Field.* Nashville, TN: Cumberland House, 2005.

Royko, Mike. *Chicago and the Cubs: A Lifelong Love Affair.* New York: Polygram, 198. [videotape]

Rubenstein, Bruce A. *Chicago in the World Series, 1903–2005: The Cubs and the White Sox in Championship Play.* Jefferson, NC: McFarland, 2006.

Sandberg, Ryne, and Barry Rozner. *Second to Home: Ryne Sandberg Opens Up.* Chicago: Bonus Books, 1995.

Santo, Ron, and Phil Pepe. *Few and Chosen: Defining Cubs Greatness Across the Eras.* Fwd. Ernie Banks. Intro. Ryne Sandberg. Chicago: Triumph Books, 2005.

Santo, Ron, with Randy Minkoff. *For Love of Ivy: An Autobiography.* Chicago: Bonus Books, 1993.

Schwab, Rick. *Stuck on the Cubs.* Evanston, IL: Sassafras, 1977.

Shea, Stuart, and George Castle. *Wrigley Field: An Unauthorized Biography.* Washington, D.C.: Brassey's, 2006.

Sherony, Mark. "Chicago Cubs Destiny — World Series Victory." *Nine* 11.2 (Spring 2003): 168–71.

Siporin, M. "Cavoto v. Chicago Nat'l League Ball Club, Inc.: Chicago Cubs Ticket Scalping Scandal and the Relationship Between Separate Corporate Entities Owned by a Common Parent." *DePaul Business & Commercial Law Journal* 2.4 (2004): 723–59.

Skipper, John C. *The Cubs Win the Pennant! Charlie Grimm, the Billy Goat Curse, and the 1945 World Series Run.* Jefferson, NC: McFarland, 2004.

_____. *Take Me Out to the Cubs Game: 35 Former Ballplayers Speak of Losing at Wrigley.* Jefferson, NC: McFarland, 2000.

Slater, Eric. "Classic Fall Instead of Fall Classic." *Los Angeles Times* 16 Oct. 2003: A1.

Snyder, John. *Cubs Journal: Year by Year and Day by Day With the Chicago Cubs Since 1876.* Cincinnati, OH: Emmis Books, 2005.

Staudohar, Paul D. "Tinker to Evers to Chance: Poetry in Motion." *Nine* 14.1 (Fall 2005): 114–29.

Steele, Tim. *The Cubs Chronology: A Chronological History of the Chicago Cubs*. St. Louis, MO: Stellar, 2003.

Stone, Steve. *Where's Harry?: Steve Stone Remembers 25 Years with Harry Caray*. Lanham, MD: Taylor Trade Publishing, 2000.

Stout, Glenn, and Richard A. Johnson. *The Cubs: The Complete Story of Chicago Cubs Baseball*. Boston: Houghton Mifflin, 2007.

Sullivan, Neil J. "Baseball and Race: The Limits of Competition." *The Journal of Negro History* 83.3 (Summer 1998): 168–77.

Swyers, Holly. "Community America: Who Owns Wrigley Field?" *The International Journal of the History of Sport* 22.6 (Nov. 2005): 1086–1105.

Taking Care of Business. Dir. Arthur Hiller. Prod. Geoffrey Taylor. Starring John Belushi and Charles Grodin. Hollywood Pictures and Silver Screen Partners IV, 1990.

Talley, Rick. *The Cubs of 1969: Recollections of the Team Than Should Have Been*. Chicago: Contemporary Books, 1989.

Theodore, John. *Baseball's Natural: The Story of Eddie Waitkus*. Lincoln: U of Nebraska P, 2006.

This Old Cub. Dir. Jeff Santo. Prod. Tim Comstock and Jeff Santo. Emerging Pictures, 2004.

Thomson, Cindy, and Scott Brown. *Three Finger: The Mordecai Brown Story*. Lincoln: U of Nebraska P, 2006.

Trevathan, Kim. "Greatest Moments." *Nine* 12.2 (2004): 130–36.

Veeck, Bill, with Ed Linn. *Veeck as in Wreck*. New York: Putnam, 1969.

Vitti, Jim. *The Cubs on Catalina*. Bay City, CA: Settefrati Press, 2003.

Wagner, Will. *Wrigley Blues: The Year the Cubs Played Hardball with the Curse (But Lost, Anyway)*. Dallas: Taylor, 2005.

Weinreich, Craig. *The Chicago Cubs and the Heart of a City*. B.A. Thesis: California Polytechnic State U, 1997.

Weisberger, Bernard A. *When Chicago Ruled Baseball: The Cubs-White Sox World Series of 1906*. New York: William Murrow, 2006.

Wheeler, Lonnie. *Bleachers: A Summer in Wrigley Field*. Chicago: Contemporary Books, 1988.

Wilbert, Warren N. *The Chicago Cubs: Season at the Summit*. Champaign, IL: Sagamore, 1997.

_____. *A Cunning Kind of Play: The Cubs-Giants Rivalry, 1876–1932*. Jefferson, NC: McFarland, 2002.

Wojciechowski, Gene. *Cubs Nation: 162 Games. 162 Stories. 1 Addiction*. New York: Doubleday, 2005.

Wolfe, Rich. *For Cubs Fans Only: There's No Expiration Date on Dreams*. NC: Lone Wolfe P, 2003.

Wood, Gerald C. "(Caray)[3]: Baseball as Narrated on Television." *Baseball/Literature/Culture*. Ed. Peter Carino. Jefferson, NC: McFarland, 2004. 124–35.

Wrigley, William, Jr. *The Man and His Business*. Self-published, 1935.

Zingg, Paul J. "Diamond in the Rough: Baseball and the Study of American Sports History." *The History Teacher* 19.3 (May 1986): 385–403.

About the Contributors

Steve Andrews specializes in nineteenth-century American literature at Grinnell College, Iowa, some two and a half hours southwest of Dyersville and within a half day's reach of the Twins, Cubs, White Sox, Cardinals, and Royals — "or what's a heaven for?" His publications include book chapters on W.E.B. Du Bois, William James, and synaesthesia, as well as on the intersections of wilderness, civil rights, and race in Senate debates of 1964. He is currently at work on a book-length manuscript on Emerson, vagrancy, and landscape.

Terry Barr teaches modern literature, film studies, and ethnic studies at Presbyterian College. He has published creative and scholarly essays in *The American Literary Review, Studies in American Culture, Southern Jewish History, The Journal of Popular Film and TV*, and has recently had a creative nonfiction essay included in the anthology *Half/Life: Jew-ish Tales from Interfaith Homes*. He lives in Greenville, South Carolina, with his wife, Nilly, and their two daughters, Pari and Layla, all of whom he's converted into Yankees baseball fans.

David Bohmer is director of the Pulliam Center for Contemporary Media and Media Fellows Program at DePauw University, as well as a lifelong Cleveland Indians and longtime Cubs fan. A Ph.D. in American history, Bohmer was both a published historical researcher and a corporate executive before accepting his position at DePauw. The last six years he has taught classes on baseball history and presented papers at baseball conferences. He celebrates birthdays with kids and grandkids at Cubs games.

Bob Boone left the public schools in 1976 to work with at-risk youth and to write. Since then he has published several textbooks and dozens of articles. In 1991 he founded Young Chicago Authors, a program that encourages young people from the city to write. In 2002 he was named a Chicagoan of the Year by *Chicago Magazine*.

Brian Carroll is an assistant professor of journalism at Berry College in Mount Berry, Georgia, specializing in print media and digital media. His book on the black press and the Negro leagues, *When to Stop the Cheering*, was published by Routledge in 2006.

George Castle has written nine books on baseball, including *I Remember Harry Caray, Sammy Sosa: Clearing the Vines, The Million-to-One Team: Why The Cubs Haven't Won the Pennant Since 1945* (a history of Cubs management and ownership since P.K. Wrigley's era), *Throwbacks: Old-School Players in Today's Game*, and *Where Have All Our Cubs Gone?* In 2007 Castle published *Baseball and the Media* and *Entangled in Ivy: Inside the Cubs' Quest for October*, a sequel to *The Million-to-One Team*. For the last fourteen years Castle has hosted the syndicated weekly "Diamond Gems" radio show. He also covers the Cubs and White Sox for the *Times of Northwest Indiana.*

James Davis is an assistant professor of theatre and performance studies at Kennesaw State University. His research focuses on the use of theatrical conventions in popular culture performance. His father made him a Cubs fan, and he has done the same to his two sons. The cycle of abuse continues.

Margaret Gripshover is an adjunct associate professor of geography at the University of Tennessee, where she teaches courses in cultural, economic, world regional, and Tennessee geography. A Cincinnati native, she earned her B.S. and M.S. degrees in geography at Marshall University and her Ph.D. from the University of Tennessee. Her primary research interests include cultural landscape evolution, equine and companion animal studies, popular culture, and urban historical geography. Gripshover is an award-winning teacher and published author. A lifelong baseball fan, she attended her first major league game at Crosley Field, and her most recent at Wrigley Field. She is currently working on a biography of Charles H. Weeghman, the man who brought the Chicago Cubs to Lake View.

Jerry Grunska was English department chairman at Highland Park High School until 1985. Soon after he retired from teaching, he moved to Colorado where he continued to write. Along with many pieces of local history, he has written extensively about sports officiating. His articles about football refereeing have been widely acclaimed.

Andrew Hazucha is an associate professor of English at Ottawa University, where he teaches classes in British literature. A native of the northwest suburbs of Chicago and a lifelong Cubs fan, he has published essays on William Wordsworth, Nelson Algren, the Irish cultural historian David McWilliams, and the author of the 1969 Cubs' collapse, Leo Durocher.

Ron Kates is an associate professor of English at Middle Tennessee State University. He has published articles in sports literature, popular culture, service-learning, film studies, and composition studies. Two of his baseball-themed essays have appeared in the proceedings of the former Indiana State University Conference on Baseball in Literature and Culture, a conference he now hosts at Middle Tennessee State University.

William F. McNeil has written several books on baseball, including *The King of Swat* (1997), *Ruth, Maris, McGwire and Sosa* (1999), *Baseball's Other All-Stars* (2000), *Cool Papas and Double Duties* (2001), *The California Winter League* (2002), *The Single Season Home Run Kings* (2003), *Gabby Hartnett* (2004), and *Backstop* (2005). In his spare time, McNeil is an active member of the Society for American Baseball Research (SABR).

Tim Morris is professor of English at the University of Texas at Arlington. He is the author of *Making the Team: The Cultural Work of Baseball Fiction* (Illinois, 1997) and is the nonfiction editor of *Aethlon: The Journal of Sport Literature*. He compiles the on-line *Guide to Baseball Fiction.*

Rick Moser is vice president of corporate communications at Abbott Laboratories, so he relishes the opportunity of writing something that doesn't require ten approvals. Cursed with Cubs DNA from a lifetime in the northern suburbs of Chicago, he waits.

Shawn O'Hare is an associate professor of English at Carson-Newman College, editor of the scholarly journal *Nua: Studies in Contemporary Irish Writing*, and a lifelong fan of the New York Mets.

Joseph L. Price is the C. Milo Connick Professor of Religious Studies at Whittier College, the author of *Rounding the Bases: Baseball and Religion in America* (2006), and the editor of *From Season to Season: Sports as American Religion* (2001). His forays to Wrigley Field include witnessing Rennie Stennett's 7-for-7 performance in the Pirates' record-setting shutout of the Cubs, catching a foul pop up off the bat of Ed Kirkpatrick, and singing the National Anthem for a Cubs night-game victory over the Phillies.

Curt Smith, the author of twelve books, is "the voice of authority on baseball broadcasting," says *Gannett News*. He has written more speeches than anyone else for President George H.W. Bush, aired XM Satellite Radio and ESPN-TV programming, and hosted series at the Smithsonian Institute and Baseball Hall of Fame. The award-winning host of "Perspectives" radio teaches English at the University of Rochester.

Holly Swyers is an assistant professor of anthropology at Lake Forest College. She received her Ph.D. from the University of Chicago in 2003, where she did work on high school culture and community. Her work on Cubs fans includes an article entitled "Community America: Who Owns Wrigley Field?" in the *International Journal of the History of Sport* (2005) and a forthcoming book, *And Keep Your Scorecard Dry*.

Gerald C. Wood edited a collection of one-act plays by Horton Foote (1989), the Garland casebook on Foote (1998), and *Neil LaBute: A Casebook* (2006). He also wrote the critical studies *Horton Foote and the Theater of Intimacy* (1999) and *Conor McPherson: Imagining Mischief* (2003). He is presently writing a biography, *Smoky Joe: The Life and Times of Howard Ellsworth Wood*. Wood is dean of humanities at Carson-Newman College, where he also serves as film editor of *Nua: Studies in Contemporary Irish Writing*.

Index